A HISTORY OF No.10 SQUADRON ROYAL NAVAL AIR SERVICE IN WORLD WAR I

A HISTORY OF No.10 SQUADRON ROYAL NAVAL AIR SERVICE

IN WORLD WAR I

Mike Westrop

Schiffer Military History
Atglen, PA

Acknowledgements

This book would not have been possible without the support and encouragement of my wife and children, and the enthusiasm and assistance of many friends and contacts around the world. I would like to mention the following who have so generously provided help and research materials, and spurred me on:

Les Rogers, Stuart Leslie, Trevor Henshaw, Norman Franks, Andrew Smith, Steve Drew, Mike O'Neal, Hugh Halliday, Jim Du Bois-Tyson, Stewart Taylor, the late Don Neate, the late Jack Bruce, the late Phil Markham, Jan Keohane at the Fleet Air Arm Museum, and staff at the Royal Air Force Museum. I must especially thank Mark Miller for his wonderful illustrations, and Frank Cheesman for proofreading the work.

Book design by Robert Biondi.

Library of Congress Catalog Number: 2004104463.

Printed in China.
ISBN: 0-7643-2055-6

Published by Schiffer Publishing Ltd.
4880 Lower Valley Road
Atglen, PA 19310
Phone: (610) 593-1777
FAX: (610) 593-2002
E-mail: Info@schifferbooks.com.
Visit our web site at: www.schifferbooks.com
Please write for a free catalog.
This book may be purchased from the publisher.
Please include $3.95 postage.
Try your bookstore first.

In Europe, Schiffer books are distributed by:
Bushwood Books
6 Marksbury Ave.
Kew Gardens
Surrey TW9 4JF
England
Phone: 44 (0)20 8392-8585
FAX: 44 (0)20 8392-9876
E-mail: Bushwd@aol.com.
Free postage in the UK. Europe: air mail at cost.
Try your bookstore first.

CONTENTS

INTRODUCTION

This book is the first in a series outlining the history of the Royal Naval Air Service squadrons, and the naval derived Royal Air Force squadrons of the Great War. I have chosen to start with one of the most famous, but paradoxically, least known naval squadrons, No.10 Squadron, RNAS.

No.10 Squadron RNAS, often informally referred to as No.10 Naval Squadron, Naval 10, and No.10(N) Squadron, and its successor, No.210 Squadron, Royal Air Force, have always been something of an enigma. Everyone with an interest in World War I aviation has heard of Raymond Collishaw's legendary "Black Flight" of Sopwith Triplanes, and no book dealing with Sopwith Camels is complete without a photograph of a brightly striped Naval 10 Camel, but what else is really known of the squadron? When compared to equivalent RFC squadrons, or even one of the more popular naval squadrons, No.10 Squadron RNAS has been unjustifiably ignored by historians and researchers for many years.

My aim in this work, is to address this omission, starting with a discussion of the RNAS expansion at Dunkerque and working through to RNAS and RFC amalgamation on the 1st April 1918 to form the fledgling Royal Air Force. The book deals with the people, the machines, the places, the incidents and the day-to-day victories and losses. The Black Flight is dealt with in what I hope is a dispassionate manner, and will certainly be at variance with the hyperbole that has been published in the past. I have taken a detailed look at the unprecedented incident that provided the impetus for the famous striped colour scheme to come into existence, and shown that at least one Camel continued to carry stripes for far longer than other authors have surmised. Many of the squadron's pilots who survived the war came to post war prominence in vastly differing fields, and, where appropriate, I have detailed their post war successes and failures.

Readers should be aware that the author takes a sceptical view of combat claims and where the original documentation does not support them the more outrageous claims, made by or on behalf of certain pilots, have been discounted. The reference to original documentation is significant, much of the content of this work being based upon original squadron documents, backed up by pilot's log books, letters written by the pilots, and transcripts of interviews. The author does not wish to be dragged into disputes over how many victories a certain pilot did or did not score. For this reason the following notes may clarify the criteria used in the presentation of this aspect of the work.

Combat claims were generally regarded as either "decisive" or "indecisive". A decision that was initially made by the Squadron's Commanding Officer after reviewing the combat and associated reports. The ultimate decision of whether a claim was granted would not be made until the claim and all associated evidence had been considered by Wing HQ and RNAS HQ, or in the situation where a naval squadron was working for the RFC, by Wing, Brigade and then RFC HQ. Evidence might well be obtained from sources such as balloon observers, infantry and artillery units, intelligence agencies and other flying units.

A decisive claim generally fell into one of two camps:

• "Destroyed" where an enemy machine was seen to break up in the air, fell in flames, or was seen to crash.

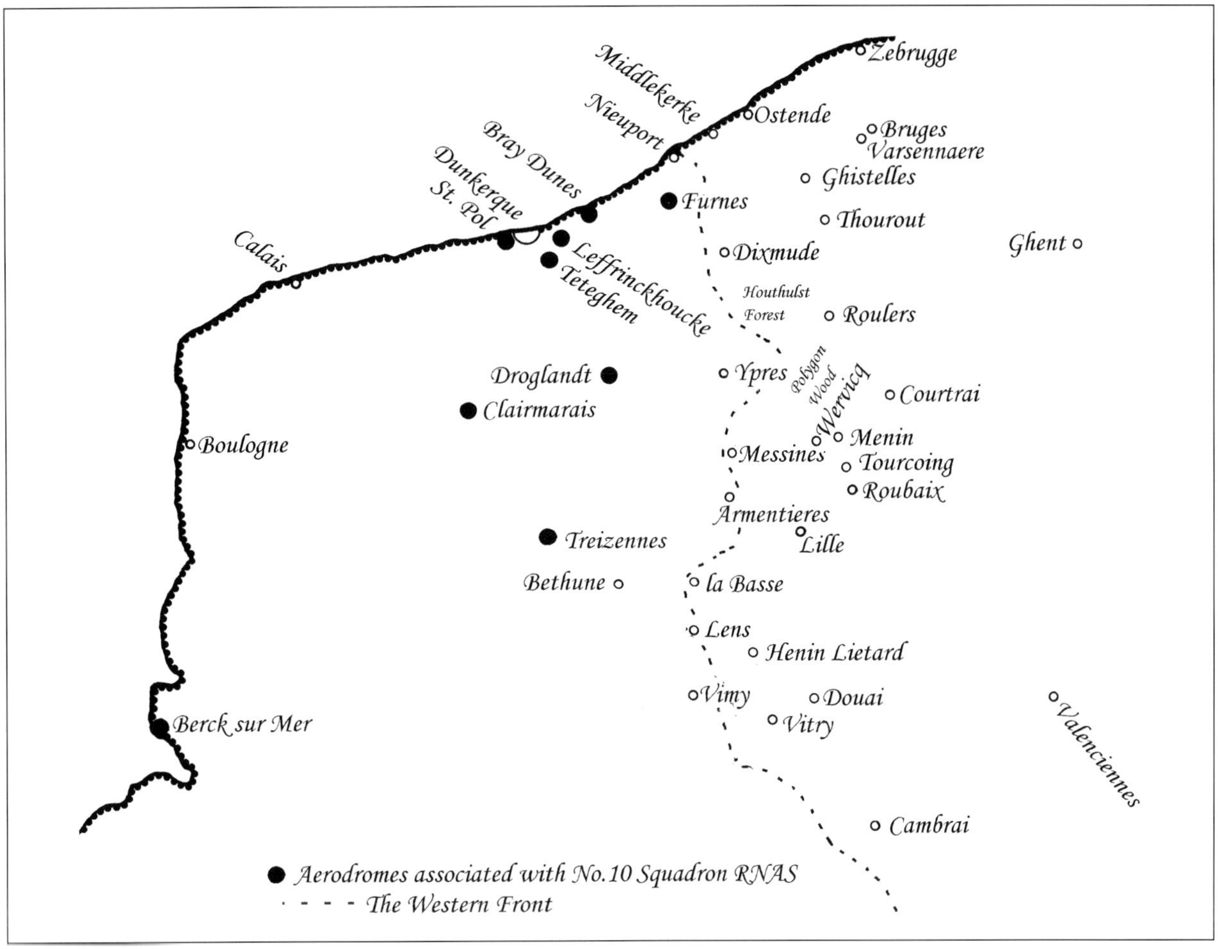

Sketch map showing the area of operations for No.10 Squadron RNAS, 1917-1918.

• "Out Of Control" where an opponent's machine was considered to fall in an uncontrolled manner with little chance of recovery.

Of course, the second category was open to significant personal interpretation and abuse. It must be remembered however, that whether an opponent left the battle zone in an inverted spin and after a fright recovered at a much lower altitude or simply stalled his machine and spun away to fight another day, he ceded the battle zone to the victor. An important objective of a scout machine was to make the sky safe to enable the observation, spotting and bombing machines to go about their normal business. An "Out Of Control" achieved this objective. When discussing victory claims, it helps to remember a few truths:

• Most encounters took place over enemy territory making verification difficult.

• We now know that gross over-claiming on the part of the Allies was a regular occurrence.

• When trying to match Allied claims with German losses, unless the German machine was destroyed completely, or the German pilot was unable to return to his unit, no loss was recorded in the German records.

• In the heat of battle, even the most experienced pilot sometimes made mistakes in observation.

The claims presented in this book are pilots' declarations, *not* corroborated victories. The claims are all supported by primary documentation sources, squadron record books and Combat Reports. This work does not place a strong emphasis on RNAS and RFC Communiqués which were basically summaries produced by clerical staff and were often unreliable. It does not place any emphasis at all upon secondary published sources, many of which have fed off their predecessors.

GLOSSARY

AA	Anti-Aircraft
AAP	Aircraft Acceptance Park
AD	Aeroplane Depot
ADD	Aircraft Depot Dunkerque (situated at St. Pol)
AFC	Air Force Cross
AM	Air Mechanic
AP	Aeroplane Park
ASD	Aeroplane Supply Depot
Bde	Brigade
Capt	Captain
CBE	Commander of the British Empire
Cdr	Commander
CFS	Central Flying School
COL	Crashed on landing
CPO	Chief Petty Officer
Cpl	Corporal
CSD	Central Supply Depot
DD	Driven Down
DFC	Distinguished Flying Cross
DFM	Distinguished Flying Medal
DFW	*Deutsche Flugzeug-Werke*
DSC	Distinguished Service Cross
DSM	Distinguished Service Medal
DSO	Distinguished Service Order
EA	Enemy Aircraft
Eng Lt	Engineering Lieutenant
F.A.U.	Friends Ambulance Unit
FCdr	Flight Commander
FIS	Flying Instructors School
FLt	Flight Lieutenant
FSgt	Flight Sergeant
FSL	Flight Sub-Lieutenant
Fw	*Feldwebel* (Sergeant)
FwLt	*FeldwebelLeutnant* (Master Sergeant)
GHQ	General Headquarters
HA	Hostile Aircraft
Haupt	*Hauptmann* (Captain)
HOP	High Offensive Patrol
Hp	Horsepower
HQ	Headquarters
Hrs	Hours
Jasta	*Jagdstaffel* (scout unit)
KB	Kite Balloon
LAM	Leading Air Mechanic
LFG	*Luftfahrzeug Gesellschaft*
LM	Leading Mechanic
Lt	Lieutenant
2Lt	Second Lieutenant
Ltn	*Leutnant* (2nd Lieutenant)
LVG	*Luft-Verkehrs Gesellschaft*

MBE	Member Of the British Empire
MC	Military Cross
MM	Military Medal
NAD	Naval Aeroplane Depot
NADD	Naval Aeroplane Depot Dunkerque
NAP	Naval Aeroplane Park
OBE	Order Of The British Empire
Oblt	*Oberleutnant* (1st Lieutenant)
Offstlvtr	*OffizierStellvertreter* (Warrant Officer)
OOC	Out Of Control
OP	Offensive Patrol
PFO	Probationary Flying Officer
PFSL	Probationary Flight Sub-Lieutenant
POW	Prisoner of war
PRO	Public Records Office (National Archive)
RAE	Royal Aircraft Establishment
RAF	Royal Air Force
RFA	Royal Fleet Auxiliary
RFC	Royal Flying Corps (Military Wing)
Rittm	*Rittmeister* (Cavalry Captain)
RN	Royal Navy
RNAS	Royal Naval Air Service/Royal Naval Air Station
RNR	Royal Naval Reserve
RNVR	Royal Naval Volunteer Reserve
R/T	Radio Telephony
SCdr	Squadron Commander
SD	Stores Depot
SDF	Seaplane Defence Flight
TDS	Training Depot Station
TPFO	Temporary Probationary Flying Officer
TPFSL	Temporary Probationary Flight Sub-Lieutenant
TS	Training Squadron
Uffz	*Unteroffizier* (Corporal)
Vzfm	*Vizeflugmeister*
Vzfw	*Vizefeldwebel* (Sergeant Major)
WCapt	Wing Captain
WCdr	Wing Commander
W/T	Wireless Telegraphy

CHAPTER ONE

EXPANSION OF THE RNAS AT DUNKERQUE

The history of the Royal Naval Air Service's presence at Dunkerque is beyond the scope of this book. However, in order to understand why new scout squadrons were introduced during 1916 and 1917, we need to briefly look at the policies and re-organisation of the Dover-Dunkerque command.

By the late summer of 1915, Wing Captain C.L. Lambe was in charge of two reconnaissance squadrons at Dover, and six squadrons at Dunkerque. The town of Dunkerque was, of course, a port and the aerodromes associated with Dunkerque, St. Pol, Petite Synthe and Coudekerke were situated in outlying suburbs. The Dunkerque squadrons comprised two spotting and reconnaissance squadrons, two bombing squadrons, and two fighter squadrons. Lambe had ambitious plans for his command, and by December 1915 had obtained Admiralty approval to form two more Wings, each comprised of four squadrons, to concentrate on offensive operations.

During 1916 the Dover-Dunkerque command expanded rapidly under Lambe's direction. Its three main objectives were:

- To protect the cross-channel supply routes of the British expeditionary force
- To harass enemy submarines using Belgian ports
- To take offensive action against the Channel end of the German lines

By mid 1916, 1 Wing was situated at St. Pol, 4 Wing at Petite Synthe, and 5 Wing at Coudekerke. The Wings were structured as follows:

1 Wing	A Squadron	No.1 Flight
		No.2 Flight
	B Squadron	No.3 Flight
		No.4 Flight
	C Squadron	No.14 Flight

Responsibilities included photo-reconnaissance, artillery spotting (by day and night), and fighter patrols over Front and Fleet.

4 Wing	A Squadron	No. 9 Flight
		No. 10 Flight
	B Squadron	No. 11 Flight
		No. 12 Flight

Responsibilities included bombing, and fighter patrols.

5 Wing	A Squadron	No.5 Flight
		No.6 Flight
	B Squadron	No.7 Flight
		No.8 Flight

Responsibilities primarily bombing but included some fighter patrols and reconnaissance.

In June 1916, the two flights of A Squadron 1 Wing moved nearer to the front at Furnes aerodrome, the squadron quickly becoming known as the "Detached Squadron". The Detached Squadron was equipped solely with Nieuport single-seat scouts and was the first uniformly equipped squadron in the RNAS.

Due to the closer proximity to the front, the Squadron took on new duties of providing French reconnaissance and artillery spotters with fighter escort.

In the Autumn of 1916, the RFC was experiencing difficulties on the Somme. In October, Wing Captain Lambe agreed to lend a squadron to assist the RFC. Each of the Dunkerque Wings contributed a Flight, Sopwith Pups from 1 Wing, Nieuport Scouts from 4 Wing, and Sopwith 1 1/2 Strutters from 5 Wing. The new squadron was designated No.8 Squadron.

In a subsequent re-organisation, all of the RNAS Dunkerque Squadrons were re-designated with numbers:

A Squadron 1 Wing became No.1 Squadron.
B Squadron 1 Wing became No.2 Squadron
C Squadron 1 Wing became No.3 Squadron.

A Squadron 4 Wing became No.6 Squadron.
B Squadron 4 Wing became No.7 Squadron.

A Squadron 5 Wing became No.4 Squadron.
B Squadron 5 Wing became No.5 Squadron.

Wing Captain Lambe's successful expansion of the Dunkerque squadron's offensive capability was a double edged sword. By the Autumn of 1916, the Germans had introduced the Albatros DI and DII twin gun scouts, precipitating a crisis for the RFC. Major-General Trenchard requested a substantial strengthening of the fighter squadrons attached to each British army. Nothing was done until December 1916 when it rapidly became obvious that any realistic action would be too late. The War Office made a request to the Admiralty for the loan of four fighter squadrons to assist the RFC, and material help in the form of engines and aircraft. The Admiralty was not really in any position to object, being in the "overkill" situation of having eight newly restructured squadrons attached to Dunkerque.

The RNAS Dunkerque "Order of Battle" at the end of 1916 for landplane scout/fighting squadrons is shown below:

No.1 Squadron: Reformed from A Squadron 1 Wing on 6th December 1916. Re-equipping with Sopwith Triplanes at Furnes. Carrying out coastal protection.

No.3 Squadron: Reformed from C Squadron 1 Wing on 5th November 1916. Initially equipped with Sopwith 1 1/2 Strutters.

No.4 Squadron: Re-formed from A Squadron 5 Wing at Coudekerke on 31st December 1916. Initially equipped with Sopwith 1 1/2 Strutters.

No.6 Squadron: Reformed from A Squadron 4 Wing on 12th December 1916 at Petite Synthe. Re-equipping with Nieuport scouts.

No.8 Squadron: Formed on 25th October 1916 with a flight each from 1 Wing, 4 Wing, and 5 Wing. On secondment to the RFC at Vert Galant. Initially equipped with Sopwith Pups, 1 1/2 Strutters, and Nieuports, but re-equipping with Sopwith Pups.

From the naval point of view, five fighter squadrons, even when fully equipped, would not be adequate to meet the commitment to the RFC, and provide coastal and fleet protection. Wing Captain Lambe therefore embarked upon another round of expansion:

No.9 Squadron: Formed at St. Pol on 1st February 1917 by taking a core of experienced personnel from C Flight No.8 Squadron. Initially equipped with a variety of different Nieuport scouts and a couple of Sopwith Pups. No.9 Squadron performed coastal defence duties until seconded to the RFC in June.

No.10 Squadron: Formed at St. Pol on 12th February 1917 under No.4 Wing. Built up from scratch, but reinforced in April and May with pilots from the disbanding No.3 Wing. Initially equipped with Nieuport 2-seaters and Sopwith Triplanes. Performed coastal defence duties from Furnes until seconded to the RFC at Droglandt on 15th May 1917.

No.11 Squadron: Formed at Petite Synthe on 8th March 1917 under No.4 Wing. Intended to be an operational training unit and pilot's pool. Called upon to provide patrols in support of defence of Dunkerque. Equipped with Nieuport scouts, Sopwith Pups and Triplanes.

Further expansion took place in June 1917 to strengthen the coastal defence and training provision:

No.12 Squadron: Formed at Hondschoote on 8th June 1917 under No.5 Wing. Served primarily as an operational training unit and pilot's pool, with occasional port defence duties. Equipped with Pups, Triplanes and Camels.

No.13 Squadron: Formed at St. Pol on 30th June 1917 as the Seaplane Defence Flight with coastal and fleet protection duties. Became the Seaplane Defence Squadron on 23rd September 1917 and No.13 Naval Squadron on 15th January 1918. Initially equipped with Sopwith Pups.

As stated earlier, No.8 Squadron had been attached to the RFC since the end of October 1916. The squadron was withdrawn to Dunkerque control early in February 1917 for re-equipping and reallocation of some officers and other ranks to new squadrons. On the same day, No.3 Squadron came under RFC control, and took responsibility for both 8 Squadron's duties and their aircraft. Secondment of the Naval squadrons to the RFC in 1917 took place as shown below:

No.1 Squadron Seconded to the RFC on 15th February 1917, initially based at Chipilly. Returned to RNAS control on 2nd November 1917.

No.3 Squadron Seconded to the RFC and took over No.8 Squadron's Sopwith Pup aircraft at Vert Galant on 3rd February 1917. Returned to RNAS control on 18th June 1917.

No.6 Squadron Seconded to the RFC on 11th March 1917, initially based at La Bellevue. Disbanded on the 28th August 1917 with the pilots and aircraft transferring to No.9 Squadron and No.10 Squadron. No.6 Squadron would be resurrected in 1918 as a bombing squadron.

No.8 Squadron Brought back under RNAS control and returned to Dunkerque on 3rd February 1917 for rest and re-equipping with Sopwith Triplanes. Seconded to RFC on the 14th February 1917, initially based at Furnes. Returned to RNAS control on 1st March 1918.

No.9 Squadron Seconded to RFC on 15th June 1917, initially based at Flez. Returned to RNAS control on 28th September 1917.

No.10 Squadron Seconded to RFC on 15th May 1917, initially based at Droglandt. Returned to RNAS control on 20th November 1917.

When the new RNAS scout squadrons started to form in late 1916, the intention was to maintain a squadron strength of 20 pilots. However, losses sustained by the squadrons serving on the Western Front were considerably higher than the RNAS had previously experienced. With a much lower recruiting intake than the RFC, the RNAS found it impossible to keep their squadrons staffed at their optimum level. On numerous occasions new recruits were thrown into the fray with no time allowed for adjustment, the inevitable outcome depleting numbers even further. For much of 1917 squadron strength hovered around a core of 15 pilots, sometimes dropping as low as 10 or 11.

By August 1917, it had become apparent that the RNAS could not support five scout squadrons on the Western Front, and on 28th August 1917, No.6 Squadron was disbanded, its pilots and Sopwith Camel aircraft being used to strengthen No.9 and No.10 Squadrons. No.11 Squadron was disbanded on 27th August 1917, as there simply were not enough new pilots coming through to support two operational training units.

CHAPTER TWO

FORMATION AND EARLY DAYS OF No.10 SQUADRON, RNAS

When the new RNAS scout capability was being expanded the approach taken was generally either to strengthen and re-equip an existing squadron, or to take a Flight from an existing squadron or Wing and use its experienced pilots as the core of a new squadron. By the time that No.10 Squadron was formed these approaches were no longer practical.

According to popular folklore, in order to start No.10 Squadron off with an experienced core of personnel, each existing Wing was asked to contribute 1 or 2 officers to the fledgling squadron. Of course, human nature being what it is, each Wing Commander donated those personnel that they considered they could most easily do without.

Unfortunately, this story is completely without foundation, as the squadron was, with one exception, staffed by officers from Cranwell and Eastchurch with little or no combat experience. The exception was FCdr George Thom, the only officer with previous combat experience gained with 5 Wing, and with No.8 Squadron RNAS.

Officially formed at St. Pol on the 12th February 1917, under Squadron Commander C.D. Breese, No.10 Squadron was equipped by the 27th of February with a handful of obsolescent Nieuport 12s and a single Sopwith Triplane. The Nieuports were ostensibly 2-seaters, but at least two of the machines had been converted to single seat form by the simple expedient of sheeting over the observer's cockpit.

By the 1st March, the core roster of officers was as follows:

SCdr C.D. Breese, Commanding Officer
Lt. RNVR C.A. McIlroy, Record Officer
WO A.E. Case, Stores and Engine Officer
FCdr A.R. Cox, A Flight Commander
FCdr G. Thom, B Flight Commander
FSL W.S. Oliver
FSL E.B.J. Walter
FSL L.E.B. Wimbush
FSL G.E. Nash
FSL C.A. Narbeth

The squadron commander, Charles Dempster Breese did not appear to be a particularly forceful officer, his approach to training being best described as "relaxed". Breese left the squadron on the 13th April to take command of No.6 Squadron, due to the death of SCdr J.J. Petre in a flying accident. During his brief tenure Sopwith Triplanes were initially in very short supply and Breese tended to restrict flights in them to himself and the more capable pilots. Less proficient pilots had to train on the obsolescent Nieuport 12 2-seaters.

Of Breese's flight commanders FCdr A.R. Cox had no operational experience and appeared reluctant to devote time to training his Flight, and FCdr G. Thom, an experienced veteran of No.5 Wing and No.8 Squadron RNAS, was in poor health and finding it difficult to perform his duties. Thom had left the squadron by 4th April 1917.

Warrant Officer Case, the Stores and Engine Officer had left the squadron on the 19th April, and was replaced by Warrant Officer E.P. Dampier who had previously been with Naval 6. WO Dampier was appointed Stores Officer, with Warrant Officer H. Poyntz-Gaynor appointed Engine Officer from 12th May.

The five Flight Sub Lieutenants, most of them straight out of the RNAS training system, had no combat experience

Naval 10's first home, the aerodrome at St. Pol near Dunkerque. This is a view of the east end of the aerodrome with Nieuport 17's belonging to the French Navy parked to the centre right. *Courtesy JMB/GSL Collection*

and, with the exception of FSL Nash who was allowed access to the Sopwith Triplane, received little practical training with the squadron. FSL Narbeth was on sick leave by the 1st March having crashed a Nieuport 17bis scout belonging to No.9 Naval Squadron on the 16th February.

Not surprisingly, the junior flying officers failed to develop their skills at the rate that would normally be expected.

The supply of new Triplanes improved over the following weeks, and new pilots were gradually received as follows:

15th March	FSL K. Ogden	injured and transferred out on 9th May
15th March	FSL A.H. Munday	injured 16th April and hospitalised
15th March	FSL O.B. Ellis	transferred to Naval 1 by 27th April
17th March	FSL K.G. Boyd	
28th March	FSL R. McDonald	transferred to Naval 8 by 4th April
30th March	FSL E.D. Roach	transferred to Naval 8 by 4th April
1st April	FSL G.G. Bowman	transferred to Naval 1 by 30th April
1st April	FSL E. Dickson	transferred to Naval 5 by 29th April
1st April	FSL A.Mc.B. Walton	transferred to Naval 6 by 4th April
2nd April	FSL Q. Shirriff	
3rd April	FSL H. leR. Wallace	transferred to Naval 1 by 7th April
3rd April	FSL W.H. Chisam	transferred to Naval 1 by 7th April
18th April	FSL R.F. Collins	
21st April	FSL M.W.W. Eppstein	

As can be seen, many of these new pilots were moved on to reinforce other squadrons almost immediately. The continuous "poaching" of No.10 Squadron pilots seriously affected the squadron's progress towards combat readiness, and the author is of the opinion that the decision had already been taken to use many of the experienced pilots from the disbanding 3 Wing to bring No.10 Squadron up to strength at a later date.

February 1917

Whilst the squadron was formed on the 12th February as part of 4 Wing, the first aeroplane did not arrive until the 24th. The few flights made before this date were performed using Nieuport scouts and Sopwith Pups borrowed from No.9 Naval Squadron, a practice that was temporarily stopped when FSL Narbeth wrote off a Nieuport 17bis on the aerodrome on the 16th February. After the 24th February, a couple of local familiarisation flights were made with No.10 Squadron's own aircraft, but training and patrols did not get underway until March.

The facilities provided to Squadron Commander Breese are probably best described as primitive. The squadron personnel spent their first days at St. Pol attempting to rectify this situation.

On the 19th February, the squadron head count was as follows:

SCdr Breese
FCdr Cox
FSL Nash
FSL Wimbush
FSL Narbeth (by now on sick leave)
WO Case
3 Petty Officers
3 Leading Mechanics
17 Aircraft Mechanics

The work carried out on the 19th comprised:

- Constructing Mess tables and benches
- Moved the wash house to the other side of a sand bank (water running away from the wash house was causing a problem)
- Digging foundations for stays to be used with Bessoneaux hangars
- Workshop duties

An aerial view of the St. Pol complex. Closely packed hangars, workshops and storage facilities show why it was a popular target for German night bombing raids. *Courtesy E.F. Cheesman*

Another view of the facilities at St. Pol, these buildings forming part of the RNAS quarter. *Author's collection*

As aircraft filtered in the squadron was ill equipped to work on them and the men were set to work constructing trestles, chocks and boxes. The infrastructure also continued to need work, roads were widened, the heads (lavatories) were rebuilt and more mess and office furniture was constructed.

March 1917

1st March

The first patrols were flown on the 1st. At 10.55, FCdr Cox flew Triplane N5352 on an uneventful patrol from St. Pol to Nieuport then 10 miles out from Nieuport to Gravelines and back to St. Pol. FSL Wimbush and FSL Oliver carried out brief patrols as far as Nieuport and back but both were restricted to using Nieuport 12s. Cox carried out a second patrol later in the afternoon at 16.40.

2nd March
Bad weather prevented all flying activity.

3rd March
Bad weather restricted flying to just one test flight.

4th March
Initially, practice was restricted to the pilots making numerous short flights of less than 10 minutes duration around the immediate environs of the aerodrome. It was not until the 4th that Wimbush, Walter and Oliver were sent up together to practice formation flying in the old Nieuports.

5th March
The weather had closed in again on the 5th. Very bad visibility was reported by FCdr Cox who made a 5 minute test flight at 14.00.

FSL Walter carried out a ten minute test flight in Sopwith Pup, serial 9900, at 16.00. This particular machine was on the strength of No.9 Squadron and was presumably borrowed.

6th March
FSL Oliver was obviously considered to show promise as he was allowed a 25 minute practice flight in Triplane N500.

Several test and practice flights were carried out during the day.

7th and 8th March
Bad weather shut down all flying activity.

9th March
FSL Walter made another practice flight in a Sopwith Pup belonging to No.9 Squadron. SCdr Breese made a short test flight in one of the Nieuports and FSL Oliver took Triplane N500 up for a 25 minute practice flight.

10th March
The weather again prevented any flying activity.

11th March
The sky was overcast on the 11th, but the wind had dropped to 10 miles per hour and the pilots were able to carry out nine local test and practice flights during the course of the day. FSL Walter was allowed his first brief practice flight in Triplane N500.

12th of March
Rain set in on the 12th and no flying took place.

13th March
Ten practice and test flights were carried out in the afternoon, none of them lasting longer than 20 minutes.

Lt. Cecil Birch, the squadron's new Armament Officer, arrived on the 13th.

14th March
The weather was unsuitable for flying. SCdr Breese was able to make one short test flight in a Triplane in the afternoon.

15th March
SCdr Breese performed a remarkably brief fighter patrol in Triplane N5352 at 08.35, covering Gravelines to Nieuport. Breese was airborne for 35 minutes and reported an uneventful patrol.

The rest of the day was given over to the usual short test and practice flights. However, it was a notable day for FSL Wimbush who was able to make his first flight in a Triplane.

16th March
SCdr Breese took off at 06.45 to perform another fighter patrol. His 40 minute patrol took him 15 miles east and 15 miles west of Dunkerque and was completely uneventful.

New pilots FSL Ogden, FSL Ellis and FSL Munday had arrived the day before and were set to work making the regulation short practice flights in the squadron's Nieuport 12 aircraft. A total of twenty test and practice flights were completed during the course of the day.

17th March
The wind which was 15 miles per hour in the morning, picked up to 30 miles per hour later in the day. All practice and test flights were cancelled, however Breese and his flight commanders each carried out a fighter patrol. FCdr Cox flew at 05.35, Breese at 07.30 and FCdr Thom at 16.05. No enemy machines were seen.

FSL Boyd arrived at the squadron during the day.

18th March
Two fighter patrols were flown on the 18th, FCdr Thom at 06.05 and FSL Nash at 17.25. Neither pilot observed any enemy aircraft.

Sopwith Triplane N5350, the first machine to be produced by Clayton & Shuttleworth, delivered to Naval 10 on 16th March 1917, but pictured here prior to delivery. FSL RF Collins was flying this machine over the English Channel on the 23rd April 1917 when it suffered from engine failure and Collins was forced to ditch in the sea near Boulogne. *Author's collection*

Three short test and practice flights were carried out in the early evening.

19th March
The wind was blowing at 30 miles per hour on the 19th; the only flight carried out being a brief test by FSL Nash at 09.20.

20th March
The wind speed had increased to 40 miles per hour. No flying took place.

21st March
At 14.30, FSL Walter delivered Nieuport 12 serial 3923 to No.8 Naval Squadron at Furnes. FSL Nash flying Nieuport 12 serial No.8728, accompanied Walter presumably with the intention of bringing him back to St. Pol. Nash had to land his machine near Bray Dunes where he damaged the Nieuport's propeller.

22nd March
Five local test and practice flights were carried out despite the wind being at 30 miles per hour.

23rd March
Ten local test and practice flights were flown on the 23rd, all but one in Nieuport 12s and all less than 35 minutes duration.

The squadron's flight structure was officially recorded for the first time on the 23rd:

A Flight
FCdr A.R. Cox, Flight Commander
FSL G.E. Nash
FSL L.E.B. Wimbush
FSL E.B.J. Walter
FSL W.S. Oliver

B Flight
FCdr G. Thom, Flight Commander
FSL K. Ogden
FSL O.B. Ellis
FSL A.H. Munday
FSL K.G. Boyd

24th March

The squadron's first fatality occurred on the 24th; FSL W.S. Oliver was sent to Dover to pick up new Triplane N5473. Oliver was killed when a wing broke off in the air whilst he was testing the new machine.

SCdr Breese carried out a fighter patrol at 10.30, travelling along the coast to Ostende. No hostile aircraft were observed.

Four local test and practice flights were also flown during the course of the day.

25th March

The squadron's first tentative contact with enemy aircraft took place during a fighter patrol being flown by FCdr Cox. Flying Triplane N5438, Cox took off at 10.03 and was at a point 6 miles out to sea and 10 miles northeast of Nieuport when he observed 2 seaplanes making for Ostende. He attempted to cut them off and fired 25 rounds at the last machine from long range.

FSL Ellis performed his first fighter patrol in one of the old Nieuports at 10.20. No hostile aircraft were observed.

Five local test and practice flights were carried out in the morning and early part of the afternoon.

26th March

Heavy rain and strong winds prevented any flying. Nieuport 12, serial 8711, was wrecked, presumably damaged by the storm.

27th March

The squadron moved to Furnes in Belgium. Nieuport 12 serial 8728 was wrecked but the responsible pilot was not identified.

28th March

No flying took place; the squadron spent the day settling in to their new aerodrome.

29th March

FSL Ellis made a brief 10 minute test flight at 15.05.

The aerodrome at Furnes, presumably shot from the bell tower of the nearby village church. *Author's collection*

Two remarkably short hostile aircraft patrols were carried out in the evening. SCdr Breese took off at 18.40 and FCdr Cox at 18.45. Both pilots returned at 19.10.

30th March

Five hostile aircraft patrols were flown during the day, FSL Nash at 06.30 and 09.15, FSL Wimbush at 07.35 and 17.50, and FCdr Cox at 15.45.

Nine local test and practice flights were flown during the day. New pilots FSL R. McDonald and FSL E.D. Roach made their first flights with the squadron getting 15 minute hops in a Nieuport 12.

31st March

Four hostile aircraft patrols were flown in the morning, FCdr Thom at 07.20 and 08.00, SCdr Breese at 08.05 and FSL Wimbush at 08.50.

The usual local test and practice flights took place throughout the day.

April 1917

By the end of March, SCdr Breese had dropped B Flight, replacing it with C Flight:

A Flight
FCdr A.R. Cox, Flight Commander
FSL G.E. Nash
FSL L.E.B. Wimbush
FSL E.B.J. Walter

Another shot of the aerodrome at Furnes, taken whilst A Squadron No.1 Wing was in residence during the summer of 1916. The distinctive church can be seen to the right. *Author's collection*

C Flight
FCdr G. Thom, Flight Commander
FSL K. Ogden
FSL O.B. Ellis
FSL A.H. Munday
FSL K.G. Boyd

1st April
FSL Nash carried out a hostile aircraft patrol at 08.39.

The rest of the day was taken up by thirteen test and practice flights, all except one being made using Triplanes. The exception was new pilot FSL G.G. Bowman's first flight, predictably made in a Nieuport 12.

2nd April
FSL Wimbush and SCdr Breese carried out short fighter patrols at 06.20 and 10.30 respectively.

Two training landmarks were achieved on the 2nd, the first when FCdr Cox took FSL Boyd and FSL Ogden up for 45 minutes of practice formation flying. This was the first time that any sort of organised instruction had been given.

The second landmark occurred when new pilots FSL Walton and FSL Shirriff made their first flights with the squadron in one of the Triplanes, the Nieuport 12's finally being relegated to "pleasure" flights.

A total of eleven test and practice flights were performed during the course of the day.

FSL Oliver Bernard Ellis had arrived at the squadron on the 22nd March. Ellis fitted the stereotypical image of a fighter pilot. He came from an upper-middle class background, attended Sidcot school (a private boarding school), and was an accomplished athlete. During his time with No.10 Squadron he wrote numerous letters to his family, some of which were smuggled out and avoided the censor. These letters paint a fascinating picture of a young Flight Sub Lieutenant's life during the early days of the squadron:

10 Squadron
RNAS
C/o GPO London
2/4/17

Dear Mother,

Thanks so much for your letter of the 24th – received yesterday – and also for Pater's received just after I posted my last one – if you leave out the "No 1 Wing" they will get thro' quicker I think.

I have just been having a chat with the Censor and he tells me that he won't mind if I point out that when we moved we didn't go far, but we are not now in the same country as we were before we moved, and as you know where I was before we moved, you will be able to draw your own conclusions as to where I am now, very subtle isn't it!

Please don't think that I'm not having a bearable existence here, because life here is far preferable to the sort of aimless life we used to lead in England, in fact I am having an extremely nice time here – with by no means too much to do.

As for the weather – it hasn't been all it might be – but when its really thick we sit round the fire in the mess and at other times we can go up for a flip if we want to – and the cloud effects are sometimes jolly fine – and what more could one wish for?

Has Pater developed those photographs he took of me in Khaki?

3rd April

Bad weather restricted flying on the 3rd. There was no flying during the morning but conditions improved enough for three hostile aircraft patrols to be flown in the afternoon and evening. SCdr Breese performed a patrol at 14.40 and another at 18.40, and FSL Wimbush flew a patrol at 16.55.

In his second letter FSL Ellis refers to the F.A.U., this was the Friends Ambulance Unit, an organisation run and staffed by Conscientious Objectors:

10 Squadron
RNAS
C/o GPO London
3/4/17

Dear Pater,

I hope you have got the small parcel I sent you. Unfortunately my flight commander – Mr Thom – has gone sick and has had to return to England, so our flight will not get along very fast for a day or two. The weather was simply awful this morning – snow and wind and rain, and everything else beastly – but this afternoon it has cleared up and is beautifully fine. I went out to see some of the F.A.U. men and came across another old Sidcot man who was at school with Colin.

I may be able to get down to the [ ] Stores sometime and if so I'll see if they can do any better about that knapsack. Did I tell you that Mr Hills has gone home to get a job at the Admiralty!

I'll write again soon.

Thy affectionate son,
Oliver B Ellis

p.s. Please send me a note book – with stiff covers – for a diary – ruled like this paper and just a little smaller – something about 100 pages I should think – I can't get anything of the sort here – I don't want the ruling as wide as this tho' – perhaps about 2/3rds of it. Well again goodbye and the best of luck for Easter.

4th April

Hostile aircraft patrols were flown by FSL Ogden at 12.00 and at 14.30, and by SCdr Breese at 15.53.

A total of sixteen local test and practice flights were carried out including first flights by FSL Dickson, FSL Chisam, and FSL Wallace.

FSL R McDonald and FSL E.D. Roach were transferred to No.8 Squadron on the 4th. McDonald however, would return in June, borrowed from No.8 Squadron to assist A Flight for a week.

5th April

Four hostile aircraft patrols were flown, two by FSL Ogden at 07.00 and 11.17, and two by FSL Shirriff at 12.50 and 19.25.

FCdr Cox and FSL Ogden provided an escort for a brief photographic reconnaissance mission at 11.44.

At 14.10, FCdr Cox led Wallace, Wimbush and Shirriff on a practice formation patrol, but he only kept them aloft for twenty minutes.

A total of seventeen local test and practice flights were carried out during the day.

6th April

FSL Shirriff carried out a hostile aircraft patrol at 10.30.

The squadron flew just three local test and practice flights during the morning.

FSL Ellis was keeping up a prolific flow of letters home, reporting on the squadron's ceremony to celebrate Easter, having a bath and finding somewhere to wash his laundry!:

10 Squadron
4 Wing RNAS
C/o GPO London
6/4/17

Dear Mother,

The mails take an awful time to get thro' seemingly – I had a letter from Aunt Edith on the 4th – written on the first saying that you had not heard from me for a week –

which is a pity because I expect you will get several letters in a bunch – anyhow that's what I'm hoping for – some letters seem to get thro' in fairly reasonable time – but anyhow it's all a bit of a gamble and it makes the mails more exciting! We are having quite a nice time – with just enough to do to stop things being dull, and not enough to make it seem like work.

We had two Padres down to celebrate the day – and I have just celebrated it again tonight by having a bath, and now I'm going to sew some buttons on – please send me some name labels and some more khaki thread, if you have any handy – if not any old thread will do, and please don't forget about the note book I asked for in my last – I haven't had a letter since I got yours and Paters last Sunday – so I don't know whether you are sending the various things – or whether you have got my letters – so you must forgive me if I repeat some of my requests.

This is a really lucky day – altho' it's a Friday – I've had a bath – I've had a letter – from Pierce – and last but not least – I've found a place to send my washing – which was slowly becoming a serious proposition – I might have had to fly over to the town I was at not long ago, with my washing – and get it seen to there. I did fly over the other day and buy a football – I didn't know the word for football – but I got one in the end – we hope to get some games started shortly – altho' April is rather a funny month to begin – we seem to get plenty of days fit only for such an occupation.

Well I must stop this or I will have no buttons for my tomorrow.

Your loving son
Oliver B Ellis

7th April
FSL Wallace carried out a hostile aircraft patrol at 12.45 during which an unidentified aircraft was seen 3 miles northwest of Nieuport.

FCdr Cox led FSL Boyd and FSL Ogden on a formation hostile aircraft patrol at 14.10. The route flown was from Ghistelles to Bruges, along the coast to Blankenberghe and return. No enemy aircraft or shipping was observed but two trains were seen near Ostende.

FSL Ellis carried out several local flights in a Nieuport 12 in the evening. It is believed that these were short "joyrides" for members of his ground crew.

A view across the aerodrome at Furnes, showing another line of hangars on the far side. This photograph also dates from 1916 when A Squadron No.1 Wing was in residence. *Author's collection*

FSL Chisam and FSL Wallace were transferred to Naval 1 on the 8th of April.

8th April
SCdr Breese led Wimbush and Nash on an offensive patrol at 10.05. A circuitous route was flown from Nieuport to Bruges, Ostende, Zeebrugge, Nieuport, Dixmude, Thourout, back to Nieuport and return to Furnes. One hostile machine was observed over the coast to the west of Ostende. Breese returned with a very detailed list of ground observations ranging from trains to anti-aircraft batteries and troop movements.

FSL Ellis and FSL Nash performed an offensive patrol at 13.40 but Nash was forced to land immediately, and Ellis proceeded alone.

FSL Ogden performed a short offensive patrol at 19.33.

9th April
Bad weather set in on the 9th making flying impossible.

Oliver Ellis managed to smuggle a letter home, together with a parcel of negatives. He was still enjoying his experience with No.10 Squadron:

9/4/17

Dear Pater,

I am sending this note across with a fellow going home on leave – it may get thro' to you quickly, but if this storm lasts he may not get across for some days – anyhow, I'm taking the off chance.

I have packed up a parcel of negatives and given them to an old Sidcot man in the F.A.U. who is crossing next Saturday – he will post them to you in England, and so I hope you will get them sometime early next week – I should very much like you to send me prints of them if they come out at all – all of them – also keep a numbered copy your side – I will let you know where the places are and what they are – I will tell you the following code – A Dunkirk – B La Panne – E Furnes – G Nieuport – H our aerodrome here – and J our aerodrome at Dunkirk. I'll talk to the censor so he will let me send that thro' alright.

I expect some of the fellows out here will want some of the photographs – so if you keep numbered prints and give Young the negatives I'll send him an order for the ones I want (I know what trouble it is to do lots of prints).

I am keeping splendidly fit out here and altho' the weather is variable – we don't much mind – the letter accompanying the parcel was written yesterday – so it will be a little out of date by the time you get it I'm afraid.

Well I must stop – goodbye

Your affectionate son
Oliver B Ellis

10th to 12th April

The bad weather continued, and no flying was possible.

13th April

The commanding officer of No.6 Squadron, SCdr J.J. Petre, was killed in a flying accident when he pulled the wings off his Nieuport at a gunnery range on the 13th April. SCdr Breese was ordered to take command of No.6 Squadron and left Furnes on the same day. Breese's replacement, SCdr Bertram Charles Bell, an Australian, would not arrive to take command of No.10 Squadron until the 21st April. FCdr Cox had temporary charge of the squadron pending Bell's arrival.

Triplane N5351 shown here at RNAS Cranwell in February, was delivered to the squadron on the 13th April 1917 and led a relatively quiet life until sent back to the depot on the 10th May. N5351 did however have a significant effect upon two of Naval 10's officers; FSL J.A.M. Allan had crashed N5351 at take off on the 11th March 1917, whilst serving with Naval 8 and FSL L.E.B. Wimbush, serving as an instructor at RNAS Chingford, was killed when he pulled the wings off N5351 whilst performing an impromptu aerobatic display at Birkhampstead Grammar School on the 27th March 1918. *Author's collection*

The weather improved sufficiently for several short test and practice flights to be carried out.

14th to 15th April
The weather closed down all flying activity.

16th April
Four individual offensive patrols were flown, FSL Wimbush at 08.35, FSL Bowman at 09.25, FSL Ogden at 10.17 and FSL Dickson at 11.10.

The lack of leadership and failings of Breese's relaxed training regime were dramatically illustrated when FSL Wimbush led FSL Ellis and FSL Bowman on an offensive patrol at 10.30. The patrol headed towards Dixmude, north towards St. Georges, east over Ghistelles and Varssenaere towards Bruges, northwest towards Blankenberghe and back to the aerodrome. At 11.10, when between Bruges and Blankenberghe, Wimbush observed a 2-seater diving on the Triplane on his left wing. He turned and fired 200 rounds at it without effect but received a burst from the observer in reply. Bowman and Ellis left Wimbush struggling with the 2-seater to pursue another machine which ultimately turned out to be a Belgian Nieuport. Finding himself abandoned and in opposition to a skilfully piloted 2-seater, Wimbush sensibly broke off and made a run for home but was forced to suffer the embarrassment of being pursued as far as the lines by his aggressive enemy. FSL Ellis tried to remedy his mistake by following the 2-seater which was chasing Wimbush but was unable to catch up.

FSL Nash led Walter and Boyd on an offensive patrol at 11.25, crossing the lines north of Dixmude then heading for St. Georges, Ghistelles, Nieuport and return. No enemy machines were observed.

Several local test and practice flights were carried out, during which FSL Munday crashed Nieuport 3923 when landing and was hospitalised.

FSL Walter, one of the squadron's founding pilots was transferred to No.8 Squadron on the 16th.

17th April
The weather was unsuitable for flying.

18th April
Just three local flights were carried out.

FSL RF Collins arrived at the squadron on the 18th.

Oliver Ellis's next letter home fell foul of the Censor but it was obvious that he was depressed, certainly upset at Breese's departure and by Munday's accident and possibly licking his wounds after the admonishment he must have received after deserting his patrol leader during the offensive patrol on the 16th:

4 Wing
c/o GPO London
18/4/17

Dear Mother,

[ ] You also ask if there are a decent lot of fellows here – if you'd asked me that a little while ago I should have unhesitatingly said "Yes" – but now I feel rather inclined to put "fellows" in the singular – perhaps it is not quite as bad as that but the authorities have been [ ] that there are [ ] – and now [ ] – we hope he may return – but the odds are heavily against it, I'm afraid. Your fourth question is answered by NO. I am hoping to get up a game of football against the F.A.U. next Sunday afternoon if possible.

I should rather like you to send me something of the weekly touch – The Spectator or something. We don't get many papers here.

The note book arrived quite safely thanks. I am looking out for the photographs every mail – I hope they came out all right.

I am sorry I didn't finish this yesterday but I got a letter from you and one from Peter enclosing some prints for which many thanks. I'll try and write again tomorrow – but I'm going to make certain of getting this off so I'll finish it off now (Wednesday night) and get it posted.

I remain,
Thy loving son
Oliver B Ellis

19th April
Reports were received of enemy aircraft in the vicinity of Ramsgate. This was the first torpedo attack in UK waters made by seaplanes from the German naval air unit at Zeebrugge, the target being shipping in the Goodwin Sands area. Five pilots left between 08.36 and 08.43 to patrol singly in a general northwesterly direction over the sea. FCdr Cox reported the visibility as being extremely bad. No enemy machines were observed. Upon his return, FSL Wimbush landed at Hondschoote.

20th April

Five individual offensive patrols were carried out in the morning, two by Ellis at 07.50 and 09.00, and one each by Nash, Bowman, and Wimbush at 09.04, 09.04 and 11.25 respectively. Bad visibility prevented any observations being made.

FSL Wimbush led FSL Ellis and FSL Bowman on an offensive patrol at 13.25. The patrol crossed the lines at Dixmude and headed towards Thourout, Bruges, Blankenberghe, Ostende and Nieuport. As usual, no hostile aircraft were seen. The formation was well kept, but on their return, due to bad visibility, Wimbush led the patrol too far west. At Dunkerque, Ellis and Bowman left him and returned to the aerodrome. Wimbush was forced to land at St. Pol to refuel, returning later.

A number of local test and practice flights were carried out during the day, notable amongst them being a 30 minute formation practice by Boyd, Nash and Dickson, and a test flight performed by FSL Collins in N5359 at 18.16. Collins lost his way and landed at Rubroucke damaging a wheel and axle.

FSL Eppstein arrived at the squadron on the 20th.

21st April

The squadron "scrambled" seven Triplanes at 12.45 in response to a signal from No.4 Wing reporting three seaplanes off Middlekerke. FSL Bowman had to abandon the mission almost immediately when the wire on the gun's firing handle came off as he tested the gun. Of the remaining six pilots only FSL Eppstein, flying the second Sopwith prototype N504, made contact with the enemy.

When 4 miles out to sea off La Panne Eppstein encountered two small seaplanes 500 feet above him heading towards Westende.

He climbed under their tails and fired 100 rounds at a range of 200 to 400 yards without effect. He reported the visibility as very poor, and that the hostile machines were very difficult to see in the cloud. During the engagement, four of N504's ignition leads broke, and Eppstein was forced to break off and glide back to the aerodrome.

FSL E. Dickson suffered from the first of a number of incidents that were to blight his time with No.10 Squadron, crashing Triplane N5357 when landing after a practice flight.

FSL Nash was driven to the site of FSL Collins heavy landing at Rubroucke where he fitted new components to N5359, and flew the machine back to Furnes.

A late hostile aircraft patrol was carried out by Eppstein, Nash and Boyd at 20.00 when a report was received of three hostile machines over Dunkerque.

Oliver Ellis sent a long rambling letter to his mother in which he seemed to be in better spirits than a few days earlier. He wrote at length about football and cricket and personal matters, but he closed the letter with the comment:

21/4/17

....

....

....

We are getting a new Squadron Commander this afternoon. I've never met him before so I don't know at all what he'll be like.

I remain

Your affectionate son

Oliver B Ellis

As Ellis had related to his mother, the new Squadron Commander arrived on the 21st of April. Bertram Charles Bell was a somewhat abrasive Australian with a blunt manner that did not endear him to subordinates. Whilst statements made after the war indicate that Bell was not liked by many of his pilots it should be remembered that a commanding officer was not appointed to be popular, he was placed in command to prosecute the war. Bell was an extremely able administrator and his "no nonsense" attitude gave his superiors confidence that they could depend upon him to "get on with the war".

In the ten weeks since its formation, No.10 Squadron had singularly failed to develop into an effective fighting unit. It was Bell's job to stop the rot, implement a cohesive structure with effective training and to imbue the squadron with an offensive spirit in preparation for the move to the Western Front in support of the RFC.

Bell's previous posting had been as senior Flight Commander with No.3 Squadron RNAS with a record of 4 victories flying Sopwith Pups all achieved in one month. Bell had been an aggressive pilot and in his new role he expected those serving under him to display the same commitment that he had shown. He was completely intolerant of those whom he felt were not giving their all and was often rude to, or would totally ignore, those officers that he felt were not pulling their weight. However, Bell was extremely supportive of pilots that conformed to his ideals and made strenuous efforts to ensure they received rapid promotion and official recognition.

After the relaxed atmosphere engendered by the benign SCdr Breese it is little wonder that the intensity of SCdr Bell's approach caused resentment amongst some of his junior officers.

As will be seen, Bell was spectacularly successful at instilling the squadron with an offensive spirit, although it was achieved at a very high cost in terms of casualties.

22nd April

FSL Nash, FSL Boyd and FSL Eppstein took off at 13.20 to pick up three Sopwith 1 1/2 Strutter bombers above Bray Dunes aerodrome at 13.30. The Triplanes escorted the bombers up the coast towards Flushing and maintained formation until 14.55 when one of the bombers turned back. Boyd also left the formation to accompany the returning 2-seater. At 15.10, the remaining two Triplanes were compelled to return due to low fuel levels.

FSL Ellis and FSL Collins carried out an offensive patrol at 14.45, covering Dixmude, Nieuport, Ostende, Bruges and Varssenaere. One enemy machine was seen at Dixmude at high altitude heading eastwards.

FSL Wimbush carried out a hostile aircraft patrol at 16.20 on report of a hostile machine over Dunkerque.

FCdr Cox led Ellis and Bowman on an offensive patrol at 18.00. Cox took the patrol six miles out to sea off Nieuport, then to Westende, Dixmude and back to Nieuport. No enemy machines were observed.

23rd April

If SCdr Bell was not previously aware of No.10 Squadron's lack of preparation the day's activities would have left him in no doubt.

The squadron flew six individual offensive patrols at 04.50, following a course from Furnes to the sea in a north easterly direction as far as Zeebrugge. FCdr Cox suffered engine trouble before he reached Ostende and returned. FSL Eppstein patrolled in the vicinity of Zeebrugge for 45 minutes when he encountered an enemy seaplane to the northeast of Zeebrugge. He was unable to engage it before it reached the protection of an enemy anti-aircraft battery. FSL Bowman inadvertently crossed the channel and was forced to land at Dover and returned later in the day. FSL Collins in N5350 came down in the English Channel and was rescued by a French patrol boat.

FSL Nash, FSL Wimbush and FSL Dickson left on an offensive patrol at 13.04. Dickson, flying N5356, clipped a tree on take off, damaging his propeller and snapping undercarriage and centre section wires. He eventually landed at St. Pol and had to leave the machine there for repairs. Nash and Wimbush continued to Nieuport and then to Ostende, Wenduyne, Bruges, Ghistelles, Dixmude and back to Nieuport. Nash reported several enemy machines parked in front of hangars at Ghistelles aerodrome. With the exception of Nash and possibly Eppstein, SCdr Bell could not have been overly impressed with the performance exhibited by his new squadron.

At 17.35, FSL Ellis flew to Ostende and Zeebrugge to observe destroyer activity. Four destroyers were seen entering Zeebrugge harbour.

FSL Boyd was despatched at 18.30 to search for a disabled seaplane that was reported to be under attack to the northeast of Nieuport. Boyd failed to find any machines, friendly or hostile.

24th April

FSL Wimbush and FSL Bowman carried out an offensive patrol at 07.45. Wimbush suffered engine trouble and was forced to return but Bowman continued to Nieuport, then out to sea along the coast to Zeebrugge and return.

FSL Ellis led FSL Boyd and FSL Bowman on a bomber escort mission. They picked up three Sopwith bombers off La Panne at 11.00 and accompanied them up the coast to Ostende where they turned in. The formation was well kept until the bombers separated. Ellis accompanied a bomber to Zeebrugge and back, Boyd returned from Ostende with another, and Bowman followed the third machine to Zeebrugge where he lost it in the clouds. No hostile aircraft were seen.

Oliver Ellis wrote to his father on the 24th, by now having completely forgotten his earlier sorrows:

24/4/17

Dear Pater,

Thanks very much for your letter dated 21st enclosing stamps, which I received last night. This is just a short note to say that I'm enjoying myself hugely and am keeping as fit as anything. We are getting beautifully bright weather with large white clouds floating round, and generally a pretty fresh breeze. Time doesn't hang very heavily on ones hands nowadays – there always seems something to do – by the way those novels have come in very convenient – it was warm enough today to sit out in the sun (out of the wind) and read! It sounds almost like a nursing home – but if I don't get anything more strenuous than a rest cure during the war – I shan't do so badly.

I saw a little owl tonight and heard lots of partridges calling – it was a simply ripping evening and I almost expected to see an old curlew flying over! I should think there ought to be some quite good "flighting" about here in the winter – a lot of people in this war would have benefited from some really good duck flighting – tho' personally I'm afraid that in future my sympathies will be all with the duck!

Well good night – I'm afraid I must go to bed now.

I remain thy loving son
Oliver B Ellis

25th April

Bad weather prevented any flying.

Oliver Ellis's next letter was smuggled out; some of the information detailed in the letter would have been regarded as quite sensitive, and it was obvious that first impressions of his new Squadron Commander were not favourable! It should also be remembered that the taking of photographs was a military offence; Ellis needed some means of getting his illicit films processed and developed. After he'd finished the letter, but before he despatched it, Ellis received news that he was not at all pleased to get:

April 25th 1917

Dear Mother,

I'm afraid I haven't been very communicative lately but I have been waiting for a wet day which has at last arrived – much to everyone's satisfaction.

I have been having a ripping lot of flying – during the last five days I have put in 12 hours in the air – and have spent most of that time at an average height of 14000 feet. We have done patrols all over Belgium, right up to Flushing, and inland about 15 miles the other side of Bruges and the worst of it is that we have never even sighted a Hun.

Yesterday I had to rush up and lead a formation of 3 machines flying in a V – pick up some bombing machines at La Panne, and escort them up the coast while they dropped their bombs on Ostende and Zeebrugge – we flew a little above and behind them so that we could see and drive off any hostile machines – it was a beautiful clear day and you could see for miles and miles – but no Huns put in an appearance – so they dropped their bombs and came back quite happily! The other day I was up on a 2 hour patrol at about 7 o'clock in the evening – it was beautifully clear with white clouds hanging about 4000 feet up – and above that absolutely nothing. The sun went lower and lower and eventually set over England! And at that time I could see Holland, Belgium, France and England all at once! Not bad was it.

I expect we shall be moving in about 3 weeks, and will either go down somewhere near Colin – or move only about 20 miles south, anyhow it will be a change for the better I think.

I am having a big "PETER" painted on my machine, and the man who flies next to me is having "BENJAMIN" on his – and we are both having rabbits painted on them. Another man is going to have "FLOPSY" and a rabbit on his and so our flight will be a real Belgian Rabbit flight!

I am enclosing some photographs that I have taken – I'm not taking quite so many nowadays, partly because I've exhausted most of the subjects about here, and partly because I've had other things to do.

We have got a new Squadron Commander, who has just come up from the Somme and is fearfully full out – but things are going along quite well and as long as he doesn't worry us when flying is a wash out, I'm perfectly satisfied. Have you heard from Colin lately, I must write to him again – now that I've got a chance of getting a letter posted in England – this time it is a man who has got nerves and is going home on sick leave. He may not be going for several days so I cant quite say when this letter will get home. You never mention anything about those photographs you got developed and printed for me – can you make anything out of them – perhaps the enclosed will help you – I've lettered them – so that I can order any of these from Young as well

One of our men lost himself above the clouds up by Flushing the other day. So he came west for 20 minutes – dropped down thro' the clouds and found he was out to sea just off Dover – so he landed there – had breakfast and flew back here when the weather cleared. While he was there he arranged to have a supply of daily and weekly papers sent over to the mess – so I expect I shall see them before I would get any you send over.

The same day I was sent out to look for some Hun destroyers off Zeebrugge – it took me 40 minutes to get up there – out to sea – I saw what I wanted and came back in 10 minutes (30 miles) so you see there must have been very nearly an 80 mph wind "up top sides" that day – some travelling isn't it. I put her nose down and fired a few rounds off at Ostende coming back – just to put the wind up them! And while crossing the lines I had the opportunity of watching friend Fritz loosing off a gas attack – which incidentally failed. It makes you feel like a Daily Mail reporter being right away out of sight and danger, and watching all these funny little hates go on right away in the distance – and then come back to comfortable quarters and princely food!

Tell Uncle Robert where I am, and where I may be going to – because if he does happen to be anywhere near I shall be able to look him up

Well I must stop before I tell you anything I oughtn't to !

I remain,
Your affectionate son,
Oliver

p.s. My C.O. has just told me that in all probability I shall have to transfer to No.8 Squadron (also Triplanes) which is stationed just north of Arras, tomorrow – 26th – if so my address will be

No.8 Squadron RNAS
C/o 40 Marine Parade
Dover

I'm hoping against hope that I don't have to go, because I've just got properly settled down here and it will be awfully sickening to start right again – but I'll let you know for certain before I post this letter.

p.s. My address is

No.1 Squadron RNAS
C/o 40 Marine Parade
Dover

26th April

Shortly after Bell's arrival, FSL Raymond Collishaw was posted to No.10 Squadron after a brief spell of sick leave. Collishaw was rapidly building a reputation and had already accumulated several victories flying Sopwith 1 1/2 Strutter fighters with 3 Wing and Pups with No.3 squadron. Bell and Collishaw had served together in No.3 Squadron and it is not unreasonable to surmise that Bell had requested Collishaw's posting to the new squadron. Prior to, and immediately after Collishaw joining the squadron a number of new pilots started to filter in, most of them experienced personnel from No.3 Wing which was now in the process of disbanding:

25/4/17	FSL J.A. Glen	ex 3 Wing and No.3 Squadron, posted back to No.3 Squadron after 4 days
26/4/17	FSL R. Collishaw	ex 3 Wing and No.3 Squadron
27/4/17	FSL W.M. Alexander	ex 3 Wing
27/4/17	FSL E.V. Reid	ex 3 Wing
27/4/17	FSL J.A. Page	ex 3 Wing
27/4/17	FSL A.B. Holcroft	ex 3 Wing
30/4/17	FSL J.E. Sharman	ex 3 Wing

FSL Collishaw's arrival on the 26th April marked the turning point for the squadron. Despite Collishaw's rank of Flight Sub-Lieutenant, SCdr Bell appointed him Commander of B Flight. He immediately had Bowman, Wimbush, Nash and Eppstein up for a 1 1/2 hour formation practice flight.

FSL Boyd led Collins and Glen on a bomber escort mission at 15.25. The patrol accompanied five bombers to Zeebrugge. After their attack, they broke formation for their return. FSL Collins returned with two but at 16.15, one of the bombers was attacked by a seaplane. Collins opened fire from 300 yards

A desperately poor copy, but it has to be included for its significance. This photograph was taken by Oliver Ellis just before he left Naval 10, and is believed to depict N5490, a new Triplane that was allocated to FSL R. Collishaw when he arrived to take charge of B Flight. *Author's collection*

and continued firing until within 20 yards at which point the seaplane broke off its attack. At 16.25 off Nieuport, Collins encountered two seaplanes dropping bombs on an Allied seaplane which appeared to be disabled and was floating on the sea. Collins engaged one seaplane at 50 yards range and fired 100 rounds, causing it to break off its engagement. At 16.40, after seeing the bombers back to La Panne, Collins saw that the disabled seaplane was again under attack. He turned back and opened fire on the attacking machine at 100 yards range. When Collins disengaged Glen attacked the hostile seaplane. He returned to the aerodrome at 16.45 and almost immediately took off again accompanied by FSL Collishaw to find and protect the disabled seaplane. Glen found the seaplane and circled above it for 1 1/2 hours until it finally drifted ashore near Westende. Collishaw failed to find the seaplane but continued on towards Ostende. When just off the Ostende basin at 17.50, Collishaw sighted an enemy 2-seater at 12000 feet, he manoeuvred into the sun and attacked but after 40 rounds suffered a gun jam. Collishaw had seen tracers enter the engine and by the time he had cleared the stoppage the enemy machine was gliding towards Ostende. After firing several more rounds he noticed the enemy observer lying prone across his gun. Collishaw followed the 2-seater down to 6000 feet but could not get the gun to fire more than 4 rounds at a time. The enemy machine started to spiral and the Triplane's gun jammed completely, forcing Collishaw to abandon the engagement.

27th April

Bad weather made flying difficult, the only flight of the day being a brief test flight carried out by FCdr Cox.

FSL OB Ellis was transferred to Naval 1 on the 27th, where he started to show great promise, gaining several victories before his untimely death. He wrote to his parents on the 28th April, and had the following to say about No.10 Squadron:

I was very sorry to leave No.10 – but now I've gone, it isn't as bad as I'd expected, after all, No.10, as I knew it, was entirely different from the No.10 as it is today and before long I don't expect there will be any of the original people left at all. I am flying the same sort of machines here; but I don't expect to get properly in working trim, so to speak, for some time to come.

At last we've got a really nice day – I mean comparatively warm – and it is so nice, after the cold nip the wind always had at my last place. I am hoping that the time of frost bites is over for the present at any rate now – I didn't get frost bitten myself but I think that was more by good luck than good management

I remain

Your affectionate son

Oliver B Ellis

28th April

FSL Collishaw led Bowman and Wimbush on an offensive patrol at 10.00 but Wimbush dropped out almost immediately with engine trouble and 15 minutes later Bowman lost touch with Collishaw and proceeded alone. At 10.50, whilst flying at 10000ft over Ramscappelle, Bowman saw two scouts at 5000 feet, he shut off the engine and made a diving attack. He attacked the higher of the two machines and fired 40 rounds at

FSL R.F. Collins was killed in Triplane N5438 on the 28th April 1917, when he crashed whilst attempting to land. *Author's collection*

100 to 150 yards range. The other aircraft came up and attacked him on the port side, firing continuously until within 50 yards, and then passed over him. Bowman's gun jammed, and he was unable to clear it so climbed away in a left-hand spiral.

A bombing escort mission was scheduled for 15.40 but the five Triplanes were unable to locate the bombers. The patrol continued as a formation practice, upon completion of which, FSL Collins bounced his Triplane when trying to land, took off again, stalled and side-slipped in from 50ft wrecking the machine, Collins subsequently died of his injuries.

Collishaw, Wimbush and Reid took off at 16.21 with the intention of trying to pick up the bomber escort which had left earlier, Collishaw intercepted the escort at 8000 feet to the northwest of Nieuport but failed to attract their attention.

FSL Alexander, FSL Holcroft, and FSL Page, new pilots from 3 Wing, made their first flights in a Sopwith Triplane. Making an inauspicious start with the squadron, Alexander took N5359 up for a 17 minute practice flight but upon landing turned it over on its nose breaking the propeller and damaging the cowling.

29th April

The squadron was unable to fly on the 29th, not because of adverse weather but because the aerodrome was being used for a Belgian sports meeting!

30th April

FSL Nash led Eppstein and Holcroft on an offensive patrol at 07.25 from Nieuport to Ostende, Zeebrugge, Bruges and Dixmude. Holcroft lost the formation in cloud between Ostende and Bruges and returned alone landing at St. Pol at 09.50. Visibility was reported as indifferent, and no enemy aircraft were seen.

The squadron's first confirmed victory was scored when FSL Collishaw led FSL Alexander and FSL Page on an offensive patrol at 16.00. They followed a route from Nieuport to Ostende, Thourout and Dixmude and on the second circuit, at 17.30, they were attacked over Cortemarck. A hostile 2-seater was seen to dive on FSL Alexander who was flying on Collishaw's left wing. Collishaw attempted to engage the attacker, but it was 500ft above him and he lost speed and stalled. By the time he had recovered he was under attack from an enemy scout. Collishaw was able to out-manoeuvre the scout and shot it down seeing it strike the ground near the railway junction east of Cortemarck. Page, flying on Collishaw's right wing attacked the 2-seater after seeing Collishaw's aircraft spin away. He got in 1 burst from beneath and received a heavy but inaccurate reply from the observer's gun. Alexander's machine collected a few bullets but was not badly damaged and after his initial surprise at being attacked he was also able to climb above and behind the 2-seater and fire 50 rounds at it. The 2-seater dived away and escaped.

FSL Wimbush was transferred to No.8 Squadron.

May 1917

In later years, Collishaw wrote that when he arrived at No.10 Squadron, it was staffed with "odds and sods" with no fighting spirit. He also claimed that he was instrumental in getting them transferred out of the squadron to be replaced by experienced pilots from the disbanding 3 Wing. As we have seen, one Flight Commander showed little interest in war flying or in training new Flight Sub Lieutenants, but the majority of the pilots were young and inexperienced, and simply lacked appropriate training. Many of the squadron's pilots had been taken as reinforcements for the established naval squadrons, in fact during March and most of April, No.10 Squadron was effectively being used as a "Pilot's Pool". Collishaw's assertion that he was responsible for the influx of 3 Wing pilots can be discounted, they had already started to arrive before he joined the squadron. It was much more likely that the decision to utilise the experienced pilots returning from the disbanded 3 Wing was taken at a much earlier stage by Wing Captain Lambe. It is quite possible however, that Collishaw made recommendations to Bell that certain resident pilots be transferred out of the squadron.

Many of the new pilots arriving from 3 Wing were from Canada, and within a few weeks the squadron was almost entirely manned by Canadian pilots. The arrival of new pilots continued into May as follows:

5/5/17	FSL C.E. Pattison	ex 3 Wing
5/5/17	FSL D.F. Fitzgibbon	ex 3 Wing
5/5/17	FSL J.H. Keens	ex 3 Wing
5/5/17	FSL L.G. Steel	ex 3 Wing
5/5/17	FSL Morrison	ex 3 Wing
8/5/17	FSL A.C. Dissette	ex 3 Wing
8/5/17	FSL L.H. Parker	ex 3 Wing
9/5/17	FSL P.G. McNeil	ex 3 Wing and No.3 Squadron

The squadron's work-rate picked up noticeably in May, Collishaw appearing to be involved in almost everything that was carried out. Contact with enemy aircraft was much more commonplace, with Collishaw, Sharman, and Page regularly in combat. FCdr Cox was still in evidence though he seemed to suffer an inordinate amount of engine trouble which caused him to regularly abandon patrols.

1st May

Collishaw and Sharman flew individual offensive patrols at 11.45 and 12.00 respectively. They followed a general route of Nieuport to Ostende, Thourout, Ghistelles, and back. Collishaw saw nothing but Sharman picked up a Pup and a Caudron out to sea northwest of Ostende and accompanied them for some time.

Collishaw led Page and Sharman on an offensive patrol to Ostende, Thourout and Dixmude at 14.00. At 15.00, an enemy machine was sighted off Ostende and engaged briefly by Collishaw and Sharman.

Nash and Eppstein took off at 18.30 upon report of four enemy aircraft over Nieuport. At 18.50, Nash, flying at 12000 feet sighted all four enemy machines flying 500 feet below him. One machine turned to engage, Nash dived and fired, observing his tracers entering the fuselage. The enemy machine broke off his attack and dived for Westende, Nash followed but eventually lost him. Upon returning, Nash was unable to locate the remaining three machines. Eppstein accompanied a formation of Belgian Nieuports over the Nieuport, Ostende, Dixmude, Bruges, Thourout sector. At 19.40 an enemy formation was sighted over Roulers, but the mixed formation was unable to bring them to action.

Four hostile aircraft patrols were flown in the evening, by FSL Boyd at 19.05, FCdr Cox at 19.20, FSL Holcroft at 19.25 and FSL Nash at 19.35. The visibility was very bad and no enemy machines were observed.

2nd May

FSL Collishaw led Sharman and Page on an offensive patrol at 07.00. The Triplanes traversed a line between Westende and Middlekerke on the coast to a point half way between Dixmude and Thourout. At 08.00, on the second pass over the line, the formation engaged two Halberstadt scouts to the east of

Nieuport. Collishaw manoeuvred the flight into the sun and attacked. One scout dived away and escaped but the patrol caught the other machine. Collishaw fired 150 rounds into the scout from close range when his empty ammunition belt unstowed itself from the drum, and wrapped around him and his aircraft's controls. Collishaw's Triplane then suffered a severe fuel leak compelling him to break away from the engagement and return to the aerodrome. Page and Sharman continued the attack, driving the scout down into a long spin. They followed the machine down, firing as opportunity presented. Eventually, the scout recovered from the spin and dived steeply away towards Ostende.

FSL Sharman carried out a hostile aircraft patrol at 10.45 in response to a report of an enemy machine over Nieuport Bains. Sharman patrolled the coast between Nieuport and Dunkerque without sighting an enemy machine.

FSL Nash performed a hostile aircraft patrol between Calais and Gravelines at 12.30. The visibility was very bad and no hostile aircraft were seen.

FSL Sharman carried out another hostile aircraft patrol over Nieuport Bains at 13.02. At 13.40, Sharman encountered an enemy machine near Nieuport. When approached the intruder dived steeply away towards Westende.

FSL Eppstein led Holcroft and Boyd on an offensive patrol between Nieuport and Dixmude at 16.10. At 16.45 the formation was attacked by two Albatros scouts; Holcroft immediately dropped out of the engagement when he lost his engine and lost 2500 feet before recovering. After their initial attack the Albatros scouts dived away eastwards towards Ostende, FSL Boyd was the only pilot within range and he fired at them from 75 yards observing tracers enter one machine without effect. Boyd's gun suffered an un-clearable stoppage and he was forced to return to the aerodrome to get it rectified.

At 17.30, FSL Collishaw led a bomber escort mission. Four Sopwith 1 1/2 Strutters from No.5 Naval Squadron were picked up at La Panne at 17.45, and escorted to Ostende and back. Upon the bomber's return, one machine broke away and headed inland, Collishaw directing two of the escort to accompany the machine, whilst the rest of the patrol escorted the remaining three bombers back to Dunkerque. Although this dispersal seemed to be normal practice for Naval 5 pilots upon their return, Collishaw was not impressed and made a formal complaint.

Eppstein, Collishaw and Nash carried out individual hostile aircraft patrols just after 20.00, when reports were received of hostile aircraft overhead. The pilots covered the line between Nieuport and Dunkerque at heights between 10000 and 15000 feet. A number of Sopwith Pups were observed but no enemy aircraft.

3rd May

FSL Nash carried out a hostile aircraft patrol at 08.00 upon receipt of a signal reporting an intrusion over Nieuport Bains. Upon arrival, Nash found three Sopwith Pups, but no hostile aircraft.

FSL Collishaw carried out a hostile aircraft patrol at 08.10 taking off in response to a signal reporting six enemy aircraft crossing the lines. He patrolled between La Panne and Dunkerque, traversing the line for considerable distances to north and south without encountering any enemy aircraft.

FSL Eppstein led Boyd and Holcroft on an offensive patrol at 09.10, over the route from Zarren to the coast. At 09.45, when at the northern end of the patrol, an enemy machine was encountered and followed to Ostende.

FSL Collishaw led Nash and Page on an offensive patrol between Middlekerke and Zarren at 11.00. No enemy machines were encountered, but the patrol came under heavy and accurate anti-aircraft fire at Westende and Nash's Triplane, N5354, was damaged by shrapnel passing through the main planes.

4th May

FSL Eppstein led Boyd and Holcroft on an offensive patrol over the Nieuport-Zarren line at 07.00. Formation was well kept until 07.35 when Holcroft became sick and was forced to return to the aerodrome and then Eppstein and Boyd became separated.

Hostile aircraft patrols were flown by FSL Page and FSL Collishaw at 10.48 and 13.38 respectively. Page took off to look for an enemy machine reported from Nieuport Bains, and Collishaw attempted to locate an enemy machine reported from Westende. Neither pilot was successful and Collishaw was forced to curtail his patrol when his machine developed a fuel leak.

FSL Nash took the squadron's last Nieuport 12 back to the depot.

5th May

Eppstein scored the squadron's second victory when leading Boyd and Holcroft on an offensive patrol at 16.35 over Nieuport-Zarren-Dixmude. Boyd had a problem with his Triplane and returned to Furnes to exchange the machine but he was unable to pick-up the patrol again. Nash suffered engine trouble and was forced to return to Furnes. Eppstein decided to continue the patrol on his own and at 18.05 he sighted a formation of nine Halberstadt scouts flying at 19000 feet over Zarren. He manoeuvred between the enemy machines and the sun and followed them until they broke up. Eppstein closed with the rear machine of the right wing and it turned across him presenting a large target. Eppstein fired 75 to 100 rounds at which point the Halberstadt's petrol tank exploded and the machine turned over and fell away erratically. Eppstein was unable to watch it further as he was attacked by three other machines from the formation and had to take evasive action.

FLt H.G. Travers arrived at Furnes on the 5th. Whilst not regarded as being attached to the squadron he was recorded as being on strength by the Recording Officer. Travers brought the prototype Sopwith Camel N517 to Furnes and carried out several test flights during his brief stay, he also assisted the squadron when Triplanes needed to be delivered to the depot.. Travers and his Camel remained at Furnes with No.9 Squadron when No.10 Squadron moved to Droglandt on the 15th.

6th May

Unfavourable weather curtailed all flying activities.

7th May

Eppstein led Holcroft and Pattison on an offensive patrol at 08.00. The course flown was from Nieuport to Zarren and Dixmude. Pattison was forced to drop out with engine trouble after an hour. No enemy aircraft were sighted but six kite balloons were observed and a large howitzer was seen in action at Oostnieuwkerke.

Pattison and Eppstein carried out hostile aircraft patrols at 11.55 and 12.50 respectively. Neither pilot was able to detect the reported intruders.

Nash led Dissette and Morrison on an offensive patrol at 20.30, covering Nieuport, Middlekerke, Zarren and Dixmude. No enemy aircraft were observed.

8th May

Dissette led Keens and Fitzgibbon on an offensive patrol at 09.00, following the route Dixmude, Roulers, Bruges, Ostende and Nieuport. Four enemy destroyers were observed heading for Ostende at 10.30 but the patrol was otherwise uneventful.

9th May

Hostile aircraft patrols were carried out by Holcroft, Steel, Parker, Nash and Fitzgibbon. All of the patrols failed to find the reported enemy machines. FSL Steel took off at 09.45 but choked the engine of N5352 and spun in. The machine was wrecked and Steel was hospitalised.

FSL Eppstein led a bomber escort mission for No.5 Squadron at 11.05. FSL Parker dropped out with engine trouble but the rest of the formation picked up the bombers off Nieuport at 11.37 and escorted them throughout the duration of their mission. No enemy aircraft were seen and Eppstein reported that the formation was well kept during the patrol.

FSL Collishaw led Eppstein, Parker, Dissette and Keens on an offensive patrol over the Middlekerke-Zarren line at 18.30. FSL Keens dropped out of the patrol with engine trouble. Collishaw encountered three Farman machines near Dixmude at 19.05, escorted them across the lines and safely back and then continued the patrol. At 19.55, to the east of Dixmude, the patrol encountered three Halberstadt scouts. Collishaw let them pass and then opened fire on the rear machine at 75 yards range. He reported seeing tracers enter the enemy machine which went into a nose-dive and side-slip so rapidly that he was unable to keep his gun trained on it. Collishaw then suffered a gun stoppage, a not uncommon problem at this time, and was forced to abandon the patrol. FSL Dissette confirmed that whilst it was in his view, the enemy aircraft was descending vertically and swaying erratically from side to side.

10th May

FSL Eppstein led a patrol comprising Boyd and Holcroft at 06.00. Holcroft dropped out with engine trouble but Eppstein continued the patrol and both he and Boyd attacked a 2-seater at 06.50. After 50 rounds, Eppstein suffered a gun stoppage so he abandoned the attack and returned to Furnes to get the stoppage cleared. After resuming the patrol, Eppstein encountered another 2-seater to the northeast of Zarren but suffered another gun jam after firing 250 rounds.

FSL Collishaw and Fitzgibbon flew as escort for a Handley Page bomber at 08.30. They picked up the bomber over La Panne, headed to Zeebrugge then turned out to sea and back towards Dunkerque, flying circuits in search of hostile shipping. No hostile aircraft were observed.

At 10.15, FSL Dissette led Keens and Pattison on an offensive patrol down to Ypres and then to Roulers, Bruges, Ostende and Nieuport. Dissette engaged a 2-seater near Nieuport at 11.15; after manoeuvring to get the sun behind him he dived on the enemy and fired a burst of 30 rounds from 100 yards but suffered a gun jam and was forced to disengage. Dissette reported that the observer opened fire on him from 200 yards.

FSL Nash and Parker carried out a repeat of the earlier bomber escort mission at 12.15. The visibility had become very poor and no enemy aircraft were observed.

At 17.10, FSL Keens observed a enemy machine flying low over Furnes and dropping bombs on the town. He was able to take off in pursuit at 17.15 and chased the enemy machine to the lines.

11th May

At 08.00, FSL Collishaw led Parker and Nash on an offensive patrol over the Middlekerke-Zarren sector. Parker suffered a gun stoppage and returned to Furnes whilst Nash lost Collishaw in thick cloud over Dixmude. At 09.40 Nash encountered an enemy machine between Zarren and Thourout. Nash dived on the hostile machine and opened fire at a range of 50 to 75 yards observing his tracers enter the fuselage. The enemy machine dived away, and Nash reported that he was unable to keep up in the dive. The enemy machine was still in a steep dive when last seen but Nash considered that it was under control.

FSL Boyd carried out a patrol between Nieuport and Ostende at 09.55. Boyd reported that the visibility was very bad due to thick haze.

Three individual hostile aircraft patrols were carried out during the day by Parker, Dissette, and Fitzgibbon. Fitzgibbon was the only pilot to encounter a reported intruder during his patrol at 10.25, the enemy machine was at great height over La Panne and heading east. Fitzgibbon gave chase and got up to 18500 feet but lost sight of the machine in the heavy haze.

Collishaw led an offensive patrol at 18.00, covering the Zarren-Dixmude-Ypres sector. Fitzgibbon was forced to drop out with gun trouble and the patrol was otherwise uneventful.

FSL McNeil led a three Triplane line patrol at the same time. Visibility was very poor and no enemy aircraft were encountered.

12th May

At 04.30, FSL McNeil led six Triplanes on a patrol to protect the fleet which was bombarding Zeebrugge; no enemy aircraft were seen. FSL Eppstein, flying N5456, failed to return. He

In the past, doubt has been cast upon the assertion that this photograph depicts FSL W.M. Alexander. Mel Alexander himself was in no such doubt! *Courtesy Jim Tyson-Dubois*

was thought to have been shot down by *Flakzug* 72 near La Ventie and crashed into the sea.

FSL Collishaw led Reid and Alexander off at 06.35 to relieve the fleet patrol. At 07.48 two seaplanes were observed off Ostende and engaged by Collishaw and Reid. Collishaw was flying at 8000ft, and the seaplane was first seen flying at 5000ft, 2 miles off shore from Ostende. The observer opened fire at long range but Collishaw closed in to fire 50 rounds at close range, and claimed to have either killed or wounded the observer. The seaplane dived steeply and headed for the shore, Collishaw followed and fired as opportunity presented. The seaplane's engine was disabled, but the pilot managed to glide into the approach to Ostende harbour, at which point two defending aircraft appeared and Collishaw broke off the engagement. The RNAS Communiqué credited Collishaw with a 2-seater crashed into Ostende harbour, however the initial sources of information, Collishaw's combat report and the squadron daily record do not specifically mention a victory. The war diary of Seeflugstation Flandern II contains the following report for the 12th May:

> *"A/c 787 flown by Vzfmst Dyck was attacked at Ostende by two Triplanes. It was forced to withdraw from the combat and dived away in a steep dive. The aircraft thereafter landed."*

Reid engaged the second seaplane, reporting that he saw tracers entering the fuselage. The seaplane dived away and escaped. FSL Alexander had been unable to keep up with the patrol, and joined up with two Sopwith Pups in pursuit of an enemy seaplane which escaped to its base at Ostende.

FSL Pattison carried out a solo patrol covering Nieuport to Ostende and then Blankenberghe to Dixmude. The visibility was again very bad and no enemy machines were observed.

FSL Nash was dispatched on a hostile aircraft patrol at 15.14 to Oost-Dunkerque. No hostile machines were observed.

Later in the day, FSL McNeil led Parker and Holcroft on a formation offensive patrol at 17.50, Holcroft in N5357 experienced engine trouble, and crashed while attempting to return to the aerodrome. At 18.50, Parker encountered an Albatros scout at 5000 feet over Roulers, Parked attacked and fired a few rounds but the enemy scout dived away and was rapidly lost in the haze. Parker then engaged a 2-seater near Ypres at 19.20, the Triplane's gun jammed, and Parker was forced to break off the attack. As Parker climbed away the 2-seater turned and chased him for some distance. At 18.50, when over Roulers, McNeil attacked an Albatros scout flying at 12000 feet. The scout dived away and McNeil found that he was unable to keep his sights trained on the enemy machine during the dive.

FSL Dissette led Keens and Fitzgibbon on an offensive patrol at 18.20. The formation covered the Nieuport to Zarren line. The patrol was not a success, with Keens suffering engine trouble and dropping out and Dissette and Fitzgibbon lost touch with each other in heavy cloud.

13th May

FSL Dissette led Keens and Fitzgibbon on an offensive patrol over the Nieuport, Zarren and Dixmude sector at 08.00. At 09.50, the patrol encountered two scouts which made a diving attack and continued their dive down past the Triplanes. FSL Keens was able to follow them down and fired 60 rounds at one machine without effect.

FSL Nash and Alexander carried out a patrol over Nieuport-Dixmude-Thourout sector at 10.30. By the time they had climbed to 8000ft the engine in Nash's Triplane had started to miss so he returned to the aerodrome. At 11.45 Alexander sighted a 2-seater 2000ft above him. Alexander climbed towards it but was seen and the 2-seater dived at him attacking on his right side. Alexander pulled up in a steep climb when the 2-seater was close, made a vertical turn and followed the 2-seater firing 30 rounds; he followed the enemy machine in its dive for about 3500ft when he noticed a drift wire had broken and he disengaged from the combat.

FSL Fitzgibbon and Keens flew hostile aircraft patrols at 12.45 and 13.48 respectively. Neither pilot encountered the reported enemy aircraft.

14th May

FSL Nash performed two hostile aircraft patrols at 09.05 and 09.50, looking for an enemy machine reported to be over Nieuport Bains. No enemy machines were encountered, possibly due to a low cloud base.

FSL McNeil led Pattison and Boyd on an offensive patrol over the Nieuport, Dixmude, Zarren sector at 17.30. Pattison suffered engine trouble and was forced to drop out of the formation at 18.15. McNeil was able to surprise a lone Albatros scout at 19.30, five miles northeast of Dixmude, he was able to fire 60 rounds at the scout before it dived away. McNeil followed the scout down to 8000 feet and was able to fire at it again when it levelled out, the scout then dived away steeply and was lost to sight.

15th May

The squadron transferred from Furnes to Droglandt, with command being handed over to 11 Wing 2 Brigade, Royal Flying Corps. Droglandt was situated in low lying terrain and to avoid problems with a high water table had runways composed of rolled ash, laid out in the form of a cross. The runway's surfaces were kept in good condition by the regular practice of marching squads of men over them.

FSL D.F. Fitzgibbon received a slight injury when landing at the new aerodrome.

CHAPTER THREE

REORGANIZATION & THE BLACK FLIGHT

Flight Structure

Although the flight structure of No.10 Squadron had initially been formally split into two Flights under FCdr Cox and FCdr Thom, the patterns of flying make it difficult to ascertain to which flight any particular pilot was attached.

After the transfer of command from the RNAS to 11 Wing 2 Brigade RFC on the 18th May, a defined flight structure started to become more readily discernible with practice flights and patrols being made under consistent leadership and with regular personnel. On the 26th May, A, and B Flights flew practice formation patrols in their final form for the first time. C Flight practiced at full strength on the 27th May.

The squadron was still short of pilots, being restricted to just 15, in three flights of five:

A Flight
FSL P.G. McNeil, Flight Commander
FSL H.W. Taylor
FSL L.H. Parker
FSL K.G. Boyd
FSL A.B. Holcroft

B Flight
FSL R. Collishaw, Flight Commander
FSL J.E. Sharman
FSL E.V. Reid
FSL G.E. Nash
FSL W.M. Alexander

C Flight
FSL A.C. Dissette, Flight Commander
FSL J.A. Page
FSL J.H. Keens
FSL D.F. Fitzgibbon
FSL Q.F. Shirriff

With the exception of Holcroft, Fitzgibbon and Squadron Commander Bell all of the pilots were from Canada.

The Black Flight

There have been many published accounts devoted to No.10 Squadron's "Black Flight" none of them, in the author's opinion, have been based on documented facts. The "Black Flight" nickname has to be used in context on occasion but as the term "Black Flight" was allegedly applied to B Flight at some undefined time after the event and "Black Flight" tends to mean something different to each individual the author will, wherever possible, refer to Collishaw's B Flight from this point onwards.

Whilst the squadron was reorganising and being strengthened by the arrival of experienced pilots from the disbanding No.3 Wing, Collishaw was assessing the capabilities and offensive spirit of his colleagues. The squadron records showing that he was involved in everything, and trying to fly with as many members of the squadron as possible. As the Flight structures developed during May it is clear that Collishaw "cherry picked" the personnel for B Flight, leaving A and C Flights in a dangerously unbalanced state.

As stated earlier, it can be safely assumed that the squadron's Flight structure was completely defined by the 26th/27th May 1917 when each Flight flew a practice formation patrol. The structure of B Flight on the 26th May was undisputedly as follows:

FSL R. Collishaw, Flight Commander
FSL J.E. Sharman, Deputy Flight Commander
FSL W.M. Alexander
FSL G.E. Nash
FSL E.V. Reid

Prior to this date the evidence indicates that Collishaw favoured FSL John Page at the expense of FSL Gerald Nash. SCdr B.C. Bell however, was having difficulty in selecting a Commander for C Flight, he eventually installed a reluctant FSL A.C. Dissette as Flight Commander and insisted that he be supported by FSL Page. Collishaw reluctantly took Nash from A Flight to replace Page.

Collishaw stated in his book, *Air Command*, that the Triplanes of each flight were "colour coded", red cowling and wheel covers for A Flight, black cowling and wheel covers for B Flight, and blue cowling and covers for C Flight. This was to provide a visual cue to the ground crew that their flight had returned. It was stated that the black did not show up sufficiently on the B Flight aircraft, so it was extended to cover all of the aluminium top cladding and side panels. It is difficult to prove or disprove Collishaw's account, however, the author finds it significant that the "Black Flight" of Naval 3 (of which Collishaw was a member) had their Sopwith Pups painted in the same fashion, and that at the end of 1917, the Camels in Collishaw's Flight in the Seaplane Defence Squadron were also painted in the "Black" tradition.

In addition to the B Flight black paintwork, "black" names (Black Maria, Black Death, Black Prince, Black Sheep, and Black Roger), were stencilled in white below the cockpits and almost certainly each aircraft carried large white letters on the fuselage side behind the cockade (C, S, A, N, & R). It is not certain if B Flight was referred to as the "Black Flight" at the time or if the name was appended at a later date.

What has never been appreciated is that "B Flight" as defined above did not stay intact for any longer than eight days and that only five flights were carried out in which all five pilots participated:

26th May 1917: Practice formation patrol and gunnery practice
28th May 1917: Practice formation patrol and gunnery practice
1st June 1917: Offensive patrol
2nd June 1917: Eight machine photographic reconnaissance escort in morning eight machine photographic reconnaissance escort in afternoon.

An aerial view of the aerodrome at Droglandt showing to good effect the rolled ash runways. Aircraft in the photograph are Nieuports of No.46 squadron RFC and RE8s belonging to No.21 Squadron RFC. *Courtesy E.F. Cheesman*

Whilst B Flight were confidently establishing themselves, the other two Flights suffered tragic losses when two Flight Commanders, FSL Dissette and FSL McNeil, were shot down and killed on the 2nd and 3rd of June respectively.

Squadron Commander Bell's immediate reaction to this disaster was to transfer FSL Sharman into C Flight, where he was evaluated against a reluctant FSL Page as a suitable Flight Commander. FSL D.F. Fitzgibbon exchanged places with Sharman and moved from C to B Flight. A Flight ceased to exist as an entity for a couple of weeks, its remaining pilots being used to support B and C Flights. For reasons unknown, other authors have never regarded Fitzgibbon, a skilled member of the squadron and a future Commander of B Flight, as a bona fide member of B Flight. The author does realize that Fitzgibbon was not Canadian, but this is not considered to be a valid reason to ignore him.

Sharman was extremely ambitious and regarded himself as being in competition with Collishaw. In an interview many years later, Mel Alexander and Nick Carter (the new A Flight Commander) stated that Sharman and Collishaw were not comfortable together as competing Flight Commanders, and they were reputed to always be arguing. Knowing this, it seems very unlikely that Sharman would paint his new Triplane in B Flight's markings, especially as he was first in line for the position of permanent C Flight Commander. Whether this surmise is correct or not, Sharman cannot be considered to be a member of B Flight from the 4th June onwards.

It might be argued that Sharman flew with B Flight after this date; however, apart from just one occasion, this was as Commander and very rarely as deputy Commander of C Flight when the two Flights patrolled together.

The next loss to B Flight occurred on the 25th June, when FSL Nash was shot down and captured. Nash flying "Black Sheep" became isolated below the patrol and surrounded by Albatros scouts, Collishaw had to sacrifice Nash to avoid putting the rest of the patrol in a dangerous position. Nash, shot down by *Ltn.* K. Allmenröder of *Jasta* 11, survived the crash and spent the rest of the war in captivity.

Sharman had been confirmed as C Flight Commander by the 3rd July and experienced rapid promotion through the ranks of Flight Lieutenant and Flight Commander but was killed on the 22nd July, apparently taking a direct hit by an anti-aircraft shell. His deputy, FLt Page, was also killed during the same patrol.

FLt Alexander was transferred from B Flight to become Commander of C Flight on the 26th July, leaving Collishaw and Reid as the last original members of B Flight. Collishaw left the squadron on the 28th July, posted on Canadian Leave, and Reid was shot down and killed, possibly by anti-aircraft fire, also on the 28th July.

During the period from 27th May to 28th July 1917, B Flight achieved an impressive record of combat claims, a record that unfortunately was embellished and exaggerated each time the story was retold. The following list of claims was derived from the squadron records, not from other published works:

B Flight's Combat Record during the period 27/5/17 to 28/7/17

1/6/17	FSL R. Collishaw	N5490	Albatros scout claimed destroyed in flames south of Wervicq, 09.20.
1/6/17	FSL E.V. Reid	N5483	Albatros C claimed destroyed in flames, southwest of Wervicq, 09.15.
2/6/17	FSL W.M. Alexander	N5487	C type out of control at St. Julien, 07.00, shared with N5490, N5483, and N5492.
2/6/17	FSL R. Collishaw	N5490	C type out of control at St. Julien, 09.00, shared with N5483, N5487, and N5492.
2/6/17	FSL G.E. Nash	N5492	C type out of control at St. Julien, 09.00, shared with N5490, N5483, and N5487.
2/6/17	FSL E.V. Reid	N5483	C type out of control at St. Julien, 09.00, shared with N5490, N5487, and N5492.
3/6/17	FSL R. Collishaw	N5490	Albatros scout claimed destroyed in flames at Roubaix, 20.15.
3/6/17	FSL E.V. Reid	N5483	Albatros scout claimed destroyed near Roubaix, 20.25.
4/6/17	FSL W.M. Alexander	N5487	Albatros scout out of control northeast of Ypres, 08.45.
5/6/17	FSL R. Collishaw	N5490	Albatros C claimed destroyed in flames at Wervicq, 08.50, shared with N5478, N6306, N5483 and N5466.
5/6/17	FSL G.E. Nash	N5478	Albatros C claimed destroyed in flames at Wervicq, 08.50, shared with N5490, N5483, N6306 and N5466.
5/6/17	FSL E.V. Reid	N5483	Albatros C claimed destroyed in flames at Wervicq, 08.50, shared with N5490, N5466, N5478 and N6306
5/6/17	FSL D.F. Fitzgibbon	N5466	Albatros C claimed destroyed at Wervicq, 08.50, shared N5490, N5478, N5483 and N6306.
5/6/17	FSL R. Collishaw	N5490	Albatros scout out of control northwest of Poelcappelle, 09.00, shared with N5466.
5/6/17	FSL D.F. Fitzgibbon	N5466	Albatros scout out of control northwest of Poelcappelle, 09.00, shared with N5490.
6/6/17	FSL W.M. Alexander	N5487	Albatros scout out of control at Polygon Wood, 11.45.

6/6/17	FSL R. Collishaw	N5490	Albatros scout claimed destroyed in flames at Polygon Wood, 10.50.
6/6/17	FSL R. Collishaw	N5490	Albatros scout claimed destroyed in flames at Polygon Wood, 11.05.
6/6/17	FSL R. Collishaw	N5490	Albatros scout out of control at Polygon Wood, 11.10.
6/6/17	FSL G.E. Nash	N5492	Albatros C claimed destroyed at Polygon Wood, 11.00.
6/6/17	FSL G.E. Nash	N5492	Albatros scout out of control at Polygon Wood, 11.15.
6/6/17	FSL E.V. Reid	N5483	Halberstadt scout claimed destroyed north of Polygon wood, 11.00.
7/6/17	FSL R. Collishaw	N5470	Albatros scout out of control between Menin and St. Julien, 8.45.
7/6/17	FSL G.E. Nash	N5492	Albatros scout out of control at St. Julien, 09.00.
7/6/17	FSL E.V. Reid	N5483	Albatros C claimed destroyed at Clercken, 09.15.
15/6/17	FSL D.F. Fitzgibbon	N5458	Halberstadt type out of control at St. Julien, c. 10.35.
15/6/17	FSL R. Collishaw	N5492	C type out of control between St. Julien and Houthem, 10.55.
15/6/17	FSL R. Collishaw	N5492	C type out of control at Menin, 17.15.
15/6/17	FSL D.F. Fitzgibbon	N5458	Albatros scout out of control at Moorslede, 17.40.
15/6/17	FSL R. Collishaw	N5492	Albatros scout out of control north of Moorslede, 17.40
15/6/17	FSL R. Collishaw	N5492	Albatros scout claimed destroyed north of Moorslede, 17.40.
15/6/17	FSL E.V. Reid	N5483	Albatros scout out of control at Moorslede, 17.45.
15/6/17	FSL E.V. Reid	N5483	Halberstadt out of control at Moorslede, 17.45.
17/6/17	FSL R. Collishaw	N5492	Hostile aircraft, probably Halberstadt, out of control at Roulers 19.10.
17/6/17	FSL E.V. Reid	N5483	Halberstadt out of control at Roulers, 19.10.
24/6/17	FSL R. Collishaw	N5492	Albatros scout claimed destroyed at Moorslede, 08.10.
2/7/17	FSL R. Collishaw	N5492	C type claimed destroyed at Poelcappelle station, 11.10.
6/7/17	FSL W.M. Alexander	N5487	Albatros scout out of control at Deulemont, 11.00.
6/7/17	FSL W.M. Alexander	N5487	Albatros scout out of control at Deulemont, 11.00.
6/7/17	FSL R. Collishaw	N5492	Albatros scout out of control at Deulemont, 11. 00.
6/7/17	FSL E.V. Reid	N5483	Albatros scout out of control at Deulemont, 11.00.
11/7/17	FSL W.M. Alexander	N5487	Albatros scout out of control at Polygon Wood, 20.45.
11/7/17	FSL R. Collishaw	N5492	Albatros scout out of control at Moorslede, 20.40.
12/7/17	FCdr R. Collishaw	N5492	Albatros scout out of control south of Polygon Wood, 07.45.
12/7/17	FSL E.V. Reid	N5483	Albatros scout claimed broke up in the air and crashed at Polygon Wood, 07.45.
12/7/17	FSL E.V. Reid	N5483	Albatros scout claimed shot down, pilot shot, seen to crash at Veldhoek, 07.45.
20/7/17	FSL W.M. Alexander	N5487	Albatros scout destroyed in flames between Menin and Messines, 08.05.
20/7/17	FCdr R. Collishaw	N5492	Albatros scout out of control, pilot shot, between Menin and Messines, 08.05.
20/7/17	FSL E.V. Reid	N5483	Albatros scout out of control, pilot shot, between Menin and Messines, 08.05.
21/7/17	FCdr R. Collishaw	N5492	Albatros scout out of control at Passchendaele, 08.00 to 08.40.
21/7/17	FCdr R. Collishaw	N5492	Albatros scout out of control at Passchendaele, 08.00 to 08.40.
21/7/17	FSL E.V. Reid	N5483	Albatros scout destroyed, edge of wood north of Becelaere, 20.20.
23/7/17	FSL E.V. Reid	N5483	Albatros scout out of control at Polygon Wood, 20.25.
27/7/17	FCdr R. Collishaw	N533	Albatros scout destroyed north of Menin, 19.45.
27/7/17	FCdr R. Colliishaw	N533	Albatros scout out of control Polygon Wood, 19.45.
27/7/17	FSL E.V. Reid	N5483	Albatros scout destroyed at Menin, 19.50.
27/7/17	FSL E.V. Reid	N5483	Albatros scout out of control at Courtrai, 20.00.
27/7/17	FSL E.V. Reid	N5483	Albatros scout destroyed at Menin, 20.05.
28/7/17	FSL E.V. Reid	N5483	Albatros scout destroyed at Dadizeele-Becelaere, 20.00.

The above list is very impressive but may seem controversial as it omits all of Sharman's "accepted" B Flight claims. This is because all of Sharman's claims were made whilst flying with C Flight. All of the flight's unsupported claims, including Collishaw's "six in one fight" claim and the ridiculous Allmenröder claim that various authors have periodically attributed to Collishaw have also been omitted. The last two mentioned incidents can be discounted for the following reasons:

Ltn. Karl Allmenröder – 27th June 1917

Ltn. Karl Allmenröder of *Jasta* 11 was killed at 09.45 on the morning of the 27th July, almost certainly shot down by anti-aircraft fire at Zillebeke. Although Collishaw did not fly until 17.30 on the evening of the 27th, many authorities have attributed Allmenröder's death to Collishaw. In Collishaw's book *Air Command*, he even seems to have convinced himself that he scored a lucky long range victory.

Six in one fight – 6th July 1917

Collishaw submitted the following Combats In the Air report on the 6th July:

While in the vicinity of Deulemont, with the three other pilots of my flight, I saw an encounter between some FE's and a number of enemy scouts. I dived and went into the fight. I saw one of my flight get an E.A. and observed it crash on the ground. At the beginning of the fight, I attacked and drove down one scout entirely out of control, the pilot appearing to be hit.

A general engagement ensued and I saw five other E.A. go out of control as a result of my fire, but I could not watch results as continual attention was required to a new attack.

I saw an enemy scout attack Flt. Sub-Lt. Fitzgibbon and drove him off. While doing so another attacked me and was in turn driven off by Flt. Lieut. Alexander.

At the bottom of Collishaw's entry on the report, SCdr B.C. Bell had written in black ink "*Decisive. One out of control.*" The official verdict was one "Out of Control" and that is what he is credited with in this work.

This was of course, the famous fight during the course of which Captain D.C. Cunnell and 2Lt A.E. Woodbridge of No.20 squadron RFC were credited with shooting down *Rittm.* Manfred von Richthofen.

When studying any list of allied victory claims the reader must be aware that the outcome of a combat could not, in most cases, be verified. Gross over-claiming and misidentification of aircraft type were unavoidable when a pilot was almost always fighting over enemy territory where the result of a combat was indeterminate.

With hindsight, we can compare allied claims and German losses and in the case of B Flight's claims for destroyed aircraft there are very few matching German losses. However, this should be tempered by the fact that unless a German pilot was killed or injured and required hospitalisation or the machine was a total write-off, the surviving records do not indicate a crash or forced landing due to combat.

A full list of squadron claims can be found in Appendix D.

CHAPTER FOUR

WORKING FOR THE RFC

Settling In and Training

The transfer to RFC Control on the 15th May 1917 was initially something of an anti-climax with bad weather curtailing any flying activity for 2 days. The first patrol under RFC control took place at 11.55 on the 18th May, however, practice flights and gunnery practice were still regular events.

16th May

Bad weather, no flying took place.

17th May

Heavy rain in the morning, thick clouds throughout the day, no flying.

18th May

FSL Collishaw led Nash and Reid on an uneventful formation line patrol from Ypres to Armentières at 11.55.

FSL McNeil led Boyd, Holcroft and Pattison on a similarly uneventful line patrol at 17.00, followed by a line patrol flown by FSL Shirriff and FSL Dissette at 17.25 and another flown by Sharman and Alexander at 18.25.

19th May

No.10 Squadron would be called upon to carry out far more escort duties than they had previously experienced. The RE8's of No.21 Squadron RFC were made available to make the training exercises as valuable as possible and in the morning, FSL Collishaw led Parker, Sharman, Alexander and Reid, and FSL McNeil led Pattison, Fitzgibbon and Dissette on practice escort patrols.

20th May

The first enemy opposition was encountered when FSL McNeil led Parker and Pattison on a line patrol from Ypres to Armentières at 08.30. McNeil claimed a scout out of control to the east of Armentières at 09.50 and Pattison claimed another out of control, but then had to make a forced landing at La Lovie after the combat, damaging his machine. During the

An annoyingly poor shot of Naval 10 Triplanes at Droglandt. A variety of different markings can be seen, but the fourth machine carried the letter "A" on the fuselage side and is believed to be FSL W.M. Alexander's Triplane N5487. *Author's collection*

Triplane N5366 was flown by FSL C.E. Pattison of A Flight on the 20th May when he made an Out Of Control claim. Pattison was seriously wounded during the combat and made a forced landing, damaging the Triplane. N5366 had a long life with Naval 10, FSL Sharman claimed a scout destroyed on 24th June and a 2-seater out of control on the 26th June, and FSL G.L. Trapp claimed an Albatros scout out of control on the 21st August. *Author's collection*

combat Pattison received injuries that required hospitalisation and resulted in his being struck off the squadron strength.

Further uneventful line patrols over the same section were carried out by Collishaw and Reid at 09.45, Sharman and Alexander at 11.00, Dissette and Page at 12.10 and Shirriff, Keens and Fitzgibbon at 16.35. Collishaw led Sharman and Nash at 18.00 but suffered engine trouble and was forced to return early.

FSL Nash carried out a hostile aircraft patrol at 19.35 when an enemy machine was reported to be over Ypres. No hostile machines were seen.

At 20.10, Collishaw and McNeil took the opportunity to get some gunnery practice at the Clairmarais range.

21st May

FSL Nash and FSL Alexander performed a line patrol from Ypres to Armentières at 09.10, however, the pilots became separated in heavy mist and cloud. Nash ran into 5 Albatros scouts and claimed one destroyed between Ypres and Staden at 10.30. Due to the heavy mist Nash was forced to land at the aerodrome of No. 2 Naval Squadron at St. Pol. FSL Alexander landed at Hondschoote following an indecisive engagement with an enemy machine.

During the course of the day most of the pilots took part in gunnery practice using the Clairmarais range. Both Sharman in N5485 and McNeil in N5365 crashed during the practice session.

FSL Reid escaped the first day's gunnery practice, having flown N6297 to Cassell for comparative testing against a captured Albatros scout, Baby Nieuport, and a Sopwith Pup. Reid reported that the Triplane was far superior in speed and climbing power and seemed to handle equally quickly as any other.

22nd May

Further gunnery practice was carried out at Clairmarais during the day.

23rd May

In the morning, FSL Boyd and FSL Holcroft performed a practice line patrol from Poperinghe to Merville, Boyd also flew to Clairmarais for gunnery practice.

The same pattern was repeated in the afternoon when Fitzgibbon, Dissette and Keens flew a practice line patrol, followed by gunnery practice.

FSL Alexander and Nash took off at 19.00 on a hostile aircraft patrol. The reported enemy machine was not observed.

24th May

FSL Keens and Shirriff flew to Clairmarais for gunnery practice at 10.20.

25th May

FSL Keens and Fitzgibbon performed a hostile aircraft patrol at 07.15. They patrolled the area from Poperinghe to Merville at 15000 feet but the reported enemy machines were not observed.

FSL Parker took off at 09.05 on a hostile aircraft patrol, when he tested his gun it was found to be jammed and he was forced to return.

Most of the day was taken up with practice line patrols, gunnery practice, and practicing aerial tactics.

Two hostile aircraft patrols were flown at 18.50 to the coast off Ostende, searching for enemy aircraft returning from bombing Dover. FSL Dissette with Keens and Page did not encounter any hostile machines but FSL McNeil accompanied by Boyd and Parker encountered enemy scouts 15 miles off Ostende, McNeil and Parker both claimed a scout shot down out of control at 19.45.

26th May

FSL Holcroft and FSL Taylor carried out a hostile aircraft patrol at 06.28, they became separated and Holcroft patrolled from Poperinghe to Merville on his own, the reported enemy machine was not seen. Taylor was forced to land at Hondschoote due to bad visibility. Upon his return he encountered a hostile machine near Poperinghe which dived away to the east upon his approach.

FSL Alexander performed a hostile aircraft patrol at 09.00. No enemy machines were seen and Alexander reported that the visibility was very bad.

At 18.05, Collishaw led the full complement of B Flight in the air for the first time, carrying out a practice formation patrol, and finishing off with gunnery practice at Clairmarais.

In similar exercises at 19.15, McNeil led A Flight out at full strength for the first time.

27th May

At 05.50, enemy aircraft patrols were flown by McNeil, Parker, Dissette, Fitzgibbon, Collishaw and Sharman. Each patrol stayed out for 90 minutes but no enemy aircraft were seen.

FSL Shirriff carried out a hostile aircraft patrol at 09.15, the reported enemy machine was not seen.

At 18.45, FSL Dissette led the full complement of C Flight pilots on a practice formation patrol between Poperinghe and Merville.

FSL McNeil led Taylor and Holcroft on another practice patrol at 19.00, finishing the patrol with gunnery practice at Clairmarais.

28th May

In the morning, Boyd, and Parker flew hostile aircraft patrols at 09.50 and 10.20 respectively, the reported enemy aircraft were not seen.

FSL Boyd flew another hostile aircraft patrol in the afternoon at 14.10, no enemy aircraft were observed.

All three flights carried out a formation patrol and gunnery practice, A Flight at 17.50, C Flight at 18.50, and B flight at 19.45.

29th May

FSL Parker flew Triplane N6306 to No.20 Squadron RFC for comparative tests with an FE and various Nieuport machines.

Sharman and Nash took advantage of further gunnery practice at the Clairmarais range at 19.25.

30th May

Another day of practising. Keens and Fitzgibbon flew a practice patrol from Poperinghe to Merville, Shirriff and Dissette flew to Clairmarais for gunnery practice at 17.30, McNeil led Parker and Taylor on a formation practice followed by gunnery practice at 19.10.

31st May

FSL Dissette led C Flight on a line patrol from Ypres to Armentières at 18.30. Shirriff's machine suffered engine trouble and he was forced to return, the patrol was otherwise uneventful. Fitzgibbon got away late and completed the patrol on his own.

FSL Holcroft carried out a hostile aircraft patrol at 19.30. The reported enemy machine was not seen.

June 1917

In June, the Allied forces concentrated their efforts in Flanders, the ultimate intention being to liberate the Belgian coast and bring pressure to bear on the enemy's northern flank. The first objective was the capture of the Messines-Wytschaete Ridge. With control of Messines, the Ypres battlefields and the Lys valley could be overlooked.

The British 2nd Army were tasked with taking the Messines ridge and the battle was scheduled to start on the 7th June. No.10 Squadron were to support the second army in the forthcoming battle. The opposing German forces were well aware of the Allied intent and were also moving air units to the north. The German presence doubled during June and July. Of great significance was the appearance of Richthofen's *Jagdgeschwader* 1 fighter wing comprising *Jastas* 4, 6, 10, and 11. No.10 Squadron's first positive contact with JG 1 occurred on the 23rd June.

In order to prevent enemy aircraft from crossing the balloon line between Perenchies and Langemarck, the concept of northern and southern offensive patrols was introduced whereby two patrols simultaneously flew a northern and southern route to meet up approximately above the centre of the battlefield. Any enemy machines breaking through would be reported by wireless and hopefully intercepted by hostile aircraft patrols.

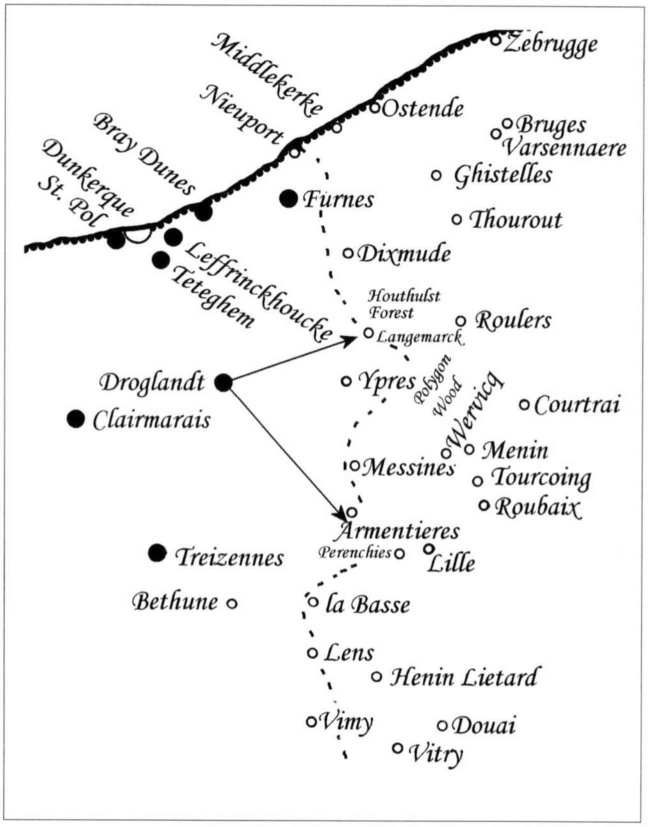

Sketch map showing area of operation from Droglandt and the path of simultaneous Northern and Southern Offensive Patrols which swept round to meet up over the Messines battlefield.

The battle opened as planned on the 7th June with the detonation of 19 mines which had been laid beneath the German positions on the Messines ridge. 400 tons of Ammonal had been placed after months of careful tunnelling. The attack on the ridge was almost completely successful by the 8th and by the 10th fighting had generally died down.

1st June

C Flight were allocated hostile aircraft patrols on the 1st. FSL Shirriff took off at 04.50 but failed to see any enemy machines.

Dissette, Page and Fitzgibbon all took off at 06.30 upon receipt of a report of a spotting machine working to the southeast of Ypres. Dissette and Page encountered the spotting machine and claimed it driven down out of control at 07.15. The patrol then drove away another spotting machine and recorded an indecisive engagement with eight Albatros scouts.

B Flight carried out a distant offensive patrol at 07.30. Reid claimed a 2-seater shot down in flames to the south of Wervicq at 09.15 and Collishaw claimed a scout shot down in flames to the southwest of Wervicq at 09.20. Nash engaged an enemy machine and saw his tracers entering its fuselage. The enemy machine spun away but Nash was not sure that it was out of control.

FSL McNeil's A Flight carried out an offensive patrol between Becelaere and Quesnoy at 17.20. The visibility was reported as poor and both Holcroft and Taylor lost the formation in cloud and returned early.

2nd June

FSL McNeil, Parker, Boyd and Holcroft took off at 07.40 on a hostile aircraft patrol. The Triplanes patrolled at heights from 12000 to 14000 feet but the reported enemy machines were not encountered.

Collishaw led Reid, Alexander and Nash on another hostile aircraft patrol at 09.20. The flight attacked a spotting machine over St. Julien, Collishaw followed it down to 8000 feet and it was last seen going down in a spin. Collishaw, Alexander, Reid and Nash shared the out of control claim.

Later that morning, at 11.18, B and C Flights provided a combined escort for two FE's from No.20 Squadron RFC. The

FEs abandoned their photographic reconnaissance mission due to heavy clouds and landed at Droglandt. The C Flight Commander, FSL A Dissette, flying Triplane N6294 failed to return from the mission. Dissette was shot down and killed over Coxyde, his Triplane broke up and crashed in a wood near Proven. *Ltn.* Gustav Nolte of *Jasta* 18 has been credited with shooting down Dissette.

The FEs made another attempt at their photographic reconnaissance mission at 15.48. Collishaw led B Flight and McNeil joined Page and Keens of C Flight to provide the escort. Upon their return, one of the FEs made a forced landing to the west of Ypres.

3rd June

Three hostile aircraft patrols were flown in the morning. Collishaw, Reid, Sharman and Alexander took off at 06.00; one hostile machine was observed over St. Julien and another over Hooge. Both dived away eastwards before the patrol could bring them to action.

Shirriff, Fitzgibbon, Keens and Page carried out the second patrol at 06.45. A 2-seater was encountered to the southeast of Ypres at 07.30 and driven down over Lille. The observer returned fire for a short time but suddenly stopped. Another 2-seater was attacked at 07.50, but it dived beneath the patrol and was not seen again.

The third hostile aircraft patrol was carried out by Collishaw, Sharman, Reid and Alexander at 08.10. The patrol found two spotting machines working over St. Julien, but was unable to bring them to action before they dived away to the east.

At 10.05, FSL McNeil led six Triplanes on a distant offensive patrol to Becelaere, Menin and Quesnoy, providing an escort for Sopwith 1 1/2 Strutters of No.45 Squadron. Apart from anti-aircraft fire over Tourcoing, the mission was uneventful.

FSL McNeil led Taylor and Parker on a northern offensive patrol at 17.00, whilst Page, Sharman and Keens carried out the southern offensive patrol. McNeil's patrol encountered twelve Albatros scouts at 18.00, Parker shot down one scout which was seen to crash between Ypres and Courtrai by FSL Taylor, and Taylor engaged another indecisively. The Flight Commander, FSL McNeil was shot down and killed near Moorslede, believed to be the victim of *Offstlvtr* St. Klein of *Jasta* 27. Page, Sharman and Keens made an indecisive attack on the rear part of a formation of nine Albatros scouts.

At 17.45 FSL Boyd was dispatched on a hostile aircraft patrol to the north of Ypres. No enemy machines were observed.

A northern and southern offensive patrol was flown at 18.50. Collishaw led Reid and Alexander on the southern patrol, whilst Nash led Holcroft and Fitzgibbon on the northern patrol. The northern patrol encountered four Albatros scouts and engaged one indecisively. The patrol then met up with the southern patrol near Roubaix where five scouts were engaged. Collishaw claimed one scout shot down in flames at 20.15 and Reid shot another down which was seen to crash in a small field at 20.25.

The loss of two flight commanders on consecutive days was devastating and demonstrated the inadvisability of using personnel with insufficient experience of scout operations as flight commanders, an error that would be repeated again before the year was out. Squadron Commander Bell's immediate response to the loss of the two flight commanders was to move Sharman into C Flight, Fitzgibbon into B Flight and to use the remaining A Flight pilots to support B and C Flights to create larger patrols when necessary. As the year progressed, SCdr Bell would follow this pattern whenever a flight was weakened, either by combat losses or scheduled leave, he would run two Flights and use the spare pilots from the weakened Flight to reinforce the other two when necessary.

To provide the squadron with more versatility during the week after the start of the battle of Messines, A Flight was briefly resurrected from the 7th to the 12th June, by borrowing FSL R. McDonald from Naval 8 as a temporary Flight Commander.

In the following weeks, Sharman was effectively the leader of C Flight, although SCdr Bell sometimes appointed Page to take command for the occasional patrol.

4th June

The squadron was placed on readiness to respond to wireless reports during the morning of the 4th. Two new pilots, FSL Winter and FSL Prewett were unceremoniously dumped straight into the action.

Six pilots took off at 05.40 in response to reports of numerous incursions by spotting machines and scouts. A 2-seater and three scouts were encountered to the north of the salient and driven off and another 2-seater was found to the south of Ypres and driven away without a fight.

Four pilots were dispatched at 06.25; a spotting machine and six scouts were encountered and driven off.

Boyd performed a hostile aircraft patrol over Cassel at 07.04, no enemy machines were observed.

Taylor and Parker performed a hostile aircraft patrol at 07.40 in response to reports of a hostile machine over St. Omer. The patrol failed to find the intruder.

At 08.20, Fitzgibbon, Alexander, Reid and Winter took off in response to signals reporting enemy aircraft. They encountered an observation machine escorted by nine scouts to the northeast of the salient, the patrol drove off the 2-seater but was attacked by its escort. Fitzgibbon's machine was badly shot about, but Alexander was able to claim one scout driven down out of control. The new pilot, FSL Winter, had returned to the aerodrome suffering from airsickness.

Holcroft took off at 09.05 but failed to find the reported intruder.

Collishaw carried out a hostile aircraft patrol at 10.05 and discovered a hostile machine near Ypres. Collishaw drove the enemy machine off, firing 50 rounds at it.

Page and Sharman were dispatched at 10.25 and observed an enemy machine being shelled by an anti-aircraft battery. The intruder dived away before the Triplanes could get close to it.

Keens and Shirriff left at 10.30, Shirriff saw nothing but Keens encountered an enemy machine near Armentières which dived away before he was able to bring it to action.

Four pilots carried out a hostile aircraft patrol at 12.00, covering Langemarck to Becelaere and Tenbrielen. No enemy machines were seen.

Holcroft, Prewett and Keens performed a central offensive patrol at 13.20. No enemy aircraft were observed.

At 18.00, C and B Flights carried out high southern and northern offensive patrols. C Flight encountered a 2-seater near Hollebeke, the enemy machine dived away to the east when the patrol attempted to attack. B Flight observed five separate hostile 2-seaters in the vicinity of Ypres, all were driven off before they could be approached. The patrol also observed two large formations of enemy aircraft to the east.

5th June

B Flight flew a high northern offensive patrol and C Flight the southern patrol at 08.05. Collishaw, assisted by Boyd, Nash and Fitzgibbon, shot down a 2-seater in flames near Wervicq at 08.50, and at 09.40, Collishaw and Fitzgibbon attacked another 2-seater over Poelcappelle, sending it down out of control. At 08.45, C Flight went to the rescue of a flight of FEs which were engaged with four enemy scouts. After a brief engagement two of the enemy machines went down spinning but they were not thought to be out of control. FSL Shirriff in Triplane N6303 suffered engine trouble and made a forced landing at Poperinghe, damaging the machine.

At 13.00, Taylor, Boyd and Winter flew a northern offensive patrol whilst Prewett, Holcroft and Parker covered the southern area. Winter returned suffering from airsickness again. Taylor engaged an enemy machine between Dixmude and Nieuport at 14.10 and shot it down in flames. Boyd encountered an enemy machine to the northeast of Ypres but the encounter was inconclusive and Boyd was forced to return with a gun stoppage. Prewett lost formation and returned early. The depleted southern patrol encountered an enemy machine which was engaged at long range without effect.

6th June

A major engagement took place over Polygon Wood between B and C Flights and an estimated fifteen to twenty enemy machines. Between 10.50 and 11.05, Collishaw had claimed two Albatros scouts shot down in flames and an Albatros scout sent down completely out of control with the pilot apparently dead. Alexander fired 20 rounds into an Albatros scout from a range of 75 feet, all of his tracers entered the enemy's fuselage in the region of the seat. The machine fell in a spinning vertical nosedive. Nash attacked a 2-seater which he followed down to 3000 feet. Nash observed the machine hit the ground and burst into flames. Immediately afterwards he fired at an enemy scout from very close range, the scout went down and was last seen in a vertical dive within 500 feet of the ground. Reid was attacked by four scouts at 11.05 and fought them down to 5000 feet, at this point he obtained a good position on one machine and followed it down firing into it until it crashed nose first into the ground. Page fired at an enemy scout at a range of 50 to 75 feet, observing his tracers go into the pilot's back. The scout went down immediately and was seen to crash by FSL Taylor. Keens claimed a scout driven down completely out of control at 10.50. Sharman, who was leading C Flight, fired at an Albatros scout from a range of 50 feet observing his tracers enter the fuselage immediately behind the pilot, the scout went down completely out of control. These claims should be tempered by the fact that German losses reported for the 6th of June totalled one pilot killed and one wounded, neither of them remotely close to the engagement over Polygon Wood.

C and B Flights carried out northern and southern offensive patrols at 16.00. Heavy thunderstorms were building in the Ypres to Armentières area so both patrols moved north into the Dixmude area. Conditions were difficult with storms encountered everywhere.

7th June

This was the opening day of the Battle of Messines. Page led C Flight off at 07.15, followed by Collishaw's B Flight at 07.30. The two flights carried out offensive patrols over the section from Lille to Ypres and followed six Albatros scouts to St. Julien and Clercken where they were seen to attack an allied formation. Another formation of twelve enemy machines was observed at 10000 feet and Collishaw led B Flight against the latter formation at 08.45. Collishaw attacked a scout which was about to attack Nash and sent it down out of control. Nash fired 50 rounds into a scout at close range, observing his tracers enter the fuselage, the enemy scout stalled, side slipped and fell out of control.

FSL Reid became separated from the patrol during the engagement. At 09.15 he encountered a 2-seater near Clercken, fired a few rounds and hit the pilot who fell forward. The machine went into a nosedive and was seen to crash in a field.

C Flight was also involved in the morning's activity, Sharman shot down an Albatros scout at 09.15, seeing it crash and shot the pilot of another scout, sending it down out of control. Sharman's machine, N6307, was damaged by gunfire and he was forced to land at Coudekerke. FSL Keens was shot in the chest but managed to land at Chateau Lovie aerodrome.

B and C Flight performed another northern and southern offensive patrol at 13.30. The area covered comprised Poelcappelle, Passchendaele, Wervicq and Perenchies. The weather had closed in with thick cloud and poor visibility. No enemy machines were encountered.

Collishaw crashed and damaged Triplane N6302 during a test flight.

FSL R. McDonald arrived at No.10 Squadron, on secondment from Naval 8 for a week; he arrived with his own Triplane, N6301, which carried the legend "Dusty II".

McDonald was placed with A Flight and was soon in action when he participated in a seven machine offensive patrol at 20.10. The Triplanes of A and C Flights patrolled the area from Poelcappelle to Wervicq and Perenchies, with the intention of finding enemy kite balloons. FSL Taylor attacked a kite balloon near Gheluvelt and fired 90 rounds into it without effect.

8th June

A Flight took off at 04.08, followed by C Flight at 04.10, the two flights carrying out southern and northern offensive patrols over the area from Poelcappelle to Wervicq and Perenchies. No enemy aircraft were encountered. Prewett suffered engine failure in N5372 and damaged the machine when he made a forced landing in a field near the aerodrome.

At 09.30, B Flight and C Flight were involved in northern and southern offensive patrols. A 2-seater was observed over St. Julien at 10.15, another 2-seater was seen over Veldhoek

FSL R. McDonald with his Naval 8 Triplane N6301, Dusty II. McDonald and his Triplane were seconded to Naval 10's A Flight on the 7th June 1917. This enabled SCdr Bell to be able to field three Flights during the first week of the battle of Messines. *Author's collection*

at 10.35 and six scouts were seen to the north of Menin with twelve more high above them at 10.45. At 11.15, Page and Alexander attacked an enemy machine which turned beneath them and was lost to sight.

B Flight and C Flights carried out a northern and southern offensive patrol in the afternoon. B flight encountered and engaged a formation of Albatros scouts which proved to be a trap. Collishaw was fortunate to survive a crash after N5490's controls were shot away when he sprung the trap.

9th June

Enemy activity had subsided and the next few days saw a dramatic drop in the amount of contact with enemy aircraft.

Heavy cloud reduced visibility on the 9th. B Flight left on a hostile aircraft patrol at 06.55, the reported enemy aircraft was not observed.

A Flight took off in bad conditions at 20.12 after a signal was received reporting an intrusion. No hostile machines were seen.

10th June

Heavy rain interfered with all flying activity.

11th June

C Flight attempted to carry out an offensive patrol at 05.40, light cloud was encountered at 100 feet, turning to heavy cloud at 6000 feet. The patrol was forced to return when heavy rain was encountered. FSL Saunders flying N5361 got lost in rain clouds and landed at Hondschoote.

12th June

The weather was improved by the 12th, but enemy aircraft proved difficult to bring to action.

Northern and southern offensive patrols were carried out at 07.30 by B and A Flights. Both patrols reported considerable numbers of hostile machines seen well behind their own lines.

C Flight were dispatched on an enemy aircraft patrol at 09.35 in response to a reported intrusion. Immediately after take-off, Shirriff suffered engine failure in N5368 and damaged the machine in the subsequent forced landing. Page lost the patrol but encountered an enemy 2-seater to the southeast of Ypres and drove it back behind its own lines. The rest of the patrol failed to find any hostile machines.

McDonald led A Flight on an enemy aircraft patrol at 10.24. No enemy aircraft were found in the reported area.

B Flight took-off at 11.03 on another enemy aircraft patrol. The reported intruder was found over Westhoek and driven off.

The last enemy aircraft patrol of the day was flown by Sharman, Prewett, Boyd and Holcroft at 12.25. The reported machine was not found but the patrol observed an encounter between FEs and enemy aircraft to the southeast of Ypres. By the time the Triplanes reached the area, the enemy machines had gone east and the FEs were returning.

At 15.30, B and C Flights carried out northern and southern offensive patrols. A heavy thunderstorm caused the patrols to break up and return, Shirriff landed at Petite Synthe and Page and Sharman landed at Bray Dunes.

FSL R. McDonald and his Triplane "Dusty II" returned to Naval 8 after their brief stay with A Flight.

13th June

A change in command structure took place on the 13th, with control transferring to 22 Wing 5 Brigade.

Northern and southern offensive patrols were flown at 05.30, Boyd led A Flight and Sharman was in charge of C Flight. Visibility was again impaired by heavy cloud between Ypres and Armentières, extending from 6000 to 10000 feet, with more cloud above and rainstorms below. Two machines returned almost immediately, one with a broken centre section wire and the other with engine trouble. The patrols were abandoned after 45 minutes.

B Flight carried out an enemy aircraft patrol at 07.50, the visibility was very bad and no enemy aircraft were seen.

Sharman led an enemy aircraft patrol at 08.18. The patrol crossed the lines between two heavy layers of cloud, and dived through the lower bank over the search area. An enemy 2-seater was working over Langemarck but escaped eastwards when approached.

Holcroft and Parker carried out an enemy aircraft patrol at 09.11, the area was thoroughly patrolled but no enemy machines were seen.

At 11.30, B and C Flights carried out high northern and high southern offensive patrols. The visibility was still bad and no enemy aircraft were encountered.

FSL Page led a seven Triplane offensive patrol over Passchendaele, Wervicq and Perenchies at 17.25. Pegler, flying Triplane N5478 lost the formation and made a forced landing near Bailleul, damaging his machine.

14th June

FSL Boyd led a six Triplane offensive patrol at 04.15 and immediately ran into thick cloud and mist. The patrol was scattered with most of the pilots getting lost, Boyd landed at Herzeele, Prewett made a forced landing at Oost Cappelle, Taylor landed at Zouafques and Shirriff ended up at Manston in Kent. Only Parker and Holcroft found their way back to the aerodrome.

B and C Flights carried out an offensive patrol at 08.35. Two scouts and a 2-seater were observed in an engagement with a flight of FEs over Menin at 09.45. The patrol attacked and engaged the enemy machines; Collishaw fired 50 rounds at one machine which went down in a spin but was seen to recover and dive away to the east. Reid fired a couple of rounds and then suffered a gun stoppage, his opponent dived away to the east. Sharman fired a number of rounds into an enemy machine and saw tracers enter its fuselage, his opponent spun away under control. Later during the patrol, a 2-seater was encountered over the lines near Armentières and driven off after a brief engagement at long range.

Sharman led C Flight on an offensive patrol at 18.00 and encountered 6 Albatros scouts over Zonnebeke at 19.20. Sharman and Page were both credited with a scout driven down out of control but FSL Parker was shot down and killed in Triplane N5470. Parker is believed to have been the victim of Vzfw Krebs of Jasta 6.

15th June

Sharman led a C Flight offensive patrol at 08.20 but lost Boyd almost immediately with engine trouble. The patrol was further weakened when Shirriff dropped out for the same reasons. Sharman pressed on with Page and Saunders and encountered three 2-seaters over Houthem, and a 2-seater accompanied by three scouts over Poelcappelle. Sharman and Page both claimed a 2-seater out of control at Houthem at 09.40. The patrol encountered a 2-seater being pursued by a Belgian Nieuport near Poelcappelle at 10.25. Sharman dived to assist the Nieuport but the 2-seater was able to escape eastwards. Sharman then led the patrol against five enemy scouts with indecisive results.

Collishaw, newly promoted to Flight Lieutenant, led a six machine patrol at 09.25. Holcroft was compelled to drop out of the patrol with engine trouble and landed at Coudekerke. The patrol encountered two 2-seaters over Lille at 10.30 and engaged them without result. At 10.55, a general engagement took place with five Halberstadt scouts near St. Julien. Collishaw attacked one machine from behind and fired 50 rounds at close range. The enemy machine dropped into a nosedive and Collishaw believed that the motor had been hit or the pilot was wounded. Fitzgibbon was able to fire a long burst into a scout from a favourable position, it was seen to turn on to its back and then fall out of control in a series of stalls and spins.

At 16.00, B and C Flights carried out an offensive patrol. Five 2-seaters were encountered over Menin, one was driven down out of control by Collishaw at 17.15. At 17.40 over Moorslede several 2-seaters and ten to fifteen Halberstadt and Albatros scouts were encountered and a general engagement took place. Collishaw attacked an Albatros scout from very close range at 17.45. The enemy machine turned on its side and went down in a series of spins, stalls and sideslips. Collishaw then got in position behind a scout which was attacking Alexander, after firing 100 rounds Collishaw observed the scout's right hand planes break away and the machine fell in pieces. Whilst Collishaw dived to attack, Fitzgibbon remained above the fight and attacked another scout which had dived towards the engagement. Fitzgibbon opened fire whilst the enemy machine was broadside on, the scout turned on its side and then fell away out of control. Reid attacked a scout and observed his tracers enter the fuselage near the pilot, the machine went down in a nosedive, turned over on its back, and fell completely out of control. Reid then went to the rescue of another Triplane, obtaining a good position behind the enemy scout. Reid fired from a range of 30 yards observing his tracers enter the top of the fuselage just behind the pilot. The pilot fell back with his head on one side and the machine fell absolutely out of control. Alexander attacked a 2-seater and fired 30 rounds at close range, he observed his tracers hitting the observer in the chest and head. The 2-seater dived away very steeply, but appeared to be under control.

Sharman led a five Triplane hostile aircraft patrol at 20.18 to intercept enemy bombers returning from England. Holcroft's machine suffered engine failure after take-off and he was compelled to land immediately. The visibility was very poor due to mist and no enemy machines were seen. Owing to the onset of darkness, Sharman landed at Wormhoudt, and Pegler damaged N5367 when he turned it over whilst landing.

16th June

Collishaw led an uneventful offensive patrol at 08.05. The visibility was reported as very bad.

Sharman led an offensive patrol at 09.35. One enemy machine was seen over Polygon Wood, when approached it headed eastwards. A flight of enemy machines were occasionally seen at great height.

Sharman and Collishaw led further offensive patrols at 18.00 and 18.35 respectively. The visibility was reported as indifferent and neither patrol observed any enemy aircraft.

New pilot FSL Kent arrived at the squadron.

17th June

Sharman and Collishaw led offensive patrols at 08.10 and 09.35 respectively. The B Flight patrol encountered 3 enemy machines about ten miles east of Ypres, these headed eastwards when approached. Five 2-seaters were observed later at 17000 feet over Wulverghen, as soon as the patrol started to climb, the enemy machines turned away to the east.

Collishaw led a six Triplane offensive patrol at 18.00. A patrol of five SPADs linked up with the Triplanes at Armentières and at 19.10, when over Roulers, the combined patrols attacked 8 enemy machines. Collishaw attacked a scout that was firing at a SPAD and drove it down out of control. Reid claimed a scout out of control with the pilot hit and a SPAD claimed a scout driven down.

Sharman led C Flight on an offensive patrol at 19.05. The patrol encountered a flight of FEs being attacked at Houthem at 20.00 and went in above the FEs to keep the enemy scouts away from them. Sharman kept the patrol out for half an hour beyond the normal patrol time to stay with the FEs.

18th June

Collishaw led an offensive patrol at 08.00 and encountered five enemy 2-seaters in the vicinity of Perenchies, the hostile machines were engaged and driven off to the east.

Sharman led an offensive patrol at 09.20. Shirriff in N5357 suffered engine trouble after take-off and was compelled to make a forced landing in a field near the aerodrome. Saunders also dropped out of the patrol and returned to the aerodrome. The visibility was bad, one enemy machine was seen over the west end of Polygon Wood but it dived away to the east when approached.

19th June

Storms were present throughout the day and no flying took place.

20th June

The weather was still unsettled. Collishaw led a local patrol over Herzeele at 11.05 but was forced to return due to very low clouds and an approaching storm.

21st June

The squadron put on an uncharacteristically poor show on the 21st. Sharman led C Flight and Collishaw led B Flight on an escort and offensive patrol at 07.34. The patrols were arranged to enable two DH4 reconnaissance machines to be escorted over the lines, however, the DH4 pilots failed to wait for the escort and the Triplane pilots were unable to get into the proper formation at the start. On reaching the lines, but whilst still scattered, the Triplanes encountered a number of enemy aircraft at Ypres. Collishaw, Fitzgibbon and Boyd all suffered engine or gun trouble and were forced to return to the aerodrome to exchange their aircraft. Taylor flying Nash's Black Sheep, N5376, was shot down by anti-aircraft fire but was able to make a successful forced landing.

22nd June

Bad weather again affected operations over the next couple of days. All flying was abandoned on the 22nd.

23rd June

Sharman was promoted to Flight Lieutenant on the 23rd.

B and C Flights again attempted to escort a pair of DH4s over the lines at 07.30. The DH4s quickly abandoned their mission due to the weather but the Triplanes attempted offensive patrols over Staden, Roulers, Menin and Comines. Low cloud and an approaching storm resulted in the patrols being abandoned.

FSL Holcroft led an inner patrol at 10.30, a 2-seater was seen to the north of Ypres but the patrol was unable to bring it to action.

B Flight attempted a patrol at 18.40 but heavy clouds and snow at 8000 feet made conditions difficult.

C Flight left on a patrol at 18.40 but three of the pilots lost formation in the cloud. Sharman and Pegler encountered an RE8 being pursued by six red painted enemy scouts near Pilken at 20.30. The two Triplanes kept station above the RE8 until it could get away. Pegler then had to abandon the patrol due to engine trouble, Sharman teamed up with a SPAD and at 20.40 they saw flight of three Sopwith 1 1/2 Strutters being attacked by the same enemy machines. Sharman engaged one scout at long range without result and was then forced to break

off the engagement when he came under attack from two other scouts from the formation. The Sopwith 1 1/2 Strutters were able to escape whilst the enemy machines were occupied with Sharman and the SPAD.

24th June

B and C Flights flew another escort and offensive patrol mission at 07.35. The two DH4 photographic reconnaissance machines were escorted over the lines but ran into trouble when 15 to 20 brightly coloured scouts were encountered over Zonnebeke and Moorslede at 8.05. Combats ensued which resulted in 2 scouts being shot down, Collishaw claimed a machine destroyed at Moorslede at 08.10 and Sharman clamed a scout destroyed at Zonnebeke, also at 08.10. Both scouts were seen to break up in the air. Pegler reported seeing another enemy scout going down out of control and still spinning when within 200 to 300 feet of the ground. Reid and Taylor suffered engine trouble and were forced to return early. Saunders and Holcroft both failed to return from the patrol. Saunders was shot down and killed over Moorslede in N5358, and Holcroft was shot down in N6306 at Zonnebeke. Holcroft was wounded and became a prisoner of war. *Jasta* 11's *Ltn*. K. Allmenröder and *Ltn.* Groos both claimed Triplanes destroyed during the engagement. Naval 1 had a patrol in the vicinity and reported seeing a Triplane breaking up in the air.

FSL Fitzgibbon had become separated from B Flight during the general engagement, at 09.00 he observed a 2-seater over the lines to the south of Ypres and engaged it from below. Fitzgibbon's gun suffered repeated stoppages and he was compelled to break of the attack.

Despite the seemingly conclusive claims made by Collishaw and Sharman, the German Air Service admitted no losses in the area.

FSL Reid led a patrol at 10.00; a 2-seater was driven away from Ypres at 11.25. Prewett in N5361 failed to pick up the formation and landed at Hondschoote.

C Flight carried out an offensive patrol at 18.00 over the inner and outer areas. Sharman flying Reid's Triplane, Black Roger, N5483, suffered engine failure and was compelled to make a forced landing, damaging the Triplane.

25th June

C Flight and B Flight carried out offensive patrols over the inner and outer areas at 10.10 and 10.15 respectively. Thick cloud obscured the entire area. Pegler in N5359 suffered engine failure and made a forced landing at La Lovie, wrecking the machine.

Because of bad weather, and acting on instructions, B Flight carried out a line patrol at 7000 to 8000 feet between Armentières and the Dixmude floods. The patrol took off at 17.30 and encountered 3 scouts near Hollebeke where several indecisive combats took place. Kent lost formation and returned to the aerodrome. Nash in N5376 "Black Sheep" also lost formation and was shot down to the east of Messines by *Ltn*. K. Allmenröder of *Jasta* 11. Nash was wounded and spent the remainder of the hostilities as a Prisoner of War. In an interview many years later, W.M. Alexander stated that Collishaw had refused to allow the other members of the patrol to go down to help Nash, an incident that caused Alexander to feel resentment for the rest of his life.

Left: FSL R.G. Saunders was shot down and killed over Moorslede in Triplane N5358 during an engagement with *Jasta* 11 on the 24th June. *Courtesy E.F. Cheesman* Right: FSL Holcroft, flying N6306, a C Flight triplane, was also shot down during the engagement with *Jasta* 11 on the 24th June. Holcroft survived this crash and became a prisoner of war. N6306 had been on the squadron strength since the 24th May, FSL L.H. Parker making two out of control claims, one on the 25th May and the second on the 3rd June, and FSL K.G. Boyd shared a claim in a 2-seater destroyed in flames on the 5th June. *Author's collection*

FSL Holman and FSL Drummond joined the squadron on the 25th.

26th June

Sharman led C Flight on an offensive patrol at 15.31. At 16.00, the patrol was at 7000 feet over Messines when an enemy 2-seater was observed at 12000 feet, the enemy machine moved away eastwards before the patrol could climb to its altitude. Another 2-seater was observed over Ypres at 17.00, this machine also retired to the east.

Collishaw led an offensive patrol at 17.20 and reported seeing enemy aircraft to the east of Menin. Taylor was compelled to change aircraft at the start of the patrol and failed to pick up the formation. He engaged a 2-seater near Wervicq at 19.45 and drove it down out of control. Taylor landed at Berre, east of Hazebrouck at 20.20.

27th June

Sharman led C Flight on an offensive patrol at 15.42. Drummond and Shirriff were delayed when their engines proved difficult to start and Page subsequently suffered from engine failure and made a forced landing at Proven. Seven scouts were encountered over Houthulst Forest at 16.30, the formation moved away before it could be approached. At 17.00, two formations of enemy scouts were encountered over Moorslede but the patrol was unable to close with them. At 17.35, anti-aircraft fire was observed near allied kite balloons and one balloon was seen to catch fire. The patrol was unable to get within firing distance of the enemy scout as it retreated back across the lines at Boesinghe.

Collishaw led B Flight on an offensive patrol at 17.22, the patrol indecisively engaged an enemy 2-seater over the lines to the north of Armentières at 18.10. One hour later a formation of three scouts was attacked without result over Fortuin. A storm then forced the patrol to descend to a lower altitude.

28th June

Bad weather prevented all flying until the evening. Both C and B Flights patrols had been delayed due to an approaching storm but reports were received of a large number of enemy machines over Ypres and Hooge. B Flight took off at 17.52, followed by C Flight at 17.58; a lone enemy machine was observed over Ypres at 18.00 and another was seen over Clercken at 18.50. Both machines dived away to the east before they could be approached. The patrols reported that visibility was very bad and that rainsqualls had been encountered.

29th June

Weather conditions again prevented any flying until the evening when B and C Flights carried out high offensive patrols at 18.05. Four enemy machines were observed several miles behind Roulers heading in an easterly direction.

30th June

Bad weather prevented all flying activity.

July 1917

Preparations for the Flanders offensive continued through July. Whilst the opening infantry assault was planned for the 25th July, the air offensive was intended to begin on the 8th July. Five Brigade RFC were to support the British 5th Army, No.10 Naval Squadron, No.23 Squadron, No.29 Squadron and No.32 Squadron were to provide the fighter cover.

The opening infantry assault in the 3rd Battle of Ypres was eventually delayed until the 31st July. The appalling weather made offensive patrols almost impossible and scout squadrons were restricted to ground attacks and strafing of enemy positions.

1st July

Bad weather, no flying.

2nd July

A special squadron strength offensive patrol was flown at 10.00 using all eleven available pilots. Shirriff and Allan returned with motor trouble and left again immediately with different machines. Collishaw shot down a 2-seater at 11.10 near to Poelcappelle station but suffered gunfire damage to his engine and was forced to return. Sharman engaged a 2-seater indecisively over Houthem on the allied side of the lines at 11.30. Page and Reid engaged two 2-seaters indecisively.

Two further offensive patrols were carried out, one by C Flight at 15.30 and one by B Flight at 17.35. Neither patrol observed any enemy aircraft.

New pilots FLt A.W. Carter and FSL Barnes arrived on the 2nd July. Carter was a very experienced pilot having served with 3 Wing and flown Sopwith Pups with No.3 Squadron. SCdr Bell put Carter in charge of A Flight. Carter would go on to have a long association with No.10 Squadron and No.210 Squadron RAF, taking 210 to its final days in 1919 with the rank of Major.

3rd July

C Flight carried out an offensive patrol over the inner area at 05.25. Sharman reported layers of broken cloud at 5000 and at 6000 feet. The patrol was flown at 14000 feet; at 06.20, five enemy aircraft were observed over Roulers. These machines kept well to the east when the patrol tried to approach. FLt Page flying N5380 suffered engine failure and was compelled to make a forced landing in a field, the machine struck a ridge, overturned and was damaged.

B Flight covered the inner area at 08.20 at altitudes of 15000 to 17000 feet. A formation of enemy machines was observed to the east of Roulers.

At 15.10, B Flight carried out an offensive patrol over the inner area to guard allied artillery spotters working between Ypres and Hetsas.

C Flight, accompanied by FLt Carter, carried out an offensive patrol at 19.42. The flight patrolled the inner area and the lines between Ypres and Hetsas. A large number of enemy scouts were observed patrolling at various heights over Houthulst Forest between 20.25 and dusk.

FLt Carter flying N5381 experienced engine trouble and landed at No.7 Squadron RFC, damaging the Triplane slightly.

4th July

With A Flight now reformed, the squadron structure was as follows:

A Flight
FLt A.W. Carter, Flight Commander
FSL J.P. Barnes
FSL J.A.M. Allan
FSL C.R. Pegler
FSL C.M.R. Prewett

B Flight
FLt R. Collishaw, Flight Commander
FSL W.M. Alexander
FSL E.V. Reid
FSL D.F. Fitzgibbon
FSL H.W. Taylor

C Flight
FLt J.E. Sharman, Flight Commander
FLt J. Page
FSL R.L. Kent
FSL C. Lowther
FSL Q.S. Shirriff

B Flight took off at 04.06 to carry out an inner offensive patrol and cover the line between Ypres and Hetsas. The visibility was bad and no enemy aircraft were seen.

C Flight carried out a similar patrol at 06.53. Approximately fifteen enemy scouts were encountered over Roulers at 08.00, three scouts which were detached from the main formation were indecisively attacked.

FSL Prewett performed an enemy aircraft patrol at 08.20. The start of his mission was delayed after the signal reporting the intruder was received, due to difficulty in starting his Triplane's engine.

FLt Carter led the reformed A Flight on an offensive patrol at 09.44. The patrol again covered the inner area and the line from Ypres to Hetsas and also provided protection for two RE8s which were spotting to the south of Ypres. Heavy rain set in at 10.30 and Carter abandoned the patrol.

C Flight attempted to patrol the same area at 15.18. The visibility was extremely bad with very low cloud and heavy weather approaching from the north.

5th July

The weather prevented any war flying until the late afternoon when A Flight patrolled the inner area at 16.50.

B and C Flights covered the inner area at 19.45. Heavy cloud covered the whole area and visibility was reported as very bad.

6th July

B and C Flight attempted to fly a combined patrol at 09.40. FLt Sharman suffered engine trouble and had to return to change his machine. Lowther and Kent misunderstood Sharman's signals and followed him back to the aerodrome. B Flight continued alone and encountered considerable enemy activity over the area from Warneton to Deulemont and Quesnoy. A patrol of FEs from No.20 Squadron RFC was being attacked and a large number of enemy scouts were observed. Collishaw led B Flight into the fight and a general engagement ensued in which one scout was seen to crash and at least three others were believed to be out of control. Collishaw felt that he had personally accounted for six "out of controls" during the course of the engagement, however, after the combat reports were analysed, Squadron Commander Bell credited Alexander with two scouts out of control and Collishaw and Reid were each credited with one scout out of control. During the course of the engagement, Captain DC Cunnell and 2/Lt A.E. Woodbridge of No.20 Squadron RFC shot down and wounded *Rittm.* Manfred von Richthofen. The engagement was carried out at a height of 8000 feet at 11.00. All of the No.10 Squadron pilots returned safely.

A Flight carried out an offensive patrol at 12.15, four enemy aircraft were observed at 13.45 to the south of Ypres. The enemy machines appeared to be heading towards a flight of RE8s but rapidly retired eastwards at the approach of the Triplanes.

C Flight took off at 15.05 and escorted two RE8s from Ypres to Polygon Wood. One enemy machine was observed over Ypres at 16.20 and five more over Courtrai. FSL Lowther flying N5354 experienced a problem with his machine and landed at No.12 Naval Squadron.

A and B Flights carried out a combined offensive patrol at 18.20. Barnes returned with engine trouble, and Allan in N5375 had engine failure and was unable to reach the aerodrome. Allan made a forced landing on bad ground and wrecked the machine. The patrol observed eight enemy aircraft to the east of Deulemont but was unable to bring them to action.

7th July

A Flight carried out an offensive patrol at 05.25. A scout was observed over Tourcoing at 06.15 but the patrol was unable to close with it. Two 2-seaters were engaged between Moorslede and Roulers at 06.45, FSL Pegler submitted a combat report stating that he fired 40 rounds at one of the 2-seaters and observed tracers hit the tail, the 2-seater then started to spin towards the ground. Although the squadron record book described the incident as inconclusive, the RFC Communiqué for the 7th July optimistically credited Pegler with driving one of the 2-seaters down out of control.

Sharman led C Flight on an offensive patrol at 08.10 and encountered significant enemy activity with a large number of enemy machines seen over Polygon Wood at 08.45. The patrol dived on a flight of seven 2-seaters which retreated to the east. A patrol of seven scouts was engaged near Comines at 09.05 without result. During this combat FLt Page became separated from the flight and joined up with a French SPAD. The pair encountered three Albatros scouts and followed them over Lille. At 09.40, Page dived on one scout and fired 40 rounds at a range of 40 to 60 yards. Page saw his tracers enter the machine which fell completely out of control, when last seen, the scout was going down in a vertical dive.

B Flight performed an offensive patrol at 11.00. Five enemy scouts were observed at great height to the east of Messines at 12.00 and a single enemy machine was observed crossing the lines at St. Julien at 12.10, then crossing back near Messines.

A Flight were dispatched at 11.38 to intercept bombers returning from England. The patrol lay off the coast near Flushing with a large number of allied aircraft spread westwards from that point. No enemy machines were seen. Running low on fuel on their return, Carter, Pegler and Allan landed at Dunkerque, and Glasgow landed at Petite Synthe.

B and C Flights carried out a combined offensive patrol at 16.40. Whilst over the lines the patrol reported two machines seen falling on fire, one just after the other. At 17.05, four machines were seen travelling east and at 17.50, C Flight encountered a 2-seater to the south of Armentières. Sharman and Page closed with the 2-seater, Sharman fired 200 rounds but suffered seven gun stoppages and Page fired 100 rounds and then suffered a stoppage. Both Sharman and Page reported that they believed the observer was either killed or severely injured during the engagement.

8th to 10th July

Bad weather for three days curtailed all operational flying. Collishaw and Sharman were both promoted to the rank of Flight Commander.

11th July

FLt Carter led A Flight on an early offensive patrol at 04.20, covering the inner area at heights of 14000 to 15000 feet. There was a complete absence of enemy aerial activity but anti-aircraft fire was reported as particularly heavy between Warneton and Hollebeke.

B and C flights carried out a combined offensive patrol at 07.15 but found heavy cloud building up as the patrol progressed. At 07.45, a 2-seater was observed over Bailleul at 18000 feet, the machine moved away to the east before the patrol could reach its height.

A Flight carried out an inner offensive patrol at 09.45; the entire area was obscured by heavy cloud at 3000 to 4000 feet.

A Flight went out again at 15.20, visibility was much better than earlier with the cloud at 3000 feet breaking up. Despite the improved conditions no enemy aircraft were seen.

B and C Flights carried out a combined patrol at 19.15 and ran into heavy enemy activity between Wervicq and Zonnebeke at 20.00. About forty Albatros scouts were seen at different heights and a number of engagements took place throughout the sector. Between 20.40 and 20.45, FCdr Collishaw and FLt Alexander both claimed an enemy machine shot down out of control and a further ten indecisive combats were reported. FSL Kent flying N5357 was in combat with an Albatros scout over Polygon Wood, he was seen to dive at

FLt John Page claimed a scout out of control over Lille on the 7th July whilst flying C Flight Triplane N5379. *Courtesy JMB/GSL Collection*

Wervicq with an enemy machine on his tail and was brought down at 20.45. Kent's Triplane made a successful forced landing and photographs of his machine in German hands show that it was relatively undamaged. Kent was captured and became a prisoner of war.

12th July

Sharman and Collishaw led C and B Flights on offensive patrols at 06.33 and 06.40 respectively. Enemy activity was high with approximately thirty multicoloured Albatross scouts encountered between Menin and Polygon Wood. A running fight developed during which Reid destroyed a scout which was seen to break up in the air and shot the pilot of another which was seen to crash on a house near Veldhoek. FCdr Collishaw claimed a third machine, a red painted scout, which fell away out of control with the pilot apparently shot. Numerous indecisive engagements took place from 07.45. Pegler flying N5368 was in combat with three scouts at Zillebeke at 07.45, he was seen to spin over Polygon Wood but thought to be under control. Pegler, however, was shot down and killed, possibly by *Ltn*. W. Güttler of *Jasta* 24.

A Flight carried out an offensive patrol at 08.15, considerable activity being observed. The patrol encountered twelve scouts attacking a flight of DH5s to the east of Ypres at 09.15. A number of indecisive engagements took place until the area was cleared. FSL J.A.Mc.D. Allan in N5364 received leg injuries from an anti-aircraft shell splinter and was forced to land at No.306 Siege Battery.

B and C Flights flew offensive patrols at 11.05. A couple of Albatros scouts were seen to the south of Ypres near Houthem and a 2-seater accompanied by three yellow and green Albatros scouts were encountered to the south of Polygon Wood. A general engagement took place between 12.15 and 12.25, during which FCdr Sharman destroyed a scout which was seen to break up in the air by FLt Page.

At 13.45, Carter, Barnes and Glasgow carried out an offensive patrol, Barnes made two abortive attempts to stay with the patrol, returning the first time with a broken drift wire and the second time with engine trouble. Carter and Glasgow engaged four 2-seaters with indecisive results at 15.00 over the lines to the east and southeast of Ypres. The engagement attracted the attention of 2 RE8s that joined the

Above: FSL Kent's Triplane, N5357, was brought down at Wervick on the 11th July by *Ltn.* W. Blume of *Jasta* 26. Kent made a successful forced landing and spent the rest of the war in captivity. *Courtesy L. Rogers*

Below: Another shot of N5357 in enemy hands. It was common practice to cut away the sections of fabric bearing the cockade and the serial number for souvenirs. *Courtesy E.F. Cheesman*

fight. Carter saw one of the RE8s shoot down one of the enemy 2-seaters which crashed near the lines to the east of Ypres.

FLt Carter led another patrol at 19.34 over the inner area. No enemy aircraft seen in the area, but seven or eight were seen high up and far to the east.

13th July

B Flight carried out an offensive patrol of the inner area at 07.35. Enemy activity was reported as being quieter than observed over the previous two days, but two scouts were encountered four miles east of Polygon Wood at 07.50 and five scouts accompanying three 2-seaters were seen over the Wood at 08.10. These machines retreated to the east when approached by the patrol.

C and A Flights combined for an offensive patrol at 08.35. Eight enemy scouts were encountered over Langemarck at 10.00 but no engagements occurred.

B Flight escorted an RE8 reconnaissance machine over Langemarck at 12.42 and then went on to cover the area. Seven enemy machines were observed at 13.40, however, these kept well to the east.

FCdr Sharman led six Triplanes flown by pilots from all three Flights on an uneventful inner patrol at 18.15.

14th July

Sharman led C Flight on an offensive patrol at 05.35. The visibility was poor but the patrol encountered a 2-seater over Polygon Wood at 06.25 and drove it off.

B Flight ran into a thunderstorm during their 15.10 offensive patrol, the visibility was very bad and no enemy machines were seen. Collishaw's machine, N5492, was damaged by anti-aircraft fire and he had to make a forced landing at No.21 Squadron RFC.

A and C Flights performed an outer offensive patrol at 19.30, the visibility was bad with heavy cloud. About 20 enemy scouts were observed over Polygon Wood in several formations at differing heights. Several indecisive engagements took place at 20.20, before the enemy machines dived away to the east.

15th July

B and C Flights carried out offensive patrols over the outer area at 10.45, the visibility was fair but no enemy aircraft were seen. FCdr Collishaw flying N5379 suffered engine trouble, made a forced landing at Moeres and damaged the Triplane's axle. After repair, Collishaw was returning to Droglandt at 12.00 when he encountered a combat between a Nieuport scout and an Albatros. Collishaw dived on the Albatros scout and fired 150 rounds, suffering several gun stoppages. The Albatros spun away for 6000 feet then recovered and made off to the north. Collishaw's engine then failed completely and he made a forced landing in a field near Vinckes to the northeast of Hondschoote.

FLt Carter led Alexander, Lowther and Glasgow on an offensive patrol at 16.00. The patrol encountered five enemy scouts over Polygon Wood at 17.15. Carter dived and attacked, firing at three of the scouts in succession. He was close to the third machine when his gun suffered a stoppage. The enemy machines dived away to the east.

C Flight carried out an inner offensive patrol at 17.35. New pilot FSL Holmes returned to the aerodrome suffering from air sickness. FSL Weir failed to pick up the patrol from the start and patrolled the lines until it was time to return. Sharman and Page continued the patrol and observed eight enemy scouts at great height over Poelcappelle at 18.00.

Reid, Fitzgibbon and Trapp carried out an uneventful inner offensive patrol at 18.40.

16th July

Layers of heavy cloud made flying conditions difficult. B and C Flights attempted an outer offensive patrol at 06.35 but found that conditions made if difficult to navigate. No enemy aircraft were observed.

The squadron mounted a 12 machine patrol at 17.15 with all three Flights participating. No enemy aircraft were seen. FSL Taylor in N5429 failed to pick up the formation as his engine was down on power. He joined up with a flight of French machines and encountered four scouts to the north of Polygon Wood at 18.00. An engagement took place in which Taylor shot down an enemy scout which was seen to break-up in the air. This may have been *Vfw*. Fritz Krebs of *Jasta* 6 who was killed in action that evening.

17th July

Carter led A Flight on an offensive patrol at 05.20, Glasgow dropped out with engine trouble and Taylor lost the formation in cloud. Carter and Lowther continued the patrol and attacked five scouts to the southeast of Polygon Wood at 06.45, Lowther fired a burst into an Albatros scout and observed his tracers entering the fuselage close to the seat. The pilot fell forward and the machine side-slipped, nose dived and went down completely out of control. The two pilots were attacked by five more scouts from above, both Triplanes suffered gun stoppages, necessitating a hasty retreat across the lines.

Collishaw led B Flight on an offensive patrol at 08.00. Several flights of hostile machines were observed at great height and well to the east. The patrol stayed low to provide cover for a flight of DH5 aircraft working at 11000 feet.

FSL Reid took off at 09.50 on a hostile aircraft patrol. The enemy machine passed north of the aerodrome and was observed by Reid just after he left the ground but was lost shortly afterwards in the clouds.

C Flight carried out an offensive patrol at 10.05, and observed an engagement over Polygon Wood between enemy machines, DH5s and SPADs. The patrol attacked a flight of three Albatros scouts without result and at 11.20, drove off an enemy reconnaissance machine working over Houthulst Forest.

A Flight performed an offensive patrol at 19.45 and encountered a large number of allied machines. At 20.00, a large number of enemy aircraft were encountered at 13000 feet over the Roulers sector. A long general engagement followed during which Carter drove an Albatros scout down out of control. Lowther flying N5381 escaped injury when he damaged his aircraft during a forced landing southeast of Polygon Wood.

18th to 19th July

Two days of bad weather prevented any operational flying. Two new pilots arrived at the squadron, FSL TC May and FSL McLachlan.

20th July

B and C Flights carried out an offensive patrol at 06.45. The patrol encountered fifteen to twenty Albatros scouts over the Menin-Messines sector at 08.00 and immediately engaged them. Collishaw and Reid each claimed an enemy aircraft driven down out of control, the pilot being shot in both instances. Alexander shot one machine down in flames, and a further six indecisive combats occurred before the enemy machines were driven off. Fitzgibbon flying N5458 suffered engine trouble and made a successful forced landing at No. 23 Squadron RFC.

Sharman and Carter led their flights on an offensive patrol at 14.47. Three enemy scouts were indecisively attacked over Houthulst Forest. Weather conditions were deteriorating, with heavy cloud from 3000 feet and bad visibility.

A and B Flights carried out an offensive patrol at 19.00 and observed approximately twenty-two enemy scouts over Courtrai at 19.45. Several of the Camel pilots were experiencing engine trouble and a strong southwest wind was blowing. Because of these two factors, Collishaw decided to refrain from attack. May had to return to the aerodrome with engine problems and Taylor's machine also left the patrol when he was unable to keep up. On his way back, Taylor had an engagement with an enemy machine near the lines to the southeast of Ypres and sustained a flesh wound in his left arm.

21st July

Carter led A Flight on an offensive patrol at 16.30. May lost the patrol and landed at Proven. Glasgow suffered from engine trouble and also lost the patrol. Carter and Lowther continued the patrol and encountered five enemy scouts over Tourcoing at 17.40 and two more to the southeast of Ypres at 17.55. Three indecisive engagements took place and the enemy machines withdrew.

B and C Flights carried out an offensive patrol at 19.05. A large engagement involving twenty Albatros scouts, No.10 Squadron, and other allied machines took place between 20.00 and 20.40, spread from Passchendaele to Polygon Wood, Becelaere and Houthulst Forest. In the course of this engagement, Collishaw claimed two scouts shot down out of control, one with the pilot shot and Reid shot down a scout, seeing it crash at the edge of a wood, north of Becelaere. Reid described his opponent as being painted grey with a thin black stripe around the fuselage. A further twenty indecisive combats took place.

Earlier in the day at 16.40, FCdr Collishaw collected a twin gun Triplane, serial N533, from the depot. This aircraft would subsequently become his third "Black Maria" with No.10 Squadron.

22nd July

The structure of A and C Flights had changed somewhat since the beginning of July, and the squadron strength was now down to 12 pilots:

A Flight

FLt A.W. Carter, Flight Commander
FSL H.W. Taylor
FSL T.C. May
FSL T.L. Glasgow

B Flight

FCdr R. Collishaw, Flight Commander
FLt W.M. Alexander
FSL E.V. Reid
FSL D.F. Fitzgibbon

C Flight
FCdr J.E. Sharman, Flight Commander
FLt J. Page
FSL C.H. Weir
FSL G.L. Trapp

FLt Carter led A Flight on the early offensive patrol at 06.20. Five enemy machines were encountered over Menin and two indecisive engagements took place.

The squadron suffered a major setback later in the morning when FCdr Sharman led C flight on an offensive patrol at 07.25. The patrol encountered enemy aircraft between Ypres and Messines. As Sharman was engaging one of the enemy machines, his Triplane broke up in the air, apparently taking a direct hit by an anti-aircraft shell. The deputy Flight Commander, FLt Page, also failed to return from the patrol having been shot down and killed near Becelaere, possibly by *Ltn.* O. Brauneck of *Jasta* 11. Trapp reported seeing an enemy machine going down out of control after combat with a Triplane, and a flight of DH5s reported seeing an enemy machine go down and break up in the air after combat with a Triplane. As there were no other claims made, Page was credited with one enemy destroyed and another out of control. The German records indicate no matching losses, so it is quite possible that the DH5 pilots saw Sharman's Triplane break up in the air, not an enemy machine.

Two more patrols were flown during the day. B Flight carried out a patrol at 08.45, numerous enemy machines were observed but the patrol was unable to bring them to action.

A and B flight flew a combined patrol at 18.35, six enemy machines were observed over Becelaere at 19.15 but they dived away to the east when approached.

23rd July

A and B Flights performed an offensive patrol at 14.55. Collishaw's machine suffered from engine trouble and he returned for another Triplane which proved to be just as bad. The patrol continued without him and attacked six enemy machines over Quesnoy at 16.10, the enemy aircraft were able to dive away and escape when the Triplanes suffered from gun stoppages.

A and B Flights carried out another offensive patrol at 19.00. A large number of scouts were encountered in the region of Polygon Wood; two sections of these were attacked by the Triplanes. Reid claimed one machine out of control with the pilot shot. A number of indecisive combats took place before the enemy machines dived away to the east. Alexander's machine, N5487, suffered from engine trouble and was compelled to land at the aerodrome of No.53 Squadron RFC.

24th July

A and B Flights carried out offensive patrols at 11.30. FLt Carter's flight observed two enemy aircraft attacking a British artillery spotter over Langemarck at 12.10 and drove them away; at the same time, the patrol was attacked by four scouts which dived through the clouds onto the Triplanes. Carter led the patrol westwards, gained height, then returned and attacked the scouts. Carter claimed one scout shot down out of control and the remaining scouts were driven off.

A Flight attempted to perform another offensive patrol at 17.30 but the visibility was very bad due to heavy mist.

FLt Alexander led Reid and May on an offensive patrol at 18.35, Collishaw and Fitzgibbon took off at 19.00 to join up with them. The patrol observed three Albatros scouts over Moorseele at 19.15, three more over Polygon Wood at 19.55 and one to the north of Hetsas at 20.05. Five indecisive engagements took place, gun stoppages being blamed for the lack of success. At 19.15 over Moorslede, Alexander and Reid saw May's Triplane falling and breaking up in the air. Both pilots were sure this was not due to enemy action.

25th July

A and B Flights performed an offensive patrol at 19.00, visibility was reported as bad and no enemy aircraft were seen.

26th July

SCdr Bell reformed C Flight around the leadership of FLt WM Alexander:

C Flight
FLt W.M. Alexander
FLt H.J.T. Saint
J.A. Cole
FSL H. Day
FSL A.M.O. McLachlan

FLt Alexander took his new flight up for practising formation flying and patrolling the lines. The practice session was reported to be successful.

A and B Flights carried out an offensive patrol at 19.00. At 19.45 the patrol observed ten enemy aircraft to the southeast of Ypres at 16000 feet, three of these came down but kept out

On the 12th July, New Zealand pilot, FSL J.A.M. Allan of A Flight made a forced landing in N5364 after being wounded in the left leg by fragments from an exploding anti-aircraft shell. FSL T.C. May was killed on the 24th July when N5364 broke up in the air during combat with *Ltn* H. Dilthey of *Jasta* 27 to the south of Passchendaele. *Author's collection*

of fighting range. At 20.20 to the west of Roulers, FLt Carter indecisively engaged an enemy scout. FCdr Collishaw was flying the twin gun Triplane N533 and suffered repeated gun stoppages, after leaving the patrol to clear his guns he encountered and engaged two white scouts over Polygon Wood at 20.15. Both guns again jammed and Collishaw was forced to abandon the engagement. FSL Trapp flying N 5354 got lost in the mist and landed at the aerodrome of No.23 Squadron RFC.

27th July

The day started with difficult conditions and bad visibility. A and B Flights attempted to perform an offensive patrol at 08.00, B Flight returned after 20 minutes but A Flight persevered for 90 minutes. No enemy machines were observed.

New pilot FSL G. Roach arrived at the squadron and after a brief practice flight, was assigned to A Flight and placed straight into the action.

At 18.40 the squadron mounted a twelve Triplane patrol with A, B and C Flights. Between 19.45 and 20.00, a large number of enemy aircraft, mostly Albatros scouts, were encountered from Courtrai across to the lines. A general engagement ensued in which Reid shot down a machine at Menin which broke up in the air, claimed another our of control with the pilot shot at Courtrai, and a third destroyed at Menin. Collishaw, again flying the twin gun Triplane N533, destroyed one machine, which broke up in the air, and shot down another out of control with the pilot shot. Carter also claimed a machine out of control. A further sixteen combats took place without decisive result. Alexander reported seeing FSL Roach being attacked and his machine falling out of control near Moorslede at 19.45 Roach was shot down and killed, to the south of Moorslede, attributed to *Ltn*. K. von Schonebeck, *Jasta* 11.

Replacement pilot FSL Pownall arrived at the squadron.

28th July

The 28th was FCdr Collishaw's last day with No.10 Squadron, he left on Canadian Leave, and upon his return to France in November, he was briefly posted to the Seaplane Defence Squadron before taking command of No.3 Squadron, RNAS. B Flight ceased to exist as an operational Flight for several weeks.

A and C Flights carried out offensive patrols at 06.45. Alexander rescued an allied spotting machine when he drove off an attacking Albatros scout near Warneton at 07.50. Carter's flight attacked five enemy scouts between Roulers and Polygon Wood between 07.45 and 08.00, continual gun stoppages again being blamed for a lack of decisive results.

Carter and Alexander carried out another offensive patrol at 18.30. The patrol encountered twelve enemy aircraft at 12000 feet over Dadizeele at 19.50. Alexander and Cole engaged two of the machines. Cole fired 60 rounds into a scout,

N533 was Collishaw's third Triplane named "Black Maria". This was a twin gun machine, and Collishaw initially experienced considerable trouble with gun stoppages. On the 27th July however, he was able to claim one enemy machine destroyed and another out of control with the pilot believed shot. After Collishaw departed for Canadian leave, N533 was briefly flown by FLt W.M. Alexander before becoming SCdr B.C. Bell's personal aircraft. *Author's collection*

the machine went down in a vertical dive but Cole was unable to say that it was out of control. Alexander attacked one scout, firing 60 rounds from a range of 75 yards, he observed his tracers entering the fuselage around the seat. The scout went into a nosedive, turned on its back and fell completely out of control. Alexander observed another machine falling in pieces, this was thought to have been shot down by Reid. Reid flying N5483 failed to return having been last seen at 20.00 between Dadizeele and Roulers when the engagement was over and the sky clear of enemy aircraft. Alexander had attempted to join him, but engine trouble forced him to head for the lines and the other pilots followed him. It is thought that Reid may have been shot down by *K.Flak* 21 near Armentières.

29th July

Bad weather and poor visibility for the next week severely affected war flying.

A and C Flights carried out an offensive patrol at 19.00. The visibility was bad with heavy cloud covering the area. No enemy aircraft were seen.

30th July

Bad weather prevented operational flying.

31st July

FLt Carter, flying the twin gun Triplane N536, led A Flight on a special offensive patrol at 15.35, with the purpose of attacking personnel and transport in support of the start of the ground offensive at Ypres. The conditions were bad with cloud from 1000 to 8000 feet; when over Menin the patrol was attacked from above by five scouts, Carter and Trapp were forced into the clouds below, Carter lost his engine which did not pick up until he was down to 1000 feet. At this point the clouds were down to 600 feet and it was raining. Trapp also had engine trouble and did not recover until he was down to 800 feet. At 16.10 Trapp attacked a body of infantry and transport on a road between Menin and Gheluvelt, but he suffered a gun jam after firing a short burst. Weir lost his way in the clouds and landed at No.1 Squadron, RNAS.

August 1917

The appalling weather at the start of August stopped the Allied advance in its tracks, the battlefield having turned into a sea of clay slurry. Flying proved impossible and the loss of observation and ground support was another blow to the hard pressed troops.

The ground offensive resumed on the 16th August, with fighting lasting for three days. Conditions for air support were again unfavourable, with heavy overcast. The offensive planned to rely heavily on low-flying infantry support and ground attack and whilst No.10 Squadron was not involved in these activities at this juncture due to the Triplane's inability to carry bombs, the squadron would be heavily involved in such operations in the near future.

No.10 Squadron collected its first Sopwith Camel on the 26th August and on the 30th, the squadron strength was dramatically increased by the arrival of pilots and Sopwith Camels from the disbanded No.6 Squadron RNAS.

1st to 3rd August

Bad weather at the start of August curtailed all flying activities for 3 days, and interfered with operations thereafter.

4th August

C Flight attempted to carry out an offensive patrol at 14.28 but thick cloud and rain on the lines made an effective patrol impossible. The pilots were unable to maintain formation, and all returned at different times.

A and C Flight carried out offensive patrols at 20.05. The visibility was still very bad due to clouds and heavy ground mist and the patrols returned after fifty minutes.

FSL Munro made a forced landing in N6290 to the northwest of Proven during a practice flight in the evening, damaging the machine but escaping injury.

5th August

Thick cloud from 3000 feet to 14000 feet again made patrols all but impossible. A and C Flights attempted to carry out a patrol at 15.30 but lost FSL Pownall. Pownall in N5379 landed at Dunkerque and presumably damaged his aircraft as he did not return to the squadron until the 10th August.

A further patrol was attempted by A and C flights at 18.45, visibility was very bad due to a thick haze. A single enemy 2-seater was observed several miles east of Polygon Wood at 20.00.

6th August

The weather again stopped all flying activities.

New pilots FSL Broughall and FSL Lloyd arrived at the squadron.

7th August

A and C Flights carried out an offensive patrol at 18.12 with orders to attack ground targets of opportunity, both Carter and Alexander were flying twin gun Triplanes. The visibility was very bad and considerable difficulty was experienced in keeping bearings and the preservation of formation proved impossible. No enemy aircraft were seen. Due to the area of the patrol being totally obscured by cloud cover no suitable ground targets were observed either. Glasgow and Lowther landed near Bray Dunes and Day landed at Volkerinckhove to the northwest of St. Omer.

N6295 "B", flown by FSL H.S. Broughall in A Flight during the first two weeks of August 1917, displaying the A Flight colour scheme of red cowling, wheel covers, and fin. Broughall and N6295 moved over to C flight towards the end of the second week of August, and N6295 was shortly thereafter taken over by FCdr Saint, who claimed a 2-seater out of control on the 21st August, and a scout out of control on the 25th August. *Courtesy Les Rogers*

8th August

A and C Flights carried out an offensive patrol at 10.42. Between 11.00 and 12.00 they encountered thirty to forty enemy aircraft patrolling a north-south line at high altitude east of Menin and up towards Houthulst Forest. These machines were all in close touch but made no attempt to attack the patrol. The patrol kept close to allied spotting machines to protect them from attack.

Broughall and Lloyd performed a special mission at 11.50 to try to intercept an enemy 2-seater operating over the Poperinghe area. The visibility was very bad and the pilots were unable to locate the enemy machine. Broughall got lost in the clouds and eventually landed at Petite Synthe.

C Flight carried out an offensive patrol at 15.00 but the visibility was bad and got worse as the patrol progressed.

9th August

Carter and Alexander led their flights on an offensive patrol at 07.00. The weather had improved and visibility was reported as good. The patrol observed ten enemy aircraft at 17000 feet to the south of Roulers at 07.30 but were 4000 feet below and unable to get close. At 08.10 an enemy scout was seen 5000 feet below the patrol to the north of Messines. FLt Alexander dived on the scout but it dived steeply away and was seen to land east of Wervicq.

The two flights carried out another offensive patrol at 10.40. Just after 12.00 over Polygon Wood four scouts dived from above and one attacked Munro in N6290. FLt Saint attacked the scout in turn, sending it down out of control. The other three scouts escaped to the east. After the initial attack Munro was seen by Saint to be going down in a spin into the clouds below. Munro was shot down and killed, probably by *Ltn*. W. Güttler of *Jasta* 24.

Another combined offensive patrol was carried out at 17.55; several machines were affected by engine trouble. No enemy machines were encountered,

10th August

Alexander and Carter led their flights on an offensive patrol at 07.00. Several flights of enemy machines were seen but they dived away eastwards before the patrol was able to close with them. At 08.06, Alexander encountered two Albatros scouts near Wervicq and dived to attack firing 30 rounds at one from a range of 100 yards. Alexander reported seeing his tracers entering the fuselage around the pilot's seat and the machine dropped into a nosedive, sideslipped, and then fell completely out of control. Although Alexander was not credited with this claim, there were two reports of German pilots injured in the general area of the engagement. FCdr Saint reported that one member of C Flight was attacked by a 2-seater at

Another view of the pristine N6295 being examined by French officers, the location possibly Petite Synthe when Broughall lost his way and landed at No. 12 squadron on the 8th August 1917. *Courtesy Les Rogers*

08.15 when east of Polygon Wood. The 2-seater dived away when other Triplanes of the patrol attempted to engage it.

Another offensive patrol was performed by A and C Flights at 12.15. The two flights crossed the lines in the neighbourhood of Ypres and patrolled the 2nd Corps front at a low altitude. They then joined with a flight of SPADs and carried out an outer offensive patrol at up to 16000 feet altitude. Weir of A Flight in N5477 had to make a forced landing at Houthem near Hondschoote, damaging his machine.

Pownall and Lloyd flew a special mission at 16.10 to protect the balloon line. No enemy machines were seen but at 17.25 allied anti-aircraft batteries were seen to be shelling a single aeroplane to the northwest of Ypres. The patrol approached the machine, only to find that it was a Nieuport.

A and C Flights performed a third offensive patrol at 19.05. No enemy machines were encountered.

11th August

W.M. Alexander was promoted to the rank of Flight Commander on the 11th.

A Flight performed an offensive patrol at 8000 feet over Polygon Wood. Glasgow was forced to return early with engine trouble. The depleted patrol encountered five enemy aircraft at 14.35 near Roulers. A heavy rainsquall intervened and the patrol went north to try to get around the storm and pick up the enemy aircraft. Whilst over Houthulst Forest at 14.55, the patrol was attacked by six enemy aircraft which dived on them from the clouds above and forced them into the cloud layer below. The enemy aircraft broke off the attack when heavy rain set in. At this point the patrol was abandoned due to the weather.

A and C Flights combined to perform an outer offensive patrol at 19.15. The cloud layer was at 10000 feet, and no enemy machines were found above or below this layer.

12th August

A and C Flights carried out an outer offensive patrol at 06.45. The patrol encountered five enemy aircraft near Courtrai and followed them to Roulers, at 07.45 the enemy formation was attacked. Trapp drove one machine down out of control. All of the pilots experienced gun stoppages which prevented further success. At 08.00 five more enemy aircraft were sighted over Polygon Wood at 10000 feet, FCdr Alexander engaged one indecisively but the other pilots were unable to use their guns making a sustained attack impossible.

C Flight flew an outer offensive patrol at 10.40 and at 11.30 encountered a formation of five hostile aircraft over Wervicq. The formation was attacked and three engagements took place, Day drove one machine down out of control, Broughall observed the machine falling.

FSL McLachlan was dispatched at 14.45 to intercept an enemy machine. He patrolled the lines to the north and south of Ypres but failed to see the intruder. The allied anti-aircraft batteries had been firing at the enemy machine just before McLachlan took off and firing was again observed after he landed.

Lloyd and Cole flew a ground patrol at 17.30. Cole flying N536 suffered problems and returned for another machine. The line was patrolled north and south of Ypres. No suitable ground targets were seen, however, a single enemy aircraft was seen low down and far across the lines north east of Ypres.

New pilot FSL Manuel arrived at the squadron.

13th August

A and C Flights performed an outer offensive patrol at 06.45. The lines were crossed at 14000 feet and the patrol found a large number of allied machines working but no enemy aircraft. At 07.40, a scout was seen over Wervicq, this machine dived away before it could be approached.

Lloyd and Cole carried out a ground patrol at 09.50. They encountered two enemy aircraft over Becelaere at 10.45 which dived away to the east when approached. At 11.00, Lloyd fired fifty rounds into the enemy trenches from 400 feet altitude northwest of Polygon Wood. He observed a crashed aircraft which he identified as a Nieuport.

FLt Carter led A Flight on an inner offensive patrol at 12.30. The patrol kept low, flying between 1000 and 7000 feet. At 13.45 a 2-seater was encountered over Houthulst Forest, after a short indecisive engagement the enemy machine retreated eastwards at a very low altitude. At 13.10 Carter fired two bursts into Zonnebeke village from 1000 feet. Trapp had lost the formation in mist and descended to 100 feet and fired 100 rounds at a small party of enemy troops northeast of Polygon Wood.

C Flight flew an inner offensive patrol at 15.10, carried out from 200 to 8000 feet. At 16.18, when over Houthulst Forest, the patrol was surprised by five scouts which came down through the clouds. FSL McLachlan was attacked by a scout which was in turn attacked and driven off by Broughall. Prior to this engagement, Alexander had dropped out of the patrol with engine problems.

Lloyd and Cole performed a ground patrol at 17.45. Lloyd attempted to attack a kite balloon at 18.50 but he broke off the attack when the balloon was hauled down. On his return he was diving to attack enemy trenches when he was attacked from above and behind by a scout, he tried to turn and climb, only for his engine to fail. He was fortunate to be rescued by two DH5s which drove his assailant off. At 19.00, Lloyd saw an RE8 being attacked by an Albatros scout to the east of Ypres. Lloyd climbed and attacked the scout, driving it off.

14th August

A and C Flights carried out an outer offensive patrol at 09.45. At 10.30 when over Roulers the patrol encountered four enemy observation machines flying at a higher altitude. The enemy machines climbed up above the upper cloud layer but the patrol did not pursue them, having orders to stay low. At 11.00, three scouts were briefly engaged to the east of Wervicq at 4000 feet, four indecisive combats took place before the enemy machines dived away to the east.

Manuel and FSL Lloyd flew a ground patrol at 11.50, keeping low over the lines to the north and south of Ypres. Lloyd lost Manuel in clouds at 12.45 and at 12.55 he observed four enemy aircraft 1 1/2 miles behind enemy lines northeast of Ypres. No other enemy machines were seen, the visibility was bad with heavy low cloud and rain on the lines. Manuel flying N5370 got lost in the clouds and landed at No 15 Squadron RFC.

FLt Saint led a four Triplane C Flight inner offensive patrol at 15.18. At 16.15, accompanied by two of his pilots, Saint dived to attack three Albatros scouts flying at 10000 feet above Houthulst Forest. This proved to be a trap as the Triplanes were attacked from above by five more Albatros scouts. In the ensuing engagement Saint got into a good position behind a red Albatros scout and fired 60 rounds into it from very close range. The enemy machine burst into flames and went down vertically. FSL S.H. Lloyd who had been flying the twin gun Triplane N536 for the first time, was shot down and killed, probably by *Uffz*. K. Steudel of *Jasta* 3 who claimed a Triplane shot down at 16.20 (BST) over Langemarck.

FSL Manuel returned from No.15 RFC at 15.30, he reported having seen two enemy 2-seaters and an Albatros scout to the north of Langemarck at 13.10.

FLt Carter led an uneventful line patrol at 20.20.

15th August

Carter and Alexander led their flights on an outer offensive patrol at 05.00. At 06.15, three enemy machines were observed at 14000 feet over Houthulst Forest, these machines dived away to the east before the patrol could climb to their height. This was Carter's last flight before departing on Canadian leave, when he returned to the squadron in January 1918 he would have to rapidly learn to adapt to the unstable Sopwith Camel.

With Carter's departure for Canada, SCdr Bell moved FCdr W.M. Alexander across to take command of A Flight, whilst the relatively inexperienced FLt Saint was given command of C Flight.

FLt Saint led C Flight on an inner offensive patrol at 12.40, patrolling the inner area at 3000 to 18000 feet. Heavy clouds from 3000 to 14000 feet were encountered and no enemy aircraft were observed. Manuel flying N5370 suffered engine failure and made a forced landing between Oostvleteren and Westvleteren north of Poperinghe, damaging his aircraft.

A and C Flights performed an outer offensive patrol at 19.00. The patrol observed seven hostile aircraft high up to the east of Houthulst Forest at 19.25. The hostile machines retreated before the patrol could climb up to them. At 20.00 Saint's flight was surprised when eleven enemy aircraft dived out of the clouds to make a hit and run attack. Saint was able to fire a few rounds at extreme range as they passed. The enemy machines were seen to continue on down to attack two SPADs, and shortly after engaging the SPADs, one of the enemy machines was seen to break up in the air.

FSL Pownall collected N5381 from the depot but damaged it on landing.

The squadron structure still comprised A and C Flights, staffed as shown below:

A Flight

FCdr W.M. Alexander
FSL C.H. Weir
FSL C. Lowther
FSL T.L. Glasgow
FSL G.L. Trapp

C Flight

FLt H.J.T. Saint
FSL H. Day
FSL H.S. Broughall
FSL J.A. Cole
FSL A.M.O. McLachlan
FSL J.G. Manuel

16th August

Outer offensive patrols were flown by A Flight at 07.10 and C Flight at 07.15. The patrols were flown mostly at low altitude to protect spotter machines. A large number of enemy aircraft were patrolling the area and several engagements took place between 08.00 and 08.15. FSL Cole had become separated from his flight during an earlier engagement when he encountered a lone Albatros scout to the northeast of Zonnebeke at 08.00. After manoeuvring for position, Cole was able to fire 50 rounds into the scout's fuselage, observing several tracers hit the pilot. The enemy scout stalled, turned over on its side and then fell completely out of control. FCdr Alexander also claimed an enemy machine driven down out of control over Wervicq at 08.05. Throughout the patrols the enemy aircraft were kept away from the spotting machines. During the course of an engagement, FLt Saint received a slight flesh wound in his right thigh from enemy fire.

FSL McLachlan led C Flight on an inner offensive patrol at 14.30, encountering a 2-seater at 15.30 over Houthulst Forest which dived away to the east when approached. A patrol of seven scouts was sitting 3000 feet above the 2-seater but made no attempt to attack the Triplanes.

At 18.45, A Flight and C Flight, led this time by FSL Cole in Saint's absence, carried out an outer offensive patrol. At 20.00, when at 6000 feet over Polygon Wood, the patrol observed a combat between SPADs, SEs, and FEs, and eighteen or twenty enemy aircraft taking place over Houthulst forest at 16000 to 18000 feet. A machine was seen to fall out of control and appeared to crash. No other enemy aircraft were seen, but there were large numbers of allied machines working over the lines.

SCdr Bell flying N533 took new pilot FSL Emery on a line patrol at 19.20 to give him practice at keeping station. No enemy aircraft were seen but a large number of allied aircraft were observed working just over the lines.

FLt Howard Saint dressed for action in an unidentified Triplane. Saint held the number 1 Civil licence after the war. *Author's collection*

17th August

C and A Flights carried out outer offensive patrols at 07.35 and 07.40 respectively. Alexander led A Flight into a general engagement over Ledeghem at 08.30 with six Albatros scouts. Trapp drove a scout down out of control and eleven indecisive combats took place with several good opportunities lost due to gun stoppages. All of the enemy aircraft were driven down to the east. At 08.15 when over Polygon Wood, C Flight observed ten or twelve machines beyond Courtrai-Roulers at 18000 feet. The aircraft were too far away to identify and made no attempt to come in.

A Flight performed an inner offensive patrol at 13.50 and encountered eight Gothas coming from the direction of Roulers and Menin. The bombers came within a mile of the lines and were escorted by eight or nine scouts. A Flight kept to the lines and worked up and down to gain height, at which point the Gothas and scouts turned east. At 15.00 a combat was observed between the bomber's escort and three FEs over Hollebeke at about 12000 feet. The patrol went in and joined the fight and the enemy scouts broke off the engagement and made off through the clouds. The patrol reported four indecisive combats.

FSL Emery carried out a balloon line patrol at 16.05. No enemy aircraft were seen but Emery reported seeing a parachute descend from a balloon near Ypres immediately after a shell had burst near it.

18th August

FSL Cole led C Flight on an offensive patrol at 05.15; the patrol encountered six enemy aircraft at 06.00 to the east of Roulers at 15000 feet. The patrol climbed to 15000 feet and went in after the hostile machines but the enemy retreated to the east before they could be engaged. The lines were clear of enemy aircraft during the patrol.

FCdr Alexander led A Flight on an offensive patrol at 10.35, covering the area from 4000 to 12000 feet. FSL Lowther's engine failed immediately after take off and he damaged N5367 in the subsequent forced landing near the aerodrome. Trapp also experienced engine troubles and returned to the aerodrome. Both Trapp and Lowther resumed the patrol in different machines.

C Flight carried out an offensive patrol at 16.28; the visibility was bad with heavy cloud and intermittent rain and hail. No enemy aircraft were encountered.

A Flight performed an uneventful offensive patrol at 18.40.

FCdr Bell took FSL Nelson on a line patrol at 19.30 to give the new pilot practice in keeping station. No enemy aircraft were observed.

19th August

A Flight carried out an offensive patrol at 08.50, followed by C Flight taking off at 09.05.The patrols flew from the lines to Roulers-Courtrai at 5000 to 16000 feet. At 09.15, a 2-seater was observed to the east of Menin at 17000 feet. The patrol started to climb but the enemy aircraft dived away to the east beyond Courtrai. Between 10.05 to 10.15, about fifteen enemy machines were seen patrolling a line east of Roulers-Armentières, at this point the patrol was at the lines heading back to the aerodrome. A Flight lost FSL Glasgow, killed when he crashed in his Triplane to the east of Proven. FSL Trapp in N5354 was compelled to make a forced landing to the east of Elverdinghe, he escaped injury, but the Triplane was badly damaged.

FSL Nelson performed an uneventful balloon line patrol at 10.50.

Two more patrols were flown in the afternoon over Roulers-Courtrai-Menin and Houthulst-Roulers-Courtrai-Menin-Wervicq-Ypres, but no enemy activity was observed.

20th August

A and C Flights carried out an outer offensive patrol 07.22 covering the Roulers-Menin area. At 07.50, Alexander's flight was attacked from above by eleven scouts that did not attempt to close but dived and fired from long range then zoomed away. Lowther flying N5425 was separated from the rest of the flight owing to difficulty in keeping up and was attacked by two of the scouts and engaged one indecisively. A Flight went in towards the lines to gain height and then returned, but the enemy machines were not seen again. At 08.20, while returning to the lines, A Flight observed three enemy machines four miles northeast of Houthulst Forest. The patrol climbed to attack them but they went eastwards at high speed before they could be engaged. FLt Saint was compelled to leave C Flight when he developed a severe pain in his ear.

A Flight carried out an offensive patrol at 13.40. The visibility was poor with clouds and mist. Trapp was compelled to return to the aerodrome when his throttle control became disconnected. FSL Lowther's machine was down on power and he was unable to keep up with the formation. Alexander, Weir and Broughall carried out the patrol over Langemarck, Roulers, Menin, and Wervicq. At 15.20, when returning and near Langemarck at 10000 feet, five scouts attacked the patrol from above forcing the Triplanes down into the cloud below. On coming out of the cloud, Alexander observed three enemy aircraft still circling above the cloud. He climbed above them and followed them to Roubaix where they turned and engaged. Alexander drove one down completely out of control and the other two were driven off. Broughall lost his leader after diving through the cloud and returned alone. Weir in N5355 crashed after the initial attack, was made a prisoner of war, but subsequently died of injuries sustained during the crash.

FCdr Saint led an offensive patrol at 15.00 covering Roulers, Menin, Wervicq, and Ypres at heights up to 16000 feet. An enemy 2-seater was observed at 16.35, three miles northwest of Ypres. The patrol climbed towards it, but it dived away to the east when the patrol was still 2000 feet below it.

SCdr Bell and FSL Pownall flew a line patrol at 19.15, west of the line near Ypres. While at 18000 feet they saw an enemy aircraft being shelled by anti-aircraft defences and then attacked by allied aircraft. No other enemy aircraft were seen.

21st August

Alexander led A Flight on an offensive patrol at 05.10 on the 21st. No enemy machines were encountered until the end of the patrol when sixteen aircraft were observed getting their height several miles east of Courtrai at 06.30.

A bomber escort mission was carried out by C Flight at 06.47. The flight picked up the DH4s at 07.32 and accompanied them. Shortly afterwards at 07.40, FLt Saint surprised a 2-seater south of Roulers and drove it down completely out of control. No other enemy machines were seen.

New pilot FSL Lewis flew a solo line patrol at 10.15. Flying N5379, he made a forced landing at No.27 Squadron RFC and damaged the Triplane.

A and C Flights combined to carry out an eleven-Triplane bomber escort at 17.40. Day returned with engine trouble and left again immediately in a replacement machine. The DH4 bombers were accompanied to a point west of Menin where a general engagement took place with a number of German scouts at 18.30. In the ensuing combats, Manuel shot down two scouts, one was seen to crash and the pilot of the other was believed to have been shot in the head. Alexander and Trapp both shot scouts down out of control and a number of indecisive combats also took place. Lowther flying N5425 was shot down and killed, possibly by *Ltn.* E. Hess or *Hptm.* O. Hartman of *Jasta* 28.

22nd August

Saint led an offensive patrol at 05.04 over Houthulst, Passchendaele, Becelaere, and Polygon Wood. An enemy 2-seater was driven off from Houthulst Forest at 05.20. The same machine was indecisively engaged at extreme range by Saint at 06.05. At 06.10, eight enemy aircraft were observed gaining height east of Menin and at 06.20 seven more were observed northeast of Roulers.

A Flight carried out an uneventful offensive patrol from Houthulst Forest to Polygon Wood at 10.50.

Saint led C Flight over the same area at 15.00. The patrol observed seven 2-seaters over Ypres but they disappeared to the east. At 16.20, the same formation was seen north of Houthulst Forest but the patrol was again unable to bring them to action. A 2-seater was indecisively engaged by Saint at 16.30, this machine was attacked by a flight of SPADs after escaping from Saint. The patrol duration was extended by 20 minutes due to the presence of enemy aircraft in the sector.

FCdr Alexander led A Flight on an offensive patrol over the same area at 17.30. A machine was observed to spin into the ground at 18.30 to the east of Polygon Wood but was too far away to identify.

23rd August

FCdr Alexander left on leave on the 23rd August and was temporarily replaced as Commander of A Flight by FLt Fitzgibbon who had just returned from leave.

FLt Fitzgibbon led A Flight for the first time when A and C Flights carried out an offensive patrol at 07.30, patrolling Langemarck, Roulers, Courtrai, and Wervicq. No enemy aircraft were seen by the flight leaders, but FSL Pownall lost touch with C Flight in cloud when east of Roulers at 08.20. He was attacked by three enemy aircraft which opened fire at extreme range and then followed him for some distance without attempting to close.

A and C Flights took off on an offensive patrol at 17.15. C Flight took off first, followed by A Flight. Heavy rain set in just as A Flight left the ground and Fitzgibbon abandoned the patrol. C Flight continued and encountered two layers of heavy cloud at 4000 feet and 14000 feet. No enemy machines were seen below or above the clouds.

24th August

Bad weather prevented all operational flying.

25th August

A and C Flights performed an offensive patrol at 06.20, covering Menin, Courtrai, and Wervicq at 14500 feet. The patrol observed ten enemy aircraft well beyond Courtrai between 07.00 and 07.20. Just south of Courtrai at 07.00, C Flight observed five enemy machines below with others high above them. Saint attacked the lower formation, driving one machine down out of control. The "decoys" retreated immediately and the main flight came down with the sun behind them, forcing C Flight to retreat. At 07.30, Manuel saw three enemy aircraft near Menin, these retreated when he tried to approach them. Lewis in N5367, making his second patrol with A Flight failed to return from the patrol, he was probably shot down by *Ltn.* H.G. v. Ousten of *Jasta* 11 at 08.05. Lewis spent the rest of the war in captivity.

A and C Flights carried out an offensive patrol at 18.25 over the enemy balloon line. Throughout the duration of the patrol a large formation of enemy aircraft held station above the patrol between Langemarck and Polygon Wood. At 19.30 some of the hostile machines attacked when the patrol was north of Polygon Wood. Fitzgibbon attacked a scout which was on Nelson's tail, after firing 200 rounds into the enemy machine, it side-slipped, turned over on its back and fell completely out of control. Nelson was able to observe it fall for a long way. Emery engaged a scout that was trying to get on Fitzgibbon's tail and drove it off. All machines returned safely. FSL Trapp suffered engine trouble and returned early.

26th August

FLt Saint collected the squadron's first Sopwith Camel, B6201, from the depot and made a test flight at 19.10.

27th August

FCdr Maynard, FLt Everett and FSL Rowley of No.1 Squadron collected three of No.10 Squadron's Triplanes. No.10 Squadron's pilots flew nine of the remaining Triplanes to the depot just after mid-day.

28th to 29th August

Bad weather interfered with all flying activities.

30th August

Saint was promoted to the rank of Flight Commander. On the same day he delivered the twin gun machine N533 to the depot and FLt Jenner-Parsons of Naval 8 collected N5366, No.10 Squadron's last Triplane.

CHAPTER FIVE

CAMELS

No.10 Squadron's losses during August were such that the squadron was dangerously short of experienced pilots, this was made worse by FLt Carter being posted on Canadian Leave, and FCdr Alexander being absent on normal leave.

By the 30th August, the squadron's roster stood at 9 pilots, as follows:

FLt H.J.T. Saint
FLt D.F. Fitzgibbon
FSL H.S. Broughall
FSL J.G. Manuel
FSL H.J. Emery
FSL G.L. Trapp
FSL H.L. Nelson
FSL H. Day
FSL C.H. Pownall

Of these, only Fitzgibbon could be considered to be an experienced and skilled scout pilot. Saint, as previously stated, although experienced on bombers, was less skilled with scouts and in previous weeks his lack of judgement had run his flight into several obvious traps, nevertheless, this did not prevent him from receiving promotion to Flight Commander on the 30th August.

Of the original three flights formed in May 1917, only Alexander and Fitzgibbon were still flying operationally. Euan Dickson, a pilot not considered good enough for scouts and posted to Naval 5 was also still active. Collishaw was being rested, and would not return to operational flying until December.

The RNAS was finding it difficult to provide enough replacement pilots to equip their scout squadrons. Their intake of new pilots, always significantly lower than the RFC, simply could not keep up with the attrition faced on the Western Front. The decision was taken to disband No.6 Squadron and to use the pilots and aircraft to reinforce No.9 and No.10 Squadrons.

No.10 Squadron was re-equipped with Clerget powered Sopwith Camels during the latter part of August. As stated at the end of the previous section, No.10 Squadron's first Sopwith Camel, B6201, arrived at Droglandt on the 26th August 1917, when FLt H.J.T. Saint collected the machine from the depot. On the 30th, the squadron was allocated 13 Camels from the disbanding Naval 6, accompanied by seven of that squadron's pilots.

The following personnel were added to the No.10 Squadron roster:

FSL W.A. Curtis
FSL E.D. Abbot
FSL R.E. Carroll
FSL H. Lawson
FSL N.M. Macgregor
FSL S.A. Hamilton-Bowyer
FSL P. Wood

New pilot FSL W.C. Johnston also arrived on the 1st. A further 4 Camels were picked up from the depot, making 18 in total.

September 1917

The wet conditions experienced in August had been so bad that three weeks were required to recover and prepare for the

Sopwith Camel B3882 was inherited from No.6 Naval Squadron on the 30th August 1917, and was normally flown by FSL G.L. Trapp, the deputy Commander of A Flight. Whilst flying B3882, Trapp claimed an Albatros scout destroyed north of Moorslede on the 28th September 1917. *Courtesy GSL/JMB Collection*

third offensive. The battle for the Menin Road ridge commenced on the 20th September, the scout squadrons of 5 Brigade were required to carry out conventional offensive patrols, but to fly low on their return to seek out and attack enemy reinforcements. Low patrols in support of corps machines were also required.

The Camels of No.10 Squadron started to carry bombs and attack ground targets prior to the commencement of the ground offensive, but soon reverted to more conventional patrols followed by ground attacks upon their return, as described above.

Whilst heavy fighting continued in the vicinity of the Menin Road ridge, an assault was commenced on the 26th September into the Polygon Wood area. No.10 Squadron Camels had been despatched at first light to bomb enemy aerodromes and were again required to carry out ground attacks when returning from patrol.

On the 28th September, German air activity had noticeably dropped, and the allies carried out 20 separate bombing missions. No.10 Squadron had been tasked with performing a low level bombing attack on Rumbeke aerodrome, the mission was not performed to the satisfaction of the Commanding Officer of 5 Brigade and the ensuing repercussions are discussed in the next chapter.

The first few days of September were given over to familiarisation and practise with the new machines, although a number of patrols were flown from the 3rd to the 6th to discourage incursions by reconnaissance machines. Several engagements took place but these were indecisive due to gun stoppages.

1st September

Bad weather prevented all flying activities.

2nd September

The day was given over to familiarisation and practice flying.

FSL Manuel made a forced landing at No.5 Naval Squadron, damaging B3950.

3rd September

B Flight was reformed on the 3rd, Fitzgibbon taking Macgregor, Johnston, Broughall, Carroll and Curtis on a one hour practice formation patrol.

Saint and Abbot attempted to intercept an enemy 2-seater at 09.15. They observed ten enemy scouts at 15000 feet over Ypres. At 10.10 they observed a 2-seater to the west of Ypres being shelled by anti-aircraft defences.

Trapp and Hamilton-Bowyer performed a reconnaissance enemy aircraft patrol at 10.48. They drove off a 2-seater over Ypres at 11.00.

Macgregor and Carroll performed a reconnaissance enemy aircraft patrol at 11.00, one 2-seater was seen northwest of Ypres at 11.15.

Maund and Nelson carried out an uneventful reconnaissance enemy aircraft patrol 12.10.

Emery and Day carried out a reconnaissance enemy aircraft patrol at 13.13, a number of enemy machines were observed. FSL Emery overshot the aerodrome and damaged N6371 when landing.

Johnston, Curtis, and Broughall carried out a reconnaissance enemy aircraft patrol at 14.30. Three enemy machines were observed to the southeast of Ypres at 18000 feet. FSL Broughall made a forced landing in N6373 and damaged the aircraft.

Saint and Abbot performed an uneventful reconnaissance enemy aircraft patrol at 15.55.

Fitzgibbon had B Flight practicing formation flying again at 17.35.

4th September

FSL Trapp led a five machine reconnaissance enemy aircraft patrol at 08.30. Five scouts were encountered at 10000 feet over Houthulst Forest, the patrol attacked, Trapp and Maund both had indecisive engagements, Trapp suffering from stoppages in both guns.

FCdr Saint led an uneventful reconnaissance enemy aircraft patrol at 09.56 and FLt Fitzgibbon led another uneventful patrol at 11.00.

All of the pilots were involved in formation practise flights in the evening.

5th September

Three reconnaissance enemy aircraft patrols were flown on the 5th. Saint led C Flight over Ypres, Zillebeke, and Wormeze at 08.21. One enemy machine was observed at 17000 feet over Vlamertinghe at 09.15.

FSL Trapp led A Flight over the same area at 09.25, no enemy machines were observed.

B Flight patrolled the same area at 10.30, observing six aircraft to the east of Roulers at 11.15, these were thought to be enemy machines but the distance was too great for positive identification.

All three Flights were involved in formation and tactics practice in the afternoon and evening.

6th September

The first offensive patrol was flown by A, C, and B Flights at 06.45, 06.50, and 06.55. FSL G.L. Trapp, the deputy flight commander, led A Flight, FLt Fitzgibbon led B Flight, and FCdr Saint led C Flight. Sixteen Camels patrolled the line from Dixmude, Roulers, Moorslede, and Ypres. At 08.00, a formation of seven Albatros scouts was seen to the southeast of Dixmude at 10000ft. B Flight dived from 12000ft and attacked the enemy formation. Curtis and Broughall both claimed an enemy machine out of control and a further four indecisive engagements took place. At 08.15, four enemy scouts were observed near Houthulst Forest attacking three DH5s at 5000 feet. C Flight dived to attack but the enemy machines escaped through the clouds. Lawson made a forced landing at No.12 Naval Squadron and Johnston landed at No.9 Naval Squadron with slight engine trouble.

C Flight carried out an inner offensive patrol at 16.40, over the area Houthulst Wood, Poelcappelle and Polygon Wood. Heavy thunderclouds were forming with rain and hail over the lines.

FSL Grace attempted to make a practice flight in N6376 at 17.25 but made a forced landing immediately after take off, damaging the aircraft but escaping injury.

A Flight took off at 18.10 but were immediately recalled by Wing orders due to unfavourable weather.

7th September

FLt Fitzgibbon led an eight machine outer offensive patrol at 17.30 to cover the line Houthulst Wood, Roulers, Ledeghem and Gheluvelt. It was intended that a total of sixteen machines would perform the patrol but the second eight machines were kept back when a thick ground mist developed. Fitzgibbon brought the patrol back after 50 minutes due to the unfavourable weather conditions.

8th September

Unfavourable weather conditions, no flying.

9th September

FCdr Alexander returned from leave on the 9th. The squadron had been flying Sopwith Triplanes when he left for leave and on return he was faced with having to make a rapid conversion to the unstable Camel.

With Alexander's return, the squadron structure was as shown below:

A Flight

FCdr W.M. Alexander, Flight Commander
FSL G.L. Trapp, Deputy Flight Commander
FSL H.L. Nelson
FSL H. Lawson
FSL S.A. Hamilton-Bowyer
FSL H.B. Maund

B Flight
FLt D.F. Fitzgibbon, Flight Commander
FSL H.S. Broughall
FSL W.C. Johnston
FSL W.A. Curtis
FSL R.E. Carroll
FSL N.M. Macgregor

C Flight
FCdr H.J.T. Saint, Flight Commander
FSL H.J. Emery
FSL H. Day
FSL E.D. Abbot
FSL P. Wood
FSL J.G. Manuel
FSL E.I. Bussell

FLt Fitzgibbon led eight Camels on an outer offensive patrol at 06.04. Thick mist and cloud over the lines rendered the patrol ineffectual. No enemy aircraft were seen.

A Flight, led by Trapp, and C Flight performed an outer offensive patrol at 15.05, the patrol covered Houthulst Wood, Roulers, and Gheluvelt. At 16.30, to the east of Zonnebeke, an Albatros scout dived on the patrol and was engaged by Trapp who drove it down vertically. Trapp and Saint thought the machine was out of control but could not be sure.

Fitzgibbon took B Flight out at 18.00 to patrol over Houthulst Wood, Roulers, Ledeghem, and Gheluvelt. The patrol encountered three scouts and a 2-seater over Westroosebeke and four indecisive engagements were reported. Later during the patrol, eight scouts were observed patrolling behind Roulers at a height well above the Camels.

FCdr Alexander left at 18.10 to try and pick up the patrol but was unable to find them. He reported an indecisive attack upon a 2-seater to the northeast of Dixmude at 18.50.

10th September

FSL Grace had better luck on his second attempt at a practice flight, successfully completing a flight on the 10th.

C Flight and A Flight carried out an outer offensive patrol at 17.30. Eight enemy aircraft were observed at 17000 feet over Houthulst Wood at 18.45 but they refused to attack and withdrew to the east. Wood made a forced landing near the aerodrome in Camel N6342, damaging the aircraft.

11th September

Fitzgibbon led an eight Camel patrol on a scheduled escort mission for DH4s at 12.00. The patrol did not pick up the DH4s, so continued with an outer offensive patrol. At 12.35, Fitzgibbon led the Camels down on a patrol of eight black and white Albatros scouts but failed to overtake them. At 13.05 a 2-seater was encountered southeast of Roulers and another 2-seater was encountered at 13.40 at Westroosebeke, Fitzgibbon and Macgregor indecisively attacked both of these machines.

FCdr Alexander led a ten Camel patrol at 16.55 and patrolled the Roulers to Courtrai area, accompanied for 25 minutes by five SE5s and five DH4s. No enemy machines were seen until 18.50 as the patrol was returning.

12th September

Alexander led A Flight, and Manuel led C Flight on an outer offensive patrol at 18.05. Wood had trouble keeping up with the formation and was attacked by three enemy aircraft when to the east of Roulers. FSL Wood was driven down almost to the ground but escaped when his attacker inexplicably broke off the engagement and climbed away. Wood continued to the lines but lost his way in the failing light and had to land at No.4 Naval Squadron's aerodrome. The patrol failed to see any enemy aircraft and only Wood made any contact with the enemy.

FSL Grace carried out a practice flight at 18.40 and also managed to get lost, eventually landing in a field near Cassel.

13th September

Fitzgibbon led an eight machine patrol at 06.25. At 07.10, when returning from Roulers towards the lines, a formation of enemy aircraft dived through the clouds and performed a hit and run attack upon the rear machines in the formation. After their dive, the enemy machines zoomed up well above the patrol and would not attack again. FSL Abbot in N3933 had been flying at the rear of the patrol and was brought down during the attack. Abbot was wounded and became a prisoner of war. *Ltn.* W. von Bülow of *Jasta* 36 has been credited with the victory.

A and C Flights carried out an outer offensive patrol at 15.20. The visibility was very bad and no enemy aircraft were observed. Grace and Bussell lost the formation and returned early.

14th September

A and C Flights carried out an uneventful outer offensive patrol at 10.20.

Fitzgibbon led a formation on an outer offensive patrol at 15.45, the eight Camels crossed the lines near Houthulst Forest and followed the lines to Roulers and Ledeghem. At 16.30, eight enemy scouts were encountered near Ten-Brielen, and a general engagement took place. Fitzgibbon, Carroll, and Johnston each claimed an enemy machine out of control and several other indecisive engagements were reported.

The cloud cover thickened but A and C Flights were involved in an outer offensive patrol at 17.40. No enemy machines were encountered.

15th September

Fitzgibbon led eight machines on an escort mission at 15.15. The patrol picked up five DH4s at 16.10 and escorted them to Bryke Wood and back to the lines, and then continued as an offensive patrol. Four enemy scouts were encountered over Moorslede at 16.30 and attacked by the patrol. The attack was ineffective and the enemy scouts escaped. The patrol was then attacked from above by Albatros scouts and a Fokker Triplane and a general engagement took place in which FSL Macgregor claimed the Triplane driven down out of control, a further four indecisive engagements also took place. Although Macgregor's claim was for an "out of control", Fokker Triplane No.102/17 crashed and *Jasta* 11 ace *Oblt*. Kurt Wolff was killed.

C and A Flights performed an outer offensive patrol at 17.30. Visibility was poor due to thick mist, however, a 2-seater was observed over Houthulst Wood at 18.40. FCdr Alexander fired several rounds at long range before the machine disappeared into the mist.

16th September

Fitzgibbon led an eight machine outer offensive patrol at 05.48. The patrol attempted to cover Houthulst, Roulers, Ledeghem, and Gheluvelt but the entire area was obscured by heavy layers of cloud. The patrol returned early due to the conditions.

C and A Flights performed an outer offensive patrol at 15.15. Three Albatros scouts were encountered southeast of Roulers at 16.10. The patrol attempted to attack the scouts and FCdr Alexander engaged one machine at long range without effect. A number of enemy machines were observed during the patrol but could not be brought to action.

FLt Fitzgibbon let eight machines on a bomber escort at 17.15. The patrol waited over the aerodrome from 17.45 to 18.00 but the DH4s did not turn up. At 18.07 Fitzgibbon found six DH4s over the lines travelling west, the patrol followed them back to Cassel, then returned and patrolled over Houthulst Forest, Roulers, Ledeghem, and Gheluvelt. At 18.45, three scouts were observed behind Roulers and at 18.50 nine scouts were seen gaining height several miles beyond Roulers.

Manuel and Broughall flew a hostile aircraft patrol at 18.36 in pursuit of an enemy machine being shelled by allied anti-aircraft batteries. At 18.50 they encountered an RE8 engaged with an enemy scout, Broughall chased the enemy machine back to its own balloon line.

17th September

Bad weather over the next two days restricted flying activities.

18th September

A and C Flights attempted an outer offensive patrol at 09.50, however, as the weather was bad, the patrol was converted into a line patrol. Saint and Emery were forced to land at No.5 Naval Squadron and Nelson landed at No.9 Squadron RFC.

Squadron Commander Bell attempted to perform observation duty at 10.30, he reported that because of the weather, enemy activity was almost impossible to observe. At 11.00 he observed an enemy scout attempting to attack an RE8. Rain set in at 11.15 and all aerial activity ceased.

19th September

Fitzgibbon led an eight machine outer offensive patrol at 09.15. The patrol crossed the lines at Houthulst Forest at 09.50 and turned south. Eight enemy scouts were encountered over Hooge and at 10.00 the patrol attacked them to the east of Ypres. A fifteen minute general engagement ensued which attracted several other aircraft. Maund and Carroll both claimed a scout driven down out of control and Macgregor drove down a scout which although under control was emitting a large volume of black smoke. Several indecisive engagements were also reported. FSL E.G.V. Grace was shot down in flames and killed by *Ltn*. Adam of *Jasta* 6. The patrol continued and at 10.40, drove off three scouts which were attacking another Camel. The patrol reported seeing a number of enemy aircraft at various heights.

At 14.30, A and B Flights were despatched on a Low Road Patrol which involved attacking ground targets. Alexander, Manuel, Bussell, and Emery provided top cover, whilst Saint, Macgregor, Broughall, and Trapp carried two Cooper bombs beneath their Camels. The report of the ground attack was as follows:

FCdr Saint dropped two bombs from 2000 feet at the northwest corner of Houthulst Wood at 15.00, observing a big explosion. He then attacked enemy transport on the Staden road, firing 350 rounds from 1000 feet. He reported transport at a standstill afterwards. FSL Macgregor dropped two bombs at the same time and place as Saint and also observed a large explosion. He then attacked an active battery in Houthulst Wood from 1000 feet. FSL Broughall dropped two bombs on a crossroads south of Houthulst Wood from 2000 feet and observed one explosion at side of road, trucks stopped and men running for cover. He then flew over the Menin-Ypres road and fired 580 rounds from 700 feet at parties of men and transport. FSL Trapp lost formation in the clouds, he attacked a gun battery in the southeast corner of Houthulst Wood from 500 feet and fired 500 rounds until his gun jammed. FSL Manuel observed an enemy 2-seater and a scout diving on Broughall's Camel over Houthulst Wood. Manuel attacked the scout and both enemy machines disengaged and escaped.

The escorting machines carried out an uneventful outer offensive patrol after the ground attacks were completed.

FSL AF MacDonald arrived at the squadron and was immediately sent off on a practice flight. MacDonald had previously served with No.9 Naval Squadron, flying Pups and Triplanes, and had acquired something of a reputation for crashing his aircraft.

20th September

The squadron was again ordered to perform ground attacks on the morning of the 20th Pilots were despatched in pairs but only a few machines carried bombs.

FSL Bussell and FSL Manuel took off at 09.30. At 09.50, Bussell attacked troops moving along the main road near Poelcappelle, firing 100 rounds into them from 800 feet. At 09.55, he attacked troops and transport on the road south of Houthulst Wood passing through Vifwagen. FSL Manuel dropped 2 bombs on personnel at Vifwagen at 10.20 from 1500 feet. At 11.15, he encountered an enemy 2-seater and drove it down, reporting that the pilot was hit. Manuel followed it down and fired at it on the ground from a height of 200 feet. He reported that the pilot and observer did not get out of the aircraft.

FCdr Saint and FSL Emery took off at 10.04. At 10.35, Saint dropped a bomb on a red building which was concealing a battery. He then shot-up the area from 800 feet. Saint presumably suffered a few anxious moments when landing, as one bomb had hung up beneath the aircraft. FSL Emery observed a building on fire southeast of Houthulst Wood and from 800 feet, shot-up groups of troops in the vicinity. At 11.00, he had an indecisive engagement with a 2-seater to the east of Houthulst Wood.

FLt Fitzgibbon and FSL Macgregor took off at 10.25. Fitzgibbon attacked troops on the Poelcappelle-Westroosebeke road from a height of 800 feet. Macgregor encountered a scattered formation of enemy scouts south of Houthulst Wood and had seven indecisive engagements between 10.45 and 11.15. He reported seeing one scout being driven down into the clouds by an SE5.

FSL Johnston and FSL Carroll took off at 10.32. Johnston fired at troops marching westwards on the Menin road at 11.05. He then attacked soldiers being drilled in a field in the same vicinity. FSL Carroll attacked a gun crew in a field near the Staden road. He expended all of his ammunition from an altitude of a few hundred feet.

FSL Hamilton-Bowyer and FSL Maund took off at 10.40. Maund made attacks on several small bodies of men on the Vifwagen and Poelcappelle roads.

Hamilton-Bowyer and Maund were attacked by seven enemy scouts, one of which was driven down and forced to land in a field east of the lines.

FSL Broughall and FSL A.F. MacDonald took off at 11.05. MacDonald attacked a company of troops at a main cross-roads at 11.30. He was unable to report the location due to being new to the squadron and not yet familiar with the countryside. At 11.45, MacDonald had an indecisive engagement with an Albatros scout. He finished his patrol firing at transport from 400 to 600 feet altitude. FSL H.S. Broughall did not return from the mission. Broughall, flying B6226, was last seen northeast of Staden and was shot down and captured.

FCdr Alexander and FSL Trapp left at 11.20. Alexander attacked parties of infantry from an altitude of 400 feet. Trapp attacked troops on a cross-roads near Zonnebeke.

The squadron's work reverted to more normal offensive patrols in the afternoon, however, bombs were still carried by some pilots and patrols were ordered to attack ground targets when the opportunity arose.

FCdr Saint led C Flight on an outer offensive patrol at 13.30. Saint and Manuel dropped bombs over Poelcappelle from 5000 feet. At 14.40, over Westroosebeke, six scouts were encountered and engaged by Saint and Manuel. The scouts dived away after two indecisive engagements, presumably because of the presence of four SE5s.

FLt Fitzgibbon led B Flight off at 14.35. The first part of the patrol comprised an escort for Camels of No.70 Squadron

RFC. Carroll attacked a kite balloon over Staden without result. Johnston also attacked a kite balloon in the same locality but was unable to observe the result of his attack as he had to pull up over the balloon into clouds. The patrol fired at two anti-aircraft batteries from 800 feet.

New pilot FSL Foster made a practice flight in the evening.

21st September

The squadron was tasked with more normal duties, but was still required to attack ground targets when possible.

FCdr Saint took C Flight out at 09.35; the patrol covered the area from Houthulst, Roulers, Ledeghem, Westroosebeke, and Poelcappelle. At 11.00, five enemy scouts were encountered and followed. Saint was able to engage one scout and sent it down out of control.

A Flight carried out a patrol at 09.40, covering the Houthulst, Roulers, Legedhem area without observing any enemy aircraft. The patrol was completed by flying low over the lines. FCdr Alexander attacked a party of 60 men half a mile behind the lines, firing 250 rounds from 800 feet. FSL Trapp fired 90 rounds into a gun emplacement northeast of Ypres from a height of 25 feet.

FLt Fitzgibbon led an outer offensive patrol of 8 machines at 14.05. At 14.45, the patrol encountered a flight of six Friedrichshaven bombers accompanied by escorting scouts to the south of Ypres. The patrol followed and attacked just west of Ypres and a general engagement developed. Eight indecisive combats took place. FSL Macgregor's machine, B3833, was badly damaged by gunfire and the petrol pipe was shot through. Macgregor made a forced landing near Ypres

FSL Foster made another practice flight and landed on the sands at Hennes, near Calais.

A and C Flights went out together at 17.30 on an outer offensive patrol. Gun stoppages interfered with a number of attempted engagements, effectively ruining the patrol.

New pilots FSL De Wilde and FSL Daly arrived on the 21st. FSL R.H. Daly was an experienced pilot from the Manston War Flight and already had one victory to his credit. De Wilde and Daly were attached to A Flight.

22nd September

Fitzgibbon led a seven machine offensive patrol at 06.10. Immediately after the patrol left, a thick ground mist developed completely obscuring the area up to a height of 1000 feet.

Saint led C Flight on an inner offensive patrol to Vifwagen, Passchendaele, and Keiburg, no enemy aircraft were observed.

FCdr Alexander had his revised Flight up at 20.10 for an hour's formation practice and line patrol.

A Flight now comprised:

FCdr W.M. Alexander, Flight Commander
FSL G.L. Trapp, Deputy Flight Commander
FSL H.L. Nelson
FSL J.S. de Wilde
FSL R.H. Daly

23rd September

De Wilde and Daly were in action when A and C Flights carried out an outer offensive patrol at 10.10. Ten scouts and five 2-seaters were encountered travelling west from Westroosebeke at 11.20. Several indecisive combats took place and FCdr Saint claimed a scout driven down out of control. Considerable trouble was again experienced with gun stoppages. At 11.25, FCdr Alexander engaged a single Albatros scout and drove it down out of control. During an engagement in which Bussell claimed an enemy scout out of control, his Camel, B6216, was badly shot about and crashed. Daly landed at No.4 Naval squadron.

SCdr Bell carried out an observation patrol from 11.30 to 13.10. He reported seeing a number of enemy machines working on both sides of the lines and the lack of allied scouts in the vicinity.

FLt Fitzgibbon led an 8 machine outer offensive patrol at 13.15. The visibility was very bad and no enemy aircraft were observed. FSL Johnston failed to return, having crashed B3912 near Vlamertinghe, damaging the machine and injuring himself.

A and C Flights carried out an outer offensive patrol at 17.20. Gun stoppages again interfering with the effectiveness of the patrol.

24th September

FLt Fitzgibbon led an 8 machine outer offensive patrol at 09.15. No enemy aircraft were observed. At 10.50, Fitzgibbon fired 200 rounds at a train waiting in a siding near Stadenburg and Carroll fired 160 rounds at a gun pit in the southeast corner of Houthulst Wood. FSL Foster in B6279 failed to return, having been shot down and made a prisoner of war, possibly a victim of *Ltn*. K. Wüstoff of *Jasta* 4.

A and C Flights flew an outer offensive patrol covering Houthulst, Roulers, Ledeghem, and Gheluvelt at 11.05. At 12.30, a large formation of twin-engine bombers with a scout escort was seen heading west from Westroosebeke. The patrol joined with a flight of Nieuports to make a combined attack, but the lead Nieuport fired a red Very light and the Nieuports broke away. The Camels engaged the enemy force and four indecisive combats took place, gun stoppages again being blamed for the lack of results. It was strongly felt that if the Nieuports had joined the engagement, the bomber formation would have been split up.

Fitzgibbon led an eight machine outer offensive patrol at 14.50. Carroll reported an ineffective engagement with a 2-seater over Ypres. Fitzgibbon attacked a scout over Roulers, but yet another gun stoppage compelled him to break off and land at No.21 Squadron to get the gun cleared before rejoining the patrol. Daly attacked a 2-seater Albatros northeast of Houthulst Wood at 16.10 and brought it down out of control. Stratton landed B6225 on the Elverdinghe to Poperinghe road with his petrol tank damaged after engaging two scouts to the south of Houthulst Wood.

A number of pilots, Fitzgibbon included, carried out test flights at 18.00 to test their guns.

25th September

Saint and Alexander took C and A Flights out at 07.55 on the 25th. The visibility was reported as being very bad. Alexander had an inconclusive engagement with a 2-seater over Houthulst Wood at 08.45. Five scouts were encountered over Zillebeke Lake at 08.30, the patrol engaged them but FCdr Saint broke away due to his guns jamming. Four Triplanes from No.1 Squadron attempted to join the engagement but were unable to effectively assist.

At 11.15, Fitzgibbon led 8 Camels on an outer offensive patrol. A number of scouts and 2-seaters were seen to the east of Ypres and Houthulst Wood between 12.30 and 12.50. Three indecisive engagements were reported by Fitzgibbon, two by Macgregor, and one by Carroll. Daly was forced to land at the Seaplane Defence Flight when the pressure safety valve failed. A.F. MacDonald in B3920, received a gunshot wound in his left buttock, made a forced landing to the south of Ypres and wrecked the machine.

A and C Flights performed an outer offensive patrol at 16.15. Several enemy machines were encountered but could not be brought to action.

Flight Commander Redpath arrived at the squadron, not to take over a flight, but to run the squadron in SCdr Bell's absence.

26th September

Manuel, Macgregor, and Saint, were despatched at 05.40, 5.50, and 5.55 respectively to bomb enemy aerodromes. Saint landed at the depot at Dunkerque, and reported that he was unable to locate Ingelmunster aerodrome, but found Rumbeke West, dropped two bombs which fell in front of sheds and descended to 50 feet and fired 400 rounds into the hangars. FSL Macgregor lost his bearings in heavy cloud at 500 feet and eventually landed at No.3 Naval Squadron. FSL Manuel found Abeele aerodrome at 06.15, He dropped two bombs from 1500 feet and was fired on by a machine gun. One bomb dropped in the middle of the aerodrome and the other fell between four machines which were standing outside the sheds, at least one was badly damaged with pieces seen flying into the air. Manuel dived towards the machine gun and fired 50 rounds at it until it fell silent. Manuel then attacked a party of 500 troops near Roulers, firing 200 rounds from 800 feet. He lost his way on returning and landed at La Panne.

A and C Flights carried out an outer offensive patrol and low road patrol at 10.00, FLt Fitzgibbon standing in for the missing FCdr Saint. Several formations of enemy scouts were seen in the northern area. Between 11.00 and 11.10, nine engagements took place over Westroosebeke and Passchendaele, Fitzgibbon claimed one scout driven down out of control and Daly shot down an Albatros scout to the northeast of Houthulst Wood. Between 11.25 and 11.35, eight Gotha bombers were observed approaching the lines east of Ypres, Fitzgibbon attacked two of the Gothas without result. Daly flying N6359 was hit by anti-aircraft fire and landed at No.4 Naval Squadron, injured and with his machine badly damaged. The following ground targets were attacked:

FSL Trapp fired 250 rounds at transport at Zonnebeke.

FSL Hamilton-Bowyer fired 100 rounds into enemy trenches east of Ypres from 500 feet. He fired 80 rounds in the village of Passchendaele.

FSL Emery fired 300 rounds at men and transport to the southeast of Houthulst Wood from 1000 feet.

FSL Stratton fired 125 rounds at a field battery southwest of Westroosebeke and 50 rounds at a small party moving south on the road from Westroosebeke.

FSL Carroll fired 500 rounds at a gun battery to the southeast of Houthulst Wood from 200 feet.

At 12.20, FSL Curtis, recently returned from leave, led an outer offensive patrol and low road patrol. The patrol covered the area Houthulst, Roulers, Gheluvelt, and the lines, the visibility was very bad and no enemy aircraft were observed. The following ground targets were attacked:

FSL Curtis fired 100 rounds into a battery to the north of Westroosebeke from an altitude of 800 feet. Curtis then fired 50 rounds at trucks parked at the roadside near Westroosebeke.

FSL Maund attacked three batteries immediately north and south of Poelcappelle, firing 600 rounds from 1000 feet.

FSL De Wilde got lost in the mist and failed to find any ground targets until 14.15, when he fired 250 rounds into personnel and huts near Middlekerke. De Wilde ran out of petrol and was forced to land at No.21 Squadron RFC to refuel.

FSL A.M. Alexander did not submit a report.

A Flight carried out an outer offensive patrol and low road patrol at 15.35, covering the area from Poelcappelle to Becelaere, the visibility was indifferent and no enemy aircraft were seen. The following ground targets were attacked:

FCdr Alexander fired 350 rounds into a body of 1000 troops near Becelaere. He pressed home the attack from a height of 350 feet.

FSL Trapp attacked troops in the same area, firing 400 rounds from 200 feet. He reported that the troops were completely disorganised and considerable material loss must have been inflicted.

FSL Nelson attacked mules and horses encountered to the east of Polygon Wood. He also attacked enemy trenches but suffered stoppages in both guns.

FSL Bussell attacked transport on the road southeast of Polygon Wood, firing 100 rounds, he then fired 100 rounds into troops encountered on the Zonnebeke road. Bussell completed the patrol with an indecisive engagement against a 2-seater to the east of the Allied barrage.

FLt Fitzgibbon led B Flight on an outer offensive patrol and low road patrol at 17.10. The patrol covered the area from Becelaere to Poelcappelle, visibility was poor but a number of enemy scouts were encountered and six indecisive engagements took place. Ground targets attacked were as follows:

FLt Fitzgibbon fired into shell holes beyond the barrage from a height of 500 to 800 feet. He fired 350 rounds, until both guns jammed.

FSL Hamilton-Bowyer attacked several bodies of troops on the road between Poelcappelle and St. Julien. He pressed the attack from a height of 500 to 1000 feet and fired 400 rounds.

FSL Carroll fired 400 rounds into reserve trenches to the east of Zonnebeke.

FCdr Saint led C Flight on a balloon patrol at 18.00.

The patrol was tasked with attacking kite balloons in the Becelaere to Poelcappelle area. A solitary 2-seater was observed south of Houthulst Wood at 18.20 and indecisively engaged by Manuel. Saint, Emery, and Stratton attacked two kite balloons located 1 mile north, and 1 1/2 miles south of Westroosebeke. A total of 700 rounds were fired and the balloons were hit but did not ignite.

FSL Sutherland, a new pilot, arrived at the squadron.

27th September

Fitzgibbon led an eight machine outer offensive patrol over Houthulst Forest, Roulers, Westroosebeke, Poelcappelle and the northern area at 08.15. The visibility was very poor with the entire area covered by two thick layers of cloud at 1000 feet and 2000 feet.

Alexander and Saint led their Flights on an outer offensive patrol to Houthulst, Roulers, Ledeghem, and Polygon Wood at 12.15. The patrol escorted a flight of DH4s which were attacked by 6 Albatros scouts at 13.10 over Ledeghem. The patrol engaged the scouts and drove them off, three inconclusive engagements taking place. At 13.20, the patrol joined eight Triplanes from Naval 1 to attack four enemy scouts. FCdr Alexander reported an indecisive engagement with one of the scouts before they escaped. During the course of the engagement, Alexander noted that one of the scouts was firing from three guns, two through the propeller, and one on the top plane.

FLt Fitzgibbon led an eight machine outer offensive patrol at 14.50, covering the area Houthulst Wood, Hooglede, Roulers, Ledeghem and Polygon Wood. At 16.00, northeast of Dixmude, Curtis shot down an Albatros scout, the crash being observed by Carroll. Six enemy aircraft were engaged at 16.10 to the northeast of Westroosebeke, Fitzgibbon shot the pilot of one scout and the machine went down out of control in a cloud of smoke. Hamilton-Bowyer also drove a scout down out of control. De Wilde failed to return, he had been last seen at 15.10 lagging behind the formation. De Wilde was shot down and killed.

SCdr Bell left the squadron on sick leave, believed to be suffering from influenza.

28th September

This was Acting Squadron Commander Redpath's first day in charge of the squadron. A day that would ultimately damage Redpath's career.

At 10 minutes past midnight, FCdr Saint took off to bomb an enemy aerodrome, he returned immediately due to a ground mist obscuring visibility.

C and A Flight took off at 09.30 to perform an outer offensive patrol. The visibility was very bad, but at 10.45, four enemy scouts were engaged over Moorslede. Three combats took place, one was indecisive, but FCdr Alexander drove a machine down which landed under control but tipped over on to its nose and FSL Trapp shot a machine down which was seen to crash.

FCdr Saint led a special bombing patrol at 14.27. This mission, which initially appeared to be fairly successful and its subsequent repercussions, are fully described in the next chapter.

FSL Macgregor led an eight machine outer offensive patrol at 17.30, covering the area Houthulst Wood, Roulers, Ledeghem, and Polygon Wood. At 18.20, six Albatros scouts were encountered over Passchendaele, these performed three separate "dive and zoom" attacks from long range. No other enemy machines were encountered.

29th September

It was business as usual on the 29th, FSL Macgregor led a seven machine outer offensive patrol to Houthulst, Hooglede, Roulers, Ledeghem, and Polygon Wood at 12.35. A 2-seater was driven away over Westroosebeke at 13.45 and a number of enemy machines were observed to the south of the area at 13.50.

C and A Flights carried out an outer offensive patrol at 15.35. FSL Bramhall, a new pilot who had not been given a chance to practice was attached to Saint's flight and made a forced landing at No.6 Squadron RFC. The aircraft, B6291, was wrecked, and Bramhall received a cut on his head and was taken to hospital.

Another new pilot, FSL Wilmot, was more fortunate than Bramhall and was sent up for several practice flights.

C and A Flights performed another outer offensive patrol at 16.00, FCdr Alexander reported one inconclusive engagement with an enemy scout, hampered by gun stoppages.

30th September

Two new pilots, FSL W.N. Fox and FSL H.W.M. Cumming were sent up on practice flights.

October 1917

The next main assault on the 4th October took place despite the resumption of bad weather that effectively grounded all aircraft. The intention was to push on to Poelcappelle and Broadseinde on the Passchendaele ridge.

No.10 Squadron played no further part in the support of this battle, being withdrawn from the Front on the 5th October and relocated at Leffrinckoucke, just to the east of Dunkerque.

1st October

FSL Macgregor led a seven machine outer offensive patrol at 13.10. Four scouts were encountered northeast of Passchendaele at 14.15 and several engagements took place. FSL Curtis claimed one enemy machine shot down out of control. At 14.30, indecisive engagements were reported with three 2-seaters to the south of Houthulst Wood and further indecisive engagements took place at 14.45.

FCdr Saint carried out an enemy aircraft patrol at 20.50, an enemy machine was observed over Poperinghe at 21.20. Saint fired 100 rounds at extreme range but the enemy machine dived beneath him and escaped.

2nd October

FSL Macgregor led an eight machine outer offensive patrol at 09.30. At 11.00, three 2-seaters were attacked and 4 indecisive engagements took place.

C and A Flights were scheduled to escort bombers of No.70 Squadron at 14.05. The bombing machines failed to start and the patrol carried on as an outer offensive patrol. An enemy scout was observed protecting a couple of spotting machines, the patrol attacked and two inconclusive engagements took place.

Another new pilot, FSL McKelvey, was sent up on practice flights. No further jobs were scheduled and the rest of the day was taken up by practice flights.

3rd and 4th October

There were no jobs allocated on the 3rd and 4th, the only flying to take place being test and practice flights.

FSL Manuel, making a practice flight in B3950 on the 4th, experienced engine trouble and made a forced landing at No.9 Naval Squadron.

5th October

Control of No.10 Squadron was transferred to IV Brigade and the squadron was moved away from the Ypres area and relocated to Leffrinckhoucke, situated to the east of Dunkerque.

CHAPTER SIX

MUTINY

By the autumn of 1917, morale amongst the frontline squadrons was at a distinct ebb, an understandable sentiment in squadrons that had suffered heavy losses.

The 28th of September was Acting Squadron Commander Redpath's first day in charge of No.10 Squadron following SCdr B.C. Bell's departure on sick leave. On that day, Lieutenant-Colonel F.V. Holt, the officer in charge of 22 (Army) Wing 5 Brigade, ordered a major low level bombing and strafing attack on Rumbeke aerodrome. No.10 Squadron would spearhead the attack, with support from No.23 Squadron RFC (SPADs) and No.70 Squadron RFC (Camels). Redpath assigned FCdr H.J.T. Saint to carry out the attack and the following personnel performed the mission:

FCdr H.J.T. Saint
FSL W.A. Curtis
FSL N.M. Macgregor
FSL K.V. Stratton
FSL J.G. Manuel
FSL R.E. Carroll

The mission report is repeated below:

Special Bombing Patrol 2.27 3.20

Escorting machines Camels and SPADs picked up at La Lovie, and patrol proceeded direct to Rumbeke SW aerodrome arriving 15.05. FCdr Saint dived from 7000ft and attacked the permanent hangars to S. of aerodrome, the sheds to the east and 5 or 6 machines standing out, with machine gun fire, firing well into the midst of the latter. He fired 450 rounds in all.

FSL Macgregor dropped 2 bombs on aerodrome and fired 200 rounds at machines standing out.

FSL Curtis fired 200 rounds at machines on aerodrome standing out.

FSL Carroll dropped 2 bombs on aerodrome and fired 100 rounds at the hangars. At 15.15 from 2000ft fired 100 rounds at a train moving S. from Roulers.

FSL Stratton dropped 2 bombs on aerodrome and fired 270 rounds at hangars and machines. Observed great commotion on the ground.

FSL Manuel dropped 2 bombs on aerodrome and fired 100 rounds on sheds. Immediately after this pilot indecisively attacked a 2-seater which was attacking one of our machines. EA driven away in the clouds.

The above operation was carried out at 2000-3000ft and some of the bombs were seen to explode behind and near the hangars. All pilots particularly remark on the excellence of the escort work by all machines present for that purpose.

The attack was carried out without loss, but it came to Holt's attention that the mission was not pursued at low level. As can be seen in the squadron report, the attack was delivered from a height of 2000 to 3000 ft. Lieutenant-Colonel Holt regarded the value of the operation to have been at least halved and contacted Repath by telephone to complain. Redpath assured Holt that the failure was due to misunderstood orders and that the squadron would like the chance of repeating the mission.

On the 30th of September, Holt telephoned Redpath at 11.45 and notified him that the repeat attack was set-up for 14.00 that afternoon. To Holt's astonishment, Redpath tried to put the mission off for a day and finding that proposal unacceptable, told Holt that "his pilot's weren't for it". Holt tried to point out the seriousness of Redpath's statement and asked him if he was sure he was representing the views of his squadron.

Holt visited the squadron in the evening and again asked Redpath if he was sure that he was fairly representing his pilots. Redpath replied that they did not consider the probable results were worth the risk to machines and pilots. It must be assumed that the inexperienced Redpath adopted this stance after consulting with FCdr Saint, and taking Saint's words at face value without interviewing any other members of the squadron. Wilfrid Curtis, when interviewed by the Canadian Directorate of History after the war, professed that neither he nor the others had known what was happening and subsequent events would tend to support his statement.

Lieutenant-Colonel Holt did not order Redpath to carry out the mission, as an outright refusal would have had very serious implications. The problem was passed up through the chain of command, leaving General Trenchard with a very difficult decision. As a strict disciplinarian, Trenchard's preferred choice of action would almost certainly have been to institute formal proceedings against the responsible officers. However, the threat of unavoidable publicity and considerations of morale probably stayed his hand. He decided to discretely remove the squadron from the front, hoping that the incident would not be noted, thus avoiding repercussions amongst the remaining squadrons and in particular, the naval squadrons, under his command.

No.10 Squadron was quietly transferred to IV Brigade on the 5th of October 1917 and relocated to Leffrinckhoucke where they were left kicking their heels with little to do other than to perform practice flights and carry out relatively quiet outer line patrols. It is believed that at this point the squadron was told that the move was due to dissatisfaction with the reduced output of combat claims. On the 20th November, control was transferred back to No.4 Wing RNAS and on the 27th November, the squadron relocated to Teteghem, which was southeast of Dunkerque.

Saint was transferred out of No.10 Squadron by the 25th October 1917, leaving FSL Manuel temporarily in charge of C Flight. Redpath remained in charge of the squadron until SCdr Bell was fit to return during the early part of December, he was then transferred out and held various administrative posts at Cranwell and Redcar until the end of the war, when he took charge of No.209 Squadron.

Somewhat paradoxically, Trenchard wrote a letter of appreciation to Redpath on the 22nd November. The letter made no mention of the reason for the squadron's withdrawal from the front:

Headquarters
Royal Flying Corps
22:11:17

Dear Redpath,

I am very sorry that owing to this battle I have not been able to write to you to say how much I regret losing Number 10 Naval Squadron.

I hope you will explain to all the pilots that it was due to my having to look after this battle that I could not get this letter off earlier, and will you please thank them all from me for all the work they have done for the Army in the Field and the Flying Corps in particular. This squadron had an extraordinarily good name and the work it carried out under you and your predecessor has been of the utmost value and of the best type.

I hope that you and all your pilots will remember that if ever I can be of any use to them and I will do my best to help them, and I hope one day we may serve together again.

Yours sincerely,

Signed H. Trenchard

16th October

Saint led C Flight on an outer line patrol from Middlekerke to Praet Bosch Wood at 06.00. No enemy aircraft were encountered, but two machines in the patrol were attacked by a patrol of four French SPADs at 06.40.

A Flight covered the same route at 10.00. Two scouts were encountered to the east of Dixmude at 11.20 but they dived away towards Lichtervelde when approached.

17th October

Outer line patrols over Middlekerke to Praet Bosch Wood were flown by all three flights on the 17th. Curtis led A Flight at 06.45, the patrol encountered three enemy scouts to the west of Middlekerke at 07.50. These kept above the patrol and avoided engagement. The anti-aircraft fire in the northern area was exceptionally heavy and three machines were hit, one suffering considerable damage.

FLt Macgregor led B Flight at 09.45, the patrol encountered considerable enemy activity. Seven Albatros scouts were encountered between Keyem and Praet Bosch Wood at 10.15, Macgregor, Hamilton-Bowyer, and McKelvey recorded inconclusive engagements. At 10.40 a 2-seater was observed at 12000 feet travelling east from Nieuport, but was not engaged. Eight Albatros scouts were observed to the southeast of Dixmude at 10.55, Macgregor indecisively engaged one scout before the formation dived away to the east. A formation of 5 Aviatiks was seen at 11.10, the formation diving south over Slype. Finally, when between Nieuport and Dixmude at 11.30, a 2-seater was observed 2000 feet above the patrol.

FSL Manuel led C Flight at 12.35, but found little enemy activity, with a single enemy machine seen to the east of Ostende at 14.00.

18th October

The 18th saw a repeat of the Middlekerke to Praet Bosch Wood patrols. FCdr Macgregor led B Flight away at 06.50. Five enemy scouts were observed over Keyem at 08.15, a short general engagement took place but no decisive results were obtained. The patrol reported considerable trouble with gun stoppages.

Saint's C Flight patrol at 09.45 was uneventful.

Curtis led A Flight off at 12.42. Two 2-seaters were encountered over Middlekerke at 13.15, but they dived away beyond Ghistelles before they could be engaged. Ten enemy scouts were encountered by the patrol to the northeast of Dixmude and engaged at 13.30, no decisive results were obtained, but B3882, flown by FSL Cumming, suffered gunfire damage to its petrol tank.

Ex No.6 Squadron pilot, FSL Paynter, had arrived at the squadron a couple of days earlier and was able to carry out several practice flights on the 18th.

19th October

Curtis led A Flight on an outer line patrol over Middlekerke to Praet Bosch Wood at 09.35. Heavy cloud and very bad ground visibility caused Curtis to bring the patrol back after less than an hour.

B Flight attempted a patrol over the same area at 12.50, but there was no improvement in the weather and the patrol was abandoned after an hour.

A number of pilots were involved in test and practice flying during the afternoon.

Changes in squadron staff were reflected in the Flight structure:

A Flight
FSL W.A. Curtis, Flight Commander
FSL G.L. Trapp, Deputy Flight Commander
FSL H.L. Nelson
FSL H.W.M. Cumming
FSL J.deC. Paynter
FSL K.V. Stratton

B Flight
FLt N.M. Macgregor, Flight Commander
FSL S.A. Hamilton-Bowyer
FSL W.N. Fox
FSL W.H. Wilmot
FSL J.G. Clark
FSL M.T. McKelvey

C Flight
FCdr H.J.T. Saint, Flight Commander
FSL J.G. Manuel, Deputy Flight Commander
FSL A.G. Beattie
FSL E.I. Bussell
FSL H.B. Maund
FSL A.M. Alexander

20th October

FSL Curtis led A Flight on an outer line patrol from Middlekerke to Praet Bosch Wood at 07.40. One enemy 2-seater was observed crossing the lines near Dixmude at 09.15, the patrol climbed towards it and the enemy machine turned back and retreated to the east. FSL Cumming, flying B6297, lost his engine when returning to the aerodrome and crashed the machine. Cumming received facial injuries and was taken to Malo hospital.

B Flight covered the same area at 09.45 and reported seeing two enemy machines that were far out of range and eventually lost in the mist.

C Flight patrolled the same area at 12.40, nine enemy scouts were encountered at 13.40 to the northeast of Dixmude, the patrol engaged and followed them down. FCdr Saint claimed a machine shot down and seen to crash near Praet Bosch Wood. FSL Manuel saw the machine that he was attacking land near the same place.

21st October

FLt Macgregor led B Flight on an outer line offensive patrol at 06.45. As usual, the patrol covered the Middlekerke to Praet Bosch Wood line. At 07.30 twelve Albatros scouts were encountered over Nieuport and a general engagement ensued, but no decisive results were obtained. FSL Fox received a wound in his leg, but was able to safely return to the aerodrome. FLt Macgregor engaged a 2-seater to the east of Furnes at 08.00, Macgregor was compelled to break off the engagement when his right gun suffered a double feed after the left gun was exhausted.

C Flight covered the same area at 09.45, the patrol encountered 3 scouts over Slype, but they were not prepared to engage and remained well above Saint's patrol.

A Flight repeated the same patrol at 12.35; three 2-seaters were observed heading across the lines over Dixmude at 13.30. The patrol followed them and dived to engage, the entire Flight attacked the nearest machine which was shot down in flames and shared by Curtis, Nelson, and Emery. At 13.50 when to the northeast of Dixmude, a lone Albatros scout attacked FSL Paynter on the outside of the formation and was in turn attacked and shot down by Curtis. The 2-seater fell within allied lines and the scout was confirmed to have crashed by Belgian sources.

New pilot FSL G.J. Clark carried out his first practice flight with the squadron.

22nd October

B Flight carried out a relatively uneventful outer line patrol over the Middlekerke to Praet Bosch Wood line at 12.47. Four enemy aircraft were briefly observed beyond Ostende.

Four of Naval 10's Flight Sub Lieutenants. Left to right at rear, FSL William Henry Wilmot, and FSL Murton Tyndale McKelvey. Left to right at front, FSL John Gerald Manual, and FSL Hugh Bingham Maund. *Courtesy E.F. Cheesman*

New pilot FSL G.H. Morang made several practice flights.

23rd October

Bad weather, no flying activity.

24th October

C Flight carried out an outer line patrol over the line from Middlekerke to Praet Bosch Wood at 09.55. Heavy detached clouds from 2000 feet to 10000 feet made the visibility indifferent.

A Flight repeated the patrol at 14.10, having been delayed by the weather conditions. The visibility was poor and no enemy aircraft were seen.

The rest of the afternoon was given over to test and practice flights.

25th October

Bad weather, all flying activity was abandoned.

26th October

FSL Curtis led A Flight on an outer line patrol at 07.40. The weather delayed the planned start, but when the patrol got away it covered the line from St. Pierre Cappelle, Zarren, and Houthulst. Visibility was poor and no enemy aircraft were seen. Morang returned to the aerodrome to exchange his Camel, he crashed his second machine, B6260, when attempting to take off but escaped injury.

The rest of the day was taken up by practice flying.

27th October

B Flight carried out an outer line patrol over St. Pierre Cappelle, Zarren, and Houthulst at 06.50. Three enemy machines were observed diving down to Ghistelles at 07.15 and a further ten were seen over Roulers at 08.00.

FSL Manuel led C Flight over the same area at 09.42, reporting numerous sightings of enemy machines. Nine aircraft were observed over Praet Bosch Wood at 09.30, three 2-seaters were seen over St. Pierre Cappelle at 09.35 and several machines were seen in the distance to the southeast of Houthulst Wood. The patrol found that their guns were inoperative, thought to be caused by freezing up. FSL A.M. Alexander broke a centre section wire and returned to the aerodrome to exchange his machine. Taking replacement Camel B3919, he rejoined the patrol but made a forced landing causing minor damage to the aircraft.

A Flight repeated the patrol route at 11.35. Two 2-seaters were indecisively engaged over Zarren at 13.35, both machine diving away to the east. Six Albatros scouts were encountered at 13.20 to the northeast of Dixmude. A general engagement occurred in which one enemy machine was shot down by Stratton after being initially attacked by Curtis. Morang in N6371 was shot down in flames, by *Ltn.* H. Böhning of *Jasta* 36.

B Flight covered the same area at 13.45. The patrol observed a flight of six Albatros scouts attacking a Flight of Sopwith Pups at 15.10 to the southeast of Dixmude. The patrol dived to assist the Pups, but suffered complete failure of all machine guns, again thought to be caused by freezing up.

New pilot FSL S.K.F.P. Humphrey carried out several practice flights.

28th October

FSL Manuel led C Flight on an outer line patrol to St. Pierre Cappelle, Zarren, and Houthulst. All members of the patrol found their guns to be frozen and the patrol was abandoned.

A Flight repeated the patrol at 09.40, FSL Hall was forced to return when his guns were found to have failed, but the other member of the patrol were able to keep their guns fit for action by frequently firing short bursts.

B Flight repeated the patrol route at 13.45. One enemy machine was observed over Oostvleteren at 14.00 and another to the east of Ostende at 15.15, neither machine offered the opportunity for engagement. Hamilton-Bowyer and Carroll were forced to return when their guns failed to work at 10000 feet.

29th October

A Flight covered the St. Pierre Cappelle, Zarren, and Houthulst route at 07.03. No problems were experienced with the guns, but no enemy aircraft were encountered.

FSL Carroll led B Flight over the same patrol route at 10.50. A formation of six Gothas with accompanying scout escort was encountered to the west of Houthulst Wood at 11.20, Carroll fired 500 rounds at two or three enemy machines with no apparent effect. The patrol was attacked at 12.00 by a flight of nine scouts to the west of St. Pierre Cappelle. All of the Flight's guns failed to work and the pilots were fortunate that the enemy aircraft did not press their advantage but retired immediately.

FSL Manuel led C Flight over the same route at 14.55. The visibility was reported as very bad and no enemy aircraft were observed.

The afternoon was taken up with practice flights.

30th October

Bad weather on the 30th October interrupted all flying activities.

31st October

The squadron flew four outer line patrols over St. Pierre Cappelle, Zarren and Houthulst on the 31st.

FSL Manuel led C Flight at 07.00, the patrol observed nine enemy aircraft to the southeast of Roulers at 07.30 and five more beyond Ghistelles at 08.00. Neither formation was engaged. The lines were clear of enemy aircraft.

FSL Curtis took A Flight over the route at 09.49. The patrol reported six enemy aircraft over the Ypres sector at 10.10, ten enemy aircraft to the east of Dixmude at 10.20, a 2-seater over

Houthulst Wood at 10.45, and eight enemy aircraft to the east of Dixmude at 11.15. No engagements took place.

FSL Carroll led B Flight at 11.47, but concentrated their attention to the southern end of the line. Four enemy aircraft were observed to the east of Dixmude at 12.30, but these retired eastwards when the patrol tried to approach them.

FSL Trapp led C Flight at 13.35, but had to return after half an hour with gun problems. Beattie returned when his Camel's oil tank burst and FSL Alexander returned with a broken rocker arm. All three pilots exchanged their machines but Beattie and Alexander failed to pick up the patrol again. Manuel and Bussell observed three enemy aircraft to the east of St. Pierre Cappelle at 15.15, these dived away before they could be reached.

Eight practise flights were also carried out throughout the day.

November 1917

1st November

With the squadron having seen a number of personnel changes, the flight structure was juggled around, and now appeared as shown:

A Flight
FSL W.A. Curtis, Flight Commander
FSL H.J. Emery
FSL K.V. Stratton
FSL F.V. Hall
FSL H.L. Nelson
FSL A.A. Cameron

B Flight
FLt N.M. Macgregor, Flight Commander (on leave)
FSL R.E. Carroll, Temporary Flight Commander
FSL J.G. Clark
FSL M.T. McKelvey
FSL W.H. Wilmot
FSL S.A. Hamilton-Bowyer

C Flight
FLt G.L. Trapp, Flight Commander
FSL J.G. Manuel, Deputy flight Commander
FSL S.K.F.P. Humphrey
FSL A.G. Beattie
FSL A.M. Alexander
FSL E.I. Bussell

Newly promoted FLt Trapp led Manuel, Hamilton-Bowyer, Carroll, Hall, and Nelson on a special patrol at 15.10 to protect RE8s in the Dixmude area. The Camels crossed the lines in pairs at 1000 to 1500 feet, the visibility was very bad and no enemy aircraft were encountered. The patrol also failed to see any RE8s! Ground targets were attacked as follows:

> FLt Trapp fired 200 rounds into a German advanced position north of Dixmude from 200 feet.
>
> FSL Hamilton-Bowyer fired 300 rounds into enemy trenches near Beerst from 300 to 800 feet.
>
> FSL Nelson fired 300 rounds into enemy trenches between Beerst and Dixmude at 300 to 1000 feet.
>
> FSL Manuel fired 200 rounds into enemy trenches west of Keyem at 200 to 600 feet.
>
> FSL Carroll fired 300 rounds into enemy trenches southwest of St. Pierre Cappelle at 200 to 600 feet.
>
> FSL Hall fired 200 rounds into enemy trenches north of the Nieuport canal.

Three practice flights were flown in the morning.

2nd November

Bad weather, no flying possible.

3rd November

The weather was still bad in the morning, delaying an outer line patrol until 08.50. FLt Trapp led a C Flight patrol to the St. Pierre Cappelle to Zarren line, the sky was completely overcast and no enemy aircraft were seen. FSL Bussell lost a wheel in the air but managed to land N6330 on the beach. The machine was subsequently repaired on the spot and flown back to the aerodrome.

The seemingly obligatory practice flights took up the rest of the day.

4th November

Four line patrols over Middlekerke to Houthulst were carried out.

Curtis led A Flight away at 06.30, nine enemy aircraft were observed deep in their own territory to the east of Houthulst Wood at 07.20. The patrol was joined by seven other Camels, but the enemy machines dived away as soon as the combined force attempted to approach them.

The B Flight patrol at 08.20 became involved in a 15 minute running engagement with fifteen enemy scouts, first encountered to the north of Dixmude at 09.30. No decisive results were obtained.

C Flight's 11.05 patrol encountered a 2-seater to the west of St. Pierre Cappelle at 11.45. The patrol attempted to engage the machine, Manuel and Bussell followed it down to 4000 feet over Ghistelles but failed to obtain a decisive result. At 12.50, two scouts were observed over Beerst, with other enemy machines above them. The scouts were indecisively engaged before they made off to the east.

A Flight performed a patrol at 13.25, observing a 2-seater to the north of Dixmude at 14.50. The 2-seater dived away to the east when approached. At 15.00, seven enemy scouts were observed to the northeast of Dixmude. A general engagement ensued during which Curtis claimed two victories. Curtis fired 150 rounds into one machine at close range and drove it down out of control, then attacked another which also went down. The second machine was seen immediately after, on its nose near the canal to the northeast of Dixmude.

Several pilots reported seeing an enemy machine that resembled a Sopwith Camel and one pilot reported that an enemy machine in the final patrol appeared to be armed with four guns.

Tactics and formation practice occupied the afternoon. FSL Manuel in B3950 made a forced landing at Bray Dunes aerodrome (No.9 Squadron RNAS).

5th November

A Flight carried out an offensive patrol but immediately ran into problems when Clark in B3919 collided with A.A. Cameron in B3666 on the aerodrome. B3919 suffered enough damage to warrant its return to the depot. Cameron was in combat with an Albatros scout to the northwest of Dixmude at 13.15 which he claimed as out of control, but his machine was damaged and he was forced to land at Droglandt. Curtis was forced to return, and Manuel, Trapp and Bussell were despatched at 13.50 to reinforce the patrol.

Five practice flights were flown during the morning and afternoon.

6th November

The 6th was limited to test and practice flights.

7th November

C Flight carried out a three machine defensive patrol between Nieuport and Dixmude at 12.30. the weather was overcast with poor visibility. Three enemy aircraft were observed to the east of Dixmude at 13.30. The patrol started to climb up to the enemy formation and it immediately retired to the east.

A Flight repeated the patrol at 14.50 but had to abandon it after 30 minutes due to an approaching storm.

8th November

B Flight carried out a three machine offensive patrol between Nieuport and Dixmude at 08.20. No enemy machines were observed and the patrol was back after an hour.

C Flight performed an offensive patrol between Middlekerke and Houthulst at 10.35. Six enemy scouts were observed to the south of Leffinghe at 12.10. The patrol attacked, firing a few rounds at long range before the enemy aircraft dived away to the east.

Curtis, now promoted to Flight Lieutenant, took A Flight on a repeat of the patrol from Middlekerke to Houthulst at 13.00 and was involved in a general engagement with six enemy scouts between Beerst and Praet Bosch Wood at 13.45. The enemy aircraft were driven down, but no decisive results were obtained. Curtis reported observing a flight of Pups engaged with 5 Albatros scouts to the southeast of Middlekerke at 14.40 and seeing two of the enemy machines spinning down.

B Flight patrolled the same area at 15.15. Six enemy aircraft were encountered to the east of Zarren at 15.45. These were soon lost to sight in the clouds.

9th November

FLt Trapp led C Flight on an offensive patrol at 07.40, covering the area from Houthulst to Middlekerke. Nine enemy machines were observed beyond Ghistelles at 08.45 and at 09.15 three enemy scouts were observed attacking RE8's over Dixmude. The patrol dived to assist the RE8s and two of the enemy scouts dived away before they could be reached. The third scout was engaged and followed down to 2000 feet without decisive result. Trapp suffered gun stoppages and was forced to break off the attack.

A Flight repeated the patrol at 11.35. Two 2-seaters were indecisively engaged between Zarren and Houthulst at 12.40. At 12.50, two more 2-seaters were observed between Middlekerke and Ostende and one mile out to sea. At 13.05, four scouts were indecisively engaged to the west of Dixmude. Curtis experienced a considerable amount of trouble with his guns during the mission.

B Flight covered the same area at 13.40. Nine 2-seater bombing machines were observed over Nieuport at 14.05, the patrol climbed towards them and indecisively engaged the last two machines in the formation. A 2-seater was indecisively engaged over Middlekerke at 15.15.

10th November

Bad weather curtailed all flying activities on the 10th.

11th November

FLt Curtis led an eight Camel offensive patrol over the line between Leke and Dixmude at 13.45. The patrol reported observing four DFW and two AEG 2-seater aircraft to the south of Nieuport and well inside Allied lines at 13.55. The patrol had not made its height at that time but followed the enemy aircraft whist still climbing. The enemy formation turned back and headed in a south-easterly direction, A Flight engaged them indecisively at long range. Three enemy aircraft were observed at high altitude over Moers at 14.05.

12th November

B and C Flights carried out an offensive patrol over the Middlekerke to Houthulst line at 06.34. Fifteen enemy aircraft were observed patrolling well behind the lines to the east of Dixmude at 07.30. A flight of four scouts was seen to the north of Houthulst at 07.45, the formation was unable to attack them as the enemy flight was at a considerably higher altitude. At 08.00, a 2-seater was encountered over Couckelaere and driven down out of control by Trapp and Beattie.

A and C Flights repeated the earlier patrol at 10.30. Between 12.15 and 12.30, approximately 16 enemy aircraft were seen at various heights, occasionally crossing the lines between Dixmude and Leke. Several engagements took place but no decisive results were obtained.

C and B Flights carried out an offensive patrol at 15.05, to cover the lines from Slype to Dixmude. A 2-seater was observed near Forthem and whilst the patrol dived to attack the enemy machine, FLt Trapp's Camel, B6341, was seen to break up in the air and go down in pieces. FSL Clark flying B6225 made a forced landing at No.1 Naval Squadron with a seized engine.

13th November

FLt Curtis led Emery and Manuel on an offensive patrol over the line between Nieuport and Dixmude at 07.45. The visibility was bad with mist and cloud up to 3000 feet and no enemy aircraft were seen.

FSL Carroll led an eight machine special offensive patrol at 11.10 in an attempt to intercept enemy bombers which had been reported from the Allied side of the lines. No bombers were observed, but at 12.15, seven Albatros scouts were engaged indecisively to the east of Furnes.

A and C Flights carried out an offensive patrol at 13.38 along the line from Middlekerke to Houthulst. Two enemy 2-seaters were observed over Zarren at 14.10. On being approached these machines fired some lights, were joined by 3 scouts and then made off to the east. At 14.30, seven Albatros scouts were observed to be patrolling well to the east of Dixmude, these machines kept high and avoided engagement. Two 2-seaters were observed a considerable distance behind Middlekerke at 14.45.

New pilot FSL D.R.C. Wright carried out several practice flights.

14th November

A and C Flights carried out an offensive patrol at 08.35. The patrol covered the area from Middlekerke to Houthulst at heights between 2000 to 8000 feet. Low cloud and mist made visibility very bad, despite the conditions the upper formation of the patrol observed two enemy machines at 15000 feet over Ghistelles.

The deteriorating weather conditions prevented any further flying during the day.

15th November

FSL Carroll led B Flight on an offensive patrol at 08.00. The Flight patrolled the line from Middlekerke to Houthulst. Between 08.30 and 09.30, great enemy activity was observed between Dixmude and Houthulst with approximately thirty aircraft being seen, mostly at higher altitudes. A 2-seater was encountered northwest of Keyem at 09.40, Carroll attacked this machine without decisive results.

A and C Flights carried out an offensive patrol at 11.30, covering the same area as the earlier patrol. Five enemy aircraft were observed to the east of Houthulst at 12.10. At 12.45 near Keyem, a further four enemy machines were seen at 9000 feet with six above them at 12000 feet. These machines were attacked by the patrol, Curtis claimed one driven down out of control and Manuel claimed one driven down and crashed. The patrol then encountered a 2-seater to the west of Dixmude at 13.00, FSL A.M. Alexander attacked the machine, the gunner was put out of action and the machine driven down but Alexander then lost it in cloud. Maund engaged the same machine at 4000 feet and saw it fall out of control until very near the ground. Hall engaged a scout at 13.00 and sent it down out of control, he then suffered ignition trouble and was forced to land.

FCdr Macgregor had returned from leave and resumed command of B Flight to carry out an offensive patrol at 14.13. Four enemy aircraft were observed over Ostende at 15.00 and four more were seen in the direction of Roulers at 15.10.

FLt Curtis left to find Hall's forced landing in B6320. Curtis damaged his machine, B6202, when landing next to Hall's machine. Curtis was able to repair Hall's aircraft, B6320, and returned to the aerodrome in it leaving B6202 behind.

16th November

With Macgregor's return from leave, FSL Carroll was put in temporary charge of C Flight.

FCdr Macgregor led B Flight on an offensive patrol at 11.25, but encountered heavy low cloud and mist at 1000 feet with further heavy cloud at 3000 feet. The patrol was abandoned after 30 minutes.

FSL Carroll led C Flight on an offensive patrol over the line from Middlekerke to Houthulst at 13.10. The visibility was very bad and no other machines were encountered.

17th November

The weather was still bad on the 17th and just four practice flights were carried out during the day.

18th November

FSL Carroll led a three machine C Flight offensive patrol at 09.20, to cover the line from Nieuport to Dixmude. Three 2-seaters were observed to the east of Nieuport at 10.30. The patrol attacked and drove them off but no decisive results were obtained. Four scouts were seen in the same vicinity but not engaged.

FCdr Macgregor led B Flight along the line from Middlekerke to Houthulst at 11.30. Three scouts were encountered to the east of Slype at 12.05. These were indecisively engaged at long range, the enemy machines diving away to the east. At 12.15, six 2-seaters were encountered at 2500 feet over Middlekerke and indecisively engaged at long range.

B5658 "Cleada" was delivered from the depot on 19th November 1917, and initially used by FSL J.G. Clark in B Flight. From 26/12/17, B5658 was painted with red and white stripes, and red and white wheel covers. FSL F. Booth was killed during an engagement with Albatros scouts to the west of Lille on 3rd January 1918, believed shot down by *Uffz.* Liebert of *Jasta* 30. *Courtesy S. Taylor*

FLt Curtis led a three machine A Flight patrol at 13.15. Two 2-seaters were observed over Middlekerke at 13.25, the 2-seaters dived away before the patrol was able to get close to them.

19th November

FCdr Macgregor led B Flight on a line patrol at 11.50, covering Middlekerke to Houthulst. At 12.00, a party of 50 to 100 men were observed on the sands 1 mile east of Nieuport, the patrol fired on them from 1000 feet and scattered them.

FSL Carroll led C Flight over the line between Nieuport and Dixmude at 13.05. The visibility was bad and no enemy aircraft were observed.

Ten test and practice flights were carried out throughout the day.

20th November

The RFC handed control of the squadron back to No.4 Wing RNAS on 20th November 1917. The RFC washed its hands of a squadron that had fought with distinction during the difficult summer of 1917, because of a single mistake made by an inexperienced officer on his first day in charge of a squadron.

CHAPTER EIGHT

BACK UNDER NAVAL CONTROL

Control of the squadron reverted to No.4 Wing RNAS on 20th November 1917. Bad weather interfered with operational flying for six days and when patrols were possible, there was no contact with the enemy. The only exception being spotting machines being driven off by two Special WT patrols on the 23rd.

High offensive patrols, offensive sweeps, and the re-introduction of fleet protection patrols, or exclusive low patrols as they were known, added some much needed variety into the squadron's daily activities.

20th November

The adverse weather prevented any patrols being flown.

FSL Carroll carried out a weather test at 08.35 and two practice flights were flown in the afternoon.

21st November

No flying took place on the 21st.

22nd November

The weather prevented any patrols from being flown, but eight test and practice flights were carried out.

23rd November

The adverse weather conditions caused the morning's planned patrols to be cancelled, however, two special Wireless Telegraphy patrols were flown.

Five machines left at 10.35 upon receipt of a signal reporting enemy aircraft in the area. Three 2-seaters were encountered over Middlekerke at 10.45, escorted by three Albatros scouts. All of the enemy machines dived away before the patrol could engage them.

Five Camels were despatched at 13.15 when a signal was received reporting enemy aircraft in the area. Three 2-seaters were observed at 8000 feet over Leffinghe at 13.40, but lost to sight before the patrol was able to close with them.

A total of seven test and practice flights were also carried out.

24th and 25th November

Adverse weather conditions prevented all flying.

26th November

FSL Maund led C Flight on a high offensive patrol at 13.00. Ground visibility was reported as good but there was a heavy cloud layer from 4000 to 5000 feet. No enemy aircraft were observed.

27th November

The squadron transferred to Teteghem at 12.50, a move of just a few miles southwards.

The weather was still bad and no further flying took place on the 27th.

28th November

FLt Curtis led five machines on a high offensive patrol at 10.45. A 2-seater was observed at 8000 feet to the south of Middlekerke at 11.25. Curtis attempted to attack the machine but it made off to the northeast before he could get close enough for effective engagement. A formation of five enemy machines was seen in the distance getting their height over Roulers.

Hamilton-Bowyer, McKelvey, and Clarke performed an exclusive low patrol at 13.05. The patrol found the fleet at

Camel B5663 showing the personal markings of FLt W.A. Curtis. The Flight Leader's markings comprising the extension of the vertical white bars over the top decking are also clearly shown in this photograph. Flying B5663, Curtis claimed an Albatros scout shot down between Keyem and Leke on the 5th December 1917. *Courtesy S. Taylor*

13.30 and carried out the patrol at heights varying between 1000 to 4000 feet.

FSL Maund led C Flight on a high offensive patrol at 14.25. The patrol was uneventful.

29th November

Hamilton-Bowyer, McKelvey, and Clarke performed an exclusive low patrol at 07.55. The fleet was picked up at 08.15 off Dunkerque. There was heavy cloud cover at 1000 feet and the patrol was conducted below this height.

FSL Maund, FSL Beattie and FSL Bussell performed an exclusive low patrol at 11.10. The fleet was picked up at 11.25, 20 miles off of Ostende.

FLt Curtis led A Flight on a high offensive patrol at 11.25. The visibility was poor inland with cloud layers at 2000 feet. No enemy aircraft were seen.

30th November

No high offensive patrols were flown due to the adverse weather conditions.

Maund, Humphrey, and A.M. Alexander performed an exclusive low patrol 09.45. The fleet was picked up at 09.55. A vessel of unknown type was observed leaving Ostende harbour at 11.10.

December 1917

Squadron Commander Bell returned to the squadron in the middle of the month and whilst he may not have been welcomed back with open arms, it was clear that the squadron required a firm hand at the helm.

Bad weather throughout December seriously interfered with flying and it was during a sustained period of inactivity at Christmas that the famous (or infamous, depending upon one's point of view) striped colour schemes were rolled out. A full account of these markings can be found in Appendix A.

1st to 3rd December

No flying was possible due to adverse weather conditions.

4th December

A Flight carried out a high offensive patrol at 07.25. The start of the patrol was delayed by the weather conditions. Visibility was indifferent with cloud from 3000 to 8000 feet. No aircraft, enemy or allied, were observed throughout the patrol.

Macgregor, Wright and Wilmot performed an exclusive low patrol at 10.40. The fleet was picked up at 10.50, about ten miles off La Panne. No enemy aircraft were seen.

A total of eight test and practice flights were carried out.

5th December

FCdr Macgregor, FSL McKelvey, and FSL Clark carried out a low exclusive patrol at 07.30, the Camels were unable to find the fleet so returned to the aerodrome.

FSL Maund led C Flight on a high offensive patrol at 10.00. At 11.45, two enemy spotting machines were observed on the coast at the enemy balloon line and at 11.00, two machines from a formation of three 2-seaters came down to the patrol's level, these were attacked and driven off.

A Flight carried out a high offensive patrol at 14.20. A 2-seater was observed crossing the lines to the west of Nieuport but it dived away before the patrol could reach it. Two 2-seaters were encountered at 15.15 to the east of Zarren but the patrol was again unable to effectively engage them. At 15.35, between Keyem and Leke, a single Albatros scout from a formation of four machines attacked the rearmost Camel in the patrol. Curtis and Hall engaged the scout, both pilots fired 150 rounds into it from close range. The enemy machine went down vertically, smoking profusely and was seen to crash. A second scout was indecisively attacked by Stratton. In his combat report, Curtis described the scout as being painted black and white with a white tail. *Fw*. Hermann Seidal of *Jasta* 26 was killed on the 5th December, the *Jasta* 26 markings comprised black and white fuselage bands and a white tail. It is surmised that Seidal was flying the Albatros that Curtis shot down.

6th December

FSL Manuel led a five machine high offensive patrol at 08.00. A formation of nine enemy aircraft were observed to the east of Roulers at 08.30, the formation was travelling east at 13000 feet. At 09.00 FSL Humphrey returned with engine trouble, exchanged his Camel but failed to pick up the patrol. At 09.45, when to the south of Roulers, Humphrey encountered and engaged a 2-seater but was forced to break off when he was attacked by an escorting scout.

Curtis led a 3 machine exclusive low patrol at 11.15, the patrol was attacked by three 2-seaters and two scouts at 11.35 when 15 miles off Middlekerke. Curtis fired 20 rounds at a scout that was attacking Hall but was forced to break off due to trouble with his engine. Curtis came under attack and was forced down in a steep spiral, regaining his engine when 1500 feet above the sea. The patrol picked up the fleet at 12.15 when 15 miles off Nieuport, and remained above it until 13.00. Later in the same patrol, Curtis saw an enemy 2-seater driven down by a Belgian SPAD to the east of Nieuport. All three Camels suffered from engine trouble during the patrol, Hall was forced to land at Moeres at 13.30 and broke his tailskid in the process. Emery was forced to abandon the patrol and return to Teteghem.

FCdr Macgregor led a seven machine special reconnaissance patrol at 12.55 to try and locate Curtis and Hall who had not returned from their exclusive low patrol.

FCdr Macgregor led B Flight on a high offensive patrol at 14.30 and encountered a lone 2-seater over Houthulst Wood at 15.15. A few shots were fired at long range without effect. Four enemy aircraft were observed over St. Pierre Cappelle at 15.15, these dived away when the patrol attempted to close with them.

7th December

Adverse weather conditions prevented all flying activity.

8th December

Maund led A.M. Alexander and Humphrey on an exclusive low patrol at 09.45. The patrol picked up the fleet at 10.00, approximately 12 miles northeast of Dunkerque.

FCdr Macgregor and FSL Manuel led B and C Flights on an offensive sweep at 10.00. The patrol crossed the lines to the south of Dixmude, flew east to Bruges, then swept back passing over Slype. No enemy aircraft were observed.

FCdr Macgregor led a six machine high offensive patrol at 14.10. No enemy aircraft were reported.

9th December

Adverse weather conditions prevented all flying activities.

10th December

Emery, Hall, and Cameron performed an exclusive low patrol at 08.00, picking up the fleet immediately as it left Dunkerque. The visibility was poor and no enemy machines were encountered.

FCdr Macgregor and FSL Manuel led B and C Flights on an offensive sweep at 10.15. The patrol crossed the lines at Dixmude, headed east to Roulers and swept back over Ypres. An Albatros scout was encountered to the west of Roulers at 11.20 and attacked first by Clark and then by Macgregor who fired 100 rounds at close range. The machine burst into flames and fell completely out of control. This may have been *Ltn*. Herbert Wallner of *Jasta* 3. The patrol observed another four enemy machines at 11.05 over Thourout.

Maund, McKelvey, and FSL Wilmot carried out an exclusive low patrol, picking up the fleet at 11.15, fifteen miles off Ostende. A large seaplane was observed to the northwest of the fleet at 8000 feet, however, this turned out to be an allied machine.

This photograph was taken on the 4th February 1918 at Bray Dunes. The nearest unidentified C Flight Camel appears to have a name marked above the flight letter. The other camels from left to right are B3919 (not on squadron strength), B6202, B6299, B6204, and B6449. *Courtesy GSL/JMB collection*

FSL Maund led a five Camel high offensive patrol at 14.15. Three 2-seaters were encountered near Slype at 15.30, when the patrol approached they dived away to the east.

11th December

The visibility was bad on the 11th December, but Hall and Stratton were able to carry out a ground patrol at 10.25. The pair patrolled up the coast in the mist and turned inland when they reached Ostende. Hall observed a party of troops on the beach near Mariakerke and dived on them, firing 150 to 200 rounds from a height of 200 feet. He then proceeded inland along a road and along the Nieuport-Passchendaele canal. At 11.00 he fired 200 rounds into a trench at Nieuwendamme Old Fort but was forced to seek the safety of the clouds due to heavy machine gun fire from the ground. Hall's machine sustained considerable damage to its undercarriage while strafing trenches. FSL Stratton fired 200 rounds at ground targets of opportunity, mostly troops.

12th December

Manuel, Humphrey and Bussell carried out a low exclusive patrol at 09.40, picking up the fleet 20 miles north of Ostende at 10.05.

Wright, McKelvey, and Wilmot carried out another exclusive low patrol at 14.00. The fleet was found at 14.30, 10 miles off Nieuport.

FCdr Macgregor led a nine machine offensive sweep at 14.20, the patrol passed Nieuport five miles out to sea at 15.15, and swept round by Ghistelles and Dixmude. Hall and Stratton followed a 2-seater from the north of Dixmude to Gravelines at 15.15 and fired a few rounds at it from extreme range. At 15.40, when six miles east of Dixmude, the patrol encountered a flight of six Albatros scouts and a general engagement took place. Macgregor fired 70 rounds at one scout which had been attacking FSL Clark, the enemy machine appeared to go down out of control, but Macgregor was unable to follow it for more than 3000 feet as he was attacked by another enemy machine. FSL Clark flying N6330 was seen to go down out of control after the initial attack. Clark came down in enemy territory and was taken prisoner.

Ltn. P. Billik of *Jasta* 7 was credited with the victory over Clark.

13th December

Squadron Commander Bell returned to the squadron on the 13th.

Emery, Cameron, and Stratton carried out an exclusive low patrol at 08.05. The visibility was bad due to fog and clouds and the patrol only remained out for 1 1/4 hours.

FCdr Macgregor, FSL Wright and FSL Wilmot attempted another low exclusive patrol at 11.10 but due to the bad visibility were unable to find the fleet.

14th December

Acting Squadron Commander Redpath was posted to Headquarters No.4 Wing.

Hall, Wilmot, and McKelvey performed an exclusive low patrol at 07.25 and picked up the fleet as it left harbour at 07.50. The visibility was still bad with heavy cloud from 200 to 1000 feet.

15th December

Adverse weather conditions prevented all flying activities.

16th December

The weather conditions interfered with flying, just three test flights were made during the day.

17th December

Adverse weather conditions prevented all flying activities.

18th December

FCdr Macgregor and FSL Manuel led B and C Flights on an offensive sweep at 10.30. The patrol flew past Nieuport seven miles out to sea, turned inland at Ostende and then to Houthulst Forest and back over Ypres. Four enemy aircraft were observed over Ghistelles at 11.05, these dived away before the patrol could approach them. At 11.20, the patrol caught a 2-seater over Houthulst Forest. FSL Maund fired 200 rounds into the machine from close range and killed or injured the observer. The 2-seater tried to dive away but was attacked by Macgregor, Manuel and Wright. All three Camels were forced to break off the engagement due to gun stoppages and the 2-seater escaped.

FLt Curtis led A Flight on a high offensive patrol at 14.25. Five enemy aircraft were encountered at 15.15, five miles behind Dixmude, these dived away when the patrol tried to approach them. At 15.35, between Nieuport and Dixmude, three enemy aircraft were seen below at 8000 feet and two above at 13000 feet. The patrol was unable to attack as three Camels had dropped out with gun trouble.

19th December

B Flight performed a high offensive patrol at 07.15. A 2-seater was observed over Nieuport flying at 6000 feet at 08.15. The patrol followed and attacked, expending a total of 1000 rounds without any decisive result being obtained.

Curtis, Stratton and Hall carried out an exclusive low patrol at 09.50, the fleet was picked up off Nieuport at 10.20.

FSL Hall was despatched on a special patrol immediately after returning from the fleet patrol, anti-aircraft fire having been observed in the Dunkerque area. No enemy machines were encountered but just before returning, Hall observed a 2-seater and two scouts in the vicinity of Ypres.

FSL Emery led C Flight on a high offensive patrol at 12.00. Three enemy aircraft were observed patrolling between Middlekerke and Thourout at 12.45, when approached by the patrol the machines dived away to the east. At 13.30, a 2-seater was encountered over Middlekerke at 5000 feet, this machine also dived away when approached.

20th December

Heavy fog prevented all but a weather test and two test flights.

21st December

Heavy fog prevented all flying activities.

22nd December

Visibility was still bad to the north. Macgregor led B Flight on a high offensive patrol to the south of Ypres at 09.50. At 10.50, four Albatros scouts were encountered two miles west of Lille and engaged by the patrol. Macgregor drove one machine down vertically with a large cloud of steam escaping from the engine, and another probably damaged was seen to go down in a long gentle glide. FSL Wilmot claimed another as probably out of control, following it down to 2000 feet when it stalled and fell away in a steep side-slip. Later in the patrol, FSL Wright attacked a kite balloon firing 60 rounds from extreme range before it was pulled down.

Emery, Beattie, and Humphrey attempted to perform an exclusive low patrol at 11.10. The patrol was unable to locate the fleet, so Emery led the other two Camels on a patrol in the vicinity of Nieuport.

B and A Flights carried out an offensive sweep at 13.14 over the route Nieuport, Ghistelles, Thourout, Staden, Ypres, Dixmude, and return. A 2-seater was observed over Houthulst forest at 14.30 but dived away when approached. At 14.50, five enemy machines were observed at 6000 feet over Cortemarck, these also dived away when approached.

23rd December

Low clouds interfered with war flying on the 23rd, one patrol attempted to carry out a low fleet patrol but the bad visibility caused it to be aborted. FSL Wright flying B6291 lost control of his machine over the aerodrome and spun in. Wright was killed and the machine completely wrecked.

24th to 27th December

Mist and rain prevented all flying activity. It was during this period of enforced inactivity, that the famous striped colour schemes were applied.

A well-known photograph that is worth viewing again. This is A Flight resplendent in black and white stripes photographed at Teteghem shortly after Christmas 1917. From back to front, the aircraft are, B6289 (FSL H.L. Nelson), B5663 (FLt W.A. Curtis), B3869 (FSL S.K.F.P. Humphrey), B6320 (FSL F.V. Hall), and B6225 (FSL K.V. Stratton). B6225 was not flown in combat in this colour scheme, being transferred to Dover on the 4th January 1918. *Courtesy E.F. Cheesman*

B6289 of A Flight, flown by FSL H.L. Nelson. Nelson shared a 2-seater in flames to the northeast of Dixmude on the 21st October 1917, long before the striped markings were applied. *Author's collection*

28th December

Macgregor, Maund, and Wilmot carried out an exclusive low patrol at 07.30. As the fleet was stationary in Dunkerque harbour, Macgregor patrolled the area until 08.00 and then retuned to the aerodrome.

FSL Emery led C Flight on a high offensive patrol at 14.10. Humphrey and Booth became separated from the patrol before it crossed the lines. Humphrey flying B3869 landed at Moeres (No.2 Belgian Squadron) with engine failure and Booth landed N6341 at Bonningues.

Nelson, Hall and Cameron were temporarily stationed at Berck-sur-Mer for aerial gunnery practice, transferring at 12.40. The pilots were able to shoot at stationary, towed, and balloon targets. FSL Hall scored 123 hits from 130 rounds fired at a balloon target, a station record at that time.

29th December

Emery, Beattie, and Humphrey performed an exclusive low patrol at 07.40. The fleet was picked up off Dunkerque at 07.40.

McKelvey brought Humphrey's Camel back from Moeres, and Wilmot collected Booth's Camel from Bonningues.

30th to 31st December

Adverse weather conditions prevented all flying activities.

January 1918

Bad weather seriously interfered with flying activities during the first part of January. Hostile activity was initially sporadic but picked up as the month progressed.

1st January

It is worth examining the squadron structure again at this juncture, as a number of changes had taken place:

A Flight
FLt W.A. Curtis, Flight Commander
FSL F.V. Hall, Deputy Flight Commander
FSL H.L. Nelson
FSL R.A. Blyth
FSL A.A. Cameron
FSL K.V. Stratton

B Flight
FCdr N.M. Macgregor, Flight Commander

FSL W.H. Wilmot in B Flight Camel "ENID". This machine is believed to be B3910. *Courtesy E.F. Cheesman*

FSL H.B. Maund, Deputy Flight Commander
FSL M.T. McKelvey
FSL W.H. Wilmot
FSL F. Booth

C Flight
FSL J.G Manuel, Temporary Flight Commander
FSL H.J. Emery
FSL A.G. Beattie
FSL S.K.F.B. Humphrey
FSL A.M Alexander
FSL E.I. Bussell

FCdr Macgregor was able to lead B Flight on a delayed high offensive patrol at 10.25.

A 2-seater was observed over Ypres at 10.55 and another was seen to the south of Poperinghe at 11.15. An Albatros scout was encountered near the coast between Ostende and Middlekerke at 11.20 and another 2-seater was seen over Ypres at 11.30. The patrol was unable to bring any of these enemy aircraft to action.

The weather deteriorated and no further flying took place.

2nd January

The adverse weather conditions prevented any war flying, however, four test flights were carried out.

3rd January

FCdr Macgregor and FSL Manuel respectively led B and C Flights on a high offensive patrol at 12.30. At the time the patrol started a 2-seater was in sight, being shelled by an anti-aircraft battery. The patrol headed west over Dunkerque and

Another B Flight Camel, unfortunately unidentified. *Author's collection*

then to the lines, the enemy machine was at 18000 feet at that point whilst the patrol was at 14000 feet. Bad visibility in the northern sector forced the two Flights southwards where conditions were better. At 13.45, to the west of Lille, the patrol encountered a 2-seater which was indecisively engaged by Macgregor, Maund and A.M. Alexander. A number of enemy scouts dived onto the patrol, getting past C Flight which was supposed to protect B Flight from being "jumped". FSL Manuel suffered a stoppage in both guns and was fortunate to escape after being driven down to 300 feet and chased to Ostende by three scouts. At Ostende he was able to hide in the clouds and eventually landed at No 3 Squadron with his Camel badly shot-up. During the engagement Humphrey indecisively engaged a scout which had attacked him as he was endeavouring to attack a 2-seater. FSL Booth of B Flight and FSL Beattie of C Flight failed to return, the pilots being last seen near Lille taking part in the general engagement. Beattie, flying N6351, a blue and white striped C Flight machine, was forced down during the engagement by *Vfw*. H. Oberländer of *Jasta* 30, Beattie was wounded in the ankle and lost lateral control when trying to land, one wheel touched first and the Camel flipped over. Beattie was captured and spent the rest of the war as a prisoner. Booth flying B5658, a red and white striped B Flight machine, was shot down and killed by *Uffz*. E. Liebert, also of *Jasta* 30.

4th January

FSL Manuel led a five machine high offensive patrol at 10.00. Two enemy aircraft were observed getting their height over Ostende at 11.00 and at 11.15, four scouts were seen at 10000 feet over Thourout with another five scouts sitting above them at 18000 feet.

FCdr WM Alexander returned from Canadian leave on the 4th and was placed in charge of C Flight. FCdr Alexander wisely took his time re-acclimatising to conditions and for some time always made sure that his patrols were accompanied by one of the other experienced Flight Commanders.

The A Flight pilots returned from the Berck-sur-Mer aerial gunnery range.

5th January

The adverse weather conditions prevented all war flying.

New pilot FSL EN Gregory arrived at the squadron.

6th January

Manuel, FSL A.M. Alexander and Bussell carried out a low exclusive patrol at 08.05. The patrol picked up the fleet as it was leaving Dunkerque at 08.15, Manuel led the patrol up to 13000 feet, flew over Middlekerke and Dixmude and picked up the fleet again off Nieuport. Five enemy scouts were observed over Thourout at 08.45

Left: B5658 in red and white striped B Flight livery. FSL F. Booth was shot down and killed in an engagement with *Jasta* 30 on the 3rd January 1918. *Courtesy Les Rogers* Right: On the 3rd January, in the same engagement as FSL Booth above, FSL A.G. Beattie was shot down in N6351, a blue and white striped C Flight Camel. Beattie was forced down during the engagement by *Vfw* H. Oberländer of *Jasta* 30, he suffered a gunshot wound to his leg and lost lateral control when trying to land, one wheel touched first and the Camel flipped over. Beattie spent the rest of the war in captivity. *Courtesy Les Rogers*

FLt Curtis led A Flight on a high offensive patrol at 12.00. The patrol covered the northern area and then moved southwards. At 13.20, a new type of 2-seater resembling an LVG was encountered to the east of Houthulst forest at 4000 feet. The machine immediately dived to the east, Curtis and Nelson fired at it from long range without result. Stratton engaged an Albatros scout at the same time, also without result. Cameron had become separated from the patrol and had an indecisive engagement with a scout at 13.25, he then suffered the indignity of being chased back to the lines by four Albatros scouts which occasionally took long range shots at him.

FSL Bussell left the squadron, posted to Eastchurch.

7th to 9th January

The adverse weather conditions prevented all war flying.

10th January

The weather was still unsuitable for flying on the morning of the 10th but had improved sufficiently in the afternoon for FCdr Curtis to lead a five machine high offensive patrol at 14.05. Five enemy aircraft were observed in the distance to the east of Roulers at 14.45. The patrol reported a new type of anti-aircraft fire beyond Nieuport, it apparently comprised a green tracer of much smaller size than the ordinary "flaming onion" and appeared to be fired from a large machine gun.

11th January

Adverse weather conditions prevented all war flying.

12th January

FCdr Alexander flew his first patrol since returning from leave when he led a six machine offensive sweep at 09.50. The patrol flew over Nieuport, Ostende, Thourout, Roulers, Ypres and then returned. The patrol proved uneventful with no enemy aircraft observed.

13th January

The weather had improved enough on the 13th for the squadron to perform three patrols.

FCdr Curtis led Hall and Nelson on an exclusive low patrol over the fleet at 07.45. Curtis was flying Camel B6450 and was forced to return when his fine adjustment throttle fell off. After a quick repair he was able to rejoin the patrol.

FCdr Alexander led Macgregor, Maund, Emery and FSL Alexander on a photographic escort mission at 13.10. The escort picked the Caudron up over the aerodrome and followed it as far as its own aerodrome whereupon it went down and landed. Assuming that the ground visibility was unsuitable for photography, the patrol carried out a high offensive patrol. Three enemy machines were seen low down beyond Roulers at 14.30. During the patrol FSL Maund in B6211 suffered engine failure and made a successful forced landing to the north of Ypres.

FCdr Curtis led a second photographic escort mission at 13.35. The Caudron was picked up over Teteghem and escorted over the lines to a point between Middlekerke and Ostende. The patrol then escorted the photographic machine back to its aerodrome.

FSL R.A. Blyth and FSL G.O. Smith arrived at the squadron.

14th January

FCdr Alexander led a mixed patrol of A and C Flight machines on a high offensive patrol at 11.00. The patrol engaged six

B6449 arrived at No.10 Squadron on the 12th January, and was flown by the deputy Commander of B Flight, FLt H.B. Maund. *Author's collection*

Albatros scouts and two 2-seaters at 11.35 to the east of Houthulst Forest. FCdr Curtis attacked a black and white scout and fired 75 rounds into it from a range of 50 feet. The enemy aircraft went down in a vertical dive and then fell erratically for 4000 feet. Curtis reported another two indecisive engagements and FCdr Alexander, Emery, Nelson and Cameron all reported indecisive engagements. The 2-seaters encountered by the patrol appeared to be similar to the new type encountered on the 6th January.

FCdr Alexander led another patrol at 14.15; accompanied by FCdr Curtis, FCdr Macgregor, FSL Maund and FSL Emery, the Camels performed an offensive sweep over Nieuport, Ostende, Thourout, Roulers and Ypres. An enemy scout was observed to the south of Menin at 14.55. A little later at 15.10, two 2-seaters and an Albatros scout were observed between Roulers and Menin at 12000 feet. These machines dived away to the east before the patrol could approach. FSL Emery had to return to the aerodrome when a centre section wire broke and FSL Cameron, flying B6380, made a forced landing at No.21 Squadron RFC at 15.20.

FLt Carter arrived back at the squadron from Canadian leave. Carter would take over A Flight when Curtis left the squadron, but sensibly spent his first few days back with the squadron getting acclimatised to the handling of the Sopwith Camel.

FSL A.M. Alexander left the squadron on the 14th, posted to Eastchurch.

15th to 18th January

The adverse weather conditions prevented all war flying.

FSL Emery left the squadron on the 17th, posted to Eastchurch.

On the 18th, FSL Cameron made a test flight in B6380, immediately after leaving the ground he attempted to make a turn with insufficient airspeed and spun into the ground. The aircraft was completely wrecked and Cameron was injured and taken to Malo hospital.

19th January

Curtis, Blyth and Nelson carried out an exclusive low patrol at 08.25, picking up the fleet at 08.30 just outside of Dunkerque harbour.

FCdr Alexander, supported by FCdr Macgregor, led a five machine high offensive sweep at 14.00. No enemy aircraft were seen but the anti-aircraft fire was reported as being very active.

A total of ten test and practice flights were carried out during the course of the day.

20th January

The adverse weather conditions prevented all war flying.

21st January

FCdr Alexander accompanied by FCdr Curtis led C flight on an offensive patrol at 08.00, conditions were difficult with bad visibility and strong winds. Four enemy aircraft were seen between Ostende and Ghistelles at 09.20, but the patrol was otherwise uneventful.

A Flight carried out an exclusive low patrol at 11.20 in difficult conditions. The patrol failed to pick up the fleet.

22nd January

The weather was still uncertain on the 22nd.

FCdr Macgregor led B Flight on a high offensive patrol at 10.35. No enemy machines were encountered in the patrol area but four aircraft were seen in the distance to the east of Lille.

FCdr Alexander, accompanied by FCdr Curtis and FLt Carter, led Manuel, Blyth and Nelson on an offensive sweep at 13.45. The patrol crossed the lines over Ypres and then covered the route Roulers, Thourout, Ostende and Nieuport, no enemy aircraft were observed. The patrol then covered the high offensive patrol area, observing five enemy aircraft getting their height in the distance beyond Thourout at 15.00.

23rd January

FSL Manuel took new pilots Rice and Smith on an exclusive low patrol at 12.15, the Camels picking the fleet up off Middlekerke at 12.35. Four enemy aircraft were observed over Bruges at 13.30.

FCdr Alexander led a ten machine high offensive patrol at 14.05. At 14.50, three 2-seaters and a scout were encountered just above the clouds over Staden. The enemy aircraft dived away through the clouds and part of the patrol followed them, to be sucked into a trap set by another five Albatros scouts waiting just below the cloud cover. A general engagement ensued during which Curtis shot down a 2-seater which was seen to break up in the air by Manuel, and Alexander fired 75 rounds into the underside of an Albatros scout from 60 yards. The scout fell into the clouds out of control, Alexander followed it through the clouds and observed it still falling completely out of control. Nelson reported an indecisive combat with a scout that escaped into the clouds. Manuel saw Blyth engaged with one scout and being attacked in turn by another, whilst he was diving to assist Blyth, Manuel suffered a jam in both guns and was forced to withdraw to clear the stoppage. When he returned, he saw Blyth's machine going down out of control accompanied by an enemy machine. Both aircraft crashed simultaneously and it was surmised that Blyth and the Albatros scout had collided.

FSL RA Blythe was killed flying B5663 during an engagement with Albatros scouts near Staden on the 23rd January 1918. He was believed to have collided with an enemy machine. Note the dark painted wing tips and the light outline (white?) to the tail assembly. *Courtesy E.F. Cheesman*

24th January

FSL Nelson led Gregory and Rice on an uneventful fleet patrol at 11.00, picking up the fleet 10 miles off Ostende at 11.25.

FCdr Macgregor took B Flight out on a high offensive patrol at 12.00. The patrol was carried out at 15000 feet and at 13.00, a 2-seater was observed over Houthulst Forest at 11000 feet. Macgregor and Maund attacked the machine which immediately dived away to the east. Macgregor and Maund followed the 2-seater, both pilots firing at extreme range without result.

25th January

Heavy mist and cloud delayed the start of B Flight's high offensive patrol. The patrol eventually took off at 10.20 but found the lines and the area beyond totally enveloped in mist. Macgregor brought the patrol back after 55 minutes.

FCdr Alexander led a ten machine offensive sweep at 13.50, the patrol crossed the lines to the north of Ypres and followed a route to Houthulst, Roulers, Thourout and Ostende. No enemy aircraft were observed.

Late in the evening Dunkerque came under artillery fire. FCdr Macgregor and FSL Manuel took off at 23.25 in an attempt to find the spotting machine that was presumed to be directing the artillery fire. Manuel could not find the spotter and returned at 00.20. Macgregor was also unable to find the spotter but after crossing the lines he found an aerodrome which was thought to be Vlisseghem. Macgregor reported two hangars and a group of sheds, he attacked the hangars, firing 230 rounds from a height of 300 feet. Machine gun fire was directed at him from a point west of the sheds.

Not all of the squadron's Camels were striped at this time. This is B6202, the C Flight Commander's machine flown by FCdr W.M. Alexander. This particular Camel had originally been on the squadron strength in September and October 1917, during which time FLt D. Fitzgibbon claimed three scouts out of control and FLt W.A. Curtis claimed three enemy machines out of control and four destroyed. *Courtesy GSL/JMB Collection*

26th January

Heavy mist and low cloud prevented any war flying.

27th January

The mist and cloud persisted through the 27th, a ten machine high offensive patrol was attempted at 14.30, crossing the lines between Nieuport and Dixmude. The entire area was obscured and FCdr Alexander abandoned the patrol after 30 minutes.

FSL Rice made a test flight in B5664 and made a forced landing at No.2 Squadron, without injury to himself or damage to the machine.

28th January

FLt Carter took over the leadership of A Flight on the 28th January and led an uneventful high offensive patrol at 07.35.

McKelvey, Rice and Smith carried out an exclusive low patrol at 10.00, picking up the fleet at 10.15, fifteen miles off the coast.

A special enemy aircraft patrol was carried out by Carter, Hall and Nelson at 12.15 upon receipt of a report of enemy aircraft over Calais. The three Camels patrolled the area from the west of Dunkerque to Middlekerke at heights up to 15000 feet. No enemy aircraft were observed.

FCdr Alexander led a high offensive patrol at 12.25, five enemy aircraft were observed to the east of Dixmude at 15000 feet. A large number of allied machines were in the air and the enemy aircraft avoided engagement.

29th January

Manuel, Maund and McKelvey carried out an exclusive low patrol at 07.30, picking up the fleet at 07.40, six miles off La Panne.

FCdr Alexander led a high offensive patrol at 10.00. A large number of enemy aircraft were observed over Roulers at 10.50 and four more were seen a few minutes later in the direction of Menin. FSL Hall's Camel suffered from engine trouble and he returned to exchange his machine but failed to link up with the patrol. At 11.15, Hall observed a 2-seater being shelled by allied anti-aircraft fire and engaged it two miles out to sea off Bray Dunes. Hall was unable to make the height of the 2-seater but fired 500 rounds at extreme range to no effect. While returning from the main patrol at 11.30, FLt Carter endeavoured to reach an enemy machine that was being shelled by an Allied anti-aircraft battery between Dunkerque and Nieuport but was unable to get within 4000 feet of its height. After following it for a while, Carter was shelled by the Allied anti-aircraft battery upon his return. Carter observed another machine being shelled and upon investigation found it to be an Allied SPAD.

FCdr Alexander led a ten machine offensive sweep at 13.30, no enemy machines were seen and the patrol was completely uneventful.

FCdr Macgregor left the squadron, posted to Eastchurch.

30th January

An intake of new pilots had arrived at the squadron on the 29th, FSL A.L. Jones, FSL G.T. Steeves, FLt W.G.R. Hinchliffe, FSL H.A. Patey, FSL L.P. Coombes, and FSL R.E. Burr. These pilots were all put to work making practice flights on the 30th. During the practice flights, Patey turned B5687 over on landing, damaging the machine but escaping injury. Of the new pilots, Jones, Hinchliffe, Patey, and Coombes would develop into significant figures within the squadron and its successor, No.210 Squadron RAF.

FCdr Alexander led a five machine offensive patrol at 10.55, new pilot FLt Hinchliffe was given the number two spot despite his lack of operational experience. The patrol was uneventful, no enemy aircraft being observed.

FSL Hall took two of the new pilots, Jones and Steeves on an exclusive low patrol at 12.15. The fleet was found at 12.40, about 12 miles off Mariakerke.

FLt Carter led a high offensive patrol at 14.25, the visibility was reported as very poor and no enemy aircraft were seen.

In the afternoon, a new Camel, B7217, was delivered from Dover by FSL Burton. Burton overshot the aerodrome and turned B7217 over.

31st January

FLt Carter led a high offensive patrol at 09.25. The patrol encountered three Albatros scouts at 10.50 to the east of Dixmude and followed them. The machines were indecisively engaged over Thourout at 11.00, Carter fired 20 rounds at one machine from 50 yards before it manoeuvred out of his sights, Manuel fired 200 rounds from 500 to 150 feet without apparent effect, McKelvey and Hall fired from extreme range and Nelson fired 200 rounds from the hopelessly optimistic range of 200 yards. FSL Nelson in N6289 suffered engine trouble and made a successful forced landing at Moeres.

A heavy mist developed at midday putting an end to flying activities for the rest of the day.

February 1918

The squadron was re-equipped with Bentley Camels at the beginning of February, exchanging their old Clerget Camels with No.9 Naval Squadron who were scheduled to return to Dover to be rested. The Bentley Camel would significantly increase No.10 Squadron's scope, giving better reliability, faster climb, faster speed, and higher service ceiling.

1st February

The day was plagued by thick mist, making flying impossible.

2nd February

The mist was still evident causing the 07.30 patrol to be abandoned.

Hall, Steeves and Jones performed a low exclusive patrol at 10.15, picking up the fleet at 10.35, three miles off Bray Dunes. The visibility was poor but improved towards midday. An enemy machine was observed at 11.45 over Bray Dunes at 19000 feet. The enemy machine retired towards Ypres when the patrol started to climb towards it.

FCdr Alexander and FLt Carter led a nine machine high offensive patrol at 12.35. No enemy aircraft were observed throughout the patrol.

Nelson led Patey and Burr on an exclusive low patrol at 14.30. The fleet was picked up at 14.45, four miles off Nieuport. When the fleet returned to port, the patrol continued eastwards over the coast. Five enemy destroyers were observed off Zeebrugge at 16.00, heading towards Ostende.

During the morning, five Bentley Camels were delivered from Dover and left with the squadron in temporary custody.

FLt Carter had A Flight up for an hour's formation practice at 15.10.

3rd February

FLt Carter led a seven machine high offensive patrol at 11.00, no enemy aircraft were encountered. FSL Jones flying B3760 made a forced landing at Arques, Jones was unhurt but the machine was wrecked.

Maund led Patey and Burr on an exclusive low patrol at 12.10. The fleet was picked up at 12.30, twenty miles north northwest of Ostende, no enemy aircraft or hostile shipping was observed.

FCdr Alexander led C Flight on a high offensive patrol at 14.30. At 15.15, four Albatros scouts were engaged by the patrol over Rumbeke SW aerodrome. FCdr Alexander was compelled to break off the engagement when his engine lost pressure, he returned home making use of his hand pump. Hinchliffe lost his engine and had descended to 400 feet above Rumbeke aerodrome where he was attacked by three scouts, he recovered his engine and engaged one of the enemy aircraft firing a number of rounds into it. The machine fell out of control and crashed into a tree. Smith and Rice were involved in the initial engagement but both suffered from gun stoppages. Wilmot flying B6370 failed to return, having been shot down and killed during the engagement over Rumbeke.

4th February

FLt Carter led a seven machine high offensive patrol at 09.30. Eight enemy aircraft were sighted over Courtrai at 10.05.

The day's remaining patrols were cancelled by the Commanding Officer of No.4 Wing, and the rest of the day was spent in a complicated transference of Camels between squadrons:

- 5 Clerget Camels were ferried in from No.8 Squadron at 10.50.
- 7 Bentley Camels were ferried to No.8 Squadron at 11.55.
- 12 No.10 Squadron Clerget Camels were ferried to No.9 Squadron at 12.20.
- 12 Bentley Camels were ferried in from No.9 Squadron at 13.00.
- 1 No.10 Squadron Clerget Camel was ferried to No.3 Squadron at 14.20.
- 1 No.10 Squadron Clerget Camel was ferried to No.9 Squadron at 14.25.
- 1 Bentley Camel was ferried from No.9 Squadron at 15.25.
- 1 Bentley Camel was ferried from No.9 Squadron at 16.15.
- 2 Bentley Camels were ferried from No.1 NAP at 16.30.

Taken at Bray Dunes aerodrome on the 4th February 1918, this photograph shows B6299, FCdr N.M. Macgregor's aircraft. The B Flight livery used rather more white paint than A Flight and C Flight, with the white extending along the top to join up with the squadron marking. FLt Hinchliffe's un-striped C Flight Camel, B6204 and FLt H.B. Maund's red and white B Flight Camel, B6449, complete the line and an assortment of striped A Flight and B Flight Camels lurk in the background. *Courtesy GSL/JMB Collection*

An enlargement of the striped Camels seen in the background of the previous photograph. From left to right, B Flight's N3910 (FSL Wilmot), and from A Flight, "unknown", B6289, B6320 (now carrying deputy flight leaders markings), and FLt Carter's B6450.The wheel cover designs on several machines have been modified from their initial patterns. *Courtesy GSL/JMB Collection*

- 1 No.10 Squadron Clerget Camel was ferried to No.9 Squadron at 14.40.

5th February

No.10 Squadron's first patrol in the more powerful Bentley Camel was carried out at 07.30 when FLt Carter led five Camels on a completely uneventful patrol.

Hinchliffe, Hall, and Coombes performed an exclusive low patrol at 09.55, and picked up the fleet at 10.20, fifteen miles off Mariakerke. Three enemy aircraft were observed approaching the fleet at 11.15, the patrol climbed to intercept them and when both formations reached 17000 feet the enemy aircraft dived away toward Zeebrugge.

FLt Carter and FLt Manuel led a second high offensive patrol at 12.35. A large enemy formation was observed at 10000 feet between Roulers and Courtrai at 13.00, at the same time seven unidentified machines were seen low down between Roulers and the lines. Manuel took Maund, Nelson and Rice down to investigate and found them to be Camels. The remainder of the patrol then climbed to attack the higher formation, but the enemy machines avoided engagement and eventually dived away beyond Courtrai. Manuel observed three formations of seven, eight, and ten enemy scouts between Thourout and Aeltre at 13.45. Manuel, Maund, Nelson and Rice all reported indecisive engagements with machines from these formations between 13.45 and 14.15. FSL Smith flying B3866 made a safe forced landing at Lovie aerodrome due to an exhaust tappet breaking.

Hall, Burr, and Patey carried out an exclusive low patrol at 14.30, picking up the fleet at 14.45, eight miles off Westende. The visibility was reported as bad and no enemy aircraft or enemy shipping was observed.

6th to 14th February

Bad weather prevented all flying activities.

15th February

The weather was still bad but it was possible to perform six practice flights in the afternoon.

16th February

The flight structure had been somewhat confused for several weeks, but by the 16th, the Flights were as follows:

A Flight

FLt A.W. Carter, Flight Commander
FSL F.V. Hall, Deputy Flight Commander
FSL H.L. Nelson
FSL A.L. Jones
FSL G.T. Steeves

B Flight

FLt J.G. Manuel, Flight Commander
FSL H.B. Maund, Deputy Flight Commander
FSL M.T. McKelvey
FSL R.E. Burr
FSL H.A. Patey

C Flight
FCdr W.M. Alexander, Flight Commander
FLt W.G.R. Hinchliffe, Deputy Flight Commander
FSL E.G. Rice
FSL G.O. Smith
FSL L.P. Coombes

Unfortunately, this structure was not maintained for long.

FCdr Alexander led C Flight off on a high offensive patrol at 07.20. No enemy aircraft were reported, however, FSL G.O. Smith flying B3866 failed to return from the patrol having crashed at St. Sixte, north of Poperinghe. Smith was hospitalised with a fractured thigh and contusions on his face.

A Flight carried out a high offensive patrol at 10.25, the visibility was very good but no enemy aircraft were observed.

FLt Manuel and FSL McKelvey were despatched on a special enemy aircraft patrol at 11.10 when a report was received of an enemy machine approaching Dunkerque. The two pilots covered the lines between Nieuport and Ypres at heights up to 20000 feet. No enemy aircraft were observed.

Manuel led B Flight on a high offensive patrol at 13.25, once again there was no evidence of enemy activity.

17th February

A Flight carried out a high offensive patrol at 07.30, four enemy aircraft were seen in the far distance to the north of Roulers.

FLt Hinchliffe flew a special mission at 10.15, intending to intercept any reconnaissance machines trying to cross the lines. He was unable to find any reconnaissance machines and crossed the lines to the east of Roulers. At 11.30 he saw a 2-seater Albatros leave an aerodrome southeast of Roulers, when the enemy machine reached 10000 feet Hinchliffe attacked it out of the sun and shot the observer who fell back. At this point Hinchliffe was attacked by two scouts and had to break off the engagement with the 2-seater. The starboard lower wing of Hinchliffe's machine was hit several times but after a short engagement he was able to escape.

B Flight performed a high offensive patrol at 11.35. A 2-seater was observed over Tourcoing at 12.45, the machine dived steeply to the southeast when approached but was indecisively engaged by McKelvey and Manuel. Manuel's machine suffered a gun stoppage after he had acquired a good position.

FCdr Alexander led a high offensive patrol at 15.00. No enemy aircraft were observed throughout the patrol.

After Naval 10 disposed of its Clerget Camels, FLt Hinchliffe's B6204 eventually ended up at 207TDS Chingford where it was crashed on the 30th April 1918, still carrying Naval 10 markings. Hinchliffe's personal marking "ALLO" can be seen marked above the flight letter. Many authorities state that the marking was "ALLO LIL BIRD", but there is no evidence of this in the photograph. *Courtesy S. Taylor*

18th February

FLt Manuel led B Flight on a high offensive patrol at 08.55. Five Albatros scouts were encountered over Menin at 09.50 and a general engagement followed. Manuel fired 100 rounds from very close range into a scout, the machine stalled, spun for a short distance, then fell away out of control. Manuel then dived after the remaining scouts and fired 300 rounds without a decisive result. Hall manoeuvred into a good position on the tail of a scout and fired 200 rounds at very close range, the enemy machine side-slipped and went down absolutely out of control. Hall followed it down to 8000 feet but then had to turn away and engage another machine. After a short engagement the scout spun away then flattened out and escaped. Manuel saw the machine which he had first attacked and the first machine that had been engaged by FSL Hall both crash into the ground to the south of Menin. McKelvey attacked an Albatros scout which was engaging FSL Burr, he fired 100 rounds and the machine broke off its attack and dived away. Burr failed to return from the patrol, he was last seen after the engagement to the east of Ypres and heading towards the lines. Burr crashed on the Allied side of the lines but was seriously wounded and subsequently died of his injuries on the 20th February. Burr was possibly a victim of *Obltn*. B. Lörzer, *Jasta* 26.

C Flight and A flight carried out two further high offensive patrols at 12.00 and 14.55 respectively, both patrols were uneventful.

FLt H.T. Mellings, a very experienced scout pilot from No.2 Wing in the Aegean joined the squadron and made two practice flights.

19th February

An old familiar problem reappeared on the 19th when many machines suffered from gun problems.

FCdr Alexander led C Flight on a high offensive patrol at 07.35. A 2-seater was encountered over Houthulst Forest, when the patrol attempted to attack all pilots found their guns to be inoperative due to the cold. FLt Mellings was late getting away and failed to pick up the patrol, after flying with some RFC machines for a while, he left them and at 08.30 encountered a lone Albatros scout over Menin. He attempted to attack and also found his guns to be frozen.

A and B Flights carried out a high offensive patrol at 10.30. A 2-seater was attacked by Manuel at 11.00 over Menin, Manuel followed it down to 3000 feet but was unable to obtain a decisive result. At 11.50, four Albatros scouts were encountered on the Allied side of the lines southeast of Ypres. The enemy machines were indecisively engaged by a flight of Camels from No.1 Naval Squadron. FLt Carter climbed his patrol above them and attacked a machine on the east of the formation without effect. He then attacked a second machine and obtained a good position on its tail. Carter followed the machine down to 50 feet, firing short bursts into it. The scout crashed and burst into flames in the Ypres-Comines canal south of Zillebeke. Carter was forced to share the victory with FLt S.W. Rosevear of Naval 1. The pilot of destroyed Albatros DVa 4495/17, *Ltn.* Hans v. Puttkammer of *Jasta* 3 was taken prisoner. Carter "claimed" the rudder from the Albatros as a trophy and displayed it in the officer's mess.

FCdr Alexander led a seven machine high offensive patrol at 13.30. A 2-seater was encountered east of Messines at 14.30. Alexander tried to engage it but found his guns to be frozen. At 15.00, four scouts were encountered to the east of Roulers at 13000 feet. Manuel attacked one of the scouts, getting into a good position and fired 400 rounds at a range of 150 to 100 yards, the enemy machine stalled to the right, then dived vertically with the engine on at over 200 knots. Manuel followed it down for 7000 feet and saw it still descending in a vertical dive, he was then attacked by another machine and was unable to watch the result of his first combat.

19th to 20th February

Bad weather with strong winds prevented all flying.

21st February

The wind was still very strong and blowing from the west, however, three patrols were carried out.

Carter led a five machine high offensive patrol at 07.30. Three enemy scouts were seen to the northeast of Roulers at 08.50.

Alexander led C Flight on a high offensive patrol at 10.20, the visibility was reported as good but no enemy aircraft were encountered.

Carter led a six machine high offensive patrol at 13.25. At 14.15, anti-aircraft fire alerted the patrol to the presence of an enemy machine at 18000 feet and northwest of Dixmude. The patrol was in the Ypres sector at the time and was not able to reach the enemy machine against the strong wind before it had moved away.

22nd February

The adverse weather conditions prevented all flying activities.

23rd February

Carter led a six machine high offensive patrol at 07.30 but on crossing the lines the patrol found a thick cloud layer at 5000 feet and the entire area was completely overcast. The patrol was abandoned after 30 minutes and the patrol returned to the aerodrome.

The rest of the day's patrols were cancelled.

New pilot FSL J. Hollick made a couple of practice flights during the day.

24th February

No war flying took place due to the adverse weather conditions, however, three pilots were able to make practice flights in the morning.

25th February

The adverse weather conditions prevented any flying during the day.

FLt Hinchliffe and FSL McKelvey took off at 22.55 on the night of the 25th in an attempt to bomb Rumbeke SW aerodrome. They failed to find Rumbeke but dropped their bombs on another aerodrome that was thought to be Abeele. A total of eight bombs were dropped, at least two of which fell amongst the hangars. Both pilots were held by searchlights and subjected to machine gun fire from the ground. The pilots returned during the early hours of the 26th.

26th February

FCdr Alexander led C Flight on a high offensive patrol at 09.30. A 2-seater was observed over Houthulst Forest at 10.45. Seven Albatros scouts appeared 3000 feet above the patrol and maintained their position for 1/2 hour to protect the 2-seater.

27th February

FCdr Carter led Manuel and McKelvey on a high offensive patrol at 13.45, Carter found that the entire area across the lines was overcast and the patrol was abandoned.

Alexander led C Flight on a high offensive patrol at 14.00, the overcast was found to start at 4000 feet and the patrol was flown just below the cloud base.

Eleven test and practice flights were performed in the morning.

28th February

The squadron flew three patrols on the last day of February despite high winds, heavy cloud, and snow squalls.

FCdr Alexander led C Flight on a high offensive patrol at 08.30. FSL Rice became separated from the patrol and encountered an enemy scout in the region of Thourout. Rice fired 50 rounds at the scout from a range of 100 yards but lost the scout in the heavy cloud cover. FLt Hinchliffe also became separated from the patrol, crossed the lines on his own and fired all of his ammunition at transport and troops on the Menin road.

A and B Flights carried out a high offensive patrol at 11.25. Seven scouts were observed south of Menin at 12.10 but when the patrol started to climb towards them, they retired to the southeast.

C Flight carried out a high offensive patrol at 15.30. At 16.45, a formation of twelve scouts attacked the patrol on the Allied side of the lines northeast of Ypres. FLt Mellings obtained good position at close range and fired 100 rounds into a scout, observing his tracers enter the fuselage. The enemy machine passed from a steep dive to an inverted position and fell out of control. Mellings was unable to follow it down without becoming separated from the Flight. Alexander fired 75 rounds into another scout without result. Hinchliffe and Rice both obtained good position on a scout only to find their guns were inoperative due to the cold.

March 1918

The weather again played an important role during March, a total of 12 day's operations being lost or significantly affected.

The RAF came into existence on the 1st April 1918, the bad weather at the end of March effectively meant that No.10 Squadron, Royal Naval Air Service, finished its life in the misery of inactivity.

1st March to 4th March

The first four days of March were washed out due to unfavourable weather.

5th March

FLt Manuel led a 5 machine high offensive patrol at 13.50. The patrol was delayed for 20 minutes whilst bombs were fitted to Hinchliffe's machine. The visibility was poor and a very strong south-westerly wind was encountered at 10000 to 14000 feet. At 14.20, a large formation of enemy aircraft was observed between Lille and Tourcoing. Hinchliffe dropped two 16 lb bombs from 8000 feet near Staden at 14.35. One was seen to burst near some buildings close to the Ypres-Thourout railway line by Manuel. Hinchliffe was unwilling to descend lower to drop the bombs because of failing fuel pressure.

6th March

FCdr Alexander led C Flight on a high offensive patrol at 07.30. Four Albatros scouts were engaged by the patrol southeast of Dixmude at 09.30. Alexander fired 50 rounds into one of the scouts at 30 yards range, observing his tracers entering the fuselage. The enemy machine went straight down in a vertical dive. Hinchliffe fired 50 rounds at another scout from long range with no effect. He observed FCdr Alexander attack another machine at close range and followed it down for 3000 feet. He reported that it never came out of the vertical dive. FSL Rice had an indecisive engagement at long range and then observed FCdr Alexander's combats, seeing the enemy aircraft go down out of control.

Carter, at last promoted to Flight Commander, led five Camels on a high offensive patrol at 10.55. A 2-seater was observed 5 miles off the coast from Ostende at 12.15 but it dived away towards Zeebrugge and evaded attack.

Alexander led C Flight out again at 13.35. Six scouts were encountered over Roulers at 15.10. Alexander engaged one and fired 20 rounds from 200 yards in a head-on attack, then suffered engine failure due to falling pressure. The enemy machine returned fire then turned back to join his flight. Alexander was forced to return to the lines using his hand pump to maintain pressure.

Carter led a six machine high offensive patrol at 15.30. The weather had deteriorated with very bad visibility reported and almost complete overcast. The patrol was cut short due to the weather conditions.

7th March

FLt Hinchliffe carried out a special bombing mission at 04.30. His Camel was armed with four 16lb bombs and his target was Zeebrugge Mole. At 05.45, he dropped his bombs from 500 feet and observed three of them burst on the base of the Mole. A number of enemy aircraft were observed over Ostende at 06.30.

Carter led a five machine high offensive patrol at 06.45, the patrol returned early due to mist and clouds.

FSL Rice made a test flight at 15.30, during the flight he observed an Albatros scout east of the lines. Rice hid in the clouds until within range, then fired 100 rounds from 100 yards. The enemy machine broke away from the engagement and dived off to the east.

8th March

Enemy activity appeared to be almost non-existent on the 8th.

Alexander and Carter led high offensive patrols at 06.45 and 11.10 respectively, neither patrol encountering any enemy aircraft. At the end of A Flight's 11.10 patrol, FSL S.C. Joseph put one of B3781's wheels into a ditch when taxing after landing and stood the machine on its nose, causing some damage.

FCdr Alexander led C Flight on a photographic escort mission at 13.00. The Caudron photographic machine was picked up above the aerodrome and the patrol proceeded to the objective via Dixmude. The pilots reported seeing a giant aeroplane on Ghistelles aerodrome, standing in front of the sheds. It was described as twice the size of a Handley Page and painted yellow. This was most likely Staaken R.VI No.R.27, this machine took off on a bombing mission from Ghent on the night of the 7th March, but suffered problems due to frozen fuel lines before it crossed the coast and was compelled to make a forced landing at Ghistelles. After the mission Alexander complained about the pilot of the Caudron who made it very difficult for the escort to hold formation with his machine.

Alexander and Carter led a combined high offensive patrol at 15.00, no enemy aircraft were encountered but the pilots reported seeing a machine go down in flames to the southeast of Houthulst Forest at 16.15.

9th March

Carter led a seven machine high offensive patrol at 09.10, this proved to be completely uneventful, as did C Flight's high offensive patrol performed at 13.15.

At 13.30, C Flight provided an escort for another photographic mission. Alexander reported favourably on the Caudron pilot's performance on this mission.

C Flight carried out the last patrol of the day at 15.45, patrolling over Ghistelles aerodrome. The aerodrome had been heavily bombed by DH4s of Naval 6 in an attempt to destroy the Staaken which was parked there. At 16.20, five enemy machines were observed over St. Pierre Cappelle. The Patrol followed them to Thourout where they were joined by eleven more scouts. The enemy aircraft avoided combat but attempted to draw the Camels further east.

10th March

A, B, and C Flights fielded a twelve machine offensive patrol at 11.55, it was rapidly reduced to an eleven machine patrol when Hinchliffe's engine failed over the lines. Hinchliffe was able to glide back to the aerodrome. At 13.40, Mellings indecisively engaged a 2-seater over the allied lines near Ypres.

Another 12 machine patrol was flown at 15.00, covering Armentières, Menin, Roulers and Ypres. At 15.45, several scouts and three 2-seaters were encountered over Roulers and engaged by the patrol. FCdr Alexander and FLt Hinchliffe both claimed a 2-seater driven down out of control, though in his logbook, Hinchliffe claimed his 2-seater was crashed. At 16.00, six scouts were observed to the southeast of Dixmude, these were engaged, Manuel and Mellings both claiming an Albatros scout shot down.

11th March

Carter led a seven machine high offensive patrol at 07.20, the visibility was bad and no enemy aircraft were seen. FSL Patey crashed B5749 when landing at the end of the patrol.

FLt Mellings carried out a test flight at 10.30, and observed eleven enemy aircraft over Roulers at 11.15.

Carter led a six machine photographic escort mission at 11.45. The patrol picked up the Caudron at 12.00, and escorted it over the Ostende, Dixmude, Nieuport sector at 14000 to

15000 feet. After the French machine had been safely seen home, they proceeded to the south of Ypres and patrolled the lines at 10000 feet.

C Flight performed a high offensive patrol at 11.55. The visibility was reported as fair but no enemy aircraft were encountered.

SCdr Bell took FSL S.C. Joseph on a line patrol at 16.25. A 2-seater was encountered at 17.00 near Merckem, with 3 scouts sitting above. The enemy aircraft dived away when approached.

12th March

C Flight carried out a high offensive patrol at 10.00. Nine scouts were observed to the east of Menin at 11.30, but a large number of allied machines were in the vicinity and the enemy aircraft could not be brought to action.

A thirteen machine patrol was mounted at 14.15, an unlucky number as Hinchliffe commented in his log book. FLt Mellings in B6357 crashed from 300 feet after loosing control in a tight turn, the aircraft was wrecked and Mellings was extremely fortunate to escape with slight bruising. The rest of the patrol was uneventful.

13th March

B Flight reappeared as an entity after several weeks of its pilots having to support A and C Flights. FLt Manuel took B Flight on a high offensive patrol at 07.05. The flight joined forces with a patrol from No.1 Naval Squadron, however no enemy aircraft were observed.

A Flight encountered a 2-seater and a scout over Wervicq during their 10.05 high offensive patrol. The scout was indecisively engaged by FSL Hall at 11.25. The patrol stayed out for 1/2 hour beyond the specified time and joined up with Camels from No.1 Naval Squadron.

FCdr Alexander and FLt Hinchliffe were despatched on a special mission to intercept reconnaissance aircraft. The pilots patrolled at heights up to 16000 feet, but no enemy aircraft were encountered.

Alexander led a seven machine high offensive patrol at 13.10, no enemy machines were encountered so the patrol descended to 800 feet and fired 1500 rounds into enemy trenches near Dixmude.

FCdr Carter and FSL Hall performed a high offensive patrol at 15.20. No enemy aircraft were seen. A heavy mist rolled in from the coast towards the end of the patrol and Carter was unable to find the aerodrome, eventually reporting in from No.29 Squadron RFC.

A number of new pilots were on the squadron strength and it is worth reviewing the Flight structure at this juncture:

A Flight
FCdr A.W. Carter, Flight Commander
FSL F.V. Hall, Deputy Flight Commander
FSL S.C. Joseph
FSL G.T. Steeves
FSL A.L. Jones
FSL H.L. Nelson

B Flight
FLt J.G. Manuel, Flight Commander
FSL H.B. Maund, Deputy Flight Commander
FSL H.A. Patey
FSL J. Hollick
FSL M.T. McKelvey

C Flight
FCdr W.M. Alexander, Flight Commander
FLt W.G.R. Hinchliffe, Deputy Flight Commander
FLt H.T. Mellings
FSL L.P. Coombes
FSL E.G. Rice

14th March

Bad weather prevented all war flying.

15th March

A Flight carried out a high offensive patrol at 06.55. A 2-seater observed over Thourout at 08.15 dived away to the east before the patrol could get to it.

C Flight's high offensive patrol at 10.00 encountered two 2-seaters to the west of Ostende at 11.20, these were indecisively engaged by Alexander and Hinchliffe before they dived away steeply.

Carter led a seven machine patrol at 13.50, no enemy aircraft were encountered.

Hinchliffe performed a reconnaissance enemy aircraft patrol at 14.00, and patrolled from Ostende to Blankenberghe at heights up to 9000 feet. He engaged a 2-seater over Ostende at 14.45 and followed it down to 4000 feet without decisive result.

Mellings carried out a similar patrol at 14.50 covering Ypres to Dixmude, no enemy aircraft were observed and he descended to 1000 feet and fired 200 rounds into enemy trenches near Dixmude.

16th March

C Fight carried out a high offensive patrol at 08.15. Seven Pfalz scouts were observed at 09.30, patrolling between Roulers and Menin at 18000 feet. FLt Mellings climbed to 20000 feet and attacked one of the scouts which had climbed to 19000 feet. Mellings attacked out of the sun and fired 250 rounds at 250 to 100 yards range. The enemy machine stalled, then fell out of control in a series of dives and spins. Mellings was able to watch it fall to 5000 feet, at which point he had to evade another member of the enemy formation.

Carter led a seven machine high offensive patrol at 12.10. A 2-seater was indecisively engaged by Carter at 12.40 to the northeast of Roulers. Another 2-seater was encountered between Roulers and Menin at 13.15, this machine dived away when approached. FSL Hall's machine proved difficult to start, he missed the start of the patrol and failed to pick them up when he eventually got away. At 13.15 he encountered a 2-seater trying to cross the lines three miles south of Ypres, the machine turned back and went down when Hall approached.

FCdr Alexander led a six machine high offensive patrol at 15.45, no enemy machines were encountered and towards the end of the patrol, Alexander, Coombes and Rice descended to 800 feet and fired 650 rounds into enemy trenches near Dixmude.

New pilot FSL B.A.P.L. D'Etchegoyen made a practice flight late in the afternoon.

17th March

A high offensive patrol was flown at 06.35 by Hall, Jones and Nelson. The weather was completely overcast with thick cloud at 4000 feet and the pilots returned almost immediately.

C Flight performed a high offensive patrol at 11.15 and at 12.15 nine Pfalz and Albatros scouts were encountered over Courtrai. Several engagements took place but no decisive results were obtained.

A ten machine high offensive patrol was carried out at 15.35. No enemy aircraft were seen but at 16.15 a large explosion was observed slightly east of the centre of Houthulst Forest. FSL Hall's machine developed carburettor problems and he was compelled to make a forced landing in a ploughed field near St. Sixte. Hall managed to land without damage to the aircraft or injury to himself.

18th March

FCdr Alexander led C Flight on an offensive patrol at 08.10. A formation of eight Pfalz scouts was encountered to the east of Roulers at 09.00, these refused engagement and kept away to the east whenever C Flight approached them.

FCdr Carter led an eight machine high offensive patrol at 11.30. The patrol was attacked by a formation of eight Albatros scouts at 12.30, southeast of Courtrai. Carter, Mellings and Joseph were involved in inconclusive engagements. FSL Steeves failed to return from the patrol, he was last seen by FCdr Carter at 12.45, heading eastwards and was possibly shot down by *Ltn.* E. Thuy of *Jasta* 28. Steeves was captured and became a prisoner of war.

C and A flights carried out a high offensive patrol at 15.40. The patrol was carried out at heights up to 18500 feet in good visibility. No enemy aircraft were seen throughout the patrol.

19th March

C Flight attempted to carry out a high offensive patrol at 07.35. The patrol had been delayed by unfavourable weather conditions and when it eventually took off the entire area was found to be obscured by heavy cloud. Alexander brought the patrol back after 45 minutes.

No further flying took place.

20th March

The weather was still bad on the 20th.

A and C Flights carried out a high offensive patrol at 14.10, the entire area was overcast by clouds with the exception of a small strip of coast.

21st March

A and C Flights carried out a combined high offensive patrol at 08.15. Whilst no enemy aircraft were encountered, the patrol was far from uneventful. FCdr Carter's Camel shed a cylinder which caused the cowling to break up. Carter made a forced landing at the aerodrome of No.29 Squadron RFC and returned by car. FLt Hinchliffe also suffered engine trouble and was forced to return.

C Flight carried out a high offensive patrol at 11.55 and encountered a formation of nine Pfalz scouts at 12.40 between Roulers and Menin. The patrol was unable to close with the enemy machines but Alexander, Coombes, and Patey attacked at long range without decisive effect.

FCdr Carter led an eight machine high offensive patrol at 15.40. A 2-seater was observed at 19000 feet to the east of Houthulst Forest at 16.30. No other enemy aircraft were seen. The patrol reported a large fire raging in the docks at Ostende and several smaller fires in the town. FSL D'Etchegoyen on his first patrol became separated from the formation and landed at an RFC aerodrome.

22nd March

A and C Flights carried out a high offensive patrol at 13.55. At 15.10, two 2-seaters were observed at 6000 feet over Thourout. These machines dived away steeply when approached and FSL Hall fired 100 rounds at long range without effect.

23rd March

FSL E Swale arrived at the squadron and made a practice flight at 11.05.

A and C Flights performed a bomber escort mission at 14.30. The escort proceeded to the rendezvous over Nieuport and waited there from 14.50 to 15.30 but the bombing machines failed to turn up. When returning at 15.45, two DH9's were observed on their way back, seven miles out to sea off Ostende. FSL Patey crashed B6391 when landing at the end of the mission, damaging the aircraft.

24th March

C Flight performed a high offensive patrol at 08.15. At 09.20, a formation of seven Pfalz and Albatros scouts were encountered over the Menin-Roulers road and a 2-seater to the east of Roulers. The patrol engaged the scout formation, FCdr Alexander got on the tail on one scout and fired from 30 yards range, he saw his tracers enter the engine and immediately afterwards the propeller stopped with a jerk and put the machine out of control for a few moments. Alexander closed to within 50 feet and fired straight into the pilot. The machine went down completely out of control and was believed to have crashed. Alexander then closed to within 50 yards of another machine and observed his tracers going all round the pilot's cockpit. This machine fell out of control but recovered when 2000 feet from the ground. FLt Mellings shot down a scout which caught fire and broke up in the air and claimed another machine which turned over on its back and fell away out of control. FSL Coombes fired 250 rounds at another machine and drove it down out of control, the aircraft appeared to be on fire, emitting large clouds of black smoke. The patrol reported that some of the enemy machines were marked with large white rings containing small and narrow black crosses.

FCdr Carter led an eight machine offensive patrol at 11.50. In contrast to the earlier patrol, this one was entirely uneventful.

FLt Mellings carried out a special patrol at 13.00 in search of enemy reconnaissance aircraft. He patrolled between Nieuport and Ypres at heights up to 18000 feet. One 2-seater

Several anomalies exist with this photograph of FSL L.P. Coombes and a striped C Flight Camel. The stripes and wheel cover are clearly not blue, the engine cowling and gun covers appear to be those fitted to a Bentley Camel and the engine, although poorly focussed also appears to be a Bentley. FSL M.T. McKelvey flew B6391, a Bentley Camel, in B Flight's red and white striped livery until the 20th March 1918, when he was posted on leave. At this point B6391 was transferred to C Flight, and it is surmised that the Flight letter was changed on this date and that B6391 is the subject of the photograph. *Author's collection*

was seen at 20000 feet travelling west between Poperinghe and Ypres.

Mellings and Hall carried out another special mission at 16.00. Mellings went to Nieuport to get height and returned towards Dunkerque at 20000 feet. At 16.40 he saw a 2-seater spotting over No.10 Squadron's aerodrome. Mellings approached the spotter which turned away east, Mellings followed it to 21000 feet.

Hall headed west and returned at 18000 feet over Dunkerque and Nieuport. At 16.50, he observed a 2-seater at 19000 feet 2 miles off the coast at Nieuport. The 2-seater went down on Ghistelles aerodrome. At 17.10 he observed three enemy scouts west of Roulers.

25th March

Bad weather stopped all flying activities.

26th March

C Flight carried out an uneventful offensive patrol at 08.25. A very strong north wind made flying conditions difficult.

Alexander and Carter led a twelve machine offensive sweep at 14.25. The patrol picked up a formation of DH9s west of Dunkerque at 14.40 and accompanied them to Ostende. This took 1 1/2 hours due to the gale force wind and Alexander had to signal to the DH9s that it would be impossible to reach Bruges on the petrol supply. The bombers turned in over Ostende and the escort returned over Dixmude. FCdr Alexander landed at No.6 Squadron with broken centre section wires. FSL D'Etchegoyen, on his second patrol, made a forced landing at Eggewaertscappelle.

27th to 31st March

Bad weather set in for the rest of the month, curtailing all war flying. The last days of No.10 Squadron Royal Naval Air Service, proving to be an anti-climax.

Epilogue

After an inauspicious start, No.10 Squadron RNAS rapidly started to display the true offensive spirit demanded by its new Commanding Officer, Bertram Charles Bell. An enviable tally of combat victories was initially spearheaded by the remarkable Raymond Collishaw and his flight of black triplanes and ably continued throughout the year by many of the squadron's other pilots.

Although B.C. Bell was not a popular Commanding Officer, the inadvisability of appointing a man with a more relaxed and friendly manner was rapidly illustrated by the grave error of judgement made by Acting Squadron Commander R.F. Redpath at the end of September 1917. In the author's view, the mutinous incident would have been inconceivable under Bell's command.

After its ignominious withdrawal from the main Flanders area of conflict in early October, the squadron soldiered on in a state of low morale. It was not until Bell's return in December that the squadron regained its lost pride.

It should not be forgotten that there was a price to be paid for Bell's Offensive Spirit, a very high casualty rate, exacerbated by the Royal Naval Air Service's inability to provide enough replacement pilots throughout much of 1917. When losses were exceeding replacements, new pilots were frequently thrown straight in to the fray without time to acclimatise. Only the very best and the very lucky survived. Nevertheless, No.10 Squadron RNAS overcame their difficulties to face the future with the Royal Air Force.

On the first of April, 1918, the squadrons of the Royal Naval Air Service amalgamated with those of the Royal Flying Corps to become the Royal Air Force. For better or worse, No.10 Squadron RNAS became No.210 Squadron RAF.

CHAPTER NINE

THE ROYAL AIR FORCE

The creation of the Royal Air Force is a topic that could easily occupy several volumes, a detailed account is beyond the scope of this book and the author trusts that readers will forgive the vastly simplified outline provided below.

Politics

Whilst the need or wish for an air service, independent from the army and navy, had been a subject of bitter debate even before the start of hostilities, a succession of ineffective committees and boards failed to come to any resolution.

Following unrest after the daylight Gotha raids on London during the summer of 1917, a Government Cabinet committee was formed in August 1917, nominally chaired by Prime Minister David Lloyd George, but effectively controlled by the South African Defence Minister, Lieutenant General J.C. Smuts. Smuts had been brought into the debate, ostensibly to provide an impartial viewpoint. The committee's final report produced in October, popularly referred to as the Smuts report, recommended the formation of an Air Ministry to control and administer all aspects of the air war, and recommended the amalgamation of the Royal Flying Corps and The Royal Naval Air Service. After the appropriate Parliamentary procedures had been followed, the date of 1st April 1918 was chosen for the inauguration of the Royal Air Force.

Despite Smut's supposed impartiality, it must be emphasised that amalgamation of the RNAS and RFC was a political decision, not a military decision. As is usual with political decisions, the long-term consequences were ignored in favour of perceived short-term benefits.

It is difficult to argue against the decision to remove the RFC from Army control, after all, the Army was not comfortable with aviation. More interested in men than machines, the Army mindset showed little in the way of innovation in aerial matters. The Royal Navy on the other hand, was a technical service, used to using machinery in new and innovative ways. The RNAS was a far more modern and competent service than the RFC, and the most effective Naval aviation wing of any nation at that time. The loss of the naval air arm in 1918 was strongly resisted in some circles, but the inevitable was ultimately accepted.

The effect upon the Navy was pronounced, many of the land based scout and bomber squadrons were immediately diverted away from their naval obligations, leaving shipping and ports unprotected. After the war, it became more obvious that the Navy still needed an air arm, however, all of the experienced airmen they would need for re-building a naval air service were gone. The Air Ministry fought the Admiralty at every opportunity for funds and status and it was not until just before the start of World War II that the Navy finally clawed back control of shipboard aircraft. When Britain went to war in 1939, the new naval air service was equipped with obsolete aircraft, inexperienced airmen, and outmoded tactics.

Jan Smuts destroyed the most effective and modern naval air service in the world, and crippled Britain's credibility as a sea power. A cynic might well be justified in claiming that by killing off the Royal Naval Air Service, General Jan Smuts obtained his revenge for his defeat by Britain during the Boer War.

Practicalities

In the short term, during the spring of 1918, the most noticeable effect upon the Naval squadrons was their re-numbering by the simple expedient of adding 200 to their number, thus No.1 Squadron RNAS became No.201 Squadron RAF, and No.10 Squadron RNAS became No.210 Squadron RAF. The RNAS Wings were re-numbered by the addition of 60 to the Wing number.

The following memo from Wing Captain Lambe, was circulated on the 14th March 1918:

HEADQUARTERS,
R.N.A.S.,
14th March, 1918

No. 9423

SECRET MEMORANDUM

Owing to the formation of the AIR Force, involving the amalgamation of the Royal Naval Air Service and the Royal Flying Corps, it has become necessary to re-number the R.N.A.S. units in the Dunkerque Command. In order that the Squadrons and Wings may retain as far as possible their original identity, it has been arranged that all Squadrons will be re-numbered with the prefix 200 and the Wings will be re-numbered with the prefix 60. i.e., the existing Naval Squadron No.1 will become Squadron No.201, Naval Squadron No.2 will become Squadron No.202, etc., etc. No.1 Wing will become No.61 Wing, and Nos. 4 and 5 Wings will become nos. 64 and 65 Wings respectively.

The above nomenclature will come into force on the 1st April 1918.

C L LAMBE,
Captain, R.N.,
Senior Officer,
R.N.A.S.

Vice-Admiral, Dover patrol (for information) (2) S . O . , R.N.A.S., Dover (5)
Commodore, Dunkerque (for information)
Overseas Base Paymaster
Base Commander (for information)
Victualling Paymaster
G.A.Q.I. Sigs. — Fleet Paymaster, Dover
No.1 Wing (5) — Fleet Paymaster, Trafalgar House
No.4 Wing (3) — Drafting Commander
No.5 Wing (7) — Commanding Officer, Manstone
Warrant Officer Le Sueur, H.Q. RFC (3)
Commanding Officer, Eastchurch
Aircraft Depot (6)

The RNAS personnel adopted the military ranks used by the RFC:

Squadron Commander	became	Major
Flight Commander	became	Captain
Flight Lieutenant	became	Lieutenant
Flight Sub Lieutenant	became	2nd Lieutenant.

The uniforms changed, though, in most cases, not immediately. Some naval traditionalists such as Major Collishaw retained their naval uniforms to the end of the war.

The great naval traditions, functions that had been observed by the most land-locked naval squadrons, were killed off at a stroke-watch keeping, the ship's bell, liberty boat, officer of the watch etc. It is not recorded whether the drinking of "pink gins" was abandoned!

A slightly longer-term effect involved the supply of new pilots and the transfer of officers between squadrons. The old naval squadrons started to receive new pilots from the RFC training establishments, and much more rarely, senior officers were sometimes transferred from an ex- Naval squadron to command an ex-RFC squadron.

To the men and officers of No.10 Squadron, or No.210 Squadron RAF, the life and death struggle continued, though a move south meant that the port and fleet protection duties were a thing of the past.

For the squadron management, the plethora of memoranda being issued in advance of the amalgamation must have been very confusing. For example, the following memo was issued by RNAS Headquarters at Dunkerque on the 21st March 1918:

SECRET

H.Q. Ref. 7998 — HEADQUARTERS, R.N.A.S.,
DUNKERQUE
21.3.18.

MEMORANDUM,

TRANSFERRANCE OF NO. 10 SQUADRON

No.10 Squadron will be transferred from No.4 Wing to No.1 Wing from midnight, March 31st, and will come under the orders of C.O., No.1 Wing from April 1st.

Signed HR Aubrey Major,
Attached H.Q. R.N.A.S.,
FOR SENIOR OFFICER, R.N.A.S.

DISTRIBUTION

C.O., No.1 Wing
C.O., No.4 Wing
Base Paymaster)
Victualling Paymaster)
C.O., A.D.)
O.C., 8th A.D.D.)
H.Q., R.F.C.) For information
H.Q., R.N.A.S., Dover)
Commanders, Dunkerque)
S.O., A.,Q.,1.,G.)
H.Q. Le Sueur)

It was significant that an RFC Major, H.R. Aubrey was now seen to be issuing RNAS directives.

RNAS Headquarters obviously believed that No.1 Wing (or No.61 Wing as it would shortly become) would be controlling No.10 Squadron and although they would eventually control No.210 Squadron RAF, it would not be until July 1918.

Another memo issued from Dunkerque on the 31st March 1918 detailed orders for the squadron to move South from Teteghem to Treizennes, and informed that the squadron would now report to the 1st Brigade RFC, and although not mentioned in the memo, the reporting structure would be to No.10 Wing:

Ref. H.Q. 7958

HEADQUARTERS, R.N.A.S.,
31:3:18

MEMORANDUM.-

MOVE OF NO.10 SQUADRON
SECRET

Reference – Sheet 36A. 1/40,000 and Hazebrouck 5A. 1/100,000

1. No.10 Squadron will move to TREIZENNES tomorrow. (36A.0.1.o.) and will be accommodated on the same camp as Naval Squadron No.3.

2. Orders for machines to start will be given from H.Q., R.N.A.S.

3. C.O., M.T.P. will provide necessary transport, which will be at Teteghem tonight. Route for transport will be via BERGUES, CASSEL, ZALLON CAPPEL, and AIRE.

4. On arrival at TREIZENNES No.10 Squadron will come under the command of G.O.C. 1st. Brigade RFC.

5. On the departure of No.10 Squadron, TETEGHEM Camp and Aerodrome will be occupied by No.74 Squadron under arrangements to be made by C.O., No.4 Wing.

6. The Camp is to be left intact.

7. Completion of move to be reported to H.Q., R.N.A.S.

signed HR Aubry, Major,

Attached H.Q., R.N.A.S.
FOR SENIOR OFFICER, R.N.A.S.

Distrubution –

No.4 Wing
H.Q., R.F.C.)
1st Brigade, R.F.C.)
S.O.H.Q.)
Victualling Payr.)
Overseas Base Payr.) For Information.
C.O. N.A.D.)

H.Q.
Le Sueur)
A. Q. G.)

Wing Captain Lambe, or to give him his new rank, Brigadier General Lambe, wrote to the ex-naval squadrons on the 1st April:

On April 1st., The Royal Air Force will come into being.

After having commanded the Royal Naval Air Service Units and Dunkerque for the past two years and eight months, I wish to express my sincere thanks to all Officers and Ratings for the magnificent spirit they have displayed during the whole of this period.

The Pilots and Observers and Gunlayers have, by their skill and courage established a high reputation. The Ratings have invariable worked long hours cheerfully, and this combination could only have been achieved by the loyalty and hard work of the Ground Officers, Squadron Commanders, and Wing Commanders.

The small percentage of casualties I attribute to the great technical skill and untiring efforts of the Engine Officers and Engine Ratings generally.

The Royal Air Force will undoubtedly expand very rapidly and will, I think prove to be the deciding factor of the war.

I hope that the Naval Squadrons will maintain their old traditions, records and reputation for efficiency, under their new numbers.

In thanking every Officer and man for their loyalty and support in the past, I wish them all success in the future and can confidently rely on their doing their utmost in the Royal Air Force to win the war.

(sgd) C.L. Lambe
Brigadier-General
Royal Air Force

1st April

Major Bertram C Bell, DSO, DSC
Royal Air Force

The new No.210 Squadron Royal Air Force would go on to serve with distinction until the armistice in November 1918. It is the author's intention to produce a companion volume to this work at some time in the future, to detail the exploits of the naval men in the RAF.

APPENDICES

APPENDIX A

AIRCRAFT MARKINGS

No.10 Squadron's markings can be broken down into three distinct phases:

Triplane Markings
Camels – Official Squadron Markings
Camels – Unofficial Flight Markings

A) Triplane markings

The specified base finish for the Sopwith Triplane was PC12 (chocolate brown) on upper surfaces, with clear-doped linen on the under surface. It seems likely that when refurbished in the field, the Triplane would be finished in whatever was available, PC12 or PC10 (Olive Brown).

Until Collishaw arrived at No.10 Squadron there were no known squadron or individual markings carried on the squadron's Triplanes. On the day of his arrival it is thought that Collishaw had his Triplane painted with a personal identification mark, a large white letter "C", and many of the other pilots gradually followed suit, the individual letter, wherever possible being the initial letter of the pilot's surname.

Markings known from photographs are:

A	N5487 (conjecture)	Alexander
B	N6295	Broughall
C	N5490 (conjecture)	Collishaw
C	N533	Collishaw
H	N6306	Holcroft
K	N5357	Kent
Q	N5358	Saunders, Prewett and others

It is surmised that A was used by Alexander and that N, R, and S were taken by Nash, Reid, and Sharman respectively.

Raymond Collishaw was a traditionalist. When he served under FCdr Mack in No.3 Squadron, Mack's flight of Sopwith Pups had black painted cowls and side cladding, were marked with a large white letter representing the first letter of the pilot's surname behind the fuselage cockade, and carried "black" names, Black Tulip, Black Arrow, Black Maria, Black Prince, and Black Bess. Collishaw extended this tradition to B Flight in No.10 Squadron and would follow it again in the future when he was posted to the Seaplane Defence Squadron in November 1917.

In No.10 Squadron, the Sopwith Triplanes of Collishaw's B Flight were identified by black painted cowlings, side cladding, fin, and wheel covers. As in No.3 Squadron, each aircraft carried a "black" name stencilled in white beneath the cockpit:

N5490/N5492/N533	Collishaw	Black Maria
N5483	Reid	Black Roger
N5487	Alexander	Black Prince
N5466	Sharman	Black Death
N5492/N5476	Nash	Black Sheep

Conventional wisdom would have it that Sharman's Black Flight Triplane, "Black Death" was serial number N6307 which was not delivered to No.10 Squadron until the 3rd June 1917 and not flown until the 4th June when Sharman was in C Flight. Of course, it is possible that the ambitious Sharman, competing with the reluctant FSL Page for the leadership of C Flight, had his C Flight Triplane painted in B Flight colours. The question must be asked, however, "How likely was that to have happened?" The Triplane regularly flown by Sharman whilst he was undisputedly with B Flight was serial N5466 and lacking photographic evidence to the contrary, it must be assumed that Triplane N5466 was "Black Death".

In a similar vein, it is believed that FSL Nash's "Black Sheep" was originally N5492 as this was the Triplane regularly flown by Nash up until the middle of June 1917.

The other two flights were also identified by colour, A Flight having red wheel covers, fin, and cowlings, and C Flight having blue wheel covers, fin, and cowlings.

In his book *Air Command*, Raymond Collishaw stated the reason for Flight identification by colour was to provide a visual cue for the ground crews who were expected to run out when "their" Flight was landing to manually assist the aircraft to taxi back to the hangars.

A final point to note concerns an official proposal, on the 15th August 1917, for the adoption of official squadron markings. The marking proposed for No.10 Squadron RNAS consisted of two white vertical bars behind the national markings. The Triplanes started to be replaced by Camels from 26th August, and it is very doubtful if No.10 Squadron actually adopted this marking before the squadron was ordered by 5 Brigade to apply the more familiar marking (described in the next section) to their Sopwith Camels.

B) Camels – Official Squadron Markings

The standard base finish for No.10 Squadron Camels was usually, but not always, PC10 (olive brown) or PC12 (chocolate brown) upper surfaces, with clear-doped linen on the under surfaces. There is photographic evidence of one machine with side cladding left in natural aluminium.

An official squadron marking was allocated by 26th August 1917. This consisted of two white vertical lines on the fuselage side, one in front of the cockade and one in front of the tail. Flight markings comprised a large white Flight letter, A, B, or C, in front of the forward stripe.

The aircraft of the flight leaders and the deputy flight leaders exhibited variations to the squadron marking. In the case of the flight leader, both vertical white lines were continued up over the top decking, the most forward white line being wider than standard. The machine of the deputy flight leader was similar to that of the leader, with the exception that the rearmost stripe did not continue over the top decking.

Personal markings were often evident and photographic evidence exists of the names "Cleada", "Enid" and "Allo!" painted above the Flight letter and FCdr W.A. Curtis had white painted wheel covers with a concentric black ring on several of his machines. Photographic evidence also shows

B5663 to have wing tips painted in a darker colour that can only be red or black. Another photograph of B5663 shows the horizontal stabiliser and elevators to be outlined in a light colour, white or blue.

C) Camels – Unofficial Flight Markings

Clerget Camels

For a short period, the Camels of No.10 Squadron RNAS were possibly the most exotically painted allied aircraft of World War I. The machines bore horizontal black and white, red and white, and blue and white stripes on their cowls and side cladding, and carried individual coloured designs on their wheel covers. To discover how this evolved and was allowed to happen, we need to consider the repercussions of SCdr Repath's dispute with Lieutenant-Colonel Holt.

As related in Chapters 7 and 8, No.10 Squadron suffered the ignominy of being suddenly withdrawn from an active part of the Front and transferred to IV Brigade near the coast where they were initially given training duties. When patrols were allocated they tended to be repetitive and covered the same route from day to day.

Whilst the morale of Trenchard's command, and especially his "borrowed" RNAS squadrons, was protected from further erosion by the removal of No.10 Squadron from centre stage, the effect upon No.10 Squadron itself was not so beneficial. Whilst the light duties probably provided a welcome break for a week or so, the squadron's pride had been seriously dented. A continuation of boring duties, combined with an uncomfortable aerodrome with few amenities, saw squadron morale descend to new depths. It is not certain if the majority of the squadron's members were ever aware of the reason they had been transferred away from Droglandt. It is believed they had been told that the withdrawal was due to dissatisfaction with a reduced output of combat claims, an unpalatable reason, little better than the truth.

On the 20th November the squadron returned to the control of No.4 Wing RNAS and shortly thereafter moved to Teteghem, situated to the southeast of Dunkerque. As an aerodrome, however, Teteghem was little better than Leffrinckhoucke with uncomfortable accommodation and poor working conditions.

According to several of the squadron's Canadian pilots, the idea for giving each flight an individual striped colour scheme was devised not by the pilots but by the ground crew. They wanted to improve squadron morale and re-kindle the offensive spirit shown during the summer of 1917. The men enlisted the help of two English pilots, FSL Hall and FSL Nelson, to put the idea before higher management. Hall and Nelson were in A Flight, and they pestered their newly promoted flight commander, FLt W.A. Curtis, until he gave in and presented the idea to SCdr B.C. Bell. Bell had recently returned to the squadron following his period of sick leave, and faced an uphill task to restore morale amongst the pilots and other ranks, and possibly more difficult, to restore the confidence of higher authority. He obviously saw the proposal as a way of unifying the squadron and improving morale and somewhat surprisingly gave permission for the scheme to go ahead.

The weather was too wild for flying at Christmas 1917 so the opportunity was taken to paint the aircraft whilst the bad weather prevailed. The Camels emerged from the hangars on the 26th December resplendent in their new striped liveries. A Flight machines were painted in black and white stripes, B Fight in red and white stripes, and the two C Flight aircraft were painted in blue and white stripes. Each Flight had a distinctive pattern of stripes:

- A Flight had three white and two black stripes on each side of the cowl and side cladding.
- B Flight had the white and red stripes on the cowl and side cladding with the striping extended around the upper and lower part of the cowl and running along the top of the fuselage to the rear of the cockpit cladding.
- C Flight had blue and white stripes on the cowl and side cladding with the striping extended around the lower part of the cowl.

Additionally, the pilots had chosen individual markings in their flight colours to decorate the wheel covers.

It seems to be an accepted (but unsupported) story that a day or so later, an officer from Wing stopped by the aerodrome, saw the multicoloured Camels and ordered that the stripes be immediately removed. It is difficult to verify the truth of this story but, "stripe removal order" or not, the Camels retained their striped livery until they were exchanged for Bentley Camels on the 4th February 1918, a period of six weeks. It is also known that at least two replacement Camels received in late December and in January were painted in the new colour scheme.

Not all of the squadron's Camels were striped, FCdr W.M. Alexander returned from Canadian Leave and was given command of C Flight. He chose not to have his machine painted but kept it in standard No.10 Squadron markings. Similarly, the deputy C Flight leader, FLt W.G.R. Hinchliffe retained the standard markings but did go so far as to have the personal marking "ALLO!" painted above the flight letter "C".

As mentioned above, on the 4th February 1918, No.10 Squadron exchanged their Clerget Camels for Naval 9's Bentley Camels. Naval 9 removed the stripes, but not the squadron markings, from the Clerget Camels and used the aircraft for a day or so, before delivering the machines to Dover.

Bentley Camels

a) McKelvey's Camel

This was not the end of the striped Camel story. During a conversation with Stewart Taylor, Murton McKelvey recalled that he had been a particular favourite of SCdr Bell, and had obtained Bell's permission to have his Bentley Camel painted in the striped colour scheme. This testimony is corroborated by an extract from the squadron record book for the night of the 26th/27th February 1918 detailing a night bombing mission undertaken by FSL McKelvey and FLt Hinchliffe:

> *Special Mission (bombing)*
>
> *FLt Hinchliffe on Sop camel* *B7190* *11.55pm* *1.30am*
> *FSL McKelvey on Sop camel* *B6391* *11.55pm* *12.50am*
>
> *These pilots left, carrying four 16lb bombs each, for the purpose of attacking Rumbeke S.W. Aerodrome. Before finding it, they located an aerodrome about E. by S. or E.S.E. from Roulers, near the canal, probably Abeele. FSL McKelvey descended to 400 feet and dropped all his bombs on a line of sheds on the aerodrome. Pilot was held by searchlights for some time and subjected to heavy machine gun fire. FLt Hinchliffe was about a mile distant at this time and clearly observed FSL McKelvey's machine in the searchlights, with the stripes on the cowling and forward part of the fuselage showing up plainly. The effect of the bombs was not observed.*
>
> *FLt Hinchliffe descended to about 200ft over a line of hangars on the aerodrome. He observed his first bomb fall about 50 yards short of the hangars, the next two burst among them and the fourth among some huts about 50 yards beyond the last of the hangars. This pilot was also caught in the searchlights and heavily fired on by machine guns. After dropping his last bomb, pilot turned and fired about 20 rounds into a number of men running about among the huts.*
>
> *The two pilots proceeded to Roulers in company and found no difficulty in keeping in touch with one another, although there were no lights on their machines.*

The official squadron report clearly states that the stripes on the cowling and side panels of McKelvey's Camel could be seen in the illumination from the searchlight. In his logbook Hinchliffe does not mention the stripes but he does emphasise how clearly he could see McKelvey's machine.

FSL McKelvey regularly flew B6391 during February and the first part of March until he went on leave, the machine then being transferred to C Flight where it was flown by FSL Patey until he crashed it on the 23rd March 1918.

b) Coombes' Camel

Further evidence of a striped Bentley Camel comes from the well-known photograph of L.P. Coombes standing in front of a striped C Flight Camel. Coombes arrived at the squadron at the end of January 1918, and was not allocated a Camel until after the Clerget Camels had been exchanged for Bentley machines.

The Camel in the Coombes photograph is clearly not striped in the C Flight livery of blue and white, and the cowl is not striped in the C Flight pattern, but more closely resembles that of A Flight. Although difficult to determine with certainty, the author believes that the photograph depicts a Bentley Camel. The reasoning behind this assumption is twofold:

• The panels that cover the guns appear to extend over the cowling, rather than stopping short of the cowling as on a Clerget machine.

• The engine appears to be a Bentley having a bright shiny appearance. The cylinders of most Clerget engines looked relatively dark in comparison. The cylinders also appear to have hold down bolts.

It is surmised that the "Coombes Camel" is B6391 striped in red and white with its Flight identification letter changed from B to C on the 20th March 1918.

Profile 1
FSL R. Collishaw was allocated a new triplane, N5490, when he arrived at No.10 Squadron and was appointed B Flight Commander. By the end of May 1917 this triplane had been transformed into "Black Maria".

Profile 2
Collishaw's first Triplane named "Black Maria", he claimed ten victories in this machine before taking combat damage and crashing it on the 8th June 1917.

Profile 3
N5487 was FSL W.M. Alexander's "Black Prince". Mel Alexander claimed eight victories in this machine during June and July 1917.

Profile 4
"Black Death" is depicted here as N5466, the Triplane that FSL J.E. Sharman flew for the brief time that he was a member of B Flight. FSL Desmond Fitzgibbon, Sharman's replacement in B Flight, shared a 2-seater destroyed in flames and a scout out of control on the 5th June whilst flying N5466.

Profile 5
FSL E.V. Reid's "Black Roger", Reid claimed twenty victories in this Triplane during June and July 1917 before being shot down and killed by anti-aircraft fire on the 28th July 1917.

Profile 6
N5376, FSL G.E. Nash's "Black Sheep" was manufactured by Clayton & Shuttleworth, easily distinguished from a Sopwith built Triplane by the larger inspection panel on the metal side cladding, and a transparent inspection panel located slightly in front of and below the cockpit. Nash was shot down by Karl Allmenröder of *Jasta* 11 on the 25th June 1917. Nash was wounded and spent the rest of the war in captivity.

Profile 7
N5379 shown in the colours of C Flight. FLt J. Page, the deputy Commander of C Flight claimed an Albatros scout as "out of control" near Lille during the morning of the 7th July 1917.

Profile 8
N6306, "H", was shot down during an engagement with *Jasta* 11 over Zonnebeke on the 24th June 1917. FSL A.B. Holcroft was wounded in the crash, captured and made a prisoner of war.

Profile 9
N5357 suffered from a number of crashes during its time with No.10 Squadron, FSL E. Dickson on the 21st April, FSL A.B. Holcroft on the 12th May, and FSL Q. Shirriff on the 18th June. The triplane was brought down intact behind enemy lines on the 11th July 1917, the pilot, FSL R.L. Kent was captured and made a prisoner of war.

Profile 10
N5358 "Q". FSL R.G. Saunders was shot down and killed between Zonnebeke and Moorslede on the 24th June 1917 whilst flying this triplane.

Profile 11
N6295 "B" was with B Flight during the first two weeks of August 1918, flown by FSL H.S. Broughall. The machine was transferred to C Flight thereafter, and flown by FCdr H.J.T. Saint who claimed a 2-seater and a scout as "out of control" during the last two weeks of August.

Profile 12
N6301 "Dusty II" belonged to No.8 Squadron, but was loaned to No.10 Squadron along with its pilot, FSL R. McDonald, for the opening week of the Battle of Messines. The addition of the experienced McDonald gave SCdr Bell the opportunity to field three Flights during the crucial part of the battle.

Profile 13
Collishaw's last triplane marked as "Black Maria", the twin Vickers gun N533. Collishaw initially suffered numerous gun stoppages, but he persevered, and on the 27th July 1918 he claimed one Albatros scout destroyed, and another out of control.

Profile 14
A top view of N533, showing Collishaw's "C" identification marking repeated on the starboard stabiliser and elevator.

Profile 15
Camel B3882 flown by FSL G.L. Trapp when deputy Commander of A Flight. The deputy Commander was indicated by the forward vertical white stripe being extended over the top of the fuselage decking. Whilst flying B3882 Trapp claimed an Albatros scout crashed to the north of Moorslede on the 28th September 1917.

Profile 16
B Flight Camel B5658 "Cleada" initially flown by FSL J.G. Clark at the end of November 1917.

Profile 17
FLt W.G.R. Hinchliffe's C Flight Camel B6204, named "ALLO!" Many authorities state that this machine was named "ALLO LIL BIRD" but there is no evidence of this from contemporary photographs.

Profile 18
FCdr W.M. Alexander's C Flight Camel B6202 showing the Flight Commander's markings of both vertical white lines continuing over the fuselage decking. This Camel was Alexander's machine at the end of January and beginning of February 1918 when many of the squadron's camels were striped. Despite claims that seem to propagate from one book to another, Mel Alexander was most insistent that he never flew, or even sat in, a striped camel.

Profile 19
B5663 depicted in the black and white striped livery of A Flight. The stripes were carried from December 26th 1917 until the Clerget Camels were exchanged for Bentley camels on the 4th February 1918. FCdr W.A. Curtis flew this machine until the 4th January 1918.

Profile 20
An overhead view of B5663 showing the white outline to the tail assembly. FSL R.A. Blythe was killed in B5663 on the 23rd January 1918 during an engagement with *Jasta* 36.

Profile 21
FLt. W.A. Curtis flew B5663 when he was Flight Commander of A Flight. Photographs show the wing tips to be considerably darker than the rest of the machine, and it is considered that they were most probably painted red.

Profile 22
B3869, the A Flight Camel of FSL S.K.F.P. Humphrey.

Profile 23
B6320, the Camel of the Deputy Flight Commander of A Flight, FSL F.V. Hall.

Profile 24
B6225, this camel was not flown in combat in the striped colour scheme as it was transferred to Dover on the 4th January 1918. FSL K.V. Stratton shared an Albatros scout crashed to the northeast of Dixmude on the 27th October 1917, two months before it received its stripes.

Profile 25
FSL H.L. Nelson's Camel B6289. Nelson shared a 2-seater destroyed in flames to the northeast of Dixmude on the 21st October 1917.

Profile 26
B6299, FCdr N.M. Macgregor's aircraft. The B Flight livery used rather more paint than A Flight and C Flight, with the stripes extending along the top to join up with the squadron marking.

Profile 27
Camel B6499 flown by FLt H.B. Maund, the deputy leader of B Flight. This machine arrived at No.10 Squadron on the 12th January 1918.

Profile 28
B3910 "ENID" flown by FSL W.H. Wilmot.

Profile 29
B5658 in red and white striped B Flight livery. FSL F. Booth was shot down and killed in an engagement with *Jasta* 30 on the 3rd January 1918

Profile 30
B5664 flown by FSL H.J. Emery of C Flight.

Profile 31
N6351 in blue and white striped C Flight colours. FSL A.G. Beattie was shot down and became a prisoner of war on 3rd January 1918.

Profile 32
N6391 was a red striped Bentley camel, flown in B Flight by FSL McKelvey during February and the early part of March 1918. McKelvey was posted on leave and N6391 was transferred to C Flight where FSL Patey crashed it on the 23rd March 1918.

Profile 1

Profile 2

Profile 3

Profile 4

Profile 5

Profile 6

Profile 7

Profile 8

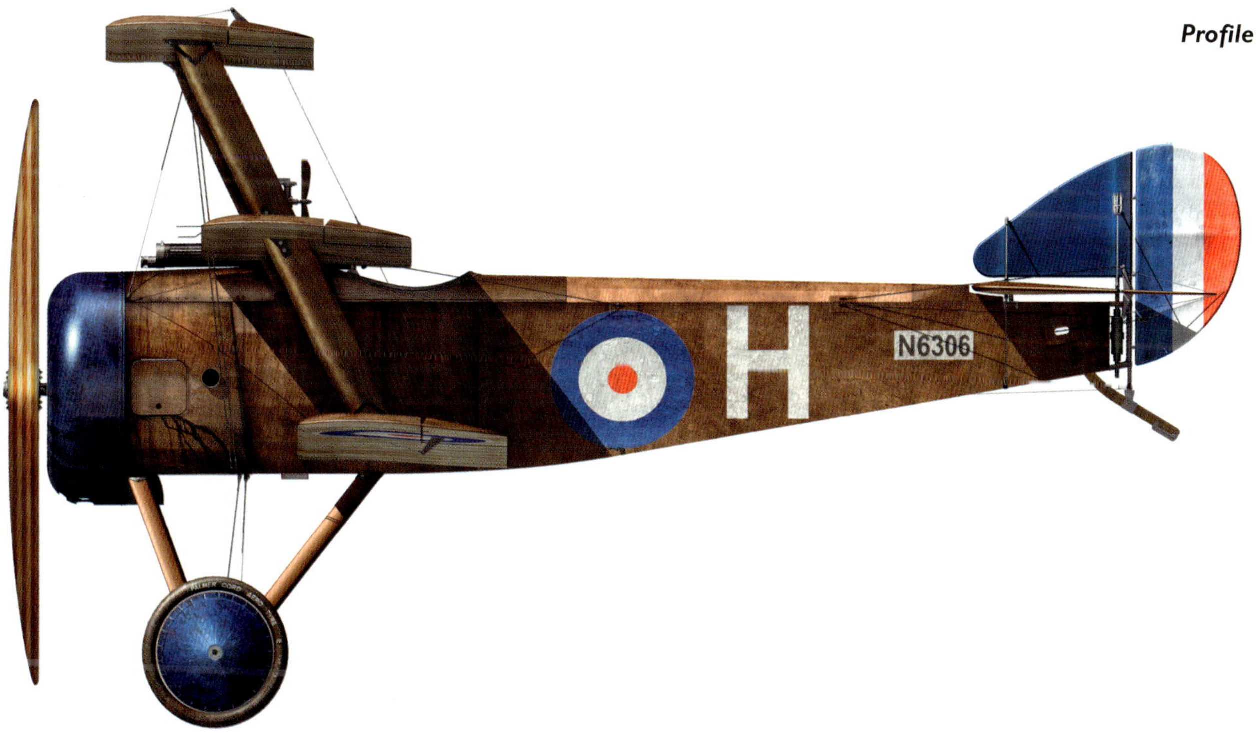

Profile 9

Profile 10

Profile 11

Profile 12

Profile 13

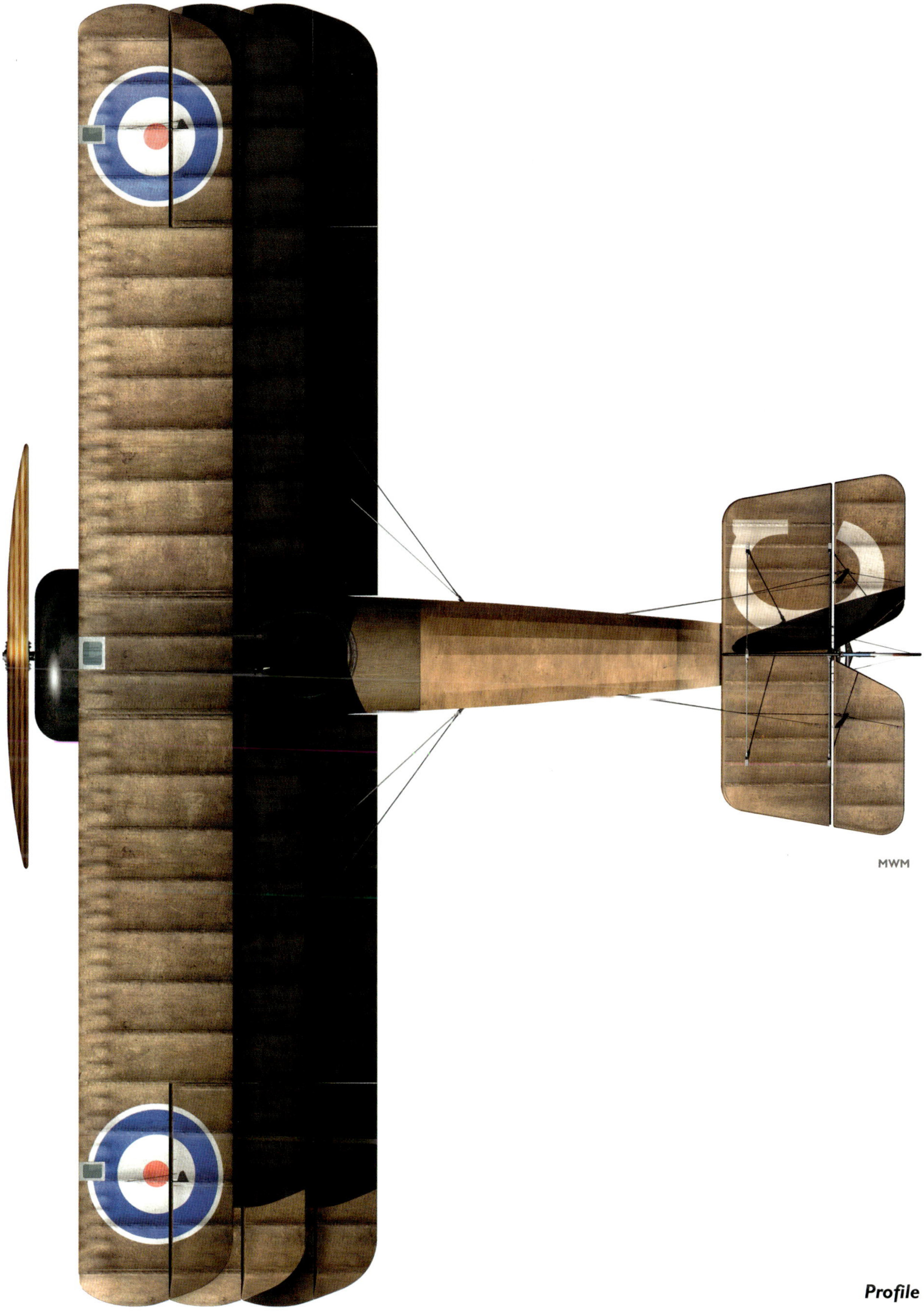

Profile 14

Profile 15

Profile 16

Profile 17

Profile 18

Profile 19

Profile 20

Profile 21

Profile 22

Profile 23

Profile 24

Profile 25

Profile 26

Profile 27

Profile 28

Profile 29

Profile 30

Profile 31

Profile 32

APPENDIX B

ROSTER OF PILOTS

When looking at the careers of many of the following pilots, readers unfamiliar with the Royal Naval Air Service may wonder why these pilots were often posted to No.11 Squadron RNAS or No.12 Squadron RNAS for just a few days. These two squadrons were operational training and holding units where pilots received a final polish and experience on the latest scout machines before being posted to an operational squadron. Both squadrons were occasionally called upon to carry out port defence duties and had limited contact with enemy aircraft.

The author has taken the possibly controversial decision to include details of the pilots' medical history whenever it is in the public domain. There is no intent to sensationalize or shock, the intention is simply to show that these young men who were away from their families, lonely, and under stress, suffered from normal human weaknesses. We should all remember that these were not supermen, but normal young men preparing to go to war, and knowing that many of their number would not return.

Abbott, Edward Dixon, FSL

Born 13th January 1897. From London.

Joined the RNAS on 4th February, 1917

Under instruction at Crystal Palace on 4th February 1917.

Under instruction at Eastchurch from 7th April 1917.

Under instruction at Cranwell from 2nd June 1917.

Dover on 23rd July 1917.

No.12 Squadron from 9th to 12th August 1917.

No.6 Squadron from 13th to 29th August 1917.

No.10 Squadron from 30th August 1917 to 13th September 1917, when shot down near Roulers. Abbot was wounded and became a prisoner of war.

FSL E.D. Abbot claimed 1 victory with No.6 Squadron RNAS.

Alexander, Alfred Mason, FSL

Born 28th March 1898, born at Doncaster, resident in London.

Joined the RNAS on 21st January 1917.

Under instruction at Crystal Palace from 14th January 1917.

Under instruction at Chingford from 17th February 1917.

Under instruction at Cranwell from 16th June 1917.

Dover on 23rd July 1917.

No.12 Squadron from 13th to 17th August 1917.

No.4 Squadron from 18th August 1917 to 21st September 1917.

No.10 Squadron from 22nd September 1917 to 14th January 1918.

RNAS Eastchurch from 15th January 1918.

On RAF unemployed list 15th April 1919.

Air Force Cross gazetted on 2nd November 1918.

Combat record with No.10 Squadron:

15/11/17	C type	West of Dixmude	13.00	OOC*

* shared with FSL H.B. Maund.

W.M. Alexander — Author's collection

Alexander, William Melville, FCdr

Born 8th November 1897 in Toronto, Ontario.

Attended Stinson school, San Antonio, Texas, 6th February to 23rd March 1916 (ACA Certificate No.447).

Joined the RNAS in Ottawa on 23rd March 1916.

Under instruction at Crystal Palace.
Under instruction at Chingford 24th April 1916.
No.3 Wing from 3rd December 1916 to 22nd April 1917.
No.10 Squadron from 26th April 1917 to 31st March 1918 (on Canadian Leave 14th October 1917 to December 1917).
No.210 Squadron RAF from 1st April 1918 to 29th May 1918
Commanded 471 Fighter Flight from 14th June 1918 to 9th November 1918.
On RAF unemployed list on 29th September 1919.
Alexander died on 4th October 1988.
Distinguished Service Cross gazetted 14th September 1917.

Combat record with No.10 Squadron:

2/6/17	C type	St Julien	09.00	OOC*
4/6/17	Albatros scout	NE Ypres	08.50	OOC
6/6/17	Albatros scout	Polygon Wood	11.45	OOC
6/7/17	Albatros scout	Deulemont	11.00	OOC
6/7/17	Albatros scout	Deulemont	11.00	OOC
11/7/17	Albatros scout	Polygon Wood	20.45	OOC
20/7/17	Albatros scout	Menin-Messines	08.05	Destroyed in flames
28/7/17	Albatros scout	Dadizeele	19.50	OOC
16/8/17	Albatros scout	Wervicq	08.50	OOC
20/8/17	Albatros scout	Roubaix	15.30	OOC
21/8/17	Albatros scout	East of Menin	18.30	OOC
23/9/17	Albatros scout	Houthulst	11.25	OOC
23/1/18	Albatros scout	Staden	14.50	OOC
6/3/18	Albatros scout	SE of Dixmude	08.30	OOC
10/3/18	C type	Roulers	15.45	OOC
24/3/18	Albatros scout	Menin-Roulers	09.20	Destroyed

* shared with Collishaw, Reid, & Nash
Captain W.M. Alexander scored a further 5 victories with No.210 Squadron RAF.

Allan, John Alexander McDonald, FSL
Born 26th November 1894. From Canterbury, New Zealand.
Joined RNAS on 25th January 1916.
Under instruction at Portsmouth from 30th January 1916.
Under instruction at Chingford 7th April 1916.
Killingholme from 24th July 1917.
East Fortune 24th September 1916.
Dover on 10th January 1917.
No.8 Squadron from February 1917 to 15th June 1917 when taken ill.
No.12 Squadron from 25th to 27th June 1917.
No.10 Squadron from 28th June 1917 to 12th July 1917, wounded in leg when hit by anti-aircraft shell splinters.
Air department duty with Commander Maguire from 23rd November 1917.
Redcar, ground duties from 3rd December 1917.
Manston War school for re-qualification on scouts on 30th January 1918.
Redcar Instructor's school from 2nd January 1918 to 20th May 1918, when killed in flying accident.

Allan — Courtesy E.F. Cheesman

Arnold, Erik Stennett, FLt
Born 23rd August 1897. From Ealing, London.
Under instruction at Crystal Palace from 18th June 1916.
Under instruction at Eastbourne from 8th July 1917.
Under instruction at Westgate (fast scout training) from 23rd November 1916.
On *Ark Royal* (No.2 Wing) from 14th May 1917.
Invalided with old leg injury whilst in Aegean.
Admitted to Chatham Hospital on 15th November 1917, and subsequently Guys Hospital on 18th February 1918.
No.12 Squadron from 25th to 30th March 1918.
No.10 Squadron on 31st March 1918.
No.210 Squadron RAF from 1st April 1918 to 11th May 1918, struck off when injured in a flying accident.
No.5 Stores Depot from 11th May 1918.
On unemployed list 1st April 1919.

Baird, Alexander, FLt
Born 24th June 1893. From Paisley, Scotland.
Under instruction at RFC Central Flying School from 6th June 1917 to 28th September 1917.
At No.2 Training Squadron (RFC) from 2nd December 1917.
At No.3 Training Squadron (RFC) from 26th February 1918.
No.12 Squadron from 28th to 30th March 1918.
No.10 Squadron on 31st March 1918.
No.210 Squadron RAF from 1st April 1918 to 5th June 1918, when wounded in action.

Barnes, James Parkinson, FSL
Born 18th March 1898. From Llandudno, Wales.
Joined RNAS on 12th November 1916.
Under instruction at Crystal Palace from 12th November 1916.
Under instruction at Vendome from 11th January 1917.
Dover from 15th June 1917.
No.12 Squadron from 25th June1917 to 1st July 1917.
No.10 Squadron from 2nd July 1917 to 17th July 1917, transferred to RNAS HQ, Dunkerque.
Calshot, seaplane instructor, from 30th July 1917.
HMS *Ark Royal* (2 Wing) from 18th October 1917.
Felixstowe from 26th March 1918.

Beattie, Andrew Gordon, FSL
Born 25th March 1898. from Ontario.
Joined the RNAS on 14th March 1917.
Under instruction at Vendome from 12th May 1917.
Under Instruction at Cranwell from 14th July 1917.
Admitted to Chatham Hospital on 16th August 1917 suffering from pharyngitis,
Under instruction at Manston War School from 20th September 1917.
No.12 Squadron from 22nd September 1917 to 13th October 1917.
No.10 Squadron from 14th October 1917 to 3rd January 1918, when forced down near Lille, wounded in foot, and lost control when trying to land. Became Prisoner of War.

Combat record with No.10 Squadron:

12/11/17	C type	Cockelaere	08.00	OOC*

* shared with Trapp.

Bell, Bertram Charles, SCdr
Born 5th April 1893. BC Bell was from Coochin Coochin Station, Boonah, Queensland, Australia.
Before joining the RNAS, Bell was a volunteer ambulance driver at the front for the Australian Hospital.
Joined the RNAS on 2nd May 1915.
Under "ground" instruction at Fishguard from 2nd May 1915.
Under instruction at Chingford from 29th May 1915.
1 Wing from 28th July 1915.
Admitted to Chatham Hospital on 24th February 1916, suffering from Gonorrhoea.
No.3 Squadron from February 1917 to 20th April 1917.
No.10 Squadron from 21st April 1917 to 31st March 1918, with a period of sick leave from 25th September 1917 to 12th December 1917.
No.210 Squadron RAF from 1st April 1918 to 8th January 1919.
DSO gazetted on 21st April 1917.
DSC gazetted on 12th May 1917.
Croix de Guerre avec Palme gazetted on 5th November 1918
B.C. Bell died on the 15th June 1941 in Brisbane.
B.C. Bell claimed 4 victories flying Sopwith Pups whilst with No.3 Squadron RNAS

Bell — Author's collection

Blyth, Ross Allison, FSL
Born 25th October 1892. From Toronto, Ontario.
Joined the RNAS on 20th July 1916.
Under instruction at Crystal Palace from 27th August 1916.
Under instruction at Chingford from 30th September 1916.
Under instruction at Cranwell from 8th January 1917.
Admitted to Boston Fever Hospital, seriously ill, suffering from Cerebral Spinal Meningitis.
Under instruction at Cranwell again from 15th October 1917.
Under instruction at Manston War School from 30th November 1917.
At Dunkerque from 23rd December 1917.
No.12 Squadron from 31st December 1917 to 12th January 1918.
No.10 Squadron from 13th January 1918 to 23rd January 1918, when killed in collision with an enemy machine during a general engagement.

Booth, Frank, FSL
Born 9th April 1899. from Crewe, Cheshire.
Joined the RNAS on 5th May 1917.
Under instruction at Crystal Palace from 6th May 1917.
Under instruction at Vendome from 9th July 1917.
Under Instruction at Cranwell from 8th September 1917.
Under instruction at Manston War school from 3rd November 1917.
At Dunkerque on 8th December 1917.
No.12 Squadron from 9th to 18th December 1917.
No.10 Squadron from 19th December 1917 to 3rd January 1918, when shot down and killed near Lille.

Boyd, Kenneth Gordon, FSL
Born 23rd March 1891. From Goodrich, Ontario.

Joined RNAS on 3rd February 1916.

Under instruction at Fishguard on 27th February 1916.

Under instruction at White City from 17th April 1916.

Under instruction at Redcar from 25th April 1917.

Under instruction at Cranwell from 5th August 1916.

Westgate from 17th October 1916.

Compass course at Slough from 21st January 1917.

Dover on 7th March 1917.

No.10 Squadron from 17th March 1917 to 3rd July 1917.

No.5 Squadron from 4th July 1917 to 12th July 1917, when admitted to Chatham Hospital suffering with Gonorrhoea.

Admitted to Chatham Hospital on 21st August 1918 suffering from Pyrexia.

Court Martialled and severely reprimanded on 10th September 1917 for breaking out of hospital whilst under treatment.

217 Squadron RAF in 1918.

Combat record with No.10 Squadron:

5/6/17	C type	Wervicq	08.50	Destroyed in flames*

* Shared with Collishaw, Reid, Nash, and Fitzgibbon

Bowman, Geoffrey Glendinning, FSL
Born 11th March 1898. From Headingley, Yorkshire.

Joined RNAS on 2nd July 1916.

Under instruction at Crystal Palace from 2nd July 1916.

Under instruction at Chingford from 22nd July 1916.

Under instruction at Cranwell from 19th September 1917.

Dover on 3rd March 1917.

No.10 Squadron from 29th March 1917 to 30th April 1917.

No.1 Squadron from 1st May 1917 to 19th May 1917, when shot down in flames and killed by Oblt Ritter Adolf von Tutschek.

Bowman *Courtesy E.F. Cheesman*

Bramhall, Charles Edgar, FSL
Born 11th October 1896. from New Brighton, Cheshire.

Joined the RNAS on 21st March 1917.

Under instruction at Crystal Palace from 28th February 1917.

Under instruction at Vendome from 14th April 1917.

Under instruction at Cranwell from 12th June 1917.

Dover on 13th August 1917.

No.12 Squadron from 1st to 15th September 1917.

No.9 Squadron from 15th to 28th September 1917.

No.10 Squadron from 29th September 1917 to 30th September 1917, admitted to hospital after receiving head injuries when making a forced landing on his first flight.

Rosyth seaplane depot, ground duties, from 12th April 1918.

Breese, Charles Dempster, SCdr
Born 23rd April 1889. From Clifton, Bristol.

Entered Royal Navy in 1905.

Royal Flying Corps (Naval Wing) in 1913, under instruction at the Central Flying School, Upavon, in October 1913.

Appointed Instructor in Theory and Construction at Central Flying School, Upavon, on 18th December 1913 to April 1916.

Instructor in Theory and Construction at Cranwell Central Depot and Training Establishment from April 1916 to 11th February 1917.

Commanding Officer of No.10 Squadron from 8th February 1917 to 14th April 1917.

Commanding Officer of No.6 Squadron from 14th April 1917 to 28th August 1917.

Central Stores Depot, Wormwood Scrubbs, from September 1917 to January 1918 with rank of Wing Commander.

Deputy Director of Training with the Air Ministry from 1st April 1918 with rank of Lieutenant Colonel.

Commandant of Central Flying School from 7th April 1919.

HQ RAF India from 28th April 1920.

Commanding Officer of Aircraft Depot, India from 9th March 1921.

Commanding Officer of Technical Training section, No.1 SoTT (Apprentices) from 9th January 1925.

Commanding Officer RAF Gosport from 3rd September 1928.

HQ Iraq Command from 11th April 1930.

Supernumerary, RAF Depot from 1st July 1932.

SASO, HQ Inland Area from 15th March 1933.

Breese *Author's collection*

AOC, No.23 Group from 16th April 1934.
AOC, No.23 (Training) Group from 1st March 1936.
AOC, No.17 (Training) Group from 5th March 1937.
AOC, No.18 (Reconnaissance) Group from 27th September 1938
Rose to rank of Air Vice Marshal in RAF, and died in 1941, when an observer in a Coastal Command Lockheed Hudson which crashed on Wick Aerodrome.
Air Force Cross gazetted on 3rd June 1918.

Broughall *Courtesy E.F. Cheesman*

Broughall, Hubert Seaton, FSL
Born 6th October 1897. Born in Toronto, Ontario, his father was the president of the Stirling Bank and the family lived in England until 1910, when they returned to Canada. Broughall was educated at Lakefield, Ontario, and attended one term at Haileybury College in England.
Originally joined Royal Sussex Regiment and awarded the Military Cross.
Relinquished Commission in Royal Sussex Regiment and joined the RNAS on 2nd December 1916.
Under instruction at Crystal Palace from 3rd December 1916.
Under instruction at Vendome from 5th February 1917.
Under instruction at Cranwell from 26th May 1917.
Dover from 23rd July 1917.
No.12 Squadron from 29th July 1917 to 5th August 1917.
No.10 Squadron from 6th August 1917 to 20th September 1917, when shot down to become a prisoner of war.
47 Squadron RAF in April 1919 during allied intervention in Russia.
Military Cross gazetted on 22nd September 1916.
DFC gazetted on 11th June 1924.
216 Squadron from 14th October 1924.
22 Squadron from 8th January 1932.
Reached rank of Group Captain.

Combat record with No.10 Squadron:

6/9/17	Albatros scout	Southeast of Dixmude	08.00	OOC

Burr, Ronald Eric, FSL
Born 22nd May 1899. From Redhill, Surrey.
Joined the RNAS on 1st July 1917.
Under instruction at Crystal Palace from 1st July 1917.
Under instruction at Eastbourne from 7th August 1917.
Under instruction at Cranwell from 29th September 1917.
Under instruction at Manston War School from 4th December 1917.
At Dunkerque on 28th December 1917.
No.12 Squadron from 24th to 28th January 1918.
No.10 Squadron from 29th January 1918 to 18th February 1918, when he was shot down, possibly by *Obltn.* B. Lörzer of *Jasta* 26. Burr was wounded, and subsequently died of his injuries on the 20th February 1918.

Bussell, Edward Irvine, FSL
Born 23rd July 1896. From Toronto, Ontario.
Joined the RNAS on 14th March 1917.
Under instruction at Crystal Palace from 14th March 1917.
Under instruction at Eastchurch from 28th April 1917.
Under instruction at Cranwell from 2nd July 1917.
At Dover on 11th August 1917.
No.12 Squadron from 1st to 6th September 1917.
No.10 Squadron from 7th September 1917 to 6th January 1918.
At Eastchurch from 7th January 1918.
At Redcar from 13th March 1918.
At Eastchurch as an instructor from 24th March 1918.

Combat record with No.10 Squadron:

23/9/17	Albatros scout	Westroosebeke	11.20	OOC

Cameron, Andrew Austin, FSL
Born 6th August 1894. From Shelburne, Ontario.
Joined the RNAS on 19th April 1917.
Under instruction at Manston Flying School from 21st May 1917.
Under instruction at Cranwell from 11th August 1917.
Under instruction at Manston War School from 28th September 1917.
At Dunkerque from 20th October 1917.
No.12 Squadron from 25th to 28th October 1917.
No.10 Squadron from 29th October 1917 to 18th January 1918, seriously injured when spun in after take off, admitted to Queen Alexandria Hospital, Malo with facial injuries and possible fractured skull.
Pronounced fit for observer duties on 23rd May 1918.

Combat record with No.10 Squadron:

5/11/17	Albatros scout	NW Dixmude	13.15	OOC

Carroll, Ralph Edward, FSL

Born 19th January 1898. From Toronto, Ontario.

Joined the RNAS on 10th November 1916.

Under instruction at Crystal Palace from 14th January 1917.

Under instruction at Vendome from 17th February 1917.

Dover on 15th June 1917.

No.12 Squadron from 25th to 28th June 1917.

No.6 Squadron from 28th June 1917 to 28th August 1917.

No.10 Squadron from 30th August 1917 to 23rd November 1917, when injured leaving Dover aerodrome, and transferred to Deal infirmary suffering from concussion and wounds to forehead. Suffered insomnia as a result of his injuries, and entered hospital in Canada in May 1918 for operation to relieve problems associated with his injuries.

Combat record with No.10 Squadron:

14/9/17	Albatros scout	Tenbrielen	16.30	OOC
19/9/17	Albatros scout	East of Hooge	10.00	OOC

R.E. Carroll claimed 1 victory with No.6 Squadron.

Carter Courtesy GSL/JMB Collection

Carter, Alfred Williams, FCdr

Born 29th April 1894, in Fish Creek, Calgary.

Enlisted in 46th Queen's University Battery as a gunner, then applied for flight training in 1915. Was discharged from the army, and took flight instruction in Florida.

Joined Royal Naval Air Service on 23rd May 1916.

No.3 Wing from 15th November 1916 to 7th March 1917.

No.3 Squadron from 7th March 1917 to 2nd July 1917.

No.10 Squadron from 2nd July to 31st March 1918 (Canadian leave from 15th August to 14th January 1918).

No.210 Squadron RAF from 1st April to 11th June.

On staff of No.4 Fighting School at Freiston from 12th June 1918 to end October 1918.

Commanded No.210 Squadron RAF from 1st November 1918 until disbandment.

On RAF unemployment list from 20th May 1919.

Appointed Air Station Superintendent with Canadian Air Board in 1920.

Air Station Superintendent in Ottawa in command of all eastern air units in 1922.

Organised Air Cadet training in Canada in 1939.

Assisted in organising the Air Cadet League of Canada in 1939 and became its first National President in 1940.

Died in Vancouver, 17th December 1986, at the age of 92.

DSC gazetted 28th August 1917.

Appointed MBE on 3rd June 1919.

Appointed OBE on 1st July 1946.

Combat record with No.10 Squadron

17/7/17	Albatros scout	Roulers	20.00	OOC
24/7/17	Albatros scout	Langemarck	12.30	OOC
27/7/17	Albatros scout	W of Tourcoing	19.30	OOC
19/2/18	Albatros scout	S of Zillebeke	11.50	Destroyed in flames*

* Shared with FLt Rosevear of Naval 1

A.W. Carter made the following claims with other squadrons:

No.3 Squadron	5
No.210 Squadron RAF	7

Chisam Courtesy E.F. Cheesman

Chisam, William Hargrove, FSL

Born 15th November 1894 in Carlisle, Cumberland, though resident in Canada.

Joined the RNAS on 4th January 1916.

Under instruction at Killingholme from 3rd January 1916,

Under instruction at Redcar from 15th February 1916.

Under instruction at Cranwell from 5th August 1916.

East Fortune from 25th September 1916.

3 Wing from 11th December 1916.

No.11 Squadron from 7th March 1917.

No.10 Squadron from 3rd April 1917 to 7th April 1917.

No.1 Squadron from 8th April 1917.

Walmer on home defence duties from 21st May 1917 to 5th August 1917.

No.3 Squadron from 6th August 1917 to 26th March 1918, when he was wounded in the hand during combat.

Chisam claimed 7 victories whilst serving with No.3 Squadron.

Clark, John George, FSL

Born 12th October 1897. From Nepean, Ottawa, family moved to Alberta in 1910.

Joined the RNAS on 19th April 1917.

Under instruction at Manston Flying School on 21st May 1917.
Under instruction at Cranwell from 4th August 1917.
Under instruction at Manston War School at 20th September 1917.
At Dunkerque from 8th October 1917.
No.12 Squadron from 9th to 14th October 1917.
No.10 Squadron from 15th October 1917 to 12th December 1917, when shot down east of Dixmude, and became a prisoner of war.

Combat record with No.10 Squadron:

10/12/17	Albatros scout	West of Roulers	11.20	Destroyed in flames*

* Shared with Macgregor

Côle, John Aubrey, FSL
Born 9th April 1892. From Birmingham, Warwick.
Joined the RNAS on 31st December 1916.
Under instruction at Crystal Palace from 31st December 1916.
Under instruction at Redcar from 27th January 1917.
Under instruction at Cranwell from 26th May 1917.
At Dover on 13th July 1917.
No.12 Squadron from 21st to 23rd July 1917.
No.10 Squadron from 24th July 1917 to 27th August 1917, transferred to RNAS HQ Dunkerque.
Admitted to Chatham Hospital on 12th September 1917 with fractured orbit, lacerated face, eyebrows, and jaw, and concussion.
Invalided out of service on 7th March 1918.

Combat record with No.10 Squadron:

16/8/17	Albatros scout	NE Zonnebeke	08.00	OOC

Collins, Ronald Felix, FSL
Born 7th April 1895. From London.
Joined the RNAS on 24th September 1916.
Under Instruction at Crystal Palace from 24th September 1916.
Under instruction at Eastchurch from 2nd October 1916.
Under Instruction at Cranwell from 9th December 1916.
Dover on 14th April 1917.
No.10 Squadron from 18th April 1917 to 28th April 1917, when crashed on landing at Furnes, suffered fracture to base of skull and fractured right leg, subsequently died of his injuries.

Collishaw, Raymond, FCdr
Born 22nd November 1893, in Nanaimo, British Columbia. Served in Canadian Fisheries Protection Service from August 1908 to October 1915.
Joined the RNAS in Ottawa on 27th May 1915.
Under instruction at Redcar from 7th February 1916.
Under instruction at Eastchurch from 16th July 1916.
3 Wing from 2nd August 1916 to 1st February 1917.
No.3 Squadron from 1st February 1917
to 24th March 1917, then on sick leave with face badly frost-bitten.
No.10 Squadron from 25th April 1917 to 3rd August 1917, then on Canadian leave.
Seaplane Defence Squadron from 23rd November 1917 to 6th January 1918.
RNAS Dunkerque from 7th January to 10th February 1918.
No.3 Squadron from 10th February 1918 to 31st March 1918.
203 Squadron RAF from 1st April 1918 to 1st October 1918.
47 Squadron in South Russia in 1919.
Commanded No.201 Group in Western Desert of Egypt and Libya during 1940-41.
Commanded No.14 Group of Fighter Command, Inverness, Scotland.
Retired to Vancouver in 1943 with rank of Air Vice-Marshal.
Raymond Collishaw died in 1976.
Croix de Guerre avec Palme gazetted 5th March 1917.
DSC gazetted on 24th July 1917.
DSO gazetted on 11th August 1917.
Bar to DSO gazetted on 21st September 1918.
DFC gazetted on 3rd August 1918
OBE gazetted on 12th July 1920.

Collishaw — Courtesy E.F. Cheesman

Combat record with No.10 Squadron:

30/4/17	Albatros scout	E Cortemarck	17.30	Destroyed
9/5/17	Albatros scout	E Dixmude	19.55	OOC
1/6/17	Albatros scout	S of Wervicq	09.20	Destroyed in flames
2/6/17	C Type	St. Julien	09.00	OOC*
3/6/17	Albatros scout	Roubaix	19.15	Destroyed in flames
5/6/17	C type	Wervicq	08.50	Destroyed in flames**
5/6/17	C Type	NW Poelcappelle	09.40	OOC***

6/6/17	Albatros scout	Polygon Wood	10.50	Destroyed in flames
6/6/17	Albatros scout	Polygon Wood	11.05	Destroyed in flames
6/6/17	Albatros scout	Polygon Wood	11.10	OOC
7/6/17	Albatros scout	Menin-St. Julien	08.45	OOC
15/6/17	Halberstadt scout	St. Julien-Houthem	10.55	OOC
15/6/17	C type	Menin	17.15	OOC
15/6/17	Albatros scout	Moorslede	17.40	OOC
15/6/17	Albatros scout	Moorslede	17.40	Destroyed
17/6/17	Albatros scout	Roulers	19.10	OOC
24/6/17	Albatros scout	Moorslede	08.10	Destroyed
2/7/17	C type	Poelcappelle station	11.00	Destroyed
6/7/17	Albatros scout	Deulemont	11.00	OOC
11/7/17	Albatros scout	Moorslede	20.40	OOC
12/7/17	Albatros scout	Polygon Wood	07.45	OOC
20/7/17	Albatros scout	Menin-Messines	08.45	OOC
21/7/17	Albatros scout	Passchendaele	20.00	OOC
21/7/17	Albatros scout	Passchendaele	20.00	OOC
27/7/17	Albatros scout	North of Menin	19.45	Destroyed
27/7/17	Albatros scout	Polygon Wood	19.50	OOC

* Shared with Reid, Alexander and Nash
** Shared with Reid, Nash, Boyd, and Fitzgibbon
*** Shared with Fitzgibbon

Raymond Collishaw made the following claims with other squadrons:

No.3 Wing	2
No.3 Squadron	2
Seaplane Defence Squadron	2
203 Squadron RAF	19
47 Squadron RAF	1

Coombes, Lawrence Percival, FSL
Born 9th April 1899 in India. From Streatham, London.
Joined the RNAS on 22nd July 1917.
Training at Crystal Palace, Chingford, and Cranwell.
No.12 Squadron from 12th to 28th January 1918.
No.10 Squadron from 29th January 1918 to 31st March 1918.
No.210 Squadron RAF from 1st April 1918 to 10th August (by which time promoted to Captain).
204TDS at Eastchurch from 10th August to March 1919.
Coombes spent the summer of 1919 barnstorming with Charles Kingsford Smith.
Obtained engineering degree at London University.
Worked at RAE Farnborough.
Worked at MAEE Felixstowe.
Technical Officer to Schnieder Trophy team in 1927.
Returned to RAE in 1930.
Established an Aeronautical Research Laboratory for Australian Government in Melbourne in 1938.
Advisor to United Nations for the establishment of Aeronautical Research Laboratory in India in 1960.
Became Chairman of CAARC, and Chief Supervisor at the Aero Research Laboratory in Australia.
Coombes died in Melbourne on 2nd June 1988.
DFC gazetted on 3rd August 1918

Coombes — Author's collection

Combat record with No.10 Squadron:

24/3/18	Albatros scout	Menin-Roulers	09.20	Destroyed in flames

Coombes went on to score a further 14 victories with No.210 Squadron RAF.

Cox, Alexander Robb, FCdr
Born Hildenborough, Kent, on 16th December 1896. Resident at Taullan, Dolgelley, North Wales.
Joined the RNAS on 16th April 1915.
Under instruction at Hendon from 16th April 1915.
Gained Royal Aero Club Certificate No.1279 on 29th May 1915 at Royal Naval Air Station Chingford.
Under instruction at Hendon from July 1915.
Chingford, staff, from 4th October 1915 to January 1916.
Cranwell Central Depot And Training Establishment from April 1916 to January 1917
No.10 Squadron from 5th February 1917 to 5th May 1917.
No.2 Squadron from May to July 1917.
Cranwell from July 1917 to October 1917.
RAF from 1st April 1918.
Air Force Cross gazetted 1st January 1919.

Cumming, Herbert William MacKarsie, FSL
Born 12th March 1898. From Cambellford Ontario, family moved to Toronto.
Joined the RNAS on 14th March 1917.

Cumming Courtesy S. Taylor

Under instruction at Crystal Palace from 14th March 1917.
Under instruction at Vendome from 28th April 1917.
Under instruction at Cranwell from 3rd July 1917.
Dover on 8th September 1917.
No.12 Squadron from 23rd to 28th September 1917.
No.10 Squadron from 29th September 1917 to 20th October 1917, when crashed on landing and received facial injuries, admitted to Queen Alexandria Hospital, Malo with a fractured nose, then transferred to Chatham hospital until 31st October 1917.
Pronounced fit for service on 12th November 1917.
No.12 Squadron from 15th November 1917 to 22nd November 1917.
No.8 Squadron from 7th December 1917 to 16th February 1918.
No.4 ASD at Wissant on 20th June 1918.
204 Squadron RAF from 22nd June 1918 to 3rd September 1918 when crashed after take off. Died of his injuries on 5th September 1918.
Cumming claimed 2 victories with 204 Squadron.

Curtis, Wilfred Austin, FCdr
Born 21st August 1893, From Havelock, Ontario. Trained at Curtiss school in Toronto 1916.
Joined Royal Naval Air Service at Ottawa on 11th August 1916.
Under instruction at Crystal Palace from 17th September 1916.
Under instruction at Cranwell from 14th October 1916.
No.12 Squadron from 6th June to 25th June 1917.
No.6 Squadron from 25th June to 28th August 1917.
No.10 Squadron from 28th August 1917 to 27th January 1918.
Served in RCAF during World War II, rising to rank of Air Marshal. Became Chief of Air Staff in Canada from 1947 to 1953.
Curtis died on the 7th August 1977.
DSC gazetted on 19th December 1917.
Bar to DSC gazetted on 16th March 1918.

Combat record with No.10 Squadron:

6/9/17	Albatros scout	SE Dixmude	08.00	OOC
27/9/17	Albatros scout	NE Westroosebeke	16.05	OOC
1/10/17	Albatros scout	NE Passchendaele	14.15	OOC
15/10/17	C type	SE Zarren	13.45	OOC
21/10/17	C type	Dixmude	13.30	Destroyed in flames.
21/10/17	Albatros scout	NE Dixmude	13.31	Destroyed
27/10/17	Albatros scout	NE Dixmude	13.20	OOC**
4/11/17	Albatros scout	N Dixmude	15.05	OOC
4/11/17	Albatros scout	N Dixmude	15.05	OOC
15/11/17	Albatros scout	Keyem	12.45	OOC
5/12/17	Albatros scout	Keyem-Leke	15.35	Destroyed***
14/1/17	Albatros scout	E Houthulst Wood	11.35	OOC
23/1/17	C type	Staden	14.50	Destroyed

* Shared with Nelson and Emery
** Shared with Stratton
*** Shared with Hall

Curtis Courtesy E.F. Cheesman

Daly, Rowan Heywood, FSL
Born 30th March, 1898, from Leigh-on-Sea, Essex.
Joined the RNAS on 13th August 1916.
Under instruction at Crystal Palace from 13th August 1916.
Under instruction at Chingford from 18th September 1916.
Under instruction at Cranwell from 2nd April 1917.
Manston War Flight from 24th April 1917.
No.12 Squadron from 11th to 17th July 1917.
No.4 Squadron From 18th July 1917 to 20th September 1917.
No.10 Squadron from 21st September 1918 to 26th September 1918, when he was wounded during combat.
Eastchurch, instructor, from 10th January 1918.
Redcar from 13th March 1918. A comment in Daly's record states "Brilliant scout pilot, but poor instructor – transferred to testing duties".
East Fortune from 27th April 1918.
No.1 Torpedo Training Squadron aboard HMS *Furious* from 30th July 1918.
47 Squadron at end of war in Russia.
RH Daly died in an aerial collision in 1923.
DSC gazetted on 11th August 1917.
DFC gazetted on 12th July 1920.

Combat record with No.10 Squadron:

24/9/17	C type	Houthulst	16.10	OOC
26/9/17	Albatros scout	NE Houthulst	11.00	Destroyed

RH Daly made the following claims with other squadrons:

Manston War Flight	1
47 Squadron (1919)	4

Day Courtesy E.F. Cheesman

Day, Harold, FSL
Born 17th April 1897. From Abergavenny, Wales.
Joined the RNAS on 28th January 1917.
Under instruction at Crystal Palace from 28th January 1917.
Under instruction at Redcar from 2nd March 1917.
Under instruction at Cranwell from 2nd June 1917.
Dover on 12 July 1917.
No.12 Squadron from 23rd to 24th July 1917.
No.10 Squadron from 25th July 1917 to 3rd October 1917. Was taken ill on 12th September 1917 and taken to No.2 CCS.
No.8 Squadron from 3rd October 1917 to 5th February 1918, killed when his Camel was seen to break up during combat near Harnes.
DSC gazetted on 22nd February 1918.

Combat record with No.10 Squadron:

12/8/17	Albatros scout	Wervicq	11.30	Destroyed

Day claimed a further 8 victories with No.8 Squadron.

d'Etchegoyen, Bryant Adalbert Paul Louis, FSL
Born 18th July 1896. From Mayenne, France.
Joined the RNAS in September 1917.
Under instruction at Greenwich from 30th September 1917.
Under instruction at Vendome from 14th October 1917.
Under instruction at Cranwell from 16th December 1917.
Under instruction an Manston War School from 1st February 1918.
Dunkerque on 23rd February 1918.
No.12 Squadron from 25th February to 4th March 1918.
No.10 Squadron from 5th March 1918 to 31st March 1918.
No.210 Squadron RAF from 1st April 1918 to 11th May 1918. Seriously injured when making a forced landing in mist, died of his injuries on 13th May 1917.

De Wilde, John Sylvan, FSL
Born 17th August 1898. From Hammersmith, London.
Joined the RNAS on 29th October 1916.
Under instruction at Crystal Palace from 29th October 1916.
Under instruction at Redcar from 16th December 1916.
Under instruction at Cranwell from 10th February 1917.
Manston War school from 22nd April 1917.
Dover on 16th August 1917.
No.11 Squadron
No.10 Squadron from 21st September 1917 to 27th September 1917, when shot down and killed.

Dickson Courtesy E.F. Cheesman

Dickson, Euan, FSL
Born 31st March 1892, in Sheffield. Emigrated to New Zealand in 1912. Returned in 1914.
Joined RNAS on 30th July1916.
Under instruction at Crystal Palace from 30th July 1916.
Under instruction at Cranwell from 14th October 1916.
Gained RAC certificate 3966 on 12th December 1916.
Dover on 3rd March 1917.
No.10 Squadron from 31st March 1917 to 29th April 1917 having been "washed out" by SCdr Bell.
No.5 Squadron from 29th April to 31st March 1918.
205 Squadron from 1st April 1918 to end May 1918.
Returned to New Zealand after the war.
First person to fly across Cook Strait on 25th August 1920.
Died at Auckland on 10th March, 1980.
DSC gazetted on 19th December 1917.
Bar to DSC gazetted on 26th April 1918.
DFC gazetted on 21st September 1918.
Dickson was "washed out" on scouts after a series of unfortunate accidents, but proved to be one of the two most successful bomber pilots of World War I with a total of 14 victories.

Dissette, Arthur Clark, FSL
Born 15th August 1886. From Toronto, Ontario.
Joined the RNAS on 3rd February 1916.

Dissette Courtesy S. Taylor

Under ground instruction at Fishguard from 27th February 1916.
Under instruction at White City from 17th April 1916.
Under instruction at Eastbourne from 25th April 1916.
Under instruction at Cranwell from 15th June 1916.
3 Wing from 4th September 1916.
Dunkerque from 23rd April 1917.
No.10 Squadron from 5th May 1917 to 2nd June 1917, when shot down and killed over Coxyd.

Combat record with No.10 Squadron:

1/6/17	C type	Southeast of Ypres	07.15	Destroyed*

* Shared with Page.

Drummond, Charles Barclay de Tothie, FSL
Born 19th July 1896. From Montreal, Quebec.
Joined RNAS on 12th January 1916.
Under instruction at Redcar from 12th January 1916.
Under instruction at Cranwell from 25th September 1916.
Under instruction at Freiston (gunnery course) from 5th February 1917.
3 Wing from 12th February 1917 to 26th April 1917.
No.9 Squadron from 28th April 1917 to 4th May 1917 (did not fly with squadron).
No.8 Squadron from 5th May to 24th May 1917.
No.12 Squadron from 22nd to 24th June.
No.10 Squadron from 25th June 1917 to 5th July 1917 when taken sick, suffering from chronic swelling of the knee joint.
Declared unfit for flying duties but fit for ground duties on 20th November 1917.
Compass Observer's course at Slough from 3rd December 1917.
Additional training at Dover from 17th December 1917 to 11th February 1918.
No.5 Squadron from 11th February 1918 to 31st March 1918, assigned to ground duties.
205 Squadron RAF from 1st April 1918 to 6th May 1918, assigned to ground duties.
Declared permanently unfit to fly on 9th July 1918, and sent back to Canada.

Ellis Author's collection

Ellis, Oliver Bernard, FSL
Born 20th June 1898 at Leicester, Leics.
Ellis attended Sidcot School in Somerset, Bootham School at York, and was admitted to St. John's College, Cambridge in May 1916, but before going into residence, he joined the Royal Naval Air Service on 16th July 1916.
Under instruction at Crystal Palace from 16th July 1916.
Under instruction at Redcar from 5th August 1916.
Under instruction at Cranwell from 4th November 1916.
No.10 Squadron from 15th March to 27th April 1917.
No.1 Squadron from 27th April to 19th May 1917, when shot down in flames and killed to the east of Arleux. It is believed that he either fell or jumped from his aircraft during its descent.
Ellis claimed 2 victories with No.1 Squadron.

Emery, Herbert James, FSL
Born 18th September 1894. From Edmonton, Alberta.
Joined the RNAS on 8th March 1917.
Under instruction at Crystal Palace from 13th March 1917.
Under instruction at Eastchurch from 21st April 1917.
Under instruction at Cranwell from 16th June 1917.
No.12 Squadron from 12th to 14th August 1917.
No.10 Squadron from 15th August 1917 to 17th January 1918.
Eastchurch from 18th January 1918.
Instructing at No.29 Training Squadron from 19th July 1918.

Combat record with No.10 Squadron:

21/10/17	C type	Dixmude	13.30	Destroyed in flames*

* Shared with Curtis and Nelson

Eppstein, Maurice William Wallace, FSL
Born 8th November 1896. From Romford, Essex.
Joined the RNAS on 10th September 1916.
Under instruction at Crystal Palace from 10th September 1916.
Under instruction at Chingford from 14th October 1916.
Under instruction at Cranwell from 5th March 1917.
Dover from 7th April 1917.
No.10 Squadron from 20th April 1917 to 12th May 1917, when shot down into the sea and killed by anti-aircraft fire. His seat, marked with his name, part of a propeller, and a glove were picked up by the French destroyer Ariflamme.

Combat record with No.10 Squadron:

5/5/17	Halberstadt scout	Zarren	18.05	Destroyed in flames

Fitzgibbon *Courtesy E.F. Cheesman*

Fitzgibbon, Desmond Fitzgerald, FLt
Born 1st November 1890. From Hampstead, London.
Joined the Royal Naval Air Service on 28th May 1916.
Under instruction at Crystal Palace from 15th June 1916.
Under instruction at Cranwell from 15th June 1916.
Under instruction at Vendome from 20th October 1916.
3(W) from 15th February 1917 to 23rd April 1917.
No.10 Squadron from 5th May 1917 to 15th October 1917. Leader of B Flight from 9th September 1917.
RNAS Cranwell, instructor, from 16th October 1917.
DSC gazetted on 2nd November 1917.

Combat record with No.10 Squadron:

5/6/17	C type	Wervicq	08.50	Destroyed in flames *
5/6/17	C type	NW Poelcappelle	09.00	OOC**
15/6/17	Halberstadt scout	St. Julien	10.55	OOC
15/6/17	Albatros scout	Moorslede	17.40	OOC
25/8/17	Albatros scout	N Polygon Wood	19.30	OOC
14/9/17	Albatros scout	Tenbrielen	16.30	OOC
26/9/17	Albatros scout	Westroosebeke	11.00	OOC
27/9/17	Albatros scout	NE Westroosebeke	16.10	OOC

* shared with Collishaw, Reid, Boyd, and Nash
** shared with Collishaw

Foster, Edgar, FSL
Born 13th November 1898. From Moseley, Birmingham.
Joined the RNAS on 11th March 1917.
Under instruction at Crystal Palace from 11th March 1917.
Under instruction at Vendome from 14th April 1917.
Under instruction at Cranwell from 19th June 1917.
Dover on 23rd August 1917
No.12 Squadron from 8th to 18th September 1917.
No.10 Squadron from 19th September 1917 to 24th September 1917, when shot down and made a prisoner of war.

Fox, William Norman, FSL
Born 15th July, 1898. From Toronto, Ontario.
Joined the RNAS in Ottawa on 14th March 1917.
Under instruction at Chingford from 19th May 1917.
Under instruction at Cranwell from 21st July 1917.
At Dover on 8th September 1917.
No.12 Squadron from 23rd to 28th September 1917.
No.10 Squadron from 29th September 1917 to 21st October 1917, when he was wounded in leg and admitted to Malo Hospital.
Still under treatment in April 1918.

Glasgow, Theodore Linscott, FSL
Born 25th May 1898. From Montreal, Quebec.
Joined RNAS on 2nd September 1916.
Under instruction at Crystal Palace from 14th January 1917.
Under instruction at Vendome from 17th February 1917.
Under instruction at Cranwell from 28th April 1917.
Dover on 22nd June 1917.
No.12 Squadron from 4th to 5th July 1917.
No.10 Squadron from 6th July 1917 to 19th August 1917, killed when crashed east of Proven.

Glasgow *Courtesy S. Taylor*

Glen, James Alpheus, FSL
Born 23/6/1890. From Turtle Mountain, Manitoba.
Joined the RNAS in Ottawa on 16th December 1915.
Under instruction at Chingford from 10th January 1916.
Under instruction at Central Flying School from 24th January 1916.
Under instruction at Eastchurch from 10th April 1916.
3 Wing from 20th April 1916 to 31st January 1917.
1 Wing from 1st February 1917 to 2nd April 1917.
No.3 Squadron from 2nd April 1917 to 24th April 1917
No.10 Squadron from 25th April 1917 to 29th April 1917.
No.3 Squadron from 30th April 1917 to 31st March 1918.
203 Squadron RAF from 1st April 1918 to 16th May 1918. Wounded in action on 18th April 1918.
253 Squadron RAF from 16th May 1918 to 2nd September 1918.
Attended staff College Course at Andover in 1923.
Retired from the RAF on 12th March 1938.
Seconded for duty with Canadian Air Board on 15th July 1920.

Glen Courtesy E.F. Cheesman

Glen died in England on the 7th March 1962.
DSC gazetted on 26th April 1918.
Bar to DSC gazetted on 7th June 1918.
Croix de Guerre avec Palme gazetted on 23rd August 1918.
Glen claimed 15 victories with No.3 Squadron/203 Squadron.

Grace, Edmond Victor Joseph, FSL
Born 13th April 1896. From Montreal, Quebec.
Joined the RNAS on 19th January 1917.
Under instruction at Crystal Palace from 18th February 1917.
Under instruction at Vendome from 31st March 1917.
Under instruction at Cranwell from 28th April 1917.
Dover on 15th August 1917.
No.12 Squadron from 23rd August 1917 to 3rd September 1917.
No.10 Squadron from 4th September 1917 to 19th September 1917, when shot down in flames and killed.

Gregory, Edmund Neil, FSL
Born 13th June 1898. From Lindsay, Ontario.
Joined the RNAS on 19th April 1917.
Under instruction at Manston Flying School from 21st May 1917.
Under instruction at Cranwell from 8th September 1917.
Under instruction at Manston War School from 3rd November 1917.
Dunkerque from 15th December 1917.
No.12 Squadron from 17th December 1917 to 4th January 1918.
No.10 Squadron from 5th January 1918 to 28th January 1918, left for medical survey.
Surveyed on 29th January 1918, and posted to Redcar.

Hall, Frederick Vincent, FSL
Born 20th March 1898. From Muswell Hill, London, educated at Eastbourne College and Highgate school.
Joined the RNAS on 2nd July 1916.
Under instruction at Crystal Palace from 2nd July 1916.
Under instruction at Chingford from 22nd July 1916.
Under instruction at Cranwell from 5th March 1917.
Dover on 17th April 1917.
No.4 Squadron from 26th April 1917 to 4th May 1917.
No.8 Squadron from 5th May 1917 to 23rd May, when wounded in combat.
Re-qualified on Camels at Manston on 20th September 1917.
No.12 Squadron from 9th October 1917 to 20th October 1917.
No.10 Squadron from 21st October 1917 to 31st March 1918.
No.210 Squadron RAF from 1st April 1918 to 15th May 1918, when Hall was killed in a collision with another 210 Squadron Camel.

F.V. Hall Courtesy E.F. Cheesman

Combat record with No.10 Squadron:

15/11/17	Albatros scout	NNE Dixmude	13.00	OOC
5/12/17	Albatros scout	Keyem-Leke	15.35	Destroyed*
18/2/18	Albatros scout	South of Menin	09.50	Destroyed

* Shared with Curtis.

F.V. Hall made the following claims with other squadrons:

No.4 Squadron	1
No.210 Squadron RAF	3

Hall, Norman Douglas, FSL
Born 26th March 1897. From Nelson, British Columbia.
Joined RNAS at Ottawa on 26th August 1916.
Under instruction at Crystal Palace from 24th September 1916.
Under instruction at Eastchurch 2nd October 1916.
Under instruction at Cranwell from 18th November 1916.
3 Wing from 13th February 1917 to 8th March 1917, (sick, suffering from tonsillitis from 25th April 1917 to 29th April 1917).
No.11 Squadron from 19th May to 23rd July 1917, Awarded medal by Dunkerque town council for bringing down enemy aircraft.
No.10 Squadron from 24th July 1917 to 26th July 1917, refused to fly triplanes.
No.11 Squadron from 27th July 1917 to 28th August 1917.
No.3 Squadron from 1st September to 3rd September 1917, when failed to return from his first patrol with the squadron and taken prisoner of war.
Hall claimed one victory with No.11 Squadron

Hamilton-Bowyer, Stanley Arthur, FSL
Born 28th August 1895. From London.
Joined the RNAS on 1st October 1916.
Under instruction at Crystal Palace from 1st October 1916.

Under Instruction at Chingford from 11th November 1916.
Under instruction at Cranwell from 11th April 1917.
Under instruction at Freiston from 11th July 1917.
Dover from 23rd July 1917 to 13th August 1917.
No.12 Squadron from 14th August to 22nd August 1917.
No.6 Squadron from 22nd to 29th August 1917.
No.10 Squadron from 30th August 1917 to 29th November 1917, transferred to Cranwell whilst on leave.
Cranwell from 15th December 1917 to 27th December 1917.
Manston War Flight from 30th December 1917 to 31st March 1918.

Combat record with No.10 Squadron:

27/9/17	Albatros scout	NE Westroosebeke	16.10	OOC

Hinchliffe Author's collection

Hinchliffe, Walter George Raymond, FLt

Born on 10th June 1894 in Liverpool. Early childhood spent in Germany.

Served with Territorial army, attached to the West Lancashire Divisional Supply and Transport Column, based at Southport. In 1915, he was forced to resign his commission, or face a court martial related to three charges of theft.

Joined the RNAS on 3rd April 1916. RAC Certificate number 3595.
Under instruction at White City from 10th April 1916.
Under instruction at Redcar from 20th May 1916.
Under instruction at Cranwell from 23rd September 1916.
Failed his graduation exams on 21st December 1916, but passed at second attempt.
Cranwell, assistant instructor from 20th January 1917.
Dunkerque from 1st January 1918.
No.12 Squadron from 23rd to 28th January 1918.
No.10 Squadron from 29th January 1918 to 31st March 1918.

No.210 Squadron RAF from 1st April to 3rd June, when he suffered facial injuries in a crash when trying to recover a Camel that had made a forced landing in a field. He lost his left eye in the incident.

Continued to instruct at Cranwell until forced to resign his commission under threat of court martial in 1919.

Became chief pilot with KLM, and later worked for Daimler Airways and Imperial Airways.

On 13th March 1928 attempted to cross the Atlantic from east to west with Elsie Mackay, the daughter of Lord Inchcape. The pair lost their lives in the attempt.

Hinchliffe's second wife, Emile became very interested in spiritualism, and the dead Hinchliffe became the subject of two "fringe" books involving psychic phenomena, *The Airman Who Would Not Die*, and *The Return Of Captain WGR Hinchliffe*.

Combat record with No.10 Squadron:

3/2/18	Albatros scout	Southwest Rumbeke	15.15	Destroyed
10/3/18	C type	Roulers	15.45	OOC

Hinchliffe claimed a further 4 victories with No.210 Squadron RAF.

Holcroft, Alan Boycott, FSL

Born 13th March 1898. From Hadley Wood, Middlesex.
Joined RNAS on 16th July 1916.
Under instruction at Crystal Palace from 16th July 1916.
Under instruction at Eastchurch from 5th August 1916.
Under instruction at Cranwell from 18th November 1916.
Dover on 16th April 1917.
No.10 Squadron from 27th April 1917 to 24th June 1917, when shot down over Zonnebeke. Holcroft was wounded and became a prisoner of war.

Hollick, John, FSL

Born 23rd January 1899. From Upminster, Essex.
Joined the RNAS on 28th July 1917.
Under instruction at Crystal Palace from 29th July 1917.
Under instruction at Vendome from 4th September 1917.
Under instruction at Cranwell from 29th October 1917.
Under instruction at Manston War School from 14th January 1918.
Dunkerque on 2nd February 1918.
No.12 Squadron from 3rd to 18th February 1918.
No.10 Squadron from 19th February 1918 to 31st March 1918.
No.210 Squadron RAF from 1st April 1918 to 18th May 1918, when shot down and killed.

Holman, Harold Spurway, FSL

Born 7th May 1898. From Westbury, Gloucs.
Joined RNAS on 26th November 1916.
Under instruction at Crystal Palace from 26th November 1916.

Under instruction at Eastchurch from 11th January 1917.
Admitted to Chatham Hospital on 8th February, suffering from Rubella.
Under instruction at Cranwell from 21st April 1917.
Dover from 11th June 1917.
No.12 Squadron from 18th to 24th June 1917.
No.10 Squadron from 25th June 1917 to 29th June 1917. Fainted, assessed as only fit to fly at low altitudes.
Air Department service from 10th September 1917, with Commander Sampson.
Yarmouth from 17th January 1918 (ground duties).
Yarmouth from 4th March 1918 (flying duties).

Holmes, Thomas, FSL
Born 10th August 1895. From Toronto, Ontario.
Joined RNAS on 20th December 1916.
No.12 Squadron from 6th to 12th July 1917.
No.10 Squadron from 13th July 1917 to 26th July 1917, when having been "washed out" on scouts, was transferred to RNAS HQ.
Under instruction on seaplane course at Calshot from 8th August 1917 to 3rd October 1917. Judged to be a capable seaplane pilot, but refused to fly seaplanes.
Appointment terminated on 9th January 1918, and was returned to Canada where he burnt his uniform.

Humphrey, Sydney Knight-Forbes Phillip, FSL
Born 27th August 1898. From Clapham Common, London.
Joined the RNAS on 14th February, 1917.
Under instruction at Crystal Palace from 11th March 1917.
Under instruction at Vendome from 14th April 1917.
Under instruction at Cranwell from 19th June 1917.
Dover on 31st August 1917.
No.12 Squadron from 16 September 1917 to 24th October 1917.
No.10 Squadron from 25th October 1917 to 18th February 1918, was hospitalised with Scabies on 26th January 1918.
At Manston to re-qualify on scouts from 10th May 1918.

Johnston Courtesy S. Taylor

Johnston, William Clarence, FSL
Born 9th November 1893. From Ontario.
Joined the RNAS on 7th November 1916.
Under instruction at Crystal Palace from 17th December 1916.
Under instruction at Eastchurch from 20th January 1917.
Admitted to Chatham hospital on 3rd March 1917 suffering from Measles.
Under instruction at Cranwell from 6th April 1917.
Dover on 22nd June 1917.
No.11 Squadron to 27th August 1917.
No.10 Squadron from 1st September 1917 to 23rd September 1917, when wounded in leg during combat, and subsequently crashed at Vlamertinghe.

Combat record with No.10 Squadron:

14/9/17	Albatros scout	Ten-Brielen	16.30	OOC

Jones, Albert Leslie, FSL
Born 19th December 1897. from Olton, Warwickshire.
Joined the RNAS on 9th March 1916.
Under instruction at Crystal Palace from 15th July 1917.
Under instruction at Chingford from 28th July 1917.
Under instruction at Cranwell from 29th September 1917.
Under instruction at Manston War School from 15th December 1917.
Dunkerque on 11th January 1917.
No.12 Squadron from 12th to 28th January 1918.
No.10 Squadron from 29th January 1918 to 31st March 1918.
No.210 Squadron RAF from 1st April 1918 to 13th August 1918, left for Home Establishment.
Jones claimed 7 victories with No.210 Squadron RAF.

Joseph, Solomon Clifford, FSL
Born 29th April 1893. From Edgbaston, Birmingham.
Joined the RNAS on 12th August 1917.
Under instruction at Crystal Palace on 12th August 1917.
Under instruction at Vendome from 15th September 1917.
Under instruction at Cranwell from 29th October 1917.
Under instruction at Manston War School from 29th January 1918.
Dunkerque on 16th February 1918.
No.12 Squadron from 25th to 27th February.
No.10 Squadron from 28th February 1918 to 31st March 1918.
No.210 Squadron RAF from 1st April 1918 to 28th November 1918.

DFC gazetted on 21st September 1918.
Bar to DFC gazetted on 2nd November 1918.
Joseph claimed 13 victories with No.210 Squadron RAF.

Keens, John Harvey, FSL
Born 14th December 1896. From Toronto, Ontario.
Joined the RNAS on 1st December 1915.
Under instruction at Hendon from 20th December 1915.
Under instruction at Chingford from 27th December 1915.
3 Wing from 24th June 1915 to 30th April 1917.
No.10 Squadron from 6th May 1917 to 7th June 1917, when shot in chest during combat, was able to return and land safely.
Acceptance Park at Dover from 4th December 1917 to 14th January 1918, performing ground duties.
Manston War School Staff, from 14th January 1918 to 14th April 1918.
RNAS Redcar from 15th April 1918.
No. 29 Training Depot Station at Beaulieu from 19th July 1918.
On unemployed list on 11th February 1919.
Regional RCAF from 10th September 1939.
Commanded No.5 Manning Depot from 1st May 1941 to 11th November 1941.
Technical Training School, St. Thomas, and promoted to Wing Commander on being given command.
Died on 22nd August 1948.

Combat record with No.10 Squadron:

6/6/17	Albatros scout	West of Polygon Wood	11.10	OOC

Kent, Raymond Leslie, FSL
Born 29th April 1898. From Highbury, London.
Joined RNAS on 10th December 1916.
Under instruction at Crystal Palace from 10th December 1916.
Under instruction at Vendome from 20th January 1917.
Under instruction at Cranwell from 28th March 1917.
Dover on 28th May 1917.
No.11 Squadron from 5th to 12 June 1917.
No.12 Squadron from 12th to 15th June 1917.
No.10 Squadron from 16th June 1917 to 11th July 1917, when brought down at Wervicq. Kent became a prisoner of war.

Knott, Edward Middleton, FSL
Born 24th April 1899. From Sutton Coldfield, Warwickshire.
Joined the RNAS on 10th March 1917.
Under instruction at Crystal Palace from 18th March 1917.
Under instruction at Chingford from 28th April 1917.
Under instruction at Cranwell from 23rd June 1917.
Dover on 15th August 1917.
No.12 Squadron from 23rd August 1917 to 1st September 1917.
No.10 Squadron from 2nd September 1917, to 3rd September 1917.
No.9 Squadron from 3rd September 1917.
Aircraft Depot Dunkerque, ferry pilot, from 28th December 1917.
Depot ferry pilot, from 1st April 1918.
FSL E.M. Knott claimed 4 victories with No.9 Squadron RNAS.

Lawson, Harold, FSL
Born 15th April 1897. From Gosforth, Northumberland.
Joined the RNAS on 11th June 1916.
Under instruction at Crystal Palace from 11th June 1916.
Under instruction at Eastbourne from 1st July 1916.
Under instruction at Cranwell from 1st September 1916.
Dover on 22nd January 1917.
No.6 Squadron to 30th August 1917.
No.10 Squadron from 30th August 1917 to 19th September 1917, transferred to 1 Wing.
RNAS Cranwell, Instructor, from 26th November 1917.
RNAS Chingford, Instructor, from 16th December 1917, No. 207 Training Depot Station after 1st April 1918.
On RAF unemployed list 23rd January 1919.

Lewis, Alfred Douglas Murray, FSL
Born 8th January 1899. From Chiswick, London.
Joined the RNAS on 21st January 1917.
Under instruction at Crystal Palace from 21st January 1917.
Under instruction at Redcar from 17th February 1917.
Under instruction at Cranwell from 26th May 1917.
Dover on 12th July 1917.

Lawson *Courtesy E.F. Cheesman*

No.12 Squadron from 9th to 19th August 1917.

No.10 Squadron from 20th August 1917 to 25th August 1917, when shot down, and made a prisoner of war.

Lloyd, Seisyllt Hugh, FSL

Born 3rd June 1898. From Southport, Lancashire, though believed to be of Welsh origin.

Joined the RNAS on 4th February 1917.

Under instruction at Crystal Palace from 4th February 1917.

Under instruction at Chingford from 10th March 1917.

Under instruction at Cranwell from 9th June 1917.

Dover on 23rd July 1917.

No.12 Squadron from 29th July 1917 to 5th August 1917.

No.10 Squadron from 6th August 1917 to 14th August 1917, when shot down and killed at Langemarck.

Lowther, Cecil, FSL

Born 27th January 1897. From Clifton, Bristol.

Joined RNAS on 3rd December 1916.

Under instruction at Crystal Palace from 3rd December 1916.

Under instruction at Vendome from 20th January 1917.

Under instruction at Cranwell from 21st April 1917.

Dover on 15th June 1917.

No.12 Squadron from 1st to 3rd July 1917.

No.10 Squadron from 4th July 1917 to 21st August 1917, when shot down and killed west of Menin.

Combat record with No.10 Squadron:

17/7/17	Albatros scout	SE Polygon Wood	06.45	OOC

MacDonald   Courtesy E.F. Cheesman

MacDonald, Alexander Forsythe, FSL

Born 16th January 1897. From London, Ontario.

Joined the RNAS on 5th September 1916.

Under instruction at Crystal Palace from 29th October 1916.

Under instruction at Chingford from 2nd December 1916.

Under instruction at Cranwell from 21st April 1917.

Dover on 28th May 1917.

No.9 Squadron from June 1917 to 29th July 1917.

Sent to England for treatment to perforated eardrum on 30th July 1917.

No.12 Squadron from 15th to 16th September 1917.

No.10 Squadron from 17th September 1917 to 25th September 1917, received gunshot wound in left buttock, lost partial function in left leg, and crashed to the south of Ypres.

Officially reprimanded for complaining about his hospital treatment.

Canadian leave from February 1918 to May 1918.

No.205 Training Depot Station as an instructor from June 1918.

MacDonald claimed 1 victory with No.9 Squadron

Macgregor   Courtesy E.F. Cheesman

Macgregor, Norman Miers, FCdr

Born 29th May 1896. From London.

Joined the RNAS on 14th February 1916.

Under instruction at Fishguard from 27th February 1916.

Under instruction at White City from 17th April 1916.

Under instruction at Chingford from 25th April 1916.

Under instruction at Eastchurch from 8th July 1916.

3 Wing from 1st August 1916.

No.6 Squadron to 29th August 1917.

No.10 Squadron from 30th August 1917 to 28th January 1918.

Eastchurch from 28th January 1918 for disposal.

Eastchurch, instructor, from 27th April 1918.

DSC gazetted on 2nd February 1918.

Combat record with No.10 Squadron:

15/9/17	Fokker DR1	Moorslede	16.50	Destroyed*
10/12/17	Albatros scout	Oostnieuwkerke	11.20	Destroyed in flames **
12/12/17	Albatros scout	East of Dixmude	15.40	OOC

* *Oblt.* Kurt Wolff of *Jasta* 11

** Shared with J.G. Clark

MacGregor also claimed 4 victories with No.6 Squadron.

Manuel, John Gerald, FLt

Born 29th March 1893. From Winnipeg.

Joined Canadian Field Artillery in 1915, to France in June 1916, and wounded on 5th October 1916.

Transferred to the Royal Naval Air Service on 7th March 1917.

Under instruction at Crystal Palace 4th March 1917.
Under instruction at Eastchurch from 7th April 1917,
Under instruction at Cranwell from 9th June 1917.
Under instruction at Freiston from 12th July 1917.
Dover on 23rd July 1917.
No.12 Squadron from 9th August 1917 to 12th August 1917.
No.10 Squadron from 12th August 1917 to 31st March 1918. Admitted to No.50 Casualty Clearing Station on 20th September 1917 with Scabies.
No.210 Squadron RAF from 1st April 1918 to 10th June 1918. Admitted to St. Omer Hospital on 10th May 1918 with fractured thumb following accident with a Very pistol. Died on 10th June 1918 after an aerial collision with Lt FC Dodd.
DSC gazetted on 19th December 1917.

Combat record with No.10 Squadron:

21/8/17	Albatros scout	East of Menin	18.30	Destroyed
21/8/17	Albatros scout	East of Menin	18.35	OOC
20/9/17	C type	Houthulst Forest	11.15	Destroyed
15/11/17	Albatros scout	Keyem	12.45	Destroyed
18/2/18	Albatros scout	South of Menin	09.50	Destroyed
19/2/18	Albatros scout	Northeast of Roulers	13.30	OOC
10/3/18	Albatros scout	Southeast of Dixmude	16.00	Destroyed

Manuel claimed another 6 victories whilst with No.210 Squadron RAF.

Manuel Courtesy E.F. Cheesman

Maund, Hugh Bingham, FSL

Born 30th May 1896. From Hampstead, London.
Served in 8th Battalion, Canadian Expeditionary Force, with rank of Lieutenant.
Joined the RNAS on 6th November 1916.
Under instruction at Crystal Palace from 10th December 1916.
Under instruction at Eastchurch from 27th January 1917.
Admitted to Chatham Hospital on 9th April 1917, with head injuries.
Under instruction at Cranwell from 13th April 1917.
Dover on 10th May 1917.
No.12 Squadron from 21st to 27th July 1917.
No.6 Squadron from 28th July 1918 to 28th August 1918.
No.10 Squadron from 30th August 1917 to 31st March 1918.
No.210 Squadron RAF from 1st April 1918 to 28th May 1918, when wounded in hands.
No.204 Squadron RAF from January 1919, becoming Commanding Officer on 23rd January, to 31st December 1919.

Combat record with No.10 Squadron:

19/9/17	Albatros scout	East Hooge	10.00	OOC
15/11/17	C type	W Dixmude	13.00	OOC*

* shared with FSL A.M. Alexander.
Maund claimed a further 9 victories with No.210 Squadron RAF.

Maund Courtesy E.F. Cheesman

May, Theodore Charles, FSL

Born 27th August 1898. From Toronto, Ontario.
Joined RNAS on 21st November 1916. Gained RAC certificate 4045 at Curtiss School, Toronto.
Under instruction at Crystal Palace from 14th January 1917.
Under instruction at Vendome from 17th February 1917.
Dover from 7th July 1917.
No.12 Squadron from 15th to 18th July 1917.
No.10 Squadron from 19th July 1917 to 24th July 1917, killed when his Triplane broke up in the air.

McDonald, Roderick, FSL

Born 31st October 1893. From St. Josephs, Nova Scotia.
Trained at Curtis School, Toronto.
Joined RNAS on 15th September 1916.
Under instruction at Crystal Palace from 17th September 1916.
Under instruction at Cranwell from 14th October 1916.
Dover on 8th March 1917.
No.8 Squadron from 25th March 1917 to 27th March 1917.
No.10 Squadron from 28th March 1917 to 4th April 1917.
No.8 Squadron from 5th April 1917 to 31st March 1918 (with period on secondment to No.10 Squadron from 7th June 1917 to 12th June 1917)
No.208 Squadron RAF from 1st April 1918 to 8th May 1918, when shot down and killed over Provin.
McDonald made the following claims with other squadrons:

No.8 Squadron	6
No.208 Squadron RAF	1

McKelvey, Murton Tyndale, FSL

McDonald Courtesy E.F. Cheesman

McKelvey Courtesy S. Taylor

McNeil Courtesy Norman Franks

Born 8th March 1898. From Turtle Mountain, Manitoba.
Joined the RNAS on 15th March 1917.
Under instruction at Redcar from 30th April 1917.
Under instruction at Cranwell.
Under instruction at Manston War School from 21st August 1917.
At Dover on 29th September 1917.
No.12 Squadron from 29th to 30th September 1917.
No.10 Squadron from 1st October 1917 to 31st March 1918.
No.210 Squadron RAF from 1st April 1918 to 11th April 1918, when wounded in ankle, forced down and made a prisoner of war.

McLachlen, Andrew McKenzie Onslade, FSL
Born 12th December 1896. From Hampstead, London.
Joined RNAS on 17th September 1916.
Under instruction at Crystal Palace from 17th September 1916.
Under instruction at Eastchurch from 2nd October 1916.
Under instruction at Cranwell from 17th February 1917.
At Dover on 22nd May 1917.
Admitted to Chatham Hospital on 7th July 1917 suffering from Gonorrhoea.
No.12 Squadron from 13th to 18th July 1917.
No.10 Squadron from 19th July 1917 to 22nd August 1917, transferred to RNAS HQ.
Commission terminated on 30th August 1917.

McNeil, Percy Gordon, FSL
Born 19th October 1891. From Gravenhurst, Ontario.
Joined the RNAS at Ottawa on 30th December 1915.
Under instruction at Eastbourne from 30th December, 1915.
Under instruction at Eastchurch Gunnery school from 18th June 1916.
3 Wing from 3rd July 1916 to 31st January 1917.
No.3 Squadron from 1st February 1917 to 4th May 1917.
No.9 Squadron from 5th May to 8th May 1917.
No.10 Squadron from 9th May 1917 to 3rd June 1917, when shot down and killed near Moorslede.
Croix de Guerre gazetted on 21st April 1917.

Combat record with No.10 Squadron:

20/5/17	Scout	East of Armentières	09.50	OOC
25/5/17	Scout	15 miles off Ostende	19.45	OOC

McNeil also claimed 1 victory with No.3 Squadron.

Mellings, Harold Thomas, FLt, DSC and Bar, DFC
Born 5th August 1897. From Ludlow, Shropshire.
Joined the RNAS on 3rd April 1916.
Under instruction at White City from 3rd April 1916,
Under instruction at Chingford from 14th April 1916,
Under instruction at Eastchurch from 30th July 1916,
Under instruction at Redcar from 16th August 1916.
2 Wing in the eastern Mediterranean from 18th October 1916, to 19th December 1917.
No.12 Squadron from 14th February 1918 to 16th February 1918.
No.10 Squadron from 17th February 1918 to 31st March 1918.
No.210 Squadron RAF from 1st April to 15th April 1918, admitted to Whitechapel Hospital with gun shot wound in left thigh. Returned to squadron until 22nd July 1918, when he was killed in action.
DSC gazetted on 22nd June 1917.
Bar to DSC gazetted on 19th December 1917.
DFC gazetted on 21st September 1918.
Hellenic Silver War Medal gazetted on 21st September 1918.

Combat record with No.10 Squadron:

28/2/18	Albatros scout	Northeast of Ypres	17.15	OOC
10/3/18	Albatros scout	Southeast of Dixmude	16.00	Destroyed
16/3/18	Pfalz DIII	Roulers	09.30	OOC
24/3/18	Pfalz DIII	Menin-Roulers	09.20	Destroyed in flames.
24/3/18	Pfalz DIII	Menin-Roulers	09.20	OOC

Mellings made the following claims with other squadrons:

2 Wing	5
No.210 Squadron RAF	5

Morang, George Heaven, FSL
Born 8th December 1897. From Toronto, Ontario.
Joined RNAS at Ottawa on 7th February 1917.
Under instruction at Crystal Palace from 7th February 1917.

Under instruction at Chingford from 28th April 1917.
Under instruction at Cranwell from 23rd June 1917.
Admitted to Chatham Hospital on 5th July 1917 with injury to right knee.
At Dunkerque on 6th October 1917.
No.12 Squadron from 12th to 20th October 1917.
No.10 Squadron from 21st October 1917 to 27th October 1917, shot down in flames and killed to the northeast of Dixmude.

Mellings Courtesy E.F. Cheesman

Morrison, Ronald Beckett, FSL
Born 3rd December 1894. From Bickley, Kent.
Joined the RNAS on 22nd September 1914, granted commission on 16th June 1916.
Under instruction at Crystal Palace from 25th June 1916.
Under instruction at Eastbourne from 15th July 1916.
Under instruction at Cranwell from 23rd September 1916.
3 Wing from 27th December 1916.
Dunkerque from 23rd April 1917.
No.10 Squadron from 6th May 1917 to 9th May, transferred to England, sick.
Dover from 21st June 1917.
Grain from 4th July 1917 to 13th July 1917, killed when crashed FE2b serial A826.

Munday, Albert Henry, FSL
Born 9th November 1892 at Melbourne, Australia. Educated in England at Eaton, and Canada at Queens University, Kingston, Ontario. Pre-war worked as a reporter with the Toronto Daily and Toronto Telegraph.
Joined the Royal Naval Air Service on 25th March 1916 in Canada.
Under instruction at White City from 26th April 1916.
Under instruction at Redcar from 20th May 1916.
Under instruction at Cranwell from 28th October 1916.
Dover on 8th March 1917.
No.10 Squadron from 15th March 1917 to 16th April 1917, when injured and hospitalised after crashing a Nieuport 12 2-seater.
Manston for re-qualification on 15th January 1918 (not recommended for scouts).
Killingholme, instruction on seaplanes, from 2nd February 1918.
Killingholme, on staff from 8th April 1918.
Member of the crew of Felixstowe F2A N4291 credited with shooting down Zeppelin L62 on 10th May 1918.
Post war activities included founding the Toronto Flying Club, and author of several books including the novel "No Other Gods", and non-fiction works *Practical Flying In War & Peace*, *The Eyes of the Army & Navy*, and *Captain of the Sky*.

Munday Courtesy E.F. Cheesman

Munro, Keith Ross, FSL
Born 10th August 1894. From Brisbane, Australia.
Originally served as a trooper in the 5th Australian Light Horse.
Joined the RNAS on 4th February 1916.
Under instruction at Eastbourne from 22nd February 1916.
Under instruction at Eastchurch from 9th June 1916.
Under instruction at Hendon from 26th June 1916.
Dover from 16th August 1916.
Cranwell from 15th June 1917.
Chingford, assistant instructor, from 7th July 1917.
Dover on 26th July 1917.
No.12 Squadron from 27th to 29th July 1917.
No.10 Squadron from 30th July 1917 to 9th August 1917, when shot down and killed over Polygon Wood.

Narbeth, Charles Anstey, FSL
Under instruction at Crystal Palace from 2nd July 1916.
Under instruction at Eastchurch from 22nd July 1916.
Under instruction at Cranwell from 7th October 1916.
Dover on 24th January 1917.
No.10 Squadron from 12th February 1917 to 16th February 1917, injured when crashed a Nieuport 17Bis borrowed from No.9 (N) Squadron.
Admitted to Haslar Hospital on 3rd March 1917.
Manston for re-qualifying on scouts from 17th July 1917.
Hendon from 13th August 1917.
Dover on 16th August 1917.
No.9 Squadron
Narbeth claimed 3 victories with No.9 Squadron.

Narbeth Courtesy E.F. Cheesman

Nash, Gerald Ewart, FSL
Born on 12th May 1896 in Jact Fleet, Ontario.
Joined the RNAS at Ottawa on 3rd February 1916.
Under instruction at Fishguard from 27th February 1916.

Under Instruction at White City from 17th April 1916.
Under instruction at Redcar from 1st May 1916.
Cranwell from 25th August 1916.
Dover on 24th January 1917.
No.10 Squadron from 15th February 1917 to 26th June 1917, when he was shot down by *Ltn.* Karl Allmenröder of *Jasta* 11.
Nash spent the rest of the war as a prisoner.
Served in RCAF during World War II, retiring as a Group Captain in 1945.
Gerald Nash died on 10th April 1976.

Combat record with No.10 Squadron:

21/5/17	Albatros scout	Ypres-Staden	10.30	Destroyed
2/6/17	C type	St. Julien	09.00	OOC*
5/6/17	C type	Wervicq	08.50	Destroyed in flames**
6/6/17	Albatros scout	Polygon Wood	11.00	Destroyed
6/6/17	Albatros scout	Polygon Wood	11.15	OOC
7/6/17	Albatros scout	St. Julien	09.00	OOC

* Shared with Collishaw, Reid and Alexander
** Shared with Collishaw, Boyd, Reid, and Fitzgibbon

Nelson, Harold Ludlow, FSL
Born 16th October 1898. From Bedford Park, London.
Joined the RNAS on 19th November 1916.
Under instruction at Crystal Palace from 19th November 1916.
Under instruction at Chingford from 30th December 1916.
Under instruction at Cranwell from 28th April 1917.
East Fortune from 22nd June to 9th July 1917.
Manston from 10th July 1917 to 15th August 1917.
Dover on 16th August 1917.
No.10 Squadron from 17th August to 31st March 1918.
No.210 Squadron RAF from 1st April 1918 to 29th April 1918, when shot down and killed by anti-aircraft fire.

Combat record with No.10 Squadron:

21/10/17	C type	Northeast of Dixmude	13.30	Destroyed in flames*

* shared with Curtis and Emery

Ogden, Kenneth, FSL
Born 7th June 1898. from Watford, Herts.
Joined RNAS on 22nd July 1916.
Under instruction at Portsmouth from 22nd March 1916.
Under instruction at Chingford from 24th June 1916.
Admitted Chatham Hospital on 30th November 1916 with Scabies.
Under instruction at Cranwell from 8th January 1917.
Dover on 31st January 1917.
No.10 Squadron from 15th March 1917 to 9th May 1917, injured and transferred back to UK.

Oliver, William Smith, FSL
Born 26th July 1891. From Toronto, Ontario.
Joined RNAS at Ottawa on 22nd March 1916.
Received ACA certificate #445 on April 5th 1916 at the Stinson school, San Antonio, Texas.
Under instruction at Eastbourne in May 1916.
Under instruction at Chingford from 24th June 1916.
Admitted to Chatham Hospital on 30th November 1916 with scabies.
Under instruction at Cranwell from 8th January 1917.
Dover on 31st January 1917.
No.10 Squadron from 22nd February 1917 to 24th March 1917, when killed at Dover during test flight of a new Triplane which broke up in the air.

Page Courtesy E.F. Cheesman

Page, John Albert, FLt
Born on 11th July 1893 at Elizabethtown, Ontario. Lived in Brockville, Ontario.
Joined the RNAS at Ottawa on 15th November 1915.
Under instruction at Eastchurch from 10th January 1916.
Under instruction at Chingford from 5th March 1916.
Under instruction at Eastchurch from 1st May 1916.
Hendon from 22nd May 1916.
Royal Naval Air Station Yarmouth in 1916 on Home Defence duties.
3 Wing from 26th June 1916 to 25th April 1917.
No.10 Squadron from 26th April 1917 to 22nd July 1918, when he was shot down in combat and killed.

Combat record with No.10 Squadron:

1/6/17	C type	Southeast of Ypres	07.15	Destroyed*
6/6/17	Albatros scout	Polygon Wood	11.15	Destroyed
14/6/17	Albatros scout	Zonnebeke	19.20	OOC
15/6/17	Albatros scout	Houthem	09.40	OOC
7/7/17	Albatros scout	Lille	09.40	OOC
22/7/17	Albatros scout	Becelaere	11.00	Destroyed
22/7/17	Albatros scout	Becelaere	11.00	OOC

* Shared with Dissette

Parker, Leslie Hunter, FSL
Born 8th December 1895. From Leeds Village, Quebec.
Joined the RNAS on 16th December 1915.
Under instruction at Chingford from 16th December 1915.
Under instruction at Cranwell from 26th April 1916.
Under instruction at Eastchurch from 18th June 1916.
3 Wing from 3rd July 1916.
Dunkerque on 23rd April 1917.
No.10 Squadron from 6th May 1917 to 14th June 1917, when shot down and killed.

Combat record with No.10 Squadron:

25/5/17	Scout	15 miles off Ostende	19.45	OOC
3/6/17	Albatros scout	Ypres-Courtrai	18.00	Destroyed

Parker Courtesy S. Taylor

Patey, Herbert Andrew, FSL
Born 25th September 1898. From West Hampstead, London.
Joined the RN Division in September 1914 and served in Egypt and Gallipolis, before being invalided home in September 1915 with Dysentery. Patey was demobilised in November 1915, as he was underage.
Joined the RNAS on 10th August 1917.
No.12 Squadron from 12th to 28th January 1918.
No.10 Squadron from 29th January 1918 to 31st March 1918.
No.210 Squadron RAF from 1st April 1918 to 5th September 1918, when he was shot down by *Ltn.* Beckmann of *Jasta* 56, and became a prisoner of war.
After release, Patey died of influenza on the 18th February, 1919.
DFC gazetted on 21st September 1918.
Patey claimed 11 victories with No.210 Squadron RAF.

Patey Courtesy GSL/JMB Collection

Pattison, Charles Edward, FSL
Born 9th May 1896, in Glasgow, (his parents were visiting relatives). Family home at Winona, Ontario.
Joined the RNAS at Ottawa on 10th January 1916.
Under instruction at Eastbourne from 10th January 1916.
Admitted to Haslar Hospital on 7th March 1916 suffering from Syphilis.
Admitted to Haslar Hospital on 9th April 1916 suffering from Syphilis.
After the periods of illness, resumed training at Eastbourne on 15th May 1916.
Under instruction at Cranwell from 12th June 1916.
3 Wing from 1st August 1916.
Admitted to Chatham Hospital on 11th September 1916 suffering from Syphilis.
Admitted to Chatham Hospital on 5th October 1916 suffering from Syphilis.
Admitted to Chatham Hospital on 24th January 1917 suffering from Syphilis.
Dunkerque on 23rd April 1917.
No.10 Squadron from 5th May 1917 to 20th May 1917, severe gunshot wound in chest during combat, and admitted to Chatham Hospital on 24th May 1917.
Sent to Canada to recuperate in September 1917.
Eastchurch from 14th November 1917.
Died on 3rd April 1918 when he crashed Camel B5720 into telephone wires at Redcar race course.

Combat record with No.10 Squadron:

20/5/17	Albatros scout	East of Armentières	09.50	OOC

FSL C.E. Pattison also claimed 1 victory with No.3 Wing.

Paynter, John de Campbourne, FSL
Born 17th May 1898. From Southsea, Hampshire.
Under instruction at Crystal Palace from 25th June 1916.
Under instruction at Chingford from 15th July 1916.
Under instruction at Cranwell from 13th November 1916.
Dover on 29th November 1916.
No.6 Squadron from February 1917 to 9th April 1917, when hospitalised following a crash.
No.12 Squadron from 9th to 15th October 1917.
No.10 Squadron from 16th October 1917 to 25th October 1917.
No.9 Squadron from 25th October 1917 to 26th October 1917.
Dunkerque, ground duties, from 26th October 1917 to 2nd January 1918
No.13 Squadron from January 1918 to 31st March 1918.

Paynter Courtesy E.F. Cheesman

213 Squadron RAF from 1st April 1918 to 18th June 1918, when fatally wounded by bomb fragments during an air raid on 213 Squadron's aerodrome. Admitted to Queen Alexandria hospital, died of perforated liver.

DFC gazetted on 17th April 1918.

Paynter made the following claims with other squadrons:

No.6 Squadron	1
No.13 Squadron/No.213 Squadron RAF	9

Payton, Clement Wattson, FSL
Born 13th April 1897. From Ashborne, Derbyshire.
Joined the RFC on 18th September 1917.
Under instruction at Halton Park from 18th September 1917.
Under instruction at No.2 Training Squadron from 28th November 1917.
Under instruction at No.3 Training Squadron from 28th December 1917.
No.12 Squadron from 30th to 31st March 1918.
No.10 Squadron on 31st March 1918.
No.210 Squadron RAF from 1st April 1918 to 2nd October 1918, when he was killed in action, being struck by ground fire.
DFC gazetted on 3rd December 1917.
Although Payton was a member of the RFC, he was posted to No.10 Squadron on the 31st March 1918, and was recorded as a Flight Sub Lieutenant. The following day he would revert to his correct rank of 2nd Lieutenant.
Payton claimed 11 victories with No.210 Squadron RAF.

Pegler, Charles Richard, FSL
Born 14th May 1893. From Wantage, Buckinghamshire.
Joined RNAS on 29th October 1916.
Under instruction at Crystal Palace from 29th October 1916.
Under instruction at Chingford from 2nd December 1916.
Under instruction at Cranwell from 2nd April 1917.
Dover on 22nd May 1917.
No.11 Squadron from 4th to 10th June 1917.
No.10 Squadron from 11th June 1917 to 12th July 1917, when shot down and killed at Zillebeke.

Combat record with No.10 Squadron:

7/7/17	C type	Moorslede-Roulers	06.45	OOC

Pownall, Charles Herbert, FSL
Born 10th August 1894. From Chester, Cheshire.
Joined the RNAS on 10th September 1916.
Under instruction at Crystal Palace on 10th September 1916.
Under instruction at Chingford from 14th October 1916.
Under instruction at Cranwell from 2nd June 1917.
Dover on 12th July 1917.
No.12 Squadron from 23rd to 26th July 1917.
No.10 Squadron from 27th July 1917 to 7th September 1917.
No.5 Squadron from 8th September 1917 to 9th November 1917, when admitted to Chatham hospital with gun shot wounds in both legs.

Prewett, Cyril Marston Roberts, FSL
Born 1st November 1893. From Wimbledon, London.
Joined RNAS on 17th September 1916.
Under instruction at Crystal Palace from 17th September 1917.
Under instruction at Eastchurch from 20th October 1916.
Under instruction at Cranwell from 17th February 1917.
Dover on 22nd May 1917.
No.11 Squadron from 28th May to 3rd June 1917.
No.10 Squadron from 4th June 1917 to 6th July 1917.
No.11 Squadron from 7th July 1917.
Calshot from 19th November 1917.
Dover, seaplane patrol from 30th January 1918.

Redpath, Ronald Francis, Acting SCdr
Born 7th July 1888. From Montreal, Quebec.
Joined the RNAS at Ottawa on 1st December 1915.
Under instruction at Chingford from 1st December 1915.
Under instruction at Eastchurch from 1st May 1916 to 6th June 1916.
3 Wing from 7th August 1916 (at Manston) to 6th March 1917.
No.11 Squadron from 7th March to 21st April 1917.
No.6 Squadron from 22nd April 1917 to 14th August 1917.
No.11 Squadron from 15th August to 1st September 1917.
No.3 Squadron from 2nd September to 24th September 1917.

No.10 Squadron from 23rd September to 14th December 1917.
Cranwell from 27th December 1917 to 10th June 1918 (became 201 training depot station on 1st April 1918).
Redcar 10th June 1918 to 22nd June 1918.
Cranwell 22nd June 1918 to 18th November 1918.
Commanding Officer of No.209 Squadron 18th November 1918 to 9th March 1919.
Cranwell 9th March 1919 to 24th April 1919.
To unemployed list on 24th April 1919.
Became a post-war director of the Canadian Air Force.
Redpath died on 11th January 1970.
Croix de Guerre gazetted on 21st April 1917.
SCdr Redpath made the following claims with other squadrons:

No.6 Squadron	1
No.3 Squadron	1

Redpath Courtesy GSL/JMB Collection

Reid, Ellis Vair, FSL
Born 31st October 1889 in Bellville, Ontario. Attended university of Toronto from 1908 to 1912, and was an architect. Joined the RNAS on 10th January 1916 at Ottawa.
Under instruction at Redcar from 7th February 1916.
Under instruction at Cranwell from 7th July 1916.
Cranwell, night flying instructor, from 4th September 1916 to 19th November 1916.
3 Wing from 20th November 1916 to 26th April 1917.
No.10 Squadron from 26th April 1917 to 28th July 1917, when he was shot down and killed by *K.Flak* 21.
DSC gazetted on 11th August 1917.

Combat record with No.10 Squadron:

1/6/17	C type	West of Wervicq	09.15	Destroyed
2/6/17	C type	St. Julien	09.00	OOC*
3/6/17	Albatros scout	Roubaix	18.15	Destroyed
5/6/17	C type	Wervicq	08.50	Destroyed in flames**
6/6/17	Halberstadt DII	North of Polygon Wood	11.00	Destroyed
7/6/17	C type	Clercken	09.15	Destroyed
15/6/17	Albatros scout	Moorslede	17.45	OOC
15/6/17	Albatros scout	Moorslede	17.45	OOC
17/6/17	Albatros scout	Roulers	19.10	OOC
6/7/17	Albatros scout	Deulemont	11.00	OOC
12/7/17	Albatros scout	Menin-Polygon Wood	08.45	Destroyed
12/7/17	Albatros scout	Veldhoek	08.45	Destroyed
20/7/17	Albatros scout	Menin-Messines	08.05	OOC
21/7/17	Scout	North Becelaere	20.30	Destroyed
23/7/17	Albatros scout	Houthulst Forest	20.25	OOC
27/7/17	Albatros scout	Menin	19.50	Destroyed
27/7/17	Albatros scout	Courtrai	20.00	OOC
27/7/17	Albatros scout	Menin	20.05	Destroyed
28/7/17	Albatros scout	Becelaere	20.00	Destroyed

* Shared with Collishaw, Alexander, and Nash
** Shared with Collishaw, Fitzgibbon, Boyd, and Nash

Reid Author's collection

Rice, Edmond Gabriel, FSL
Born 3rd June 1899. From Solihull, Warwickshire.
Joined the RNAS on 8th July 1917.
Under instruction at Crystal Palace from 8th July 1917.
Under instruction at Manston Flying School from 11th August 1917.
Under instruction at Cranwell from 17th October 1917.
Under instruction at Manston War school from 3rd December 1917.
Dunkerque on 23rd December.
No.12 Squadron from 31st December 1917 to 16th January 1918.
No.10 Squadron from 17th January 1918 to 24th January 1918, fainted whilst flying over lines at 18000 feet, recovered at 4000 feet, left for medical survey.
Surveyed on 26th March 1918, and pronounced as unfit for active service.
At Redcar Instructors School (No.2 SSF) from 29th April 1918 to 3rd May 1918 when killed in a flying accident.

Roach, Edmund Daniel, FSL
Born 12th January 1892. From Toronto.
Enlisted in Canadian Expeditionary Force, but being under age was claimed by his parents.
Gained ACA certificate #520 at Curtiss school on 5th July 1916.
Joined RNAS at Ottawa on 5th July 1916.
Under instruction at Crystal Palace from 5th July 1916.
Under instruction at Redcar from 26th August 1916.
Under instruction at Cranwell from 14th October 1916.

Dover on 12th February 1917.
No.8 Squadron to 21st February 1917.
Admitted to Chatham hospital on 22nd February 1917, with Syphilis.
No.10 Squadron from 28th March 1917 to 4th April 1917.
No.8 Squadron from 5th April 1917 to 1st May 1917, when he was shot down and killed.

Roach, Gerald, FSL
Born 23rd September 1897. From Chingford, Essex.
Joined the RNAS on 5th February 1917.
Under instruction at Crystal Palace from 4th February 1917.
Under instruction at Eastchurch from 7th April 1917.
Under instruction at Cranwell from 2nd June 1917.
Dover on 18th July 1917.
No.12 Squadron from 24th to 26th July 1917.
No.10 Squadron on 27th July 1917, shot down and killed on his first patrol.

Saint Courtesy GSL/JMB Collection

Saint, Howard John Thomas, FCdr
Born 20th January 1893 in Ruabon, North Wales.
Pre-war, saint was a student at Manchester University.
Held the rank of Chief Petty Officer with the Royal Naval Armoured Cars, and was commissioned as a Sub Lieutenant in August 1915.
Undertook flying instruction in 1916.
8 Flight B Squadron 5 Wing (later No.5 Squadron) flying bombers from September 1916 to 24th July 1917.
No.10 Squadron from 26th July 1917 to 26th October 1917.
Martlesham Heath serving as a test pilot until the end of the war.
Holder of Commercial Licence No.1.
Commercial pilot for Air Transport and Travel until 1922.
Regularly competed in air races. In June 1919, Placed 5th in the Victory Aerial Derby around London (6th on handicap) flying an Airco DH9B. In September 1919 won a race around Holland.
Rejoined the RAF in 1922, serving as a test pilot at the Royal Aircraft Factory.
Joined the Gloster Aircraft Company in 1927 as Chief Test Pilot. In 1934 the Gloster Aircraft Company was acquired by Hawker Aircraft Ltd., and Saint was replaced by P.E.G. Sayer, Hawker's Assistant Chief Test Pilot. Saint moved on to test machines for George Parnall and Company Ltd. This employment lasted just one year as Parnall and Company was acquired by Nash & Thompson Ltd. in 1935, the new company being concerned with the design and manufacture of aircraft gun turrets.
Worked for the Royal Aircraft Establishment at Farnborough as a Flying Control Officer, until his retirement when he lived at Hove, Sussex.
DSC gazetted on 2nd November 1917.

Combat record with No.10 Squadron:

9/8/17	Albatros scout	Polygon wood	15.50	OOC
14/8/17	Albatros scout	Houthulst Forest	16.15	Destroyed in flames.
21/8/17	C type	South of Roulers	07.40	OOC
25/8/17	Albatros scout	South of Roulers	07.00	OOC
21/9/17	Albatros scout	Wervicq	11.00	OOC
23/9/17	Albatros scout	Westroosebeke	11.30	OOC
20/8/17	Albatros scout	NE Dixmude	13.40	Destroyed

Saunders Courtesy E.F. Cheesman

Saunders, Robert Girling, FSL
Born 17th July 1898. From Warboys, Huntingdonshire.
Joined RNAS on 17th September 1916.
Under instruction at Crystal Palace from 17th September 1916.
Under instruction at Eastchurch from 2nd October 1916.
Admitted to Chatham Hospital on 3rd January 1917, suffering from Rubella.
Under instruction at Cranwell from 17th February 1917.
Dover on 22nd May 1917.
No.11 Squadron from 3rd to 7th June 1917.
No.10 Squadron from 8th June 1917 to 24th June 1917, when shot down and killed near Moorslede.

Sharman, John Edward, FCdr
Born 11th September 1892 in Oak Lake, Manitoba.
Joined the RNAS at Ottawa on 3rd February 1916.
Under instruction on navigation course from 25th February 1916.
Under instruction at Fishguard from 18th April 1916.
Under instruction at White city from 19th April 1917 to 24th April 1917.
Under instruction at Redcar from 25th April 1916.
Under instruction at Eastchurch from 16th July 1916.
3 Wing from 2nd August 1916 to 29th April 1917.
No.10 Squadron from 1st May 1917 to 22nd July 1917, when he was shot down and killed, probably by Flak Batterie 503. He was briefly attached to Raymond Collishaw's B Flight before being transferred

to C Flight on the 4th June. Sharman was evaluated against FSL John Page for the leadership of C Flight, until the 24th June, when he became undisputed flight leader.

DSC gazetted on 12th May 1917.
Croix de Guerre gazetted on 20th July 1917.
Bar to DSC gazetted on 11th August 1917.

Sharman Courtesy GSL/JMB collection

Combat record with No.10 Squadron:

6/6/17	Albatros scout	Polygon wood	11.10	OOC
7/6/17	Albatros scout	Moorslede	09.15	Destroyed
7/6/17	Albatros scout	Moorslede	09.17	OOC
14/6/17	Albatros scout	Zonnebeke	19.25	OOC
15/6/17	C Type	St. Julien-Houthem	10.50	OOC*
24/6/17	Albatros scout	Zonnebeke	08.10	Destroyed
12/7/17	Albatros scout	Polygon Wood	12.15	Destroyed

* shared with Collishaw

Sharman also claimed 1 victory with 3 Wing.

Shirriff, Quintin Speirs, FSL

Born 29th May 1891. From Toronto, Ontario.
Joined RNAS on 3rd February 1916.
Under instruction at Eastbourne from 6th March 1916.
Under instruction at Eastchurch from 26th August 1916.
3 Wing from 14th September 1916 to 8th March 1917.
No.11 Squadron from 9th March 1917 to 1st April 1917.
No.10 Squadron from 1st April 1917 to 17th July 1917, when left suffering from stomach ulcers.
Royal Naval Air Station Hendon from 3rd September 1917, performing ground duties.

Smith, George Oliver, FSL

Born 4th February 1899. From Tunbridge Wells, Kent.
Joined the RNAS on 17th June 1917.
Under instruction at Crystal Palace from 17th June 1917.
Under instruction at Vendome from 21st July 1917.
Under instruction at Cranwell from 29th September 1917.
Under instruction at Manston War School from 28th December 1917.
No.12 Squadron to 12th January 1918.
No.10 Squadron from 13th January 1918 to 16th February 1918, fractured thigh and contusions on face after crashing at St. Sixte, taken to No.4 Casualty Clearing Station.
Declared unfit for duty for at least 6 months.

Steel, Leonard George, FSL

Born 15th September 1894. from Newark, Nottinghamshire.
Joined the RNAS on 6th June 1916.
Under instruction at Crystal Palace from 18th June 1916.
Under instruction at Eastchurch from 8th July 1916.
Under instruction at Cranwell from 1st September 1916.
3 Wing on 25th November 1916.
Dunkerque from 23rd April 1917.
No.10 Squadron from 6th May 1917 to 9th May 1917, injured in crash when choked engine at take off from Furnes. Taken to Ocean Hospital, La Panne with knee and ankle damage.
Chingford, assistant instructor from 23rd August 1917.
2 Wing from 8th February 1918.

Steeves, Gordon Tracey, FSL

Born 26th October 1898 in Paradise, New Brunswick. Family home at Hillsboro, New Brunswick.
Joined the RNAS at Ottawa on 19th April 1917.
Under instruction at Manston Flying School from 21st May 1917.
Under instruction at Cranwell from 8th September 1917, failed to graduate at the first attempt.
Admitted to Chatham Hospital on 1st October 1917, suffering from Gonorrhoea.
Under instruction at Manston War School from 28th December 1917.
Dunkerque on 11th January 1918.
No.12 Squadron from 12th to 28th January 1918.
No.10 Squadron from 29th January 1918 to 18th March 1918, when shot down and captured to become a prisoner of war.

Stratton, Kenneth Vern, FSL

Born 3rd May 1895 in Delhi, Ontario. Family home at Aylmer, Ontario.
Joined the RNAS on 16th September 1916.
Under instruction at Crystal Palace from 17th September 1916.
Under instruction at HMS *Nimrod* (sea course) from 28th October 1916 (transferred to HMS *Starfish*).
Admitted to Shotley Hospital on 7th November 1916, suffering from scabies.
Under instruction at HMS *Starfish* (sea course) from 6th January 1917.
Under instruction at Cranwell from 20th January 1917.

Admitted to Chatham Hospital on 19th April 1917, suffering from gonorrhoea and syphilis.
Dover on 23rd August 1917.
Under instruction at Freiston from 4th August 1917.
No.12 Squadron from 5th to 13th September 1917.
No.10 Squadron from 14th September 1917 to 10th January 1918, struck off strength when admitted to Malo hospital, suffering from a kidney disease.
Still unfit for service on 1st March 1918.

Combat record with No.10 Squadron:

27/10/17	Albatros scout	Northeast of Dixmude	13.20	Destroyed*

* shared with Curtis

Sutherland, Irving Frederick, FSL
Born 5th January 1892. From Randwick, Sydney, Australia.
Enlisted in Australian Imperial Force on 5th April 1916. Served with Naval and Military expedition to German New Guinea.
Royal Aero Club Certificate No.4037.
Joined the RNAS on 15th April 1917.
Under instruction at Eastchurch from 12th May 1917.
Under instruction at Cranwell from 14th July 1917.
No.12 Squadron from 22nd to 25th September 1917.
No.10 Squadron from 26th September 1917 to 15th October 1917, when received gunshot wound in shoulder (compound fracture of humorous), to Malo Hospital, then transferred to Clapham Hospital.
Manston from 6th February 1918.
6 Wing from 3rd March 1918.
Transferred to RAF Unemployed List on 2nd September 1919.

Swale, Edwin, FSL
Born 28th June 1899. From Chesterfield, Derby.
Joined the RNAS on 19th August 1917.
No.12 Squadron from 19th to 20th March 1918.
No.10 Squadron from 21st March 1918 to 31st March 1918.
No.210 Squadron RAF from 1st April 1918 to 21st October 1918, when posted to Home Establishment.
After the war, he was prominent in local politics between 1927 and 1933, and between 1946 and 1977, becoming Mayor of Chesterfield in 1953. He received an OBE, and a CBE.
Served with the RAF in World War II as a Wing Commander.
Edwin Swale died in 1978.
DFC gazetted on 2nd November 1918.
Bar to DFC gazetted on 3rd December 1918.
Swale claimed 17 victories with No.210 Squadron RAF.

Taylor, Howard William, FSL
Born 20th May 1898. From Putney, London.
Joined RNAS on 10th September 1916.
Under instruction at Crystal Palace from 10th September 1916.
Under instruction at Cranwell from 14th October 1916.
Dover on 23rd March 1917.
No.11 Squadron from 19th to 24th May 1917.
No.10 Squadron from 25th May 1917 to 21st July 1917, wounded in left arm by enemy gunfire, and hospitalised.
Eastbourne, ground duties, from 29th October 1917.
Compass Course at Slough on 3rd December 1917.
Eastbourne, assistant instructor, from 26th January 1918.
Redcar instructor's school from 15th April 1918.
212 Training Depot Station Vendome, Instructor, from 19th April 1918.

Combat record with No.10 Squadron:

5/6/17	C type	Dixmude-Nieuport	14.10	Destroyed in flames.
26/6/17	C Type	Wervicq	19.45	OOC
16/7/17	Albatros scout	Polygon Wood	18.00	Destroyed

Thom, George, FCdr
Born 13th March 1890 at Gateside, Scotland. Moved to Merritt, British Columbia circa 1910.
Gained Certificate No.1860 at Curtiss School, Toronto on 3rd October 1915.
Joined RNAS at Ottawa on 3rd October 1915.
No.7 Flight, B Squadron, 5 Wing, from 10th April 1916.
No.5 Flight, A Squadron, 5 Wing, from 17th July 1916.
No.8 Squadron from 25th October 1916 to 23rd February 1917.
No.10 Squadron from 24th February to 3rd April 1917, left after becoming ill with nervous exhaustion.
No.11 Squadron from 4th June 1917.
No.12 Squadron from 25th June 1917 to 31st March 1918.
Redcar from 8th April 1918.

Cranwell, No.201 Training Depot Station on instructional staff from 29th April 1918 (became No.56 Training Depot Station from 27th July 1918).

Post war, George Thom was a prospector in Canada; he died when his canoe was upset in Peace River Rapids in 1924.

Air Force Cross gazetted on 3rd June 1919.

Thom *Author's collection*

Trapp, George Leonard, FLt
Born 1st July 1894 in New Westminster, British Columbia.
Joined RNAS on 19th January 1917 at Ottawa.
Under instruction at Crystal Palace from 18th February 1917.
Under instruction at Chingford from 12th March 1917.
Under instruction at Cranwell from 19th May 1917.
Under instruction at Freiston from 18th June 1917.
Dover on 2nd July 1917.
No.12 Squadron from 11th July to 13th July 1917.
No.10 Squadron from 14th July 1917 to 13th November 1917, when he was shot down and killed by *Oblt.* Bruno Justinius of *Jasta* 35.

George Trapp was one of three brothers in the flying services, all three losing their lives during the war. Trapp's sister married Raymond Collishaw.

Combat record with No.10 Squadron:

12/8/17	Albatros scout	Roulers	07.45	OOC
17/8/17	Albatros scout	Ledeghem	08.30	OOC
21/8/17	Albatros scout	East of Menin	18.35	OOC
28/9/17	Albatros scout	Moorslede	10.45	Destroyed
12/11/17	C Type	Couckelaere	08.00	OOC*

* Shared with Beattie.

Trapp *Courtesy E.F. Cheesman*

Travers, Herbert Gardner, FLt
Born 1st April 1891. From Warlingham, Surrey.
Joined the RNAS on 14th December 1915.
At Furnes attached to No.10 Squadron, but not on squadron strength, from 5th May 1917 to 15th May 1917.

Wallace, Hugh Douglas McIntosh, FSL
Born 15th July 1894. From Midland, Ontario.
Joined RNAS on 3rd February 1916.
Under instruction at Eastbourne from 6th March 1916.
Under instruction at Cranwell from 20th May 1916.
3 Wing from 15th August 1916 to 6th March 1917.
No.11 Squadron from 7th March 1917 to 3rd April 1917.
No.10 Squadron from 3rd April 1917 to 7th April 1917.
No.1 Squadron on 8th April 1917 to 7th June 1917, when crashed on take off and was killed.

Walter, Eric Blount Jackson, FSL
Born 31st October 1897 in London. Lived at 21 King's Terrace, Southsea, Hampshire.
Joined RNAS on 3rd April 1916.
Under instruction at White City from 10th April 1916.
Under instruction at Redcar from 20th May 1915, gained Royal Aero Club Certificate No. 3716, 4th October 1916.
Cranwell from 7th October 1916.
Dover on 24th January 1917.
No.10 Squadron from 22nd February 1917 to 16th April 1917.
No.8 Squadron from 17th April 1917.
Shot down and killed at Bailleul on 24th April 1917.

Walton, Arthur McBurney, FSL
Born 17th October 1896, in New York City of Canadian Parents. Schooled and resident in Toronto.
RAC Certificate #3404 obtained at Toronto Curtiss school, on 18th August 1916.
Joined RNAS at Ottawa on 18th August 1916.
Under instruction at Crystal Palace 17th September 1916.
Under Instruction at Cranwell 14th October 1916.
Dover from 3rd March 1917.
No.11 Squadron from 26th March 1917.
No.10 Squadron from 1st April 1917 to 4th April 1917.
No.6 Squadron from 5th April 1917 to 4th July 1917.

Admitted to Chatham Hospital on 20th July 1917. After disciplinary problems, submitted request to terminate Commission on 25th July 1917. Grounds were that he felt unworthy of being retained in the RNAS. Resignation was accepted on 1st August 1917.

Walton claimed 1 victory with No.6 Squadron RNAS.

Travers *Courtesy E.F. Cheesman*

Walter Author's collection

Wilmot Courtesy E.F. Cheesman

Wimbush Author's collection

Weir, Charles Haddon, FSL
Born 30th January 1892 in Vancouver. Resident at Alberta.
Gained RAC Certificate 4048 at Curtiss school Toronto on 26th November 1916.
Joined RNAS at Ottawa on 26th November 1916.
Under instruction at Crystal Palace from 11th February 1917.
Under instruction at Vendome from 19th March 1917.
Under instruction at Cranwell from 17th May 1917.
Dover on 2nd July 1917.
No.12 Squadron from 11th to 13th July 1917.
No.10 Squadron from 14th July 1917 to 20th August 1917, when shot down at Langemarck. Weir was made a prisoner of war, but subsequently died of his wounds.

Wilmot, Wilfred Henry, FSL
Born 22nd July 1898. From Stratford on Avon, Warwickshire.
Gained RAC certificate 3698 at Bournemouth on 17th September 1916.
Joined the RNAS on 17th December 1916.
Under instruction at Crystal Palace from 17th December 1916.
Under instruction at Eastchurch from 27th January 1917.
Admitted to Chatham Hospital on 8th February 1917 suffering from Rubella.
Under instruction at Cranwell from 6th April 1917.
Dover on 8th July 1917.
No.6 Squadron to 28th August 1917.
No.12 Squadron from 23rd to 28th September 1917.
No.10 Squadron from 29th September 1917 to 3rd February 1918, when shot down and killed southwest of Rumbeke.

Combat record with No.10 Squadron:

22/12/17	Albatros scout	West of Lille	10.50	OOC*

* Apparently OOC

Wimbush, Lea Ewart Barnes, FSL
Born 25th May 1898, in London. Address: 8, St. Mark's Square, Regents Park, London.
Joined RNAS on 5th July 1916.
Under instruction at Crystal Palace from 9th July 1916.
Under instruction at Eastbourne from 29th July 1917. Royal Aero Club Certificate No. 3534, 23rd August 1916.
Under instruction at Eastchurch from 29th October 1916.
Eastchurch War Fight from 22nd November 1916.
Dover on 10th January 1917.
No.10 Squadron from 15th February 1917 to 30th April 1917.
No.8 Squadron from 30th April 1917 to 9th May 1917, wounded when shot-up and crashed at Nouex-les-Mines.
Chingford, assistant instructor from 27th July 1917 to 28th March 1918. Wimbush, an ex pupil at Berkhampstead Grammar school was performing aerobatics over the assembled crowd on the school's speech day on the 27th March 1918, when he tore the wings off Triplane N5351 after attempting three consecutive loops. Wimbush subsequently died of his injuries on 28th March 1918.

Winter, Henry Edgar, FSL
Born 27th December 1898. From Northwood, Middlesex.
Joined RNAS on 16th July 1916.
Under instruction at Crystal Palace from 16th July 1916.
Under instruction at Chingford from 12th August 1916.
Under instruction at Cranwell from 12th March 1917.
Dover from 16th April 1917.
No.11 Squadron from 19th May to 2nd June 1917.
No.10 Squadron from 3rd June 1917 to 8th June 1917. Suffered from airsickness, and posted to RNAS HQ.
Chingford, on ground and occasional flying duties from 26th November 1917.
Cranwell instructor's school from 23rd January 1918.
Chingford from 31st March 1918.

Wood, Philip, FSL
Born 9th July 1897. From Shrewsbury, Salop.
Joined the RNAS on 2nd July 1916.
Under instruction at Crystal Palace from 2nd July 1916.
Under instruction at Eastchurch from 22nd July 1916.
Under instruction at Cranwell from 7th October 1916.
Dover from 23rd February 1917.
No.6 Squadron to 28th August 1917.
No.10 Squadron from 2nd September 1917 to 17th September1917, when suffered shock and a very severe scalp wound.

Cranwell Instructor's school from 30th January 1918.
Redcar from 13th February 1918.
HMS *Furious* from 27th April 1918.
Wood claimed 1 victory with No.6 Squadron RNAS.

Wright, Douglas Ross Cameron, FSL
Born 9th July 1892 in Toronto, Ontario. Resident of New Westminster, British Columbia, Grandson of Sir MC Cameron of Toronto.

Joined the RNAS at Toronto on 29th February 1916.

Under instruction at Eastchurch from 18th September 1916. Was "washed out" as a possible scout pilot.

HP Squadron, Manston from 18th December 1916.

3 Wing, HP Squadron from 18th March 1917.

Admitted to Chatham hospital on 3rd June 1917, suffering from Gonorrhoea.

Under instruction at Chingford from 18th June 1917, reinstated into the scout programme after family influence brought to bear.

Under instruction at Cranwell from 4th August 1917, failed to graduate at first attempt.

Under instruction at Manston War school from 6th October 1917.

Dunkerque on 27th October 1917.

No.12 Squadron from 28th October 1917 to 6th November 1917.

No.10 Squadron from 7th November 1917 to 23rd December 1917, killed when he lost control of Camel B6201, and crashed on the aerodrome.

APPENDIX C

ROSTER OF NON-FLYING OFFICERS

Birch, Cecil, Lt, RNVR, Armament Officer
Born 4th March 1879. From London.
No.10 Squadron from 13th March 1917 to 24th July 1917, transferred to RNAS HQ

Case, Albert Edward, WO II, Stores Officer and Engine Officer
Born 20th August1887. From Portsmouth, Hampshire.
Joined RNAS on 1st March 1916.
No.10 Squadron from February 1917 to 19th April 1917.
No.6 Squadron from 20th April 1917 to 28th August 1917.
At RNAS Wormwood Scrubbs from 5th December 1917.
Recommended for commission as Lt. In RNVR on 23rd January 1918, but was not appointed.

Catterson-Smith, Robert Matthew, Lt, RNVR, Armament Officer
Born 29th August 1885. From Edgebaston, Birmingham.
4 Wing HQ.
No.10 Squadron from 18th October 1917 to 31st March 1918.
No.210 Squadron RAF from 1st April 1918 to 30th July 1918.

Chadwick, Ernest, Lt., RNVR, Armament Officer
Born 4th May 1875. From Bushey, Hertfordshire.
Joined RNAS in January 1915.
No.10 Squadron from 21st July 1917 to 12th October 1917, transferred to RNAS HQ.

Dampier, Ernest Patrick, WO II, Stores Officer
Born 23rd March 1897. From Gillingham, Kent.
Joined the RNAS on 1st July 1914.
Eastbourne (in charge of stores and lectures on aeroplane engines) from 6th June 1916
No.6 Squadron from February 1917 to 22nd April 1917.
No.10 Squadron from 23rd April 1917 to 23rd July 1917, transferred to AD.

McIlroy, Charles Alan, Lt., RNVR, Records Officer
Born 21st July 1867.
From Buchin.
Joined RNAS on 26th February 1917.
No.10 Squadron from 27th February 1917 to 31st March 1918.
210 squadron from 1st April 1918 to 5th April 1918, transferred to HQ 64th Wing RAF.

Poyntz-Gaynor, Hubert, WO II, Engine Officer
Born 4th January 1889. From Burslem, Staffordshire.
No.3 Wing.
No.10 Squadron from 12th May 1917 to 12th January 1918, transferred to Crystal Palace for a course.

Wolveridge, Arthur Eslinger, WO II, Stores Officer
Born 8th September 1876. From Ilford.
Joined RNAS on 21st May 1917.
At RNAS Killingholme from 21st May 1917.
No.10 Squadron from 17th July 1917 to 31st March 1918.
No.210 Squadron RAF from 1st April 1918 to 14th April 1918, transferred to HQ 7th Brigade RAF.

APPENDIX D

COMBAT CLAIMS

Date	Pilot	Serial	Details
30/4/17	FSL R. Collishaw	N5490	Albatros scout destroyed east of Cortemarck, 17.30
5/5/17	FSL M.W.W. Eppstein	N5456	Halberstadt shot down in flames at Zarren, 18.05.
9/5/17	FSL R. Collishaw	N5490	Halberstadt scout out of control east of Dixmude, 19.55.
20/5/17	FSL C.E. Pattison	N5366	Albatros scout out of control, 09.50.
20/5/17	FSL P.G. McNeil	N6297	Halberstadt scout out of control east of Armentières, 09.50.
21/5/17	FSL G.E. Nash	N5492	Albatros scout destroyed between Ypres & Staden, 10.30.
25/5/17	FSL P.G. McNeil	N6297	Halberstadt D out of control 15 miles off Ostende, 19.45.
25/5/17	FSL L.H. Parker	N6306	Halberstadt D out of control 15 miles off Ostende, 19.45.
1/6/17	FSL A.C. Dissette	N6294	Aviatic C out of control 3 miles southeast of Ypres, 07.15, shared with N5359.
1/6/17	FLt J.A. Page	N5359	Aviatik C out of control 3 miles southeast of Ypres, 07.15, shared with N6294.
1/6/17	FSL R. Collishaw	N5490	Albatros scout destroyed in flames south of Wervicq, 09.20.
1/6/17	FSL E.V. Reid	N5483	Albatros C destroyed in flames, southwest of Wervicq, 09.15.
2/6/17	FSL W.M. Alexander	N5487	C type out of control at St Julien, 09.20 - 10.25, shared with N5490, N5483, and N5492.
2/6/17	FSL R. Collishaw	N5490	C type out of control at St. Julien, 09.20 - 10.25, shared with N5483, N5487, and N5492.
2/6/17	FSL G.E. Nash	N5492	C type out of control at St. Julien, 09.20 - 10.25, shared with N5490, N5483, and N5487.
2/6/17	FSL E.V. Reid	N5483	C type out of control at St. Julien, 09.20 - 10.25, shared with N5490, N5487, and N5492.
3/6/17	FSL Parker	N6306	Albatros scout out of control, Ypres-Courtrai, 18.00.
3/6/17	FSL R. Collishaw	N5490	Albatros scout destroyed in flames at Roubaix, 20.15.
3/6/17	FSL E.V. Reid	N5483	Albatros scout destroyed near Roubaix, 20.25.
4/6/17	FSL W.M. Alexander	N5487	Albatros scout out of control northeast of Ypres, 08.45.
5/6/17	FSL R. Collishaw	N5490	Albatros C destroyed in flames at Wervicq, 08.50, shared with N5478, N6306 and N5466.
5/6/17	FSL G.E. Nash	N5478	Albatros C destroyed in flames at Wervicq, 08.50, shared with N5490, N6306, and N5466.
5/6/17	FSL K.G. Boyd	N6306	Albatros C destroyed in flames at Wervicq, 08.50, shared with N5490, N5466, and N5478.
5/6/17	FSL D.F. Fitzgibbon	N5466	Albatros C destroyed in flames at Wervicq, 08.50, shared N5490, N5478, N5483 and N6306.
5/6/17	FSL D.F. Fitzgibbon	N5466	Albatros scout out of control northwest of Poelcappelle, 09.40, shared with N5490.
5/6/17	FSL R. Collishaw	N5490	Albatros scout out of control northwest of Poelcappelle, 09.40, shared with N5466.
5/6/17	FSL Taylor	N5478	2-seater down in flames between Dixmude and Nieuport at 14.10.
6/6/17	FSL W.M. Alexander	N5487	Albatros scout out of control at Polygon Wood, 11.45
6/6/17	FSL R. Collishaw	N5490	Albatros scout destroyed in flames at Polygon Wood, 10.50
6/6/17	FSL R. Collishaw	N5490	Albatros scout destroyed in flames at Polygon Wood, 11.05
6/6/17	FSL R. Collishaw	N5490	Albatros scout out of control at Polygon Wood, 11.10
6/6/17	FSL G.E. Nash	N5492	Halberstadt destroyed in flames at Polygon Wood, 11.00.
6/6/17	FSL G.E. Nash	N5492	Albatros scout out of control at Polygon Wood, 11.15.
6/6/17	FLt J.A. Page	N5359	Albatros scout destroyed west of Polygon Wood, 11.00.
6/6/17	FSL E.V. Reid	N5483	Scout destroyed north of Polygon wood, 11.00.
6/6/17	FSL J.E. Sharman	N6307	Albatros scout out of control at Polygon Wood, 11.10.
6/6/17	FSL J.H. Keens	N5361	Albatros scout out of control west of Polygon Wood, 11.10.
7/6/17	FSL R. Collishaw	N5470	Albatros scout out of control between Menin and St. Julien, 08.45.
7/6/17	FSL G.E. Nash	N5492	Albatros scout out of control at St. Julien, 09.00.
7/6/17	FSL E.V. Reid	N5483	Albatros C destroyed at Clercken, 09.15.
7/6/17	FSL J.E. Sharman	N6307	Albatros scout destroyed near Roulers, 09.15.
7/6/17	FSL J.E. Sharman	N6307	Albatros scout out of control at Moorslede, 09.17.
14/6/17	FLt J.A. Page	N5359	Albatros scout out of control at Zonnebeke, 19.20.
14/6/17	FSL J.E. Sharman	N6307	Albatros scout out of control at Zonnebeke, 19.15.
15/6/17	FSL R. Collishaw	N5492	C type out of control at Menin, 17.15.
15/6/17	FSL R. Collishaw	N5492	Albatros scout out of control north of Moorslede, 17.45.
15/6/17	FSL R. Collishaw	N5492	Albatros scout destroyed north of Moorslede, 17.45.

15/6/17	FSL D.F. Fitzgibbon	N5458	Halberstadt scout out of control at Houthem, 10.55.
15/6/17	FSL D.F. Fitzgibbon	N5458	Albatros scout out of control at Moorslede, 17.40.
15/6/17	FLt J.A. Page	N5359	C type out of control at Houthem, 09.40.
15/6/17	FSL E.V. Reid	N5483	Albatros scout out of control at Moorslede, 17.45.
15/6/17	FSL E.V. Reid	N5483	Halberstadt out of control at Moorslede, 17.45.
15/6/17	FSL J.E. Sharman	N6307	C type out of control between St. Julien and Houthem, 09.40.
17/6/17	FSL R. Collishaw	N5492	Hostile aircraft, probably Halberstadt out of control at Roulers, 19.10.
17/6/17	FSL E.V. Reid	N5483	Halberstadt out of control at Roulers, 19.10.
24/6/17	FSL R. Collishaw	N5492	Albatros scout destroyed at Moorslede, 08.10.
24/6/17	FSL J.E. Sharman	N5366	Albatros scout destroyed at Zonnebeke, 08.10.
26/6/17	FSL H.W. Taylor	N5366	C type out of control near Wervicq, 19.45.
2/7/17	FSL R. Collishaw	N5492	C type destroyed at Poelcappelle station, 11.10.
6/7/17	FSL W.M. Alexander	N5487	Albatros scout out of control at Deulemont, 11.00.
6/7/17	FSL W.M. Alexander	N5487	Albatros scout out of control at Deulemont, 11.00.
6/7/17	FSL R. Collishaw	N5492	Albatros scout out of control at Deulemont, 11.00.
6/7/17	FSL E.V. Reid	N5483	Albatros scout out of control at Deulemont, 11.00.
7/7/17	FLt J.A. Page	N5379	Albatros scout out of control at Lille, 09.40.
11/7/17	FSL W.M. Alexander	N5487	Albatros scout out of control at Polygon Wood, 20.45.
11/7/17	FSL R. Collishaw	N5492	Albatros scout out of control at Moorslede, 20.40.
12/7/17	FCdr R. Collishaw	N5492	Albatros scout out of control south of Polygon Wood, 07.45.
12/7/17	FSL E.V. Reid	N5483	Albatros scout broke up in air, Menin-Polygon Wood, 07.45.
12/7/17	FSL E.V. Reid	N5483	Albatros scout, shot down and seen to crash into a house at Veldhoek, 07.45.
12/7/17	FCdr J.E. Sharman	N6307	Albatros scout destroyed at Polygon Wood, 12.25.
16/7/17	FSL H.W. Taylor	N5429	Albatros scout destroyed at Polygon Wood, 18.00.
17/7/17	FSL C. Lowther	N5381	Albatros scout out of control south east of Polygon Wood, 06.45.
17/7/17	FLt A.W. Carter	N6302	Albatros scout out of control at Roulers, 20.00.
20/7/17	FSL W.M. Alexander	N5487	Albatros scout destroyed in flames, Menin-Messines, 08.05.
20/7/17	FCdr R. Collishaw	N5492	Albatros scout out of control with pilot shot, between Menin and Messines, 08.05.
20/7/17	FSL E.V. Reid	N5483	Albatros scout out of control with pilot shot, between Menin and Messines, 08.05.
21/7/17	FCdr R. Collishaw	N5492	Albatros scout out of control at Passchendaele, 20.00.
21/7/17	FCdr R. Collishaw	N5492	Albatros scout out of control, with pilot shot, at Passchendaele, 20.00.
21/7/17	FSL E.V. Reid	N5483	Unidentified scout shot down and crashed at edge of wood, north of Becelaere, 20.30.
22/7/17	FLt J.A. Page	N5478	Albatros scout destroyed at Becelaere, 11.00.
22/7/17	FLt J.A. Page	N5478	Albatros scout destroyed at Becelaere, 11.00.
23/7/17	FSL E.V. Reid	N5483	Albatros scout out of control at Polygon Wood, 20.25.
24/7/17	FLt A.W. Carter	N6302	Albatros scout out of control at Langemarck, 12.40.
27/7/17	FLt A.W. Carter	N6302	Albatros scout out of control west of Tourcoing, 19.30.
27/7/17	FCdr R. Collishaw	N533	Albatros scout destroyed north of Menin, 19.45.
27/7/17	FCdr R. Collishaw	N533	Albatros scout out of control Polygon Wood, 19.45.
27/7/17	FSL E.V. Reid	N5483	Albatros scout destroyed at Menin, 19.50.
27/7/17	FSL E.V. Reid	N5483	Albatros scout out of control at Courtrai, 20.00.
27/7/17	FSL E.V. Reid	N5483	Albatros scout destroyed at Menin, 20.05.
28/7/17	FSL W.M. Alexander	N5487	Albatros scout out of control at Dadizeele, 19.50.
28/7/17	FSL E.V. Reid	N5483	Albatros scout destroyed at Dadizeele-Becelaere, 20.00.
9/8/17	FLt H.J.T. Saint	N5380	Albatros scout out of control at Polygon Wood, 12.10.
12/8/17	FSL G.L. Trapp	N5354	Albatros scout out of control at Roulers, 07.45.
12/8/17	FLt H. Day	N5437	Albatros scout destroyed at Wervicq, 11.30.
14/8/17	FLt H.J.T. Saint	N5380	Albatros scout destroyed in flames, at Houthulst Forest, 16.15.
16/8/17	FSL J.A. Cole	N5437	Albatros scout out of control northeast of Zonnebeke, 08.00.
16/8/17	FSL W.M. Alexander	N6302	Albatros scout out of control at Wervicq, 08.00.
17/8/17	FSL G.L. Trapp	N5354	Albatros scout out of control at Ledeghem, 08.30.
20/8/17	FSL W.M. Alexander	N6302	Albatros scout out of control at Roubaix, 15.30.
21/8/17	FSL W.M. Alexander	N6302	Albatros scout out of control east of Menin, 18.30.
21/8/17	FSL J.G. Manuel	N5380	Albatros scout destroyed east of Menin, 18.30.
21/8/17	FSL J.G. Manuel	N5380	Albatros scout out of control, pilot shot, east of Menin, 18.35.
21/8/17	FLt H.J.T. Saint	N6295	Albatros C out of control 1 mile south of Roulers, 07.40.
21/8/17	FSL G.L. Trapp	N5366	Albatros scout out of control east of Menin, 18.35.
25/8/17	FSL D.F. Fitzgibbon	N5389	Albatros scout out of control north of Polygon Wood, 19.30.
25/8/17	FLt H.J.T. Saint	N6295	Albatros scout out of control south of Roulers, 07.00.
6/9/17	FSL W.A. Curtis	N6342	Albatros scout out of control southeast of Dixmude, 08.00.
6/9/17	FSL Broughall	B6226	Albatros scout out of control southeast of Dixmude, 08.00.
14/9/17	FLt Fitzgibbon	B6202	Scout out of control near Ten-Brielen, 16.30.
14/9/17	FSL Carroll	N6357	Scout out of control near Ten-Brielen, 16.30.
14/9/17	FSL Johnston	B3912	Scout out of control near Ten-Brielen, 16.30.
15/9/17	FSL Macgregor	B3833	Fokker triplane 102/17 destroyed at Wervicq, 16.50.
19/9/17	FSL H.B. Maund	B6211	Albatros scout out of control to east of Ypres, 10.00
19/9/17	FSL Carroll	N6357	Albatros scout out of control to east of Ypres, 10.00
20/9/17	FSL J.G. Manuel	B3950	2-seater forced down and strafed on the ground, 11.15.
21/9/17	FCdr H.J.T. Saint	B6201	Scout out of control at Wervicq, 11.10.
23/9/17	FCdr H.J.T. Saint	N6341	Scout out of control west of Westroosebeke, 11.20.
23/9/17	FCdr W.M. Alexander	B3910	Albatros scout out of control northeast of Houthulst forest, 11.25.
24/9/17	FSL R. Daly	N6359	Albatros 2-seater out of control northeast of Houthulst forest, 16.10.

26/9/17	FLt Fitzgibbon	B6202	Scout out of control between Westroosebeke and Passchendaele, 11.10.
26/9/17	FSL R. Daly	N6359	Scout shot down northeast of Houthulst, 11.10.
27/9/17	FSL W.A. Curtis	B6244	Albatros scout shot down northeast of Westroosebeke, 16.05.
27/9/17	FLt Fitzgibbon	B6202	Scout out of control northeast of Westroosebeke, 16.10.
27/9/17	FSL Hamilton-Bowyer	N6330	Scout out of control northeast of Westroosebeke, 16.10.
28/9/17	FSL G.L. Trapp	B3882	Albatros scout shot down and seen to crash north of Moorslede, 10.45.
1/10/17	FSL W.A. Curtis	B6244	Albatros scout out of control northeast of Passchendaele, 14.15.
15/10/17	FSL W.A. Curtis	B6202	2-seater out of control southeast of Zarren,13.45.
20/10/17	FCdr H.J.T. Saint	N6341	Albatros scout shot down at Praet Bosch Wood, 13.40.
21/10/17	FSL W.A. Curtis	B6202	2-seater shot down in flames at Dixmude, 13.30, shared with B6289 and B6203.
21/10/17	FSL W.A. Curtis	B6202	Albatros scout shot down northeast of Dixmude, 13.50. Believed to be *Vzfw*. F. Bachmann of *Jasta* 6.
21/10/17	FSL F.V. Hall	B6289	2-seater shot down in flames at Dixmude, 13.30, shared with B6202 and B6203.
21/10/17	FSL J. Emery	B6203	2-seater shot down in flames at Dixmude, 13.30, shared with B6289 and BB6202.
27/10/17	FSL K. Stratton	B6225	Albatros scout shot down northeast of Dixmude, 13.20, shared with B6202.
27/10/17	FSL W.A. Curtis	B6202	Albatros scout shot down northeast of Dixmude, 13.20, shared with B6225.
4/11/17	FSL W.A. Curtis	B6202	Albatros scout out of control northeast of Dixmude, 15.00.
4/11/17	FSL W.A. Curtis	B6202	Albatros scout shot down northwest of Dixmude, 15.05.
12/11/17	FLt G.L. Trapp	B6341	2-seater out of control over Couckelaere, 08.00, shared with B5659.
12/11/17	FSL A. Beattie	B5659	2-seater out of control over Couckelaere, 08.00, shared with B6341.
15/11/17	FLt W.A. Curtis	B6202	Scout out of control near Keyem, 12.45.
15/11/17	FSL J.G. Manuel	B3869	Scout shot down and seen to crash near Keyem, 12.45.
15/11/17	FSL H.B. Maund	N6351	2-seater out of control to west of Dixmude, 13.00, shared with N6341.
15/11/17	FSL A.M. Alexander	N6341	2-seater out of control to west of Dixmude, 13.00, shared with N6351.
15/11/17	FSL F.V. Hall	B6320	Scout out of control north-northeast of Dixmude, 13.00.
5/12/17	FLt W.A. Curtis	B5663	Albatros scout shot down and seen to crash between Keyem and Leke, 15.35. Possibly *Fw*. H. Seidal of *Jasta* 26. Shared with B6320.
5/12/17	FSL F.V. Hall	B6320	Albatros scout shot down and seen to crash between Keyem and Leke, 15.35. Possibly *Fw*. H. Seidal of *Jasta* 26. Shared with B5663.
10/12/17	FCdr N.M. Macgregor	B6299	Albatros scout shot down in flames at Oostnieuwkerke, 11.20. Shared with B5658.
10/12/17	FSL Clark	B5658	Albatros scout shot down in flames at Oostnieuwkerke, 11.20. Shared with B6299.
12/12/17	FCdr N.M. Macgregor	B6299	Albatros scout apparently out of control, east of Dixmude, 15.40.
22/12/17	FSL Wilmot	B3910	Albatros scout apparently out of control west of Lille, 10.50.
14/1/18	FCdr W.A. Curtis	B6450	Albatros scout out of control east of Houthulst forest, 11.35.
23/1/18	FCdr W.A. Curtis	B6450	2-seater broke up in the air, Staden, 14.50.
23/1/18	FCdr W.M. Alexander	B3950	Albatros scout out of control at Staden, 14.50.
3/2/18	FLt W.G.R. Hinchliffe	B6204	Albatros scout destroyed at Rumbeke, 15.15.
18/2/18	FLt J.G. Manuel	B7195	Albatros scout shot down south of Menin, 09.50.
18/2/18	FSL F.V. Hall	B6351	Albatros scout shot down south of Menin, 09.50.
19/2/18	FLt A.W. Carter	B7202	Albatros scout shot down south of Zillebeke lake, 11.50, shared with FLt S.W. Rosevear of No.1 Naval squadron. Victim was *Ltn*. H. Puttkammer of *Jasta* 3 who was captured and made PoW.
19/2/18	FLt J.G. Manuel	B7195	Albatros scout out of control east of Roulers, 15.00.
28/2/18	FLt H.T. Mellings	B6357	Albatros scout out of control northeast of Ypres, 16.45.
6/3/18	FCdr W.M. Alexander	B7215	Albatros scout out of control southeast of Dixmude, 08.30.
10/3/18	FCdr W.M. Alexander	B7215	2-seater out of control at Roulers, 15.45.
10/3/18	FLt W.G.R. Hinchliffe	B7190	2-seater out of control at Roulers, 15.45.
10/3/18	FLt J.G. Manuel	B7195	Albatros scout shot down southeast of Dixmude, 16.00.
10/3/18	FLt H.T. Mellings	B6357	Albatros scout shot down southeast of Dixmude, 16.00.
16/3/18	FLt H.T. Mellings	N6376	Pfalz scout out of control between Menin-Roulers, 09.30.
24/3/18	FCdr W.M. Alexander	B7215	Pfalz scout shot down over Menin-Roulers road, 09.20.
24/3/18	FLt H.T. Mellings	N6376	Pfalz scout shot down in flames and broke up, Menin-Roulers road, 09.20.
24/3/18	FLt H.T. Mellings	N6376	Pfalz scout out of control, Menin-Roulers road, 09.20.
24/3/18	FSL Coombes	B6358	Pfalz scout out of control and on fire, Menin-Roulers road, 09.20

CASUALTIES, CRASHES AND INCIDENTS

Date	**Pilot**	**Serial**

16/2/17 FSL Narbeth 8751
FSL Narbeth crashed a Nieuport 17Bis belonging to No.9 Naval Squadron on the aerodrome at St. Pol.

24/3/17 FSL W. Oliver N5473
FSL W. Oliver was at Dover to pick up new Triplane N5473, and was killed when a wing broke off in the air whilst testing the machine

26/3/17 8711
Nieuport XII presumably damaged by a severe storm which prevented any flying activity.

27/3/17 8728
Nieuport XII was wrecked during the move to Furnes. Pilot not identified.

16/4/17 FSL Munday 3923
FSL A.H. Munday crashed and wrecked Nieuport XII serial 3923. Munday was injured and hospitalised.

20/4/17 FSL Collins N5359
Collins lost his way during a test flight and landed at Rubroucke aerodrome breaking a wheel and axle.

21/4/17 FSL E. Dickson N5357
Dickson crashed when landing after a practice flight.

23/4/17 FSL E. Dickson N5356
On take off, hit tree, landed at ADD. Damaged propeller, landing chassis and centre section wires broken, machine strained and needed complete overhaul.

23/4/17 FSL Collins N5350
Collins came down in the English Channel and was rescued by French patrol boat "Joyeuse".

28/4/17 FSL Collins N5438
At end of formation practice, Collins bounced the Triplane whilst trying to land, took off again, stalled at 50 feet, and side-slipped into the ground. The Triplane was wrecked, and Collins died of his injuries.

28/4/17 FSL W.M. Alexander N5359
At the end of his first practice flight in a Triplane, Alexander turned the machine over on its nose when landing, breaking the propeller and damaging the cowl.

2/5/17 FSL R. Collishaw N5490
During an engagement with an enemy scout, the empty ammunition belt became unstowed from its drum and wrapped itself around Collishaw and the controls, jamming the gun and hindering Collishaw's movement. Immediately after, the machine suffered a severe petrol leakage.

12/5/17 FSL Holcroft N5357
Holcroft experienced engine trouble whilst on patrol, crashed whilst attempting to return to the aerodrome.

12/5/17 FSL Eppstein N5456
Eppstein failed to return from a fleet protection patrol, it is thought that he was shot down by *Flakzug* 72 near La Ventie, and crashed into the sea near Blankenberghe.

15/5/17 FSL D.F. Fitzgibbon N5466
Fitzgibbon was slightly injured when landing at Droglandt.

20/5/17 FSL C.E. Pattison N5366
Pattison claimed a scout out of control but was wounded in combat and had to make a forced landing at La Lovie, damaging the Triplane.

21/5/17 FSL J.E. Sharman N5458
Sharman crashed N5458 during a gunnery practice session at Clairmarais.

2/6/17 FSL A.C. Dissette N6294
Dissette was shot down and killed over Coxyd, the Triplane broke up in the air and crashed in a wood near Proven. *Ltn.* G. Nolte of *Jasta* 18 has been credited with shooting down Dissette.

3/6/17 FSL P.G. McNeil N6297
McNeil was shot down and killed near Moorslede, possibly by *Offstlvtr*. St. Klein of *Jasta* 27.

4/6/17 FSL D. Fitzgibbon N5492
Fitzgibbon's Triplane was badly shot-up during an engagement with 9 scouts.

5/6/17 FSL Shirriff N6303
Engine failure and forced landing at Poperinghe, machine damaged.

7/6/17 FSL J.E. Sharman N6307
Triplane was damaged by gunfire, and Sharman made a forced landing at Coudekerke.

7/6/17 FSL Keens N5361
Keens was shot in the chest during combat, but was able to land at Chateau Lovie aerodrome.

8/6/17 FSL Prewett N5372
Engine failed when returning after patrol. Forced landing in field near aerodrome, machine damaged.

8/6/17 FSL Collishaw N5490
Controls shot away during combat, crashed and damaged.

12/6/17 FSL Q. Shirriff N5368
Forced landing due to engine failure. Machine damaged.

13/6/17 FSL Pegler N5478
Forced landing near Bailleul, machine damaged.

14/6/17 FSL Prewitt N5358
Patrol encountered thick cloud and mist, Prewitt got lost, and made a forced landing at Oost Cappelle, damaging the Triplane.

14/6/17 FSL Boyd N5359
Patrol encountered thick cloud and mist, Boyd got lost and landed at Herzeele.

14/6/17 FSL Taylor N5458
Patrol encountered thick cloud and mist, Taylor got lost and landed at Zouafques.

14/6/17 FSL Shirriff N5367
Patrol encountered thick cloud and mist, Shirriff got lost and landed at Manston in Kent

14/6/17 FSL Parker N5470
Parker was shot down and killed over Zonnebeke, possibly by Vzfw Krebs of Jasta 6.

15/6/17 FSL Pegler N5367
Turned over and damaged when landing too fast on uneven ground at Droglandt in darkness.

21/6/17 FSL Taylor N5376
Taylor was hit by anti-aircraft fire, and made a successful forced landing.

24/6/17 FSL R.G. Saunders N5358
Saunders was shot down and killed over Moorslede.

24/6/17 FSL A.B. Holcroft N6306
Holcroft was shot down over Zonnebeke, wounded, and became a prisoner of war.

24/6/17 FLt Sharman N5483
Forced landing due to engine failure.

25/6/17 FSL Pegler N5359
Forced landing at Chateau Lovie due to engine failure, machine wrecked.

25/6/17 FSL G.E. Nash N5376
FSL Nash was shot down and wounded over Moorslede by *Ltn*. K. Allmenröder of *Jasta* 11. Nash was made a prisoner of war.

3/7/17 FSL A.W. Carter N5381
Landed at No.7 Squadron RFC due to engine trouble, machine slightly damaged.

3/7/17 FSL Page N5380
Forced landing in a field due to engine failure, machine struck ridge, overturned, and was damaged.

6/7/17 FSL Lowther N5354
Unspecified problem whilst on patrol, landed at No.12 Naval Squadron.

6/7/17 FSL J.A.M. Allan N5375
Forced landing on bad ground near Droglandt, damaged machine.

11/7/17 FSL Kent N5357
Kent was shot down at Wervicq, captured and made a prisoner of war.

12/7/17 FSL Pegler N5368
Pegler was shot down and killed over Polygon Wood, possibly by *Ltn*. W. Güttler of *Jasta* 24.

12/7/17 FSL J.A.M. Allan N5364
Allan received leg injuries from an anti-aircraft shell splinter, and was forced to land at No.306 siege battery.

14/7/17 FCdr Collishaw N5492
Damaged by anti-aircraft fire, forced landing at No.21 Squadron RFC.

15/7/17 FCdr Collishaw N5379
Engine trouble and forced landing at Moeres, damaged axle.

15/7/17 FCdr Collishaw N5379
In combat during return from forced landing, engine cut, and forced landing at Vinckes.

17/7/17 FSL Lowther N5381
Following combat, forced landing to the southeast of Polygon Wood, damaging the aircraft.

20/7/17 FSL Fitzgibbon N5458
Fitzgibbon suffered engine trouble and made a forced landing at No. 23 Squadron RFC.

20/7/17 FSL Taylor N5429
Taylor in combat with an enemy scout, received a flesh wound in his left arm, returned to aerodrome and landed safely.

22/7/17 FCdr J.E. Sharman N6307
Sharman was killed when his Triplane broke up in the air, apparently after a direct hit from an anti-aircraft shell.

22/7/17 FLt J.A. Page N5478
Page was shot down and killed near Becelaere, possibly by *Ltn*. O. Brauneck of *Jasta* 11.

23/7/17 FLt W.M. Alexander N5487
Engine trouble and forced landing at No.53 Squadron RFC.

23/7/17 FSL D.F. Fitzgibbon N5458
Crashed near aerodrome.

24/7/17 FSL T.C. May N5364
May was killed when his Triplane broke up in the air over Moorslede.

27/7/17 FSL G. Roach N5492
Roach was shot down and killed on his first patrol, occurred south of Moorslede, possibly by *Ltn*. K. von Schönebeck of *Jasta* 11.

28/7/17 FSL E.V. Reid N5483
Reid failed to return from a patrol, possibly shot down and killed by *K Flak* 21 near Armentières.

31/7/17 FSL Weir N6302
Weir got lost in cloud and landed at No.1 Squadron RNAS.

4/8/17 FSL Munro N6290
Forced landing to northwest of Proven, machine damaged.

5/8/17 FSL Pownall N5379
Landed at Dunkerque after becoming lost.

7/8/17 FSL Glasgow N5464
Patrol encountered bad visibility, Glasgow landed near Bray Dunes.

7/8/17 FSL C. Lowther N5367
Patrol encountered bad visibility, Lowther landed near Bray Dunes.

7/8/17 FSL Day N5446
Patrol encountered bad visibility, Day landed at Volkerinckhove.

9/8/17 FSL Day N5446
Crashed on landing.

9/8/17 FSL Munro N6290
Munro was shot down and killed over Polygon Wood, possibly by *Ltn*. W. Güttler of *Jasta* 24.

10/8/17 FSL Weir N5477
Weir make a forced landing at Houthem near Hondschoote, damaging his machine.

14/8/17 FSL Lloyd N536
Lloyd was shot down and killed near Zonnebeke Lake, possibly by *Uffz*. K. Steudel of *Jasta* 3 or by anti-aircraft fire.

14/8/17 FSL J.G. Manuel N5370
Manuel got lost in cloud, and landed at No.15 Squadron RFC.

15/8/17 FSL J.G. Manuel N5370
Manuel suffered engine trouble, and made a forced landing between Oostvleteren and Westvleteren, damaging the Triplane.

15/8/17 FSL Pownall N5381
Pownall collected N5381 from the depot, but damaged it on landing.

16/8/17 FLt Saint N6295
Saint received a flesh wound in his right thigh from enemy fire.

18/8/17 FSL Lowther N5367
Engine failed at take off, forced landing near aerodrome, machine damaged.

19/8/17 FSL Glasgow N5464
Glasgow was killed when he crashed to the northeast of Proven.

19/8/17 FSL G.L. Trapp N5354
Trapp made a forced landing to the east of Elverdinghe, escaping injury, but damaging the Triplane.

20/8/17 FSL C.H. Weir N5355
Weir was shot down at Langemarck and was made a prisoner of war, but subsequently died of his wounds.

21/8/17 FSL A.D. Lewis N5379
Lewis made a forced landing at No.27 Squadron RFC, damaging the Triplane.

21/8/17 FSL C. Lowther N5425
Lowther was shot down and killed to the west of Menin, possibly by *Ltn*. Hess of *Jasta* 28.

25/8/17 FSL A.D. Lewis N5367
Lewis was shot down near Roulers and became a prisoner of war, possibly by *Ltn*. von der Osten of *Jasta* 11.

3/9/17 FSL Emery N6371
Overshot aerodrome when landing, damaged machine.

3/9/17 FSL Broughall N6373
Forced landing and damaged machine.

6/9/17 FSL Lawson N6355
Forced landing at No.12 Naval Squadron.

6/9/17 FSL Johnston B3912
Landed at No.9 Naval Squadron with engine trouble.

6/9/17 FSL Grace N6376
Engine failure and forced landing immediately after take-off, machine badly damaged.

10/9/17 FSL Wood N6342
Forced landing near the aerodrome, machine damaged.

12/9/17 FSL Grace N6374
Grace became lost during a practice flight, and landed in a field near Cassel.

13/9/17 FSL Abbot B3933
Abbot was shot down and wounded, possibly by *Ltn*. W. von Bülow of *Jasta* 36. Abbot became a prisoner of war.

18/9/17 FCdr Saint B6201
Patrol attempted in bad weather. Saint was forced to land at No.5 Naval Squadron.

18/9/17 FSL Emery B6203
Patrol attempted in bad weather. Emery was forced to land at No.5 Naval Squadron.

18/9/17 FSL Nelson N6339
Patrol attempted in bad weather. Nelson was forced to land at No.9 Squadron RFC

19/9/17 FSL E.V.J. Grace N6374
Grace was shot down in flames and killed, possibly by *Ltn*. Adam of *Jasta* 6.

20/9/17 FSL H.S. Broughall B6226
Broughall, last seen northeast of Staden, was shot down and became a prisoner of war, possibly by *Ltn*. Lange, *Jasta* 2.

21/9/17 FSL N.M. Macgregor B3833
Macgregor's machine was badly damaged by gunfire, and the petrol pipe shot through, necessitating a forced landing at Ypres.

21/9/17 FSL Foster B3920
Whilst on a practice flight, Foster ran out of fuel and landed on the sands at Hennes near Calais.

23/9/17 FSL Bussell B6216
Machine was badly shot-up, made forced landing at Westroosebeke and was damaged.

23/9/17 FSL R.H. Daly N6359
Forced landing at No.4 Naval Squadron, machine undamaged.

23/9/17 FSL W.C. Johnston B3912
Crashed near Vlamertinghe, Johnston injured, and machine damaged.

24/9/17 FSL K. Stratton B6225
Landed on Elverdinghe-Poperinghe road with petrol tank damaged by gunfire. Machine otherwise undamaged.

25/9/17 FSL A.F. MacDonald B3920
MacDonald made forced landing and crashed east of Ypres. MacDonald was injured and the machine badly damaged.

25/9/17 FSL R.H. Daly N6359
Pressure safety valve failed and pilot landed at Seaplane Defence Squadron

26/9/17 FSL R.H. Daly N6359
Daly wounded by anti-aircraft fire, landed at No.4 Naval Squadron, machine damaged.

26/9/17 FSL J.E. De Wilde N6355
Got lost in ground mist, landed at No.21 Squadron RFC to re-fuel.

27/9/17 FSL J.E. De Wilde N6355
Last seen at 15.10 lagging behind formation. Shot down and killed, possibly by *Ltn*. Dannhuber, *Jasta* 26.

29/9/17 FSL Bramhall B6291
Forced landing at No.6 Squadron RFC. Pilot received cut head and taken to hospital, machine wrecked.

4/10/17 FSL J.G. Manuel B3950
Forced landing at No.9 Naval Squadron.

14/10/17 FSL Wilmot N6379
Engine failed completely, machine turned over and damaged when landing on aerodrome.

15/10/17 FSL McKelvey B3910
Machine damaged when landing.

15/10/17 FSL Sutherland B6297
Pilot received gunshot wound in left shoulder, landed machine at aerodrome without damage.

18/10/17 FSL Cumming B3882
Petrol tank damaged by gunfire during combat.

20/10/17 FSL Cumming B6297
Engine failure, crashed machine on aerodrome, pilot received facial injuries and taken to Malo hospital.

20/10/17 FSL Bowyer N6330
Broken pressure pipe.

21/10/17 FSL Fox B3919
Pilot wounded in leg from hostile gunfire.

26/10/17 FSL Morang B6260
Crashed on take-off, pilot unhurt.

27/10/17 FSL A.M. Alexander B3919
Forced landing, minor damage.

27/10/17 FSL Morang N6371
Shot down in flames, pilot killed.

3/11/17 FSL Bussell N 6330
Lost a wheel in the air, landed on beach.

4/11/17 FSL J.G. Manuel B3950
Forced landing at No.9 Naval Squadron.

5/11/17 FSL Clark B3919
Collided with FSL A.A. Cameron in B5666 on the aerodrome. Machine damaged.

5/11/17 FSL A.A. Cameron B5666
Collided with FSL Clark in B3919 on the aerodrome. Machine slightly damaged.

5/11/17 FSL A.A. Cameron B5666
Machine damaged in combat and forced to land at Droglandt.

12/11/17 FLt G.L. Trapp B6341
Machine observed to break up in air and go down in pieces, possibly by *Oblt*. Justinus, *Jasta* 35.

12/11/17 FSL J.G. Clark B6225
Clark made a forced landing at No.1 Naval Squadron with a seized engine.

15/11/17 FSL F.V. Hall B6320
Hall suffered a failed ignition switch, and made a forced landing at map ref A.29.c.

15/11/17 FLt W.A. Curtis B6202
Curtis went to determine the condition of Hall's machine, B6320, and damaged his own machine when landing.

8/12/17 FSL F.V. Hall B6289
Faulty engine resulted in forced Landing at Moeres, tail skid broken.

12/12/17 FSL J.G. Clarke N6330
During a general engagement, Clark was seen to go down out of control, he came down in enemy territory and was taken prisoner. *Ltn*. P. Billik of *Jasta* 7 was credited with the victory.

18/12/17 FSL A.A. Cameron B5666
Forced landing, damaged machine.

23/12/17 FSL Wright B6201
Lost control of machine over aerodrome and spun down into the ground, pilot killed instantly and machine wrecked.

28/12/17 FSL Humphrey B3869
Engine failure, and forced landing at No.2 Belgian Squadron at Moeres.

28/12/17 FSL Booth N6341
Forced landing at Bonningues.

3/1/18 FSL A.G. Beattie N6351
Forced down during combat by *Vfw*. H. Oberländer of *Jasta* 30, Beattie was wounded in the ankle, and lost lateral control when trying to land, one wheel touched first and the Camel flipped over. Beattie was captured and spent the rest of the war as a prisoner. Credited to *Vzfw*. Oberländer, *Jasta* 30.

3/1/18 FSL F. Booth B5658
Shot down and killed by *Uffz*. E. Liebert of *Jasta* 30.

3/1/18 FLt J.G. Manuel B3950
Machine damaged in combat and landed at No.3 Squadron.

13/1/18 FSL Maund B6211
Engine failure and forced landing, machine undamaged.

14/1/18 FSL A.A. Cameron B6380
Forced landing at aerodrome of No.21 Squadron RFC, machine slightly damaged.

18/1/18 FSL A.A. Cameron B6380
Immediately after leaving ground, Cameron attempted to turn with insufficient speed, and spun into the ground wrecking the machine. Cameron was injured and taken to hospital.

23/1/18 FSL R.A. Blyth B5663
Blyth's machine observed to be going down out of control accompanied by an enemy machine. Both aircraft crashed simultaneously, and it was surmised that Blyth and the Albatros scout had collided. Possibly by *Ltn*. Wandelt, *Jasta* 36.

27/1/18 FSL Rice B5664
Forced landing at No.2 Squadron.

30/1/18 FSL Patey B5687
Turned over on landing, machine damaged.

30/1/18 FSL Burton B7217
Burton was delivering machine from Dover, overshot aerodrome and turned machine over.

31/1/17 FSL Nelson B6289
Engine trouble and forced landing at Moeres.

3/2/18 FSL A.L. Jones B3760
Forced landing at Arques, machine badly damaged.

3/2/18 FSL W.H. Wilmot B6370
Shot down and killed during an engagement over Rumbeke.

5/2/18 FSL G.O. Smith B3866
Engine trouble and forced landing at Lovie aerodrome, machine undamaged.

16/2/18 FSL G.O. Smith B3866
Crashed at St. Sixte, north of Poperinghe. Smith was hospitalised with a fractured thigh and contusions on his face.

18/2/18 FSL R.E. Burr N6347
Shot down, Burr was wounded, and died of his injuries on the 20th February. Possibly by *Obltn*. B. Lörzer, *Jasta* 26

13/3/18 FLt H.T. Mellings B6357
Lost control in a sharp turn after take-off and spun in. Machine wrecked, pilot suffered slight bruising.

13/3/18 FCdr Carter B7202
Carter was unable to find the aerodrome due to heavy mist. Landed at No.29 Squadron RFC.

17/3/18 FSL F.V. Hall B6351
Carburettor trouble, forced landing at St. Sixte in ploughed field.

18/3/18 FSL G.T. Steeves B3781
Shot down, Steeves was captured and became a prisoner of war. Possibly by *Ltn*. E. Thuy, *Jasta* 28.

21/3/18 FCdr A.W. Carter B6228
The Camel shed a cylinder which caused the cowling to break up. Carter made a forced landing at the aerodrome of No.29 Squadron RFC. No other damage to the machine.

27/3/18 FSL D'Etchegoyen B3817
Forced landing at Eggewaertscappelle, machine undamaged.

27/3/18 FCdr W.M. Alexander B3940
Landed at No.6 Squadron with broken centre section wires.

APPENDIX F

AIRCRAFT USED

Part 1: Nieuport XII 2-Seaters

Serial	Dates of service	Notes
3923	27/2/17 - 21/3/17	Converted to single seat format. From No.8 Squadron 27/2/17, back to No.8 Squadron 21/3/17
	29/3/17 - 16/4/17	Back with No.10 Squadron by 29/3/17. Crashed and wrecked 16/4/17, FSL Munday.
8711	1/3/17 - 26/3/17	Previously with 6 Flight A Squadron 5 Wing Coudekerke. From ADD by 1/3/17. Wrecked in storm, 26/3/17. To ADD by 29/3/17.
8728	25/2/17 - 27/3/17	Previously 6 Flight A Squadron 5 Wing, and No.8 Squadron. From No.8 Squadron on 25/2/17. Damaged propeller when landing at Bray Dunes, 2.50pm, 21/3/17, FSL Nash. Wrecked 27/3/17. To ADD by 29/3/17.
8737	26/2/17 - 4/5/17	Previously C Squadron 1 Wing and No.1 Squadron. From ADD by 26/2/17. To ADD 9/5/17.
9205	24/2/17 - 4/5/17	Converted to single seat format. Previously 6 Flight A Squadron 5 Wing, and 11 Flight B Squadron 4 Wing (became No.6 Squadron). From No.6 Squadron 24/2/17. To ADD 4/5/17.

Part 2: Sopwith Triplane scouts

Serial	Dates of service	Notes
N500	26/2/17 - 2/4/17	From No.8 Squadron on 26/2/17. (First Sopwith prototype) To ADD by 2/4/17.
N504	30/3/17 - 24/4/17	From No.8 Squadron on 30/3/17. (Second Sopwith prototype) To ADD on 24/4/17.
N533	21/7/17 - 30/8/17	From ADD 21/7/17. Two gun machine, coded "C", named "Black Maria". Albatros scout shot to pieces in air, and another out of control with pilot shot, north of Menin 19.45, 27/7/17, FCdr R. Collishaw. To ADD 30/8/17.
N536	28/7/17 - 14/8/17	From ADD 29/7/17. Two gun machine. Shot down by AA near Zonnebeke Lake, 14/8/17, FSL Lloyd killed. Credited to *Lt.* Steudel, *Jasta* 3.
N5350	16/3/17 - 23/4/17	From ADD on 16/3/17. Engine failure, ditched near Boulogne 23/4/17, FSL R.F. Collins. Pilot and aircraft rescued by French patrol boat Joyeuse, and taken to DNT office building at Boulogne. To Furnes for deletion by 25/4/17.

N5351	13/4/17 - 7/5/17	From ADD on 13/4/17. To ADD by 10/5/17.
N5352	28/2/17 - 9/5/17	From ADD on 28/2/17. Crashed on take off, 9/5/17, FSL L.G. Steel. Deleted ADD 14/5/17.
N5354	28/3/17 9/5/17	From ADD 28/3/17. To ADD 9/5/17
	5/7/17 - 19/8/17	From ADD 5/7/17. Landed at No.12 Naval Squadron, 6/7/17, FSL Lowther. Albatros scout out of control, Roulers, 07.45, 12/8/17. Albatros scout out of control, Ledeghem, 08.30, 17/8/17. FSL G.L. Trapp. Forced landing, crashed and damaged east of Elverdinghe 19/8/17, FSL G.L. Trapp unhurt. To ADD 19/8/17.
N5355	28/3/17 - 5/4/17	From ADD 28/3/17 - 4/4/17. To ADD by 5/4/17.
	10/8/17 - 20/8/17	From ADD 10/8/17. Patrol attacked by 5 Albatros, Langemarck, shot down, 15.20, 20/8/17, FSL C.H. Weir prisoner of war, died of injuries 20/8/17.
N5356	28/3/17 - 30/5/17	From ADD by 28/3/17. On take off, hit tree, landed at ADD 23/4/17, FSL E. Dickson. Damaged propeller, landing chassis and centre section wires broken, machine strained and needed complete overhaul. Back from ADD on 5/5/17. To ADD 30/5/17.
	22/8/17 - 27/8/17	From ADD 22/8/17. To ADD 27/8/17 - 30/8/17.
N5357	5/4/17 - 17/5/17	From ADD 5/4/17. Damaged landing, 21/4/17, FSL E. Dickson. Repaired locally by 26/4/17. Engine trouble, crashed while attempting to return to aerodrome, 12/5/17, FSL Holcroft. To ADD by 17/5/17.
	17/6/17 - 11/7/17	From ADD 17/6/17. Forced landing in field near aerodrome, 18/6/17, FSL Shirriff. Coded "K". Shot down Wervicq-Comines 21.00, 11/7/17, FSL R.L. Kent prisoner of war, unhurt. By *Ltn.* W. Blume, *Jasta* 26.
N5358	24/4/17 - 10/5/17	On strength 24/4/17. To ADD 10/5/17, and thence to No.9 Squadron.
	11/6/17 - 24/6/17	From ADD 11/6/17. Aircraft coded "Q". Damaged landing Oost Cappelle, 14/6/17, FSL CRM Prewitt. Shot down Zonnebeke-Moorslede, 08.05, 24/6/17, FSL R.G. Saunders killed. By *Ltn.* Allmenröder, or *Ltn.* Groos, *Jasta* 11
N5359	12/4/17 - 25/6/17	From ADD by 12/4/17. Broke wheel and axle landing at Rubroucke aerodrome, 20/4/17, FSL Collins. Landing accident 28/4/17, broke propeller and damaged cowl, FSL W.M. Alexander. Aviatic C out of control 3 miles south east of Ypres, shared N6294, 07.15, 1/6/17. Albatros scout crashed west of Polygon Wood, 11.00, 6/6/17. Albatros scout out of control Zonnebeke, 19.20, 14/6/17. 2-seater out of control Houthem, 09.40, 15/6/17. All FSL J.A. Page. Engine failure, forced landing, and wrecked Chateau Lovie 25/6/17, FSL C.R. Pegler. To ADD on 26/6/17 and deleted 27/6/17.
N5360	26/4/17 - 10/5/17	From ADD on 26/4/17. To ADD 10/5/17.
N5361	9/5/17 - 22/7/17	From ADD by 9/5/17. Albatros scout out of control west of Polygon Wood 11.10, 6/6/17. FSL J.H. Keens. Pilot wounded in chest, damaged landing at Chateau Lovie, 7/6/17, FSL J.H. Keens. Returned to squadron 8/6/17. Crashed and damaged at Droglandt, 22/7/17, FSL A.M.O. McLachlan. To ADD 33/7/17.
N5363	5/5/17 - 14/5/17	From ADD 5/5/17. To ADD 14/5/17.
N5364	16/6/17 - 24/7/17	Flight tested at Farnborough 15/5/17. From ADD 16/6/17. Forced landing at No.306 Siege Battery after pilot struck in leg by anti-aircraft shell splinters, 12/7/17. FSL J.A.M. Allan injured. Wings folded up in dive over Moorslede, 24/7/17, FSL T.C. May killed. Possibly shot down by *Ltn.* H. Dilthey, *Jasta* 27.

N5365	13/5/17 - 30/5/17	From ADD 13/5/17. Crashed during gunnery practice at Clairmarais 21/5/17. FSL P.G. McNeil. To ADD 22/5/17.
N5366	13/5/17 - 30/8/17	From ADD 13/5/17. Albatros scout out of control, 09.50, forced landing, slightly damaged, La Lovie 20/5/17. FSL C.E. Pattison wounded. To ADD 29/5/17. From ADD 7/6/17. Albatros scout broke up Zonnebeke, 08.10, 24/6/17, FLt J.E. Sharman. 2-seater out of control near Wervicq, 19.45, 26/6/17, FSL H.W. Taylor. Crashed on landing Droglandt 20/7/17, FSL A.M.O. McLachlan. To ADD 21/7/17. From ADD 19/8/17. Albatros scout out of control east of Menin 18.35, 21/8/17 FSL G.L. Trapp. To No.8 Squadron 30/8/17.
N5367	6/6/17 - 25/8/17	From ADD 6/6/17. Landed too fast on uneven ground in the dark, overturned and damaged, Droglandt, 15/6/17, FSL C.R. Pegler. To ADD 17/6/17. From ADD 17/7/17. Forced landing at Bray Dunes, 7/8/17, FSL Lowther. Returned to squadron 10/8/17. Engine failed at take off, forced landing near aerodrome, machine damaged, 18/8/17, FSL Lowther. Shot down near Roulers, 25/8/17, FSL ADM Lewis prisoner of war. By *Ltn.* Georg von der Osten, *Jasta* 11.
N5368	7/6/17 - 12/7/17	From ADD 7/6/17. Engine failure, forced landing and machine damaged, 12/6/17, FSL Q.S. Shirriff. Flying again 15/6/17. Shot down at Zillebeke, 08.50, 12/7/17, FSL C.R. Pegler killed. By *Ltn.* Güttler, *Jasta* 24.
N5370	10/8/17 - 16/8/17	From ADD 10/8/17. Engine failure, forced landing and damaged, between Oostvleteren and Westvleteren, North of Poperinghe, 15/8/17. FSL J.G. Manuel. To ADD 16/8/17.
N5372	30/5/17 - 15/6/17	From ADD 30/5/17. Engine failure, forced landing, damaged near aerodrome 8/6/17, FSL C.R.M. Prewitt. Crashed and damaged Droglandt 14/6/17, FSL C.R. Pegler. To ADD 15/6/17 - 19/7/17.
N5375	15/6/17 - 27/8/17	From ADD 15/6/17. Forced landing near Droglandt and wrecked, 6/7/17, FSL J.A.M. Allan unhurt. To ADD 7/7/17. From ADD 5/8/17. To AD 27/8/17.
N5376	17/6/17 - 25/6/17	From ADD 17/6/17. Named "Black Sheep". Forced landing due to flak 21/6/17, FSL H.W. Taylor. Local repairs, flying again 24/6/17. Shot down east of Messine, 25/6/17, FSL G.E. Nash wounded and prisoner of war. By *Ltn.* K. Allmenröder, *Jasta* 11.
N5379	25/6/17 - 27/8/17	From ADD 25/6/17. Albatros scout out of control near Lille, 09.40, 7/7/17, FSL J.A. Page. Engine trouble, forced landing at Moeres, damaged axle, 15/7/17, FCdr R. Collishaw. In combat during return from forced landing, engine cut, and forced landing at Vinckes, 15/7/17, FCdr Collishaw. Lost whilst on patrol, landed at Dunkerque, 5/8/17, FSL Pownall. Forced landing and crashed Clairmarais North, 21/8/17, FSL Lewis. To ADD 27/8/17.
N5380	12/6/17 - 27/8/17	From ADD 12/6/17. Engine failure, forced landing in field, struck ridge, overturned and damaged, 3/7/17, FSL J.A. Page unhurt. To ADD 4/7/17. From ADD 23/7/17. Albatros scout out of control Polygon Wood 12.10, 9/8/17. Red Albatros scout crashed in flames Houthulst Forest, 16.15, 14/8/17, FSL H.J.T. Saint. Albatros scout destroyed 18.30 and another out of control, pilot shot, 18.35, 21/8/17, Menin, FSL J.G. Manuel. To ADD 27/8/17.
N5381	26/6/17 - 27/8/17	From ADD 26/6/17. Engine trouble, landed at No.7 Squadron RFC and slightly damaged, 3/7/17, FLt A.W. Carter. Albatros scout out of control, then forced landing and damaged, southeast of Polygon Wood, 06.45, 17/7/17, FSL C. Lowther. To ADD 18/7/17.

From ADD 15/8/17, but damaged landing, FSL Pownall.
To No.1 Squadron 27/8/17.

N5389 23/7/17 - 27/8/17

From ADD 23/7/17.
Albatros scout out of control North of Polygon Wood, 19.30, 25/8/17, FSL D.F. Fitzgibbon.
To ADD 27/8/17 - 13/9/17.

N5425 16/8/17 - 21/8/17

From ADD 16/8/17.
Shot down out of control west of Menin, 18.40, 21/8/17, FSL C. Lowther killed. By *Ltn.* Hess, *Jasta* 28.

N5429 29/3/17 - 5/8/17

From ADD 27/6/17.
Albatros scout broke up Polygon Wood, 18.00, 16/7/17, FSL H.W. Taylor. Became detached from flight, pilot received flesh wound in left arm in an engagement with enemy machine, 20/7/17, FSL H.W. Taylor.
To ADD 5/8/17.

N5437 20/7/17 - 27/8/17

From ADD 20/7/17.
Albatros scout crashed Wervicq, 11.30, 12/8/17, FSL H. Day.
Albatros scout north east of Zonnebeke, out of control 08.00, 16/8/17, FSL J.A. Cole.
To ADD 27/8/17.

N5438 19/3/17 - 28/4/17

From ADD 19/3/17.
Bumped on landing from offensive patrol, took off again but stalled, side-slipped in from 50ft. machine wrecked, 28/4/17, FSL R.F. Collins died of injuries. Wreckage to ADD.

N5446 5/8/17 - 9/8/17

From ADD 5/8/17. Presentation aircraft "Manaos Britons No.1".
Crashed on landing 9/8/17, FSL H. Day.
To ADD 9/8/17.

N5447 11/8/17 - 27/8/17

From ADD 11/8/17. Presentation aircraft "Presented by the Government of the Dominican Republic".
To No.1 Squadron 27/8/17.

N5452 29/3/17 - 3/6/17

From ADD 29/3/17.
To ADD 3/6/17.

N5456 19/3/17 - 12/5/17

From ADD by 19/3/17.
Halberstadt down in flames Zarren, 18.05, 5/5/17, FSL M.W.W. Eppstein. Shot down by AA fire over Zeebrugge and crashed in sea near Blankenberghe 12/5/17, FSL M.W.W. Eppstein killed. Believed *Flakzug* 72 near La Ventie.

N5458 9/6/17 - 24/7/17

From ADD 9/6/17.
Crashed at Clairmarais during gunnery practice, 21/5/17, FSL Sharman.
Halberstadt scout out of control north of St. Julien, c. 10.55, 15/6/17. Albatros scout out of control Moorslede 17.40, 15/6/17. Crashed near aerodrome, 23/7/17. All FSL D.F. Fitzgibbon.
To ADD 24/7/17.

N5462 21/8/17 - 27/8/17

From AD 21/8/17.
To AD 27/8/17.

N5464 23/7/17 - 19/8/17

From 2AD on 23/7/17.
Out of control, forced landing, completely wrecked 19/8/17 northeast of Proven, FSL T.L. Glasgow killed.
Wreckage to ADD 19/8/17

N5466 23/5/17 - 9/6/17

From ADD 23/5/17. Named "Black Death".
Albatros C in flames Wervicq-Poelcappelle shared N5478, N5490 and N6306, 08.50, and Albatros scout out of control northwest of Poelcappelle, shared N5490, 09.40, 5/6/17, FSL D.F. Fitzgibbon. Crashed and damaged, Droglandt, 8/6/17, FSL D.F. Fitzgibbon.
To ADD 9/6/17.

N5470 23/5/17 - 14/6/17

From ADD 23/5/17. Presentation aircraft "Government Of Dominica".
Albatros scout out of control Menin-St. Julien, 08.45, 7/6/17, FSL R. Collishaw. Shot down Zonnebeke-Moorslede, 19.20, 14/6/17, FSL L.H. Parker killed. By *Vzfw.* F. Krebs, *Jasta* 6.

N5477 29/7/17 - 11/8/17

From ADD 29/7/17.
Forced landing at Houthem and damaged, 10/8/17, FSL C.H. Weir.
To ADD 11/8/17.

N5478 23/5/17 - 22/7/17

From ADD 23/5/17.
Albatros C in flames Wervicq-Poelcappelle, shared N5466, N5490, and N6306, 08.50, 5/6/17, FSL G.E. Nash.
2-seater in flames Nieuport-Dixmude, 14.10, 5/6/17, FSL H.W. Taylor.
Forced landing and damaged near Bailleul, 13/6/17, FSL C.R. Pegler.
To ADD 14/6/17.

From ADD 13/7/17.
Two Albatros scout destroyed, then shot down at Becelaere, 11.00, 22/7/17, FLt J.A. Page killed.

N5483 24/4/17 - 28/7/18

From ADD 24/4/17. Named "Black Roger".
Albatros C shot down in flames southwest of Wervicq, 09.15, 1/6/17. 2-seater out of control St. Julien, shared N5490, N5487, and N5492, 09.20 - 10.25, 2/6/17. Albatros scout crashed near Roubaix, 20.25, 3/6/17. Albatros C destroyed in flames at Wervicq, 08.50, shared with N5490, N5466, and N6306, 08.50, 5/6/17. Halberstadt scout crashed north of Polygon Wood 11.00, 6/6/17. Albatros C shot down, pilot killed, seen to crash at Clercken 09.15, 7/6/17. Albatros scout out of control and Halberstadt out of control, Moorslede, 17.45, 15/6/17. Hostile aircraft, probably Halberstadt, out of control near Roulers 19.10, 17/6/17. All FSL E.V. Reid.
Engine trouble, forced landing and damaged 24/6/17, FLt J.E. Sharman.
Albatros scout out of control Deulemont, 11.00, 6/7/17. Albatros scout broke up in air, crashed Polygon wood and Albatros scout shot down, pilot shot, seen to crash Veldhoek, 07.45, 12/7/17. Albatros scout out of control Menin-Messines, 08.05, 20/7/17. Unidentified scout seen to crash at edge of wood north of Becelaere, 20.30, 21/7/17. Albatros scout out of control, Polygon wood, 20.25, 23/7/17. Albatros scout shot down, Menin, 19.50, and Albatros scout out of control with pilot shot, Courtrai-Menin, 20.00, and another broke up in air Menin, 20.05, 27/7/17. Albatros scout shot down Becelaere, 20.00, 28/7/17. All FSL E.V. Reid. Albatros scout destroyed Dadizeele-Becelaere, 20.00, then last seen 20.40. Shot down by *K Flak* No. 21 near ArmentiÈres, 28/7/17, FSL E.V. Reid killed.

N5484 20/8/17 - 27/8/17

From ADD 20/8/17.
To ADD 27/8/17.

N5485 24/4/17 - 20/5/17

From ADD 24/4/17.
Crashed during gunnery practice at Clairmarais, 21/5/17, FSL Sharman.
To ADD 25/5/17.

N5487 24/4/17 - 5/8/17

From ADD 24/4/17. Named "Black Prince".
2-seater out of control, St. Julien, shared N5490, N5492, and N5493, 09.20 - 10.25, 2/6/17. Albatros scout out of control northeast of Ypres salient, 08.45, 4/6/17. Albatros scout out of control, Polygon Wood, 11.45, 6/6/17. Two Albatros scouts out of control at Deulemont, 11.00, 6/7/17. Albatros scout out of control, Polygon wood, 20.45, 11/7/17. Albatros scout in flames, Menin-Messines, 08.05, 20/7/17. Engine trouble, forced landing at No.53 Squadron RFC, 23/7/17. Albatros scout out of control, Dadizeele, 19.50, 28/7/17. All FSL W.M. Alexander.
To ADD 5/8/17.

N5489 10/4/17 - 17/5/17

From ADD by 10/4/17.
To ADD by 17/5/17.

N5490 26/4/17 - 9/6/17

From ADD 26/4/17. Named "Black Maria", and marked "C" behind fuselage cockade.
Albatros scout crashed near railway junction east of Cortemarck, 17.30, 30/4/17. Halberstadt scout out of control, east of Dixmude 19.55, 9/5/17. Albatros scout in flames, south of Wervicq, 09.20, 1/6/17. 2-seater out of control, St. Julien, shared N5483, N5487, and N5492, 09.20 - 10.25, 2/6/17. Albatros scout in flames near Roubaix, 20.15, 3/6/17. Albatros C in flames Wervicq-Poelcappelle, shared N5466, N5478, and N6306, 08.50, and Albatros scout out of control, northwest of Poelcappelle, shared N5466, 09.40, 5/6/17. Albatros scout in flames, 10.50, another in flames, 11.05, and another out of control 11.10, all Polygon Wood area, 6/6/17. Controls shot away, crashed and damaged, 8/6/17. All FSL R. Collishaw.
To ADD 9/6/17.

N5492 9/5/17 - 27/7/17

From ADD 9/5/17.
Albatros scout destroyed Ypres-Staden, 10.30, 21/5/17. 2-seater out of control, St. Julien, shared N5483, N5487, and N5490, 09.20 - 10.25, 2/6/17. All FSL G.E. Nash.
Badly shot about 4/6/17, FSL Fitzgibbon.
2-seater crashed on fire, 11.00 and Albatros scout out of control, 11.15, both Polygon Wood area, 6/6/17. Albatros scout out of control, St. Julien, 09.00, 7/6/17. All FSL G.E. Nash.
Named "Black Maria". 2-seater out of control, Menin, 17.45, Albatros scout out of control and Albatros scout crashed, 17.40, north of Moorslede, 15/6/17. Hostile aircraft, probably Halberstadt, out of control, Roulers, 19.10, 17/6/17. Albatros scout crashed Moorslede, 08.10, 24/6/17. Aviatic C crashed near Poelcappelle station, 11.10, but machine damaged by gunfire, 2/7/17. Albatros scout out of control, Deulemont, 11.00, 6/7/17. Albatros scout out of control, Moorslede, 20.40, 11/7/17. Albatros scout out of control, south of Polygon Wood, 07.45, 12/7/17. Damaged by Flak, forced landing No.21 squadron RFC, 14/7/17, pilot unhurt. Albatros scout out of control with pilot shot, Menin-Messines, 08.00, 20/7/17. Two Albatros scout out of control, Passchendaele, 20.00, 21/7/17. All FLt R. Collishaw.
Shot down south of Moorslede, 19.45, 27/7/17. FSL G. Roach killed. Claimed by *Ltn.* K. von Schönebeck, *Jasta* 11.

N6290 24/7/17 - 9/8/17

From ADD 24/7/17. Forced landing and damaged northwest of Proven, 4/8/17, FSL K.R. Munro uninjured.
Shot down over Polygon Wood, 12.10, 9/8/17, FSL K.R. Munro killed, by *Ltn.* Güttler, *Jasta* 24.

N6293 9/5/17 - 17/5/17

From ADD 9/5/17.
To ADD 17/5/17.

N6294	1/5/17 - 2/6/17	From ADD 1/5/17. Aviatic C out of control 3 miles southeast of Ypres, shared N5359, 07.15, 1/6/17, FSL A.C. Dissette. Left at 11.17 on PR escort, shot down over Coxyd, broke up, crashed in wood, burnt out, FSL A.C. Dissette killed. By *Ltn.* Gustav Nolte, *Jasta* 18.
N6295	25/7/17 - 27/8/18	From ADD 25/7/17. Aircraft coded "B". Albatros C out of control, 1 mile south of Roulers, 07.40, 21/8/17. Albatros scout out of control south of Roulers 07.00, 25/8/17. Both FLt H.J.T. Saint. To No.1 Squadron 27/8/17.
N6297	14/5/17 - 3/6/17	From ADD 14/5/17. Halberstadt D out of control, east of Armentières, 09.50, 20/5/17, FSL P.G. McNeil. Flown to Cassel 21/5/17 by FSL E.V. Reid for comparative tests with Albatros Scout, Baby Nieuport, and Sopwith Pup. The Triplane proved superior both in speed and climbing power, and seemed to handle equally quickly with any other. Halberstadt D out of control, 15 miles off Ostende, 19.45, 25/5/17. FSL P.C. McNeil. Shot down near Moorslede, 3/6/17, FSL P.C. McNeil killed. By *Offstvtr.* St. Klein, *Jasta* 27.
N6301	7/6/17 - 12/6/17	On temporary secondment (with pilot FSL R. McDonald) from No.8 Squadron, marked "Dusty II".
N6302	4/6/17 - 7/6/17	From ADD 4/6/17. Crashed and damaged Droglandt 7/6/17, FSL R. Collishaw. To ADD 7/6/17
	7/7/17 - 27/8/17	From ADD 7/7/17. Albatros scout out of control, Roulers, 20.00, 17/7/17. Albatros scout out of control, Langemarck, 12.40, 24/7/17. General engagement Albatros scout out of control, west of Tourcoing, 19.30, 27/7/17. All FSL A.W. Carter. Albatros scout out of control Wervicq 08.00, 16/8/17. Albatros scout out of control, Roubaix, 15.30, 20/8/17. Albatros scout out of control, east of Menin, 18.30, 21/8/17. FSL W.M. Alexander. To ADD 27/8/17.
N6303	3/6/17 - 5/6/17	From ADD 3/6/17. Engine failure, forced landing and damaged at Poperinghe 5/6/17, FSL Q.S. Shirriff. To ADD 5/6/17.
N6306	24/5/17 - 24/6/17	From ADD 24/5/17. Marked "H". Halberstadt scout out of control, 15 miles off Ostende, 19.45, 25/5/17, FSL LH Parker. Visited 20 squadron RFC St. Marie Cappelle, 29/5/17, for comparison tests with FE and Nieuport. Albatros Scout out of control, Ypres-Courtrai, 18.00, 3/6/17. FSL L.H. Parker. Albatros C destroyed in flames at Wervicq, 08.50, 5/6/17, shared with N5490, N5483, N5478, FSL K.G. Boyd. Shot down near Zonnebeke, 08.05, 24/6/17, FSL A.B. Holcroft prisoner of war and wounded. By *Ltn.* Grosse, or *Ltn.* Allmenröder of *Jasta* 11.
N6307	3/6/17 - 22/7/17	From ADD 3/6/17. Albatros scout shot down out of control, Polygon Wood area, 11.10, 6/6/17. Albatros scout shot down near Roulers, 09.15, then Albatros scout out of control near Moorslede, 09.17, damaged by gunfire, forced landing at Coudekerke,7/6/17. Albatros scout out of control near Zonnebeke, 19.15, 14/6/17. 2-seater out of control, St. Julien-Houthem, 09.40, 15/6/17. Albatros scout broke up at Polygon Wood, 12.25, 12/7/17. All FSL J.E. Sharman. Hit by AA fire while in combat, broke up and crashed west of Comines, 22/7/17, FCdr J.E. Sharman killed. Credited by Germans to *Oblt.* Reinhardt, *Jasta* 11, but thought to be due to *Flakbatterie* 503.

Part 3: Sopwith Camel scouts

Serial	Dates of service	Notes
B3760	19/1/18 - 3/2/18	Clerget Camel. Collected from 1 NAP by FCdr N.M. Macgregor at 09.30 on 19/1/18. Forced landing at Arques, badly damaged, 3/2/18, FSL A.L. Jones. To No.1 NAP on 4/2/18.
B3781	4/2/18 - 18/3/18	Bentley Camel. Collected from No.9 Squadron on at 13.05, 4/2/18, by FLt W.G.R. Hinchliffe. Damaged after putting wheel in ditch whilst taxiing after landing, 8/3/18, S.C. Joseph. Brought down over Houthulst Forest, 18/3/18, FSL G.T. Steeves taken prisoner of war. Possibly by *Ltn.* E. Thuy, *Jasta* 28.
B3808	4/2/18 - 31/3/18	Bentley Camel. Collected from No.9 Squadron on 4/2/18 at 13.00 by FSL Burr. With No.210 Squadron RAF from 1/4/18.
B3809	28/3/18 - 31/3/18	Bentley Camel. Delivered on 28/3/18 at 12.00 from No.13 Squadron by FSL Cooper. Forced landing at Eggewaertscappelle, 27/3/18, FSL D'Etchegoyen. With No.210 Squadron RAF from 1/4/18.

B3817	4/2/18 - 31/3/18	Bentley Camel. Collected from No.9 Squadron on 4/2/18 at 16.05 by FLt A.W. Carter. With No.210 Squadron RAF from 1/4/18.
B3821	4/2/18 - 15/2/18	Clerget Camel. Delivered from No.8 Squadron on 4/2/18 at 10.50 by FSL Johnston. Temporary custody till 15/2/18 when taken over by No.1 Squadron.
B3833	30/8/17 - 21/9/17	Clerget Camel. From No.6 Squadron on 30/8/17. Fokker DR1 shot down over Wervicq, 16.50, 15/9/17, (*Obltn.* K. Wolff of *Jasta* 11 killed). Albatros scout shot down smoking, east of Hooge, 10.00 to 10.15, 19/9/17. Both FSL N.M. Macgregor. Damaged by gunfire, forced landing near Ypres, 21/9/17, FSL N.M. Macgregor. To ADD for survey, 22/9/17. Destroyed by fire on night of 1/10/17.
B3866	4/2/18 - 16/2/18	Bentley Camel. Presentation aircraft "Basutoland No.2, Mokhachane". Collected from No.9 Squadron on 4/2/18 at 12.50pm by FSL G.O. Smith. Engine failure and forced landing at La Lovie, 5/2/18, FSL G.O. Smith. Crashed and wrecked at St. Sixte, 16/2/18, FSL GO Smith wounded. To 1 NAP week ending 21/2/18. Surveyed 4/3/18, deleted 13/3/18.
B3868	4/2/18 - 15/2/18	Clerget Camel. Delivered from No.8 Squadron on 4/2/18 at 10.50 by SCdr Draper. Temporary custody till 15/2/18 when taken over by No.1 Squadron.
B3869	17/10/17 - 24/1/18	Clerget Camel. Presentation aircraft "Basutoland No.5 Lerothora". From ADD on 17/10/17. Albatros scout crashed near Keyem, 12.45, 15/11/17, FSL J.G. Manuel. Engine failure and forced landing at No.2 Belgian squadron, Moeres, 28/12/17, FSL Humphrey. Delivered to NAP for overhaul on 24/1/18 at 10.10am by FLt Carter.
B3882	30/8/17 - 3/11/17	Clerget Camel. From No.6 Squadron on 30/8/17. A Flight machine, carrying deputy flight leader identification. Albatros scout crashed north of Moorslede, 10.45, 28/9/17, FSL G.L. Trapp. Damaged by machine gun fire/petrol tank holed, 18/10/17, FSL H.W. Cumming. Storm damage, 20/10/17. To No.1 NAP on 3/11/17.
B3893	4/2/18 - 15/2/18	Clerget Camel. Delivered from No.8 Squadron on 4/2/18 at 10.50 by FSL Walworth. Temporary custody till 15/2/18 when taken over by No.1 Squadron.
B3898	18/1/18 - 4/2/18	Clerget Camel. Collected from NAP, 12.50, 18/1/18, FSL Wilmot. Delivered to No.9 Squadron on 4/2/18 at 12.20 by FSL H.A. Patey.
B3910	30/8/17 - 4/2/18	Clerget Camel. New aircraft from ADD on 30/8/17. Albatros scout OOC, northeast Houthulst Forest, 11.25, 23/9/17, FCdr W.M. Alexander. Damaged on landing, 15/10/17, FSL M.T. McKelvey. Albatros scout probably OOC, 2 miles west of Lille, 10.50, 22/12/17, FSL W.H. Wilmot. Delivered to No.9 Squadron on 4/2/18 at 12.20 by FSL McKelvey.
B3912	30/8/17 - 23/9/17	Clerget Camel. From No.6 Squadron 30/8/17. Landed at No.9 Naval squadron with engine trouble, 6/9/17, FSL W.C. Johnston. Scout OOC at Ten-Brielen, 16.30, 14/9/17, FSL W.C. Johnston. Crashed/damaged at Vlamertinghe, 23/9/17 FSL Johnston injured. To ADD for survey on 24/9/17. Destroyed by fire on night of 1/10/17.
B3919	27/9/17 - 6/11/17	Clerget Camel. From ADD on 27/9/17. FSL Fox wounded in combat on 21/10/17. Forced landing, slight damage, 27/10/17, FSL A.M. Alexander. Collided with B5666 on aerodrome and was damaged on the 5/11/17 by FSL J.G. Clark. To ADD 6/11/17.
	2/2/18 - 4/2/18	From ADD on 2/2/18, in temporary custody, and delivered to No.9 Squadron on 4/2/18.
B3920	26/8/17 - 25/9/17	Clerget Camel. Delivered new from ADD on 26/8/17. Ran out of fuel, forced landing on beach at Hennes near Calais, 21/9/17, FSL Foster. Forced landing and crashed east of Ypres, FSL A.F. MacDonald injured on 25/9/17. To ADD on 26/9/17, surveyed on 3/10/17, and deleted on 8/10/17 as damaged beyond repair.
B3921	28/3/18 - 31/3/18	Originally a Clerget Camel, but converted to Bentley on 21/2/18. Delivered from No.13 Squadron on 28/3/18 at 12.00 by FSL Smith. With No.210 Squadron RAF from 1/4/18.
B3933	30/8/17 - 13/9/17	Originally a Bentley Camel, later converted to Clerget. Acquired from No.6 Squadron on 30/8/17. Shot down during engagement west of Roulers, came down between Terhand and Becelaere, FSL E.D. Abbot was wounded and became a prisoner of war, on 13/9/17. Victory claimed by *Ltn.* W. von Bülow, *Jasta* 36.

B3940	23/2/18 - 31/3/18	Bentley Camel. Collected from ADD on 21/2/18. Landed at No.6 Squadron with broken centre section wires, 27/3/18, FCdr W.M. Alexander. With No.210 Squadron RAF from 1/4/18.
B3950	30/8/17 - 24/1/18	Clerget Camel (converted to Bentley, probably at end of January 1918). Acquired from No.6 Squadron on 30/8/17. 2-seater forced down and strafed on ground, 11.15, 20/9/17, FSL J.G. Manuel. Forced landing and crashed at Middle aerodrome, 4/11/17, FSL J.G. Manuel injured. Damaged in combat, landed at No.3 Squadron, 3/1/18, FSL J.G. Manuel. Albatros scout out of control at Staden, 23/1/18, FCdr W.M. Alexander. Delivered to No.1 NAP on 24/1/18 for overhaul.
B5658	19/11/17 - 3/1/18	Clerget Camel. FSL Nelson collected from No1 NAP on 19/11/17. B Flight aircraft, named "Cleada". Painted red/white stripes, with red/white wheel cover from 26/12/17. Albatros scout shot down in flames at Oostnieuwkerke, 11.20, 10/12/17, FSL Clark, shared with B6299. FSL F. Booth killed after engagement with Albatros scouts west of Lille on 3/1/18, believed shot down by *Uffz*. Liebert, *Jasta* 30.
B5659	3/11/17 - 4/2/18	Clerget Camel. New from No.1 NAP on 3/11/17. 2-seater out of control at Cockelaere, 12/11/17, FSL A.G. Beattie, shared with B6341. Delivered to No.9 Squadron on 4/2/18 at 12.15 by FSL G.O. Smith.
B5663	23/11/17 - 23/1/18	Clerget Camel. Collected from AP Dover by FSL Hall on 23/11/17. Used by FLt W.A. Curtis A Flight leader, wheel cover marked with black concentric ring on white, with black hub both vertical white bars extended over fuselage top. From 26/12/17, painted black/white stripes. Black and white Albatros scout with a white tail shot down and crashed at Keyem-Leke, 15.35, 5/12/17, FLt W.A. Curtis, shared with B6320, this is presumed to be *Fw*. Hermann Seidal of *Jasta* 26. FSL R.A. Blythe killed after engagement with Albatros scouts near Staden on 23/1/18, believed to have collided with enemy machine. Claimed by *Ltn*. Gustav Wandelt of *Jasta* 36.
B5664	26/11/17 - 4/2/18	Clerget Camel. Delivered from AP Dover on 26/11/17 by FCdr Fall. C Flight aircraft Forced landing at No.2 Squadron, 27/1/18, FSL Rice. Delivered to No.9 Squadron on 4/2/18 at 12.20 by FSL Coombes.
B5666	20/10/17 - 18/12/17	Clerget Camel. New from ADD on 20/10/17. Collided with B3919 on aerodrome, 5/11/17. Damaged in combat, forced landing on aerodrome, 5/11/17. Crashed and damaged on 18/12/17, all FSL AA Cameron. To No.1NAP by 19/12/17.
B5667	3/1/18 - 4/2/18	Clerget Camel. Delivered from Dover 3/1/18 at 11.45 by FSL O.C. Le Boutillier of No.9 Squadron. Delivered to No.9 Squadron on 4/2/18 at 16.40 by Manuel.
B5687	2/1/18 - 30/1/18	Clerget Camel (later converted to Bentley during March 1918). Delivered from AP Dover 2/1/18 by FSL Finley at 15.15. Turned over upon landing and damaged after test flight on 30/1/18, FSL Patey. To No.1 NAP Dunkerque on 1/2/18.
B5749	4/2/18 - 11/3/18	Bentley Camel. Collected from No.9 Squadron on 4/2/18 at 13.15 by FSL HA Patey. Crashed on landing, 11/3/18 by FSL H.A. Patey. At 1 NAP Dunkerque by 12/3/18.
B5750	11/3/18 - 31/3/18	Bentley Camel. Collected from No.1 NAP Dunkerque on 11/3/18 at 17.25 by FSL Manuel. With No.210 Squadron RAF from 1/4/18.
B6201	26/8/17 - 23/12/17	Clerget Camel. New from ADD on 26/8/17. Scout out of control at Wervicq, 11.10, 21/9/17, FCdr H.J.T. Saint. On 23/12/17, FSL D.R. Wright returning from an Exclusive Low Patrol in low cloud and mist, lost control over the airfield and spun into the ground, pilot killed and aircraft destroyed. Deleted 31/12/17.
B6202	30/8/17 - 26/11/17	Clerget Camel. New from ADD on 30/8/17. Albatros scout out of control at Ten-Brielen, 16.30, 14/9/17. Albatros scout out of control at Westroosebeke-Passchendaele, 11.10, 26/9/17. Albatros scout out of control and smoking NE of Westroosebeke, 16.10, 27/9/17. All FSL D.F. Fitzgibbon. 2-seater out of control southeast of Zarren, 13.45, 15/10/17. 2-seater shot down in flames, 13.30, shared with B6203 and B6289, and Albatros scout crashed NE of Dixmude (thought to be *Vzfw*. Fritz Bachmann of *Jasta* 6), 13.50, 21/10/17. Albatros scout destroyed northeast of Dixmude, 13.20, 27/10/17, shared with B6225. Albatros scout out of control and another one crashed NW of Dixmude, 15.00 - 15.05, 4/11/17. Albatros scout out of control near Keyem, 12.45, 15/11/17. All FLt W.A. Curtis. To 1 NAP Dunkerque on 26/11/17 for overhaul.
	24/1/18 - 4/2/18	Collected from NAP 24/1/18 by AW Carter at 11.45. C Flight Commander's (FCdr W.M. Alexander) aircraft, white vertical bars extended over top of fuselage. Delivered to No.9 Squadron on 4/2/18 at 12.15 by FSL Burr.

B6203	4/9/17 - 23/11/17	Clerget Camel. New from ADD on 4/9/17. 2-seater in flames NE of Dixmude, 13.30, 21/10/17, shared with B6202 and B6289, FSL H.J. Emery. Delivered to AP Dover on 23/11/17 by FSL Hall at 11.20.
B6204	24/1/18 - 4/2/18	Clerget Camel. Collected from No.1 NAP Dunkerque on 24/1/18 at 11.45 by J.G. Manuel. C Flight aircraft flown by FLt W.G.R. Hinchliffe, carried personal marking "Allo!" painted on fuselage side. During raid on Rumbeke aerodrome, red nosed Albatros C type seen to crash into tree southwest of aerodrome, 15.15, 3/2/18, FLt W.G.R. Hinchliffe. Delivered to No.9 Squadron on 4/2/18 at 12.30pm by Hinchliffe. (This machine was crashed at 207TDS Chingford on 30/4/18, 2Lt Jackson killed, the aircraft was still carrying Naval 10 markings).
B6211	7/9/17 - 19/1/18	Clerget Camel (later converted to Bentley in February 1918). New from ADD on 7/9/17. Albatros scout out of control east of Ypres, 10.00, 19/9/17, FSL H.B. Maund. Engine failed, resulting in forced landing north of Ypres, 13/1/18, FSL H.B. Maund. To 1 NAP Dunkerque for overhaul on 19/1/18, converted to Bentley at end of February 1918.
B6216	20/9/17 - 23/9/17	Clerget Camel. New from ADD on 20/9/17. Albatros scout out of control at Westroosebeke, 11.30, aircraft shot up during encounter, and crashed at Westroosebeke, 23/9/17, FSL E.J. Bussell. To ADD on 29/9/17, where destroyed by fire on night of 1/10/17.
B6225	14/9/17 - 4/1/18	Clerget Camel. New from AD on 14/9/17. A Flight aircraft, from 26/12/17 painted black white stripes, with black star on white wheel covers. Forced landing at Elverdinghe-Poperinghe road, 24/9/17. Fuel tank damaged by gunfire, 25/9/17. All FSL Stratton. Albatros scout crashed northeast of Dixmude (shared with B6202), 13.20, 27/10/17, FSL K.V. Stratton. Seized engine, forced landing at No.1 Naval Squadron, 12/11/17, FSL K.V. Stratton. Transferred to Dover by FSL Burton on 4/1/18 at 2.25pm.
B6226	4/9/17 - 20/9/17	Clerget Camel. New from ADD on 4/9/17. Albatros scout out of control southeast of Dixmude, 08.00, 6/9/17, FSL H.S. Broughall. Lost during a Low Offensive Patrol, last seen at 11.55 northeast of Ypres, FSL H.S. Broughall captured and became a prisoner of war, 20/9/17. Claimed by *Ltn*. Lange, *Jasta* 2.
B6228	20/3/18 - 31/3/18	Clerget Camel, converted to Bentley in February 1918. Picked up from No.1 NAP Dunkerque on 20/3/18 by H.T. Mellings at 14.15. Lost cylinder in air, cowl broke up, forced landing at No.29 Squadron RFC, 21/3/18, FCdr A.W. Carter. With No.210 Squadron RAF from 1/4/18.
B6231	21/1/18 - 4/2/18	Clerget Camel (fitted with Constantinescu gun gear). Collected from No.9 Squadron on 21/1/18 at 10.55am by FCdr Macgregor, for trial of Constantinescu gear. Delivered to No.3 Squadron on 4/2/18 at 14.20 by J.G. Manuel.
B6244	26/9/17 - 4/1/18	Clerget Camel. New from ADD on 26/9/17. Albatros scout shot down northeast of Westroosebeke, 16.05, 27/9/17. Albatros scout out of control northeast of Passchendaele, 14.15, 1/10/17. Both FLt W.A. Curtis. Transferred to AP Dover by FLt le Boutillier on 4/1/18 at 09.15.
B6256	18/2/18 - 31/3/18	Bentley Camel. Delivered from No.1 AP Dunkerque on 18/2/18, after overhaul. With No.210 Squadron RAF from 1/4/18.
B6259	24/9/17 - 16/11/17	Clerget Camel. New from ADD on 24/9/17. Damaged in combat Nieuport - Dixmude line, 15/11/17, FSL R.E. Carroll. Transferred to No.1 NAP Dunkerque on 16/11/17.
B6260	24/9/17 - 20/10/17	Clerget Camel, converted to Bentley in February 1918. New from ADD on 24/9/17. Crashed on takeoff, 26/10/17, FSL G.H. Morang unhurt. To ADD on 28/10/17
B6276	4/2/18 - 31/3/18	Bentley Camel. Collected from No.9 Squadron on 4/2/18 at 12.40 by FSL Nelson. With No.210 Squadron RAF from 1/4/18.
B6279	22/9/17 - 24/9/17	Clerget Camel. New from ADD on 22/9/17. Shot down, last seen north of Houthulst Forest, 24/9/17, FSL B Foster became prisoner of war. Believed to be victim of *Ltn*. K. Wüsthoff, *Jasta* 4.
B6289	26/9/17 - 4/2/18	Clerget Camel. New from ADD, collected by FSL K. Stratton on 26/9/17. A Flight aircraft, from 26/12/17, painted black/white stripes, black/white check on wheel cover. 2-seater in flames northeast of Dixmude, 13.30, 21/10/17, shared with B6202 and B6203, FSL H.L. Nelson. Engine failure, forced landing at Moeres, broke tail skid, 8/12/17, FSL F.V. Hall. Engine failure and forced landing at Moeres, 3/2/18, FSL Nelson. Delivered to No.9 Squadron on 4/2/18, at 12.15 by FSL Nelson.

B6291	28/9/17 - 30/9/17	Clerget Camel. New from ADD on 28/9/17. Forced landing, and wrecked at No.6 Squadron RFC, 29/9/17, FSL C.E. Bramhall injured. Machine with ADD by 1/10/17.
B6297	29/9/17 - 21/10/17	Clerget Camel. New from ADD on 29/9/17. Damaged by machine gun fire, pilot wounded, 13.45, 15/10/17, FSL I.P. Sutherland. Engine failure, crashed on landing, 20/10/17, FSL HWM Cumming injured. To ADD on 21/10/17
B6299	16/11/17 - 4/2/18	Clerget Camel. New from No.1 NAP on 16/11/17. A Flight Commander's aircraft in November, B Flight Commander's aircraft thereafter. From 26/12/17, painted red/white stripes, two elliptical red rings on white wheel cover, vertical white "squadron" stripes extended over top of fuselage. Albatros scout in flames west of Roulers, 11.20, 10/12/17, shared with B5658. Albatros scout apparently out of control east of Dixmude, 15.40, 12/12/17, two Albatros scout engaged, one driven down in vertical dive, the other in gentle glide, 2 miles west of Lille, 10.50, 22/12/17, FCdr N.M. Macgregor. Delivered to No.9 Squadron on 4/2/18 at 12.20pm by J.G. Manuel.
B6320	1/11/17 - 4/2/18	Clerget Camel. New from ADD on 1/11/17. A Flight aircraft. From 26/12/17 painted black/white stripes, 10 black/white segment wheel cover. Albatros scout out of control north northeast of Dixmude, 13.00, 15/11/17. Albatros scout shot down with smoke observed, seen to crash, shared with B5663, 15.35, 5/12/17. Wheels and axles shot off while strafing trenches, near Mariakerke, 11/12/17. All FSL F.V. Hall. Delivered to No.9 Squadron on 4/2/18 at 12.15 by FSL Hall.
B6330	24/1/18 - 4/2/18	Clerget Camel, later converted to Bentley. Collected from No.9 Squadron by FSL Nelson at 15.15 on 24/1/18. Delivered back to No.9 Squadron on 4/2/18 at 12.15pm by FSL Rice
B6341	7/10/17 - 12/11/17	Clerget Camel. New from ADD on 7/10/17. 2-seater out of control at Couckelaere, shared with B5659, 08.00, 12/11/17, FLt G.L. Trapp. Patrol left 15.10 on 12/11/17, broke up in air diving to attack 2-seater, FLt Trapp killed. Credited to *Oblt.* B. Justinius, *Jasta* 35.
B6351	4/2/18 - 31/3/18	Bentley Camel. Collected from No.9 Squadron on 4/2/18 at 12.30 by FSL Hall. Albatros scout shot down south of Menin, 09.50, 18/2/18, FSL F.V. Hall. Carburettor trouble, forced landing in ploughed field near St. Sixte, 17/3/18, FSL F.V. Hall. With No.210 Squadron RAF from 1/4/18.
B6357	4/2/18 - 13/3/18	Bentley Camel. Collected from No.1 NAP at 16.15, 4/2/18, by FSL Nelson. Albatros scout out of control north of Ypres, 16.45, 28/2/18, Albatros scout crashed south east of Dixmude, 16.00, 10/3/18, FSL H.T. Mellings. Crashed on take off wrecking machine, 14.15, 13/3/18, FSL H.T. Mellings bruised. To No.1 NAP on 13/3/18, and deleted on 18/3/18.
B6358	4/2/18 - 31/3/18	Bentley Camel. Collected from No.9 Squadron at 12.45, 4/2/18, by FSL Rice. Pfalz scout out of control and smoking, Menin-Roulers, 09.20, 24/3/18, FSL L.P. Coombes. With No.210 Squadron RAF from 1/4/18.
B6370	25/1/18 - 3/2/18	Clerget Camel. Collected from No.9 Squadron on 25/1/18 at 15.10 by FCdr Curtis. FSL W.H. Wilmot killed when shot down, southwest of Rumbeke, missing circa 15.15, 3/2/18.
B6380	12/1/18 - 18/1/18	Clerget Camel. Delivered new from Air Park at Dover at 11.35 on 12/1/18 by FSL de Wilde. FSL A.A. Cameron made forced landing at 21 squadron RFC at 15.20 on 14/1/18. Aircraft slightly damaged, pilot unhurt. FSL A.A. Cameron injured in flying accident 18/1/18 at 13.35, attempted to turn with insufficient speed after take off, spun in from 200 feet, pilot seriously injured, taken to hospital, aircraft wrecked. To ADD on 18/1/18, and deleted on 21/1/18
B6391	4/2/18 - 23/3/18	Bentley Camel. Collected from No.1 NAP at 16.20 pm on 4/2/18 by FSL Hall. Red and White Striped cowl and sides, B flight aircraft, transferred to C Flight in March 1917. Night bombed Abeele aerodrome with four 16 lb bombs on 27/2/18, FSL McKelvey. Machine transferred to C Flight circa 20/3/18, and thereafter flown by FSL H.A. Patey. Crashed and damaged when landing after bomber escort to Bruges on 23/3/18, FSL H.A. Patey. To No.4 ASD on 25/3/18.
B6448	4/2/18 - 5/2/18	Clerget Camel. Delivered from No.8 Squadron on 4/2/18 at 10.50 by FSL Crundall. Temporary custody, until taken over by No.1 Squadron on 15/2/18.
B6449	12/1/18 - 4/2/18	Clerget Camel. Delivered from Air Park Dover at 12.05 on 12/1/18 by FSL Wallace. B Flight aircraft, painted red/white stripes, and red "shamrock" on white wheel cover, marked as deputy flight leader's machine with first vertical white bar extended over fuselage top. Flown by FSL H.B. Maund. Transferred to No.9 Squadron at 12.20 on 4/2/18 by Maund.

B6450 4/1/18 - 4/2/18

Clerget Camel. Delivered from Air Park at Dover via Bergues at 11.55 on 4/1/18 by FSL Bussell.
A Flight leader's aircraft, painted Black/white stripes on cowl. Both squadron vertical stripes extending over top of fuselage, wheel cover painted black concentric ring on white. Flown by FCdr W.A. Curtis, and taken over by FLt A.W. Carter.
Albatros scout out of control, east of Houthulst Forest, 11.35, 14/1/18. 2-Seater broke up Staden, 14.50, 23/1/18, both FCdr W.A. Curtis.
Transferred to No.9 Squadron at 12.15 on 4/2/18 by Carter.

B7185 2/2/18 - 4/2/18

Bentley Camel. Delivered new from Dover on 2/2/18 at 11.20 by FSL Rosevear. Temporary custody, taken to No.8 Squadron at 11.55 on 4/2/18 by FSL Johns.

B7188 2/2/18 - 4/2/18

Bentley Camel. Delivered from Dover at 11.20 on 2/2/18 by FLt Kinkead. Temporary custody, taken to No.8 Squadron at 11.55 on 4/2/18 by FSL Wallworth.

B7190 4/2/18 - 31/3/18

Bentley Camel. Collected from No.9 Squadron at 13.05 on 4/2/18 by L.P. Coombes.
Dropped 4 x 16lb bombs in night attack on Abeele aerodrome, 26/27.2.18. Dropped 4x16lb. bombs in night attack on Zeebrugge, 7/3/18. 2-seater out of control near Roulers, 15.45, 10/3/18, all FLt W.G.R. Hinchliffe.
With No.210 Squadron RAF from 1/4/18.

B7191 4/2/18 - 31/3/18

Bentley Camel. Collected from No.9 Squadron at 12.55 on 4/2/18 by H.B. Maund.
With No.210 Squadron RAF from 1/4/18.

B7192 30/1/18 - 4/2/18

Bentley Camel. Delivered from Dover at 15.00 on 30/1/18 by FCdr Booker. Temporary custody till taken over by No.8 Squadron at 11.55 on 4/2/18 by FSL Dennett.

B7195 4/2/18 - 31/3/18

Bentley Camel. Collected from No.9 Squadron at 13.15 on 4/2/18 by J.G. Manuel.
Albatros scout shot down south of Menin, 09.50, 18/2/18, FSL F.V. Hall.
Albatros scout out of control 10 miles northeast of Roulers 15.00, 19/2/18, Albatros scout crashed south east of Dixmude, 16.00, 10/3/18, both FLt J.G. Manuel.
With No.210 Squadron RAF from 1/4/18.

B7198 30/1/18 - 4/2/18

Bentley Camel. Delivered from Dover at 15.00 on 30/1/18 by FLt Rosevear. Temporary custody till taken over by No.8 Squadron at 11.55 on 4/2/18 by SCdr Draper.

B7202 4/2/18 - 31/3/18

Bentley Camel. Collected from No.9 Squadron at 12.40 on 4/2/18 by FLt A.W. Carter.
Albatros C crashed and burnt south of Zillebeke Lake, shared B6428, 11.45, 19/2/18, FLt A.W. Carter, (Baron von Putkamer wounded).
With No.210 Squadron RAF from 1/4/18.

B7203 2/2/18 - 4/2/18

Bentley Camel. Delivered from Dover at 11.20 on 2/2/18 by FCdr Rowley. Temporary custody till taken over by No.8 Squadron at 11.55 on 4/2/18 by FCdr Compstone.

B7215 4/2/18 - 31/3/18

Bentley Camel. Collected from No.9 Squadron at 16.05 on 4/2/18 by JG Manuel.
Albatros scout out of control southeast of Dixmude, 08.30, 6/3/18. 2-seater out of control, Roulers, 15.45, 10/3/18. Pfalz scout out of control, Menin-Roulers, 09.20, 24/3/18. All FCdr W.M. Alexander.
With No.210 Squadron RAF from 1/4/18.

B7217 30/1/18

Bentley Camel. Delivered from Dover at 15.20 on 30/1/18 for temporary custody by FSL Burton, but overshot when landing, and turned aircraft over. To No.1 NAP for repair on 1/2/18.

B7218 2/2/18 - 4/2/18

Bentley Camel. Delivered from Dover at 11.20 on 2/2/18 by FSL Forman. Temporary custody, till taken over by No.8 Squadron at 11.35 on 4/2/18 by FSL Johnstone.

B7220 2/2/18 - 4/2/18

Bentley Camel. Delivered from Dover at 11.20 on 2/2/18 by FSL Findlay. Temporary custody, till taken over by No.8 Squadron at 11.55 on 4/2/18 by FSL Crundall.

B7221 24/3/18 - 31/3/18

Bentley Camel. Picked up from No.1 NAP at 15.10 on 24/3/18 by H.A. Patey.
With No.210 Squadron RAF from 1/4/18.

N6330 30/8/17 - 12/12/17

Clerget Camel. From No.6 Squadron on 30/8/17.
Albatros scout out of control northeast of Westroosebeke, 16.10, 27/9/17, FSL S.A. Hamilton-Bowyer.
Lost wheel in air, landed on beach, 3/11/17, FSL Bussell.
After combat with Albatros scouts, shot down 8 miles east of Dixmude, 12/12/17, FSL J.G. Clarke taken prisoner of war. Claimed by *Ltn.* P. Billik, *Jasta* 7.

N6339 30/8/17 - 29/9/17

Clerget Camel. From No.6 Squadron on 30/8/17.
To ADD on 29/9/17.

N6341 30/8/17 - 4/1/18

Clerget Camel. From No.6 Squadron on 30/8/17.
Albatros scout out of control, Westroosebeke, 11.30, 23/9/17. Albatros scout shot down near Praet Bosch Wood, north east of Dixmude, 13.40, 20/10/17. All FCdr H.J.T. Saint.
Albatros scout out of control northwest of Dixmude, 13.15, machine damaged during the combat and forced to land at Droglandt, 5/11/17. FSL A.A. Cameron.

		2-seater out of control west of Dixmude, shared with N6351, 13.00, 15/11/17, FSL A.M. Alexander. Forced landing at Bonningues, 28/12/17, FSL F Booth. Transferred to Dover by FSL Finley at 08.55 on 4/1/18.
N6342	30/8/17 - 11/9/17	Clerget Camel. From No.6 Squadron on 30/8/17. Albatros scout out of control south east of Dixmude, 08.00, 6/9/17, FSL W.A. Curtis. Crashed and damaged near aerodrome, 10/9/17, FSL P Wood. To ADD on 11/9/17.
N6347	4/2/18 - 18/2/18	Bentley Camel. Collected at 12.55 on 4/2/18 by FSL McKelvey. Last seen after an engagement to east of Ypres, crashed on British side of lines, completely wrecked, 18/2/18, FSL R.E. Burr died of his wounds on 20/2/17. Possibly *Oblt.* B. Lörzer, *Jasta* 26. To ADD by 25/2/18 when surveyed, and deleted on 13/3/18.
N6351	30/8/17 - 3/1/18	Clerget Camel. From No.6 Squadron on 30/8/17. Crashed and damaged near aerodrome 9/9/17, FSL R.E. Carroll. To ADD on 10/9/17. Collected from ADD by FSL Hamilton-Bowyer on 27/10/17. C Flight aircraft, from 26/12/17 painted blue/white stripes. 2-seater out of control west of Dixmude, shared N6341, 13.00, 15/11/17, FSL H.B. Maund. Brought down in general engagement with Albatros scouts west of Lille, aircraft was forced down, pilot was injured in ankle and lost lateral control when trying to land, one wheel touched first and aircraft turned over, 3/1/18, FSL A.G. Beattie taken prisoner of war – credited to *Vzfw*. Oberlander of *Jasta* 30.
N6355	30/8/17 - 27/9/17	Clerget Camel. From No.6 Squadron on 30/8/17. Forced landing at No.12 Naval squadron, 6/9/17, FSL Lawson. Shot down, last seen southeast of Houthulst Forest, 15.10, 27/9/17. FSL J.E. de Wilde killed. Possibly by *Ltn.* Dannhuber, *Jasta* 26.
N6357	11/9/17 - 23/11/17	Clerget Camel. From ADD on 11/9/17. Scout out of control, Ten-Brielen, 16.30, 14/9/17. Albatros scout out of control east of Ypres, 10.00, 19/9/17. Both FSL R.E. Carroll. Delivered to AP Dover at 11.20 on 23/11/17 by FSL R.E. Carroll.
N6359	22/9/17 - 26/9/17	Clerget Camel. From ADD on 22/9/17. Albatros C out of control northeast of Houthulst Forest, 16.10, 24/9/17, FSL R.H. Daly. Albatros scout crashed northeast of Houthulst forest, 11.10, then hit by AA fire, forced landing Bray Dunes, damaged, 26/9/17, FSL R.H. Daly wounded. To ADD on 27/9/17, where destroyed by fire on night of 1/10/17.
N6371	30/8/17 - 27/10/17	Clerget Camel. From No.6 Squadron on 30/8/17. Overshot aerodrome when landing, damaged machine, 3/9/17, FSL H.J. Emery. To ADD on 4/9/17. Collected from ADD on 1/10/17. Shot down in flames by Albatros northeast of Dixmude, 13.20, 27/10/17, FSL G.H. Morang killed.
N6373	30/8/17 - 3/9/17	Clerget Camel. From No.6 Squadron on 30/8/17. Forced landing and damaged on 3/9/17, FSL H.S. Broughall. To ADD on 4/9/17.
N6374	11/9/17 - 19/9/17	Clerget Camel. From ADD on 11/9/17. Lost during practice flight, landed in field near Cassell, 12/9/17, FSL E.V.J. Grace. General combat east of Ypres, shot down in flames southeast of Houthulst Forest 10.15, 19/9/17, FSL E.V.J. Grace killed, possibly by *Ltn.* Adam, *Jasta* 6.
N6376	30/8/17 - 6/9/17	Clerget Camel, later converted to Bentley in February 1918. From NAP at 14.20 on 30/8/17 by FSL McKelvey. Engine failure at take off, forced landing in field near Aerodrome, badly damaged, 6/9/17, FSL E.V.J. Grace. To ADD 6/9/17, and thence to No.8 Squadron.
	13/3/18 - 31/3/18	From No.1 NAP on 13/3/18. Pfalz scout out of control, Roulers, 09.30, 16/3/18. Pfalz scout in flames, broke up, and another out of control, Menin-Roulers, 09.20, 24/3/18. All FLt H.T. Mellings. With No.210 Squadron RAF from 1/4/18.
N6379	30/8/17 - 14/10/17	Clerget Camel. From No.6 Squadron on 30/8/17. To ADD 6/9/17. From ADD on 7/10/17. Overturned on landing and damaged, 14/10/17, FSL Wilmot. To ADD 19/10/17.

BIBLIOGRAPHY

Books

Sopwith Camel Squadrons, L. Rogers, Albatros Productions.

British Aviation Squadron Markings of World War I, L. Rogers, Schiffer Publishing.

The Fighting Triplanes, E. Haddingham, Hamish Hamilton.

Sopwith Aircraft 1912-1920, King, Putnam.

Sopwith Aircraft, M Davies, Crowood.

Sopwith Camel - King of Combat, C. Bowyer, Aston.

Air Command, R. Collishaw, Squadron-Signal.

Royal Naval Aircraft Serials and Units, Sturdivant & Page, Air Britain.

Above the Trenches, Coles, Franks & Guest, Grub Street.

Fighter Pilot On The Western Front, E.D. Crundall, Kimber.

I Chose the Sky, L.H. Rochford, Kimber.

Canadian Airmen In The 1st World War, F.S. Wise, University of Toronto.

The Jasta War Chronology, Franks, Bailey & Duiven, Grub Street.

RFC Communiqués 1917-1918, C. Bowyer, Grub Street.

Naval Aviation in the First World War, R.D. Layman, Caxton.

The War in the Air, H.A. Jones, Imperial War Museum.

The Royal Naval Air Service, B. King, Hikoki.

Journals

Cross & Cockade (GB)

Cross & Cockade (U.S.)

Pilots Flying Log Books

FLt W.G.R. Hinchliffe

FSL W.M. Alexander

FSL R.L. Kent

FSL G.G. Bowman

FSL S.A. Hamilton-Bowyer

FSL F.V. Hall

National Archive Files

ADM273, Admiralty: Royal Naval Air Service: Registers of Officers' Services
Air1/45/15/9/21, 10 Squadron RNAS daily report of operations
Air1/92/15/9/228, RNAS 1, 6, 8, 9, & 10 squadrons collective combat reports
Air1/93/15/9/233, RNAS 10 Squadron – report on operations
Air1/93/15/9/234, RNAS 10 Squadron – officers and ratings return of arrivals and departures.
Air1/184/15/216/2, 10 Squadron RNAS daily report of operations
Air1/704/27/5/30, Technical Notes: Sopwith Triplane
Air1/770/204/4/258, Summary of Brigades, Wing and Squadron work, 1917 Oct
Air1/913/204/5/851, Policy and organisation of R.N.A.S. squadrons on loan to R.F.C
Air1/1219/204/5/2634, Combat Reports: 10 Naval Squadron
Air1/1690/204/120/54, Combat Reports: Naval Air Squadrons with the RFC
Air1/1695/204/122/1, 10 Squadron RNAS: Register of Officers
Air1/1695/204/122/2, 10 Squadron RNAS: Register of Officers
Air1/1695/204/122/5, 10 Squadron RNAS: Daily States
Air1/1695/204/122/8, 10 Squadron RNAS: Letters of appreciation
Air1/1695/204/122/9, 10 Squadron RNAS: Standing orders
Air1/1696/204/122/11, 10 Squadron RNAS; Recommendation of officers for awards
Air1/1696/204/122/12, 10 Squadron RNAS: Reports on operations, officers and aircraft
Air1/1697/204/122/18, 10 Squadron RNAS: Record book
Air1/1698/204/122/19, 10 Squadron RNAS: Combat reports
Air1/1698/204/122/20, 10 Squadron RNAS: Officers record book
Air1/1698/204/122/23, 10 Squadron RNAS: Combat Report summaries 1917 April to 1918 April
Air1/1698/204/122/24, 10 Squadron RNAS: Various returns
Air1/1698/204/122/25, 10 Squadron RNAS: Combat reports
Air76, Air Ministry: Department of the Master-General of Personnel: Officers' Service Records

Misc.

W.A. Curtis biographical file, Directorate of History & Heritage, Canadian National Defence
Transcript of conversation between W.A. Curtis and A.W. Carter
Transcript of interview with W.A. Curtis by J. Tyson-Dubois

NOTES

NOTES

NOTES

NOTES

Also from the Publisher